Technocracy and the Law

Technocratic law and governance is under fire. Not only populist movements have challenged experts. NGOs, public intellectuals and some academics have also criticized the too close relation between experts and power. While the amount of power gained by experts may be contested, it is unlikely and arguably undesirable that experts will cease to play an influential role in contemporary regulatory regimes. This book focuses on whether and how experts involved in policymaking can and should be held accountable.

The book, divided into four parts, combines theoretical analysis with a wide variety of case studies expounding the challenges of holding experts accountable in a multilevel setting. Part I offers new perspectives on accountability of experts, including a critical comparison between accountability and a virtue-ethical framework for experts, a reconceptualization of accountability through the rule of law prism and a discussion of different ways to operationalize expert accountability. Parts I–IV, organized around in-depth case studies, shed light on the accountability of experts in three high-profile areas for technocratic governance in a European and global context: economic and financial governance, environmental/health and safety governance, and the governance of digitization and data protection.

By offering fresh insights into the manifold aspects of technocratic decision-making and suggesting new avenues for rethinking expert accountability within multilevel governance, this book will be of great value not only to students and scholars in international and EU law, political science, public administration, science and technology studies but also to professionals working within EU institutions and international organizations.

Alessandra Arcuri is Professor of Inclusive Global Law and Governance at the Erasmus School of Law and Erasmus Initiative Dynamics of Inclusive Prosperity, at Erasmus University Rotterdam.

Florin Coman-Kund is Assistant Professor of European Union and Public International Law, Erasmus School of Law, at Erasmus University Rotterdam.

Transnational Law and Governance

Series Editor: Paolo Davide Farah, West Virginia University, USA and gLAWcal – Global Law Initiatives for Sustainable Development, UK

In recent years, the concepts of 'transnational law' and 'governance' have been explored by both scholars and practitioners with the terms taking on new meaning and significance, particularly in light of the ongoing economic crisis and a corresponding critical reappraisal of global institutional structures and governance. This multidisciplinary series aims to provide a home for research exploring these issues.

Transnational law covers a broad theoretical definition, which includes studies emerging from disciplines such as international law, comparative law, international economic law and administrative law undertaken by legal scholars but also features extensive research undertaken by scholars from other disciplines, including but not limited to, political sciences, international relations, public administration, sociology, history, philosophy and geography. Governance in particular is now seen as important when we refer to the general stability of the markets, to good faith and other key principles, which are fundamental to the notion of a fair market, which is responsive to the needs of governments and citizens as well as businesses.

This series features cutting-edge works, which critically analyse the relationship between governance, institutions and law from a variety of disciplinary perspectives.

Available titles in this series include:

A Radically Democratic Response to Global Governance
Dystopian Utopias
Margaret Stout and Jeannine M. Love

Sustainability and Peaceful Coexistence for the Anthropocene
Pasi Heikkurinen

Forthcoming titles:

The Transnationalization of Anti-Corruption Law
Edited by Régis Bismuth, Jan Dunin-Wasowicz and Philip M. Nichols

Technocracy and the Law

Accountability, Governance and Expertise

Edited by Alessandra Arcuri and Florin Coman-Kund

Routledge
Taylor & Francis Group
LONDON AND NEW YORK

First published 2021
by Routledge
2 Park Square, Milton Park, Abingdon, Oxon OX14 4RN

and by Routledge
605 Third Avenue, New York, NY 10158

Routledge is an imprint of the Taylor & Francis Group, an informa business

British Library Cataloguing-in-Publication Data
A catalogue record for this book is available from the British Library

Library of Congress Cataloging-in-Publication Data
A catalog record has been requested for this book

ISBN: 978-0-367-89857-1 (hbk)
ISBN: 978-1-032-00578-2 (pbk)
ISBN: 978-1-003-17476-9 (ebk)

Typeset in Galliard
by KnowledgeWorks Global Ltd.

Contents

Figures

Tables

About the editors

Alessandra Arcuri is Professor of Inclusive Global Law and Governance at the Erasmus School of Law and Erasmus Initiative Dynamics of Inclusive Prosperity, Erasmus University Rotterdam. Her research focuses on international economic law and the relationship with human rights, environmental and public health law, as well as on the global governance of risks and the emergence of global technocracy.

Florin Coman-Kund is Assistant Professor of European Union and Public International Law, Erasmus School of Law at Erasmus University Rotterdam. His research focuses on legal aspects of Union's external administrative action and actors across various policy areas, as well as on urgent issues concerning the functions and limits of law in multilevel governance, legitimacy and accountability of EU executive action, expert-based regulatory processes and the rule of law. Featured publication: *European Union Agencies as Global Actors. A Legal Study of the European Aviation Safety Agency, Frontex and Europol* (Routledge 2018).

Contributors

Paolo Davide Farah is Associate Professor at West Virginia University (USA). He is Founder, President, Director and Principal Investigator at gLAWcal – Global Law Initiatives for Sustainable Development (UK). He is also an Internationally Renowned Professor/Distinguished Professor of Law at Beijing Foreign Studies University (BFSU), Law School, China.

Osman Çağlar Dede is Post-doctoral Researcher in Philosophy, Vrije Universiteit Amsterdam, The Netherlands.

Sebastian Heidebrecht is Post-doctoral Researcher in Political Science, University of Vienna, Austri.a

Robert Howse is Lloyd C. Nelson Professor of International Law, New York University School of Law, New York, USA.

Machiko Kanetake is Assistant Professor of Public International Law, Utrecht University School of Law, Utrecht University, The Netherlands.

Jan Klabbers is Professor of International Law, University of Helsinki, Finland.

Marta Morvillo is Post-doctoral Researcher, Amsterdam Centre for European Law and Governance (ACELG), University of Amsterdam, The Netherlands.

Marijn van der Sluis is Assistant Professor of Constitutional Law, Maastricht University, The Netherlands.

Sanne Taekema is Professor of Jurisprudence, Erasmus School of Law, Erasmus University Rotterdam, The Netherlands.

Nathanael Tilahun Ali is Assistant Professor, Faculty Research Centre for Financial and Corporate Integrity, Coventry University, UK.

W. Gregory Voss is Associate Professor, TBS Business School, France.

Acknowledgements

In an academia increasingly driven by competition, we tend to forget how important collaboration is. This book is the result of the collective effort and cooperation of scholars from different parts of the world. We are grateful to all the academics who contributed to this volume or engaged in the rich conversation and exchanges during the conference paving the way to this book. The book project was born during the International Conference *Unpacking the 'Accountability Paradox' in Expert-Based Decision-Making*, organized by us on 30 November–1 December 2017, at the Erasmus School of Law, Erasmus University Rotterdam. This workshop was made possible by a small grant by the Research Programme Rethinking the Rule of Law, Erasmus School of Law and by funds from the personal EUR Fellowship awarded by the Erasmus University Rotterdam to Alessandra Arcuri for a project on 'Rethinking Global Technocracy: Towards A Theoretical Framework for the Accountability of Global Regulatory Scientific Institutions'. We are grateful to both the Rethinking the Rule of Law Research and the EUR Fellowship Programmes for their trust and generous financial support. We also owe a word of thanks to all our colleagues from the Department of International and European Union Law (IEUL), Erasmus School of Law, who have provided valuable feedback and support in many places, from the rooms of the conference to our little kitchen. In these Covid times, we miss our spontaneous and inspiring corridor chats. We also express our gratitude to Paolo Farah and all the colleagues at Routledge as well as Hannah Weber for their precious work and support throughout the publishing process.

Finally, a word of thanks goes to our families and friends, as academic life all too often breaks boundaries, invading homes, evenings, weekends and holidays. Thanks Martina, Florian, Anna, Olav and Corina for cheerfully and patiently enduring our busy schedules and confined availability.

Rotterdam, 27 November 2020
Alessandra Arcuri and Florin Coman-Kund

Foreword to technocracy and the law

Accountability, governance and expertise

Paolo Davide Farah[1]

In the current times of profound distrust for science and the crisis in global governance institutions, it is fundamental to re-evaluate the role of expert and expertise in the decision-making process.[2] Whether or not experts should be held accountable is this book's primary focus. The reliance on experts has been a fundamental trait of not only technical but also more politically driven international organizations, and, in several instances, experts have used their position to promote their agenda. The promotion of the 'epistemic community' agenda has had both, partially positive such as in the case of international standard settings[3] and negative outcomes.[4] Amongst the negative ones, politics, in various instances, have shifted on experts the legitimacy of 'purely' political decisions while in other cases, a global shared expert's agenda failed to consider or misinterpreted the impacts on particular groups, often the most vulnerable.[5] Global

1 Paolo Davide Farah, Associate Professor, West Virginia University, Eberly College of Arts and Sciences, John D. Rockefeller IV School of Policy and Politics, Department of Public Administration; West Virginia University, Center for Innovation in Gas Research and Utilization – CIGRU; West Virginia University, Institute of Water Security and Science – IWSS (USA). Founder, President, Director, Principal Investigator and Senior Research Fellow at gLAWcal – Global Law Initiatives for Sustainable Development. Internationally Renowned Professor/Distinguished Professor of Law at Beijing Foreign Studies University (BFSU), Law School, Beijing, China. Dual PhD in International Law from Aix-Marseille University (France) and University of Milan (Italy), LLM in European Legal Studies from the College of Europe in Bruges (Belgium), Maitrise (J.D.) in International and European Law from Paris Ouest La Defense Nanterre University (France). Email Addresses: paolofarah@yahoo.com; paolo.farah@glawcal.org.uk

2 Antonio Segura-Serrano (ed), *The Reform of International Economic Governance* (2017).

3 However, scholars argue that in international standard settings, national interests are often influencing the outcomes. See Walter Mattli and Tim Büthe, 'Setting International Standards: Technological Rationality or Primacy of Power?' (2003) 56 World Politics 1.

4 José E Alvarez, *International Organizations as Law-Makers* (OUP 2005) 34–35.

5 Angelica Bonfanti (ed), *Business and Human Rights in Europe: International Law Challenges* (Routledge 2019).

governance institutions are, however, resilient and adapt to changes quickly.[6] For instance, experts could: openly disagree with particular policies promoted by their organization,[7] call for changes from the inside of a particular epistemic community[8] or recognize that expertise is not enough for 'political' changes.[9]

In selecting and appointing experts, the level of technicalities and technical rigidity is the pattern used to evaluate an expert's professionalism. Ranging from law via economics to other social sciences, experts manage to find the most prominent place in driving political agenda across the globe. In addition to the expert's background, the ideological affinity with the institution also plays a key role.[10] As an example, the experts who 'build' the multilateral trading regime, proud supporters of free trade, gave little considerations in the past to the project's broader effects.[11] People and civil society organizations have been omitted from the policy debates. The financial crisis of 2007–2008 and the recent COVID-19 pandemic[12] have a role in clarifying that reality is much more complex than what a simple unique vision or a dominant paradigm let us believe. Even if it is agreed that societies and human beings' behaviour could not be foreseen, experts attempt to fill in the gap amongst politics and decision-making with tremendous and sometimes unnoticed consequences on society. The common wisdom on this topic is that, in light of the increasing interdependencies and difficulties of our world, experts and epistemic authority are the only reliable source for the betterment of society. This thought-provoking book manages to reopen this discussion to an unanswered question: Do we need to develop a normative and socially responsive accountability framework for experts?

Even though it was coined at the beginning of the last century, the term technocracy and expertise-based forms of governance is not anew suggestion. From the needed expertise in politics of the Plato's philosopher king via Classics knowledge for mandarins in Imperial China to specialized knowledge of consultors in the Roman Curia, governments have extensively relied on trusted advisors to guide and inform policies. Therefore, the relationship between politics and experts is a possible lens. While politics rests on values and normative

6 Robert Howse, 'From Politics to Technocracy-and Back Again: The Fate of the Multilateral Trading Regime' (2002) 96 The American Journal of International Law 94, 117.

7 Jonathan D. Ostry, Prakash Loungani and Davide Furceri, 'Neoliberalism: Oversold' (2016) 53 Finance & development 38.

8 Paolo Farah and Elena Cima (eds), *China's Influence on Non-Trade Concerns in International Economic Law* (Routledge 2016) 14.

9 WTO Director acknowledged '*Nothing Is Going to Change if I Stay Here*'. 'Azevedo Stepping Down Early From a WTO Already on the Brink' *Bloomberg* (14 May 2020) <https://www.bloomberg.com/news/articles/2020-05-14/wto-director-general-roberto-azevedo-is-said-to-plan-to-depart> accessed 25 June 2020.

10 David Kennedy, *A World of Struggle: How Power, Law, and Expertise Shape Global Political Economy* (Princeton University Press 2016) 5.

11 Howse (n 6) 97.

12 Ruiyun Li et al., 'Substantial Undocumented Infection Facilitates the Rapid Dissemination of Novel Coronavirus (SARS-CoV2)' (2020) Science 1.

judgements, technical knowledge requires positive policy analysis and lack of emotional attachment to the object of study. These two separate dimensions mutually influence and interfere with each other. Values and normative judgement in expert reasoning automatically eschew epistemic authority and biased decisions are taken by politicians resulting in a politicization of science. Value judgments are unavoidable in expert reasoning and they should be made explicit.[13] Same goes for the opposite. Politics should stop being guided by ideology and should consistently use tools based on statistical modelling and expert judgement,[14] even though it is clear that neither these instruments are totally neutral or impartial. In fact, the risk for advocating for neutrality is that real struggles are back-grounded and not openly disclosed to the public.

To be effective for reducing the experts' legitimacy deficit and the negative aspects that could arise from the relationship between the two dimensions, accountability should be reinforced under its legal dimension. The consequence in this case could be however problematic.

However, this book demonstrates that, along with definitory and epistemological issues, problems related with the transnationalization and globalization of technocracy are even more sparkling in today's society. Citizens lost their interest, trust and confidence over experts in particular and, more broadly in science's role for the betterment of human beings. Against this background, the very own foundations of science are challenged on a daily basis by raising populist movements with antiscientific views. Experts sitting or presiding over international decision-making bodies mediate between different stakeholders. Such organizations promote unity at the expenses of scientific paradigm shift; therefore, evidence-based decisions are often watered down for political purposes.

The year 2020 might be remembered as one additional step towards a continued loss of trust in the expertise and technocrats globally. If we look at the management of COVID-19 by the World Health Organization (WHO) and the slow and contradictory position of its director general, Tedros Adhanom, the problem of accountability seems of the utmost importance.[15] Since February 2020, the emergence of COVID-19 and the entire controversy surrounding the WHO and its role in what has been defined an international fiasco have been debated, while the numerous casualties have continued to emerge, and the number of deaths has increased. This took place despite the WHO experts telling the entire world that there is no reason to panic while these same experts have changed their opinions months later once the

13 Heather Douglas, 'The Role of Values in Expert Reasoning' (2008) 22 Public Affairs Quarterly 1.

14 Andrea Saltelli and Mario Giampietro, 'What Is Wrong with Evidence Based Policy, and How Can It Be Improved?' (2017) 91 Futures 62.

15 The case of face masks is an example of the different positions taken by the WHO during the health crisis. The Editorial Board, 'World Health Coronavirus Disinformation' *Wall Street Journal* (5 April 2020) <https://www.wsj.com/articles/world-health-coronavirus-disinformation-11586122093> accessed 5 October 2020.

pandemic had become truly global.[16] Moreover, these same experts have constantly issued guidelines and opinions that are being criticized by other experts. Those critics and negative commentators should concede that difficult position and work of the WHO at the intersection of expertise and geopolitics – and operating within a legal framework with its own limitations (slightly improved by the most recent health regulation).[17] Other countries have expressed their dissatisfaction with the role played by the WHO, others have called for the resignation of the WHO director, but only the United States (US) decided to withdraw its funding from the organization. Yet, the position of the United States should be also assessed in light of the anti-multilateral tendency of the Trump Presidency and its Administration expressed also by the withdrawal from the 2016 Paris climate Agreement.[18] The Biden-Harris duo promised they would revise both of these decisions on the first day of their administration.[19]

States did not do well in this pandemic either.[20] In fact, similarly, at a national level, virologists lead the political conversation not only on the COVID-19 but also, most alarmingly, on other aspects far from their expertise. An agreement, even on basic points such as the need of wearing facemasks, is still absent in terms of generating visible confusions and apprehension in citizens. Not only virologist but also other experts such as journalists and economists are increasingly offering their expertise regarding COVID-19 and present themselves as the most appropriate actor to manage the long term effects of the pandemic. Do we really need unaccountable experts (of any discipline) changing their minds based on political opportunities?

16 Jacqueline Howard CNN, 'WHO Stands by Recommendation to Not Wear Masks If You Are Not Sick or Not Caring for Someone Who Is Sick' (*CNN*) <https://www.cnn.com/2020/03/30/world/coronavirus-who-masks-recommendation-trnd/index.html> accessed 5 November 2020.

17 Christopher M. Weible and others, 'COVID-19 and the Policy Sciences: Initial Reactions and Perspectives' [2020] Policy Sciences 1, 10; for an overview of the problems faced by the WHO to counteract the pandemic *see*: 'COVID-19 and International Law: What Went Wrong and What Can We Learn from It?' <https://www.biicl.org/events/11373/covid-19-and-international-law-what-went-wrong-and-what-can-we-learn-from-it> accessed 5 November 2020.

18 Thomas G. Weiss, 'The UN and Multilateralism under Siege in the "Age of Trump"' (2018) 4 Global Summitry 1.

19 Julia Belluz, 'Trump Abandoned the WHO. Biden Will Rejoin the Agency on Day One in Office' (*Vox*, 9 November 2020) <https://www.vox.com/2020/11/9/21556172/trump-biden-transition-team-covid-19-who-join> accessed 9 November 2020; 'Biden Reaffirms Commitment to Rejoining Paris Agreement' (*EcoWatch*, 6 November 2020) <https://www.ecowatch.com/paris-climate-agreement-biden-2648649350.html> accessed 9 November 2020.

20 Andrea Lavazza and Mirko Farina, 'The Role of Experts in the Covid-19 Pandemic and the Limits of Their Epistemic Authority in Democracy' (2020) 8 Frontiers in Public Health <https://www.ncbi.nlm.nih.gov/pmc/articles/PMC7372112/> accessed 5 October 2020.

Furthermore, while some countries adopted one opinion of experts and entire nations have been quarantined in the last few months (like Italy, France, the United Kingdom, Spain), others like Sweden continued business as usual with the objective of establishing the herd immunity also in accordance with expert opinions.[21] In both cases, people have died. Which decision was correct is not known. Were there other suggestions that could have been adopted by the experts? Maybe. Would it lead to a better outcome? It is unclear. This is just one example of how experts and technocrats making decisions related to governance have either made bad decisions or simply did not know what the best decision is to take, despite their expertise. In fact, new issues emerged as a result of great disagreements between experts and technocrats. While experts such as doctors were pushing for the adoption of policies that save people's lives, technocrats at the government level were looking to avoid a great economic disaster and loss of jobs, which further complicated the decision-making process at state and supranational levels, where the decision of closing entire airports and borders was made only after the disaster has occurred. All these issues bring to another fundamental question: how to deal with the limits of expert knowledge in a crisis situation created by a new pandemic?

Yet, this book is not about COVID-19 and the role of experts and technocrats in this context.

In fact, the idea of this book and related conference was shaped well before COVID-19; however, the ongoing global pandemic has made clear even more than before among the non-experts and the general public opinion that the role of experts in policy and regulation making process are the cornerstone of our contemporary world and societies. Due to the effects of globalization, the decisions of Governments and International Organizations have an enormous impact on the life of communities and citizens of countries in the rest of the world. The global pandemic has just reminded us that barriers and walls might give the impression to part of the public opinion of being protected by what is unknown and 'alien'. As for fighting against climate change, the challenges of mitigation cannot be underestimated and cannot be solved by one country alone, but they require a global effort. Also, the public health is a matter that needs a global coalition to promote scientific collaboration and exchange among experts and scientists around the world to protect each and every community and family for the common future we share on this Earth.

Alessandra Arcuri and Florin Coman-Kund have worked hard to organize an International Workshop on 'Unpacking The "Accountability Paradox" in Expert Decision-Making', held at Erasmus University Rotterdam in The Netherlands on 30 November–1 December 2017, where early drafts of the various chapters of this volume were discussed. This International Workshop was organized in partnership and it was one of the scientific results of the Research Project

21 Rachel Elisabeth Irwin, 'Misinformation and De-Contextualization: International Media Reporting on Sweden and COVID-19' (2020) 16 Globalization and Health 62, 9–10.

'Rethinking The Rule of Law in an Era of Globalisation, Privatisation and Multiculturalisation' and the Research Project 'Rethinking Global Technocracy: An Inquiry into Accountability of Global Regulatory Scientific Institutions (GRSIs)'. All chapters have later developed thanks to the fruitful exchange and debate among the Workshop participants, following reciprocal comments on later updated version of the chapters, and the careful editorial review of the book editors and external reviewers.

As mentioned, these issues have become particularly important in the context of globalization and fit perfectly into the broader discussions related to the necessary changes and improvements of the international legal norms and systems of governance towards the protection of Non-Trade Concerns (NTCs).[22]

These topics are constitutive and pivotal of the gLAWcal book series on 'Transnational Law and Governance' and 'Global Law and Sustainable Development', published by Routledge Publishing (New York/London). In fact, through research, policy analysis and advocacy, gLAWcal attempts to shed new light on NTCs issues such as good and global governance, human rights, right to water, rights to food, social, economic and cultural rights, labour rights, access to knowledge, public health, social welfare, consumer interests and animal welfare, climate change, energy, environmental protection and sustainable development, product safety, food safety and security. All these values are directly affected by the global expansion of world trade and should be upheld to balance the excesses of globalization.

This book is an important addition to the gLAWcal book series on 'Transnational Law and Governance' regarding the broader meaning of good and global governance.[23]

Indeed, even before the emergence of COVID-19, the role of experts and technocrats has been questioned over the years and decades, especially in the last few years where seismic events occurred as a result. In fact, the number of events that occurred where expert opinions were incorrect and led to a complete failure of government's policies are too many that I could not mention them all in this foreword. Who can forget the 2007–2008 financial crisis that led to great economic losses where governments had to intervene to save banks and institutions that were deemed too big to fail? The crisis occurred despite having

22 Paolo Davide Farah, 'Trade and Progress: The Case of China' (2016) 30 Columbia Journal of Asian Law 51–112; Paolo Davide Farah and Elena Cima (eds), *China's Influence on Non-Trade Concerns in International Economic Law* (Routledge 2016). See also, Margaret Stout and Jeannine M. Love, *A Radically Democratic Response to Global Governance: Dystopian Utopias* (Routledge 2016).

23 For other relevant contributions in the field included in the gLAWcal book series, see Angelica Bonfanti (n 5); Jernej Letnar Černič, *Corporate Accountability under Socio-Economic Rights* (Routledge 2019) and Régis Bismuth, Jan Dunin-Wasowicz, and Philip M. Nichols (eds), *The Transnationalization of Anti-Corruption Law* (Routledge 2021).

experts telling us that the economy was great and that there was nothing to panic about.[24] Yet, things went downhill extremely fast where some countries have not recovered completely from the crisis until now, especially in the European region. Were these experts held accountable? Not really. In fact, we still do not know who exactly the 'so-called experts' were and who made the analysis and came to the conclusion that the economy was not going to be affected. Should we define experts based on particular criteria or accept that it is impossible to even reach a satisfactory definition, because it is too context dependent? This is just one example of many more where the so-called experts were not capable of using their expertise to improve the situation.[25] The current problems with globalization are another issue where experts also failed to foresee the problems that may occur as a result, such as job losses and trade wars. In fact, these same experts are perceived by a great number of the population of the countries that suffered from globalization, mainly the West, as part of the elite benefiting from this phenomenon on their expenses. In that sense, they are not seen as experts, but advocates of the new global order especially as their jobs have not been affected by globalization and, in many cases, their careers progressed as a result. The direct consequence of such perception was the election of Donald Trump in the United States as a blow to the establishment of both parties, while using a simple language that resonates with the people such as 'We will bring the jobs back' and 'We Will Make America Great Again (MAGA)'. This occurred in contrast to countless American and international experts and technocrats stating the Trump's claims and ideas were not feasible and, in many cases, may actually cause negative consequences to the country. Yet, the people who voted for him saw these same experts as the threat despite their expertise, and viewed the election of Trump, who was considered an outsider, as a great opportunity to reject the technocrats and experts in Washington, DC along with what they considered as the business as usual of both parties in the US politics.[26] This may also bring into light another important question: what is the role of trust as a factor influencing experts' legitimacy?

Another event that shook the world is Brexit. British citizens decided to withdraw from the European Union for several reasons including the loss of trust in the technocrats based in Brussels that are making decisions affecting their lives without any kind of accountability. Indeed, despite the reports and opinions of experts and technocrats in the United Kingdom as well as in Europe seeing

24 Ewald Engelen and others, 'Misrule of Experts? The Financial Crisis as Elite Debacle' (2012) 41 Economy and Society 360, 377 'We are living through compounding political disasters, the product of an elite debacle, that come after a massive misjudgement about the character and consequences of financial innovation. Technocratic elites and their political sponsors have failed in their first duty as public servants'.

25 Jens Maesse, 'Austerity Discourses in Europe: How Economic Experts Create Identity Projects' (2018) 31 Innovation: The European Journal of Social Science Research 8.

26 Ronald F. Inglehart and Pippa Norris, 'Trump, Brexit, and the Rise of Populism: Economic Have-Nots and Cultural Backlash' 6.

such move as extremely negative especially on the economy of the country, the British citizens decided to leave the European Union.[27] In fact, the Union itself faced and is still facing huge criticism because of the absence of the democratic process according to which the technocrats are being elected and the absence of accountability in the face of a great bureaucratic machine, where not one person can be held accountable. These are some of the events where experts and technocrats either failed to manage or were considered as one of the reasons for which it occurred.

In fact, the main problem that all these events highlight is related to experts and technocrats' lack of accountability. Even after the occurrence of disastrous events, these actors and players were not held accountable for their role and were not fired from their jobs, even if some at the top of the organizations and administration have resigned. It is for this reason that the general population, but also scholars, are questioning the exact role of experts and the way these experts can be held accountable for the decisions they make that affect the lives of entire populations. This is the main challenge facing international organizations and states alike as the public is increasingly voicing such concerns where solving this challenge may restore some of the legitimacy these actors have lost in the process of governing the world or the nation. Still, for the time being, it is not clear what can be done in this regard, especially as this problem is not a new one, but has been occurring over decades where numerous studies have been made attempting to provide a solution.

This book responds to this challenge where the different contributors are seeking to provide a solution to issues associated with expertise and technocracy. This book provides a comprehensive overview of this topic and the chapters address the following main points: experts and their role in policymaking; the complex relationship between policymakers and experts; the role for accountability and expertise in multilevel law and governance. Each of these matters is important. Indeed, experts play a great role in policymaking where politicians often resort to expert's opinions on different subjects and topics, and where the experts' opinion is usually essential in deciding a state's policy on a particular subject. Yet, the relation between policymakers and experts is a complicated one given sometimes the difference in priorities between these two actors and the many external factors that may shape such relation. Moreover, experts are seldom held accountable by the state or at the international level given the existence of huge bureaucracy that protects the experts, which is why questions related to how experts can be held accountable have been raised. Finally, the expertise in multilevel law and governance complicates the analysis and requires further investigation, especially as in recent years' institutions, such as the European

27 On the importance given to experts for the Remain campaign and its influence on public opinion John Clarke and Janet Newman, '"People in This Country Have Had Enough of Experts": Brexit and the Paradoxes of Populism' (2017) 11 Critical Policy Studies 101, 110–112.

Union, are being seen as detached from people's reality with the policies and measures taken by unknown experts and technocrats based in Brussels.

Technocracy shares a common point regarding accountability with populist movements because '*the interest of the whole of society has priority and therefore should not be constrained by procedures*'.[28] This book skilfully addresses how this lack in constraints at the multilateral, regional, and national level negatively affects the society. The in-depth and forward looking analysis of very diverse fields, from monetary policies via food safety and health protection to emerging technologies, cybersecurity and police, found a common pattern in accountability. Even if we are still far from both defining what is accountability and in holding at which is a satisfactory level of 'experts' to be accountable,[29] the direction is clear. This book offers rich, innovative, interdisciplinary and fresh approaches to strengthen accountability of experts. It also recognizes the importance of experts and highlights the urgent need of creating and operationalizing limits to experts, whether normative or ethical.[30] A holistic approach, in which not only experts but also social groups traditionally absent from the global agora, could help in re-shaping a socially responsible and integrative,[31] but, at the same time, a new procedural form of accountability'. An interesting outcome of the widespread promotion of a new paradigm in accountability is that populist movements could be reduced as an immediate effect.

The first part of this book provides perspectives on accountability of expertise in multilevel governance where chapters focus on the challenges facing the identification of accountability; the rule of law and expert accountability and the different dimensions of expert accountability.

The second part examines the accountability of experts in economic and financial governance where the scholars addressed issues such as uncertainty of knowledge; the connection between accountability and democracy; and accountability in the European Economic and Monetary Union, as well as with regards to international anti-money laundering and counter-terrorism financing.

The third part addresses accountability of experts in environment, health and safety governance such as in the context of transnational radiological standards; and European pesticides regulation.

28 Daniele Caramani, 'Will vs. Reason: The Populist and Technocratic Forms of Political Representation and Their Critique to Party Government' (2017) 111 American Political Science Review 54, 61.

29 'After Dallas, The Future of Black Lives Matter' *The New Yorker* (10 July 2016) <https://www.newyorker.com/news/news-desk/after-dallas-the-future-of-black-lives-matters> accessed 25 June 2020. Minneapolis showed once again that lacking accountability for police could lead to police brutality.

30 See Alessandra Arcuri and Florin Coman-Kund, 'Introduction: Breaking Taboos, Talking Accountability' (in this volume).

31 Margaret Stout and Jeannine M. Love, *Integrative Governance: Generating Sustainable Responses to Global Crises* (Routledge 2018).

The fourth part tackles accountability of experts in digitization and data protection governance for instance, in the context of the evolving role of ENISA in data protection, ePrivacy and cybersecurity as well as of Europol's accountability system.

As such, this book offers an innovative analysis of the challenges facing experts and technocrats, taking into account the developments that occurred in the last decades from technological and scientific perspectives as well as the events that took place and changed the world, especially in OECD Countries. It is in this context that the holistic overview provided in this book is very much needed, especially given the great questions surrounding the topic addressed and the debates that occurred and are currently taking place and will be taking place in the future.

Professor Paolo Davide Farah
Editor-in-Chief for the gLAWcal Book Series "Transnational Law and Governance" published by Routledge (New York/London)
West Virginia University, USA and gLAWcal – Global Law Initiatives for Sustainable Development, UK

Introduction

Breaking taboos, talking accountability

Alessandra Arcuri and Florin Coman-Kund

On 24 June 2018, *The Guardian* published an Editorial, arguing that there is little difference between Brexiters and experts: 'In fact both rabble-rousing Brexiters and experts have more in common than either would admit. Populists claim to have a special insight into the will of the people, able to dispense with debate and discussion. (…) Technocrats also argue it's necessary to insulate policies from political challenge'.[1] The last part of this passage alludes to the problem of experts exercising 'too much' power, possibly hijacking high politics and eroding democracy.[2] The disengagement of experts and expert bodies with people and politics is in many ways entangled with populism. New disintegrationist developments such as those underpinning Brexit and Trump politics (as well as other forms of populism) have been accompanied by attacks on entrenched elites and the technocratic decision-making paradigm underpinning them. From this vantage point, populism could be seen as the most acute manifestation of a legitimacy crisis affecting technocratic law and governance.[3] While we may contest the amount of power gained by experts, it is unlikely and arguably undesirable that experts will cease to play an influential role in contemporary regulatory regimes.

It is from the time of Machiavelli that the prominent role of the 'man of knowledge' in policy-making has been recognized. With the steady pace of technological progress, the engagement of experts in regulatory processes has naturally intensified. Today the reach of expert-based decision-making is capillary, and it has virtually covered all regulatory realms, from health and safety regulation to economic governance.

1 Editorial, 'The Guardian View on Hyper-populism: It's Infecting Politicians and Technocrats', 24 June 2018, *The Guardian* available at: <https://www.theguardian.com/commentisfree/2018/jun/24/the-guardian-view-on-hyper-populism-its-infecting-politicians-and-technocrats?CMP=share_btn_tw>. In the context of this Introduction, we use the term 'populism' in its pejorative connotation, which associates populism with nativism and anti-pluralism. However, we acknowledge that this use of the term may also be abused to marginalize instances of radical democracy and valid critiques of elite liberal democratic politics. For lucid analysis, see Robert Howse, 'Epilogue: In Defense of Disruptive Democracy—A Critique of Anti-populism', (2019) 17 (2) International Journal of Constitutional Law 641.

2 See Paul Tucker, *Unelected Power. The Quest for Legitimacy in Central Banking and the Regulatory State* (Princeton University Press 2018).

3 See, for example, Philip Wallach, The Administrative State's Legitimacy Crisis (2016), Brookings Institute, available at <https://www.brookings.edu/research/the-administrative-states-legitimacy-crisis/> accessed 6 July 2020, where he makes the case that the bureaucratic and technocratic nature of the American administrative state 'is at the heart of our contemporary legitimacy crisis'.

Think of the various expert bodies operating within the World Health Organization (WHO), which are crucial to regulate and constrain pandemics. Or consider the safety standards for mobile phones, nanotechnologies, foodstuffs, pesticides, computer networks and systems etc., which are co-produced by transnational bodies largely populated by experts. If the expert-policy nexus is unquestionably significant, it is also increasingly controversial. The backlash against so-called technocracy, with mounting mistrust in regulatory experts, is not only fuelled by populism. NGOs, public intellectuals and academics have also criticized the too close relation between experts and power.[4] As the integration of expert knowledge in regulatory policy remains key for well-functioning democratic institutions, it is thus crucial to interrogate how expertise can meaningfully relate to the broader society, rather than fixating on insulation. It is in this relational dimension that accountability may play a role.

While socio-legal scholars have long studied the expert-policy nexus,[5] insufficient attention has been paid to the question of their accountability.[6] The

4 See for instance, Corporate Europe Observatory, 'The Glyphosate Saga and "Independent Scientific Advice" According to Germany, the UK & France' (Corporate Europe Observatory, 2 April 2015) <https://corporateeurope.org/en/foodand-agriculture/2015/04/glyphosate-saga-independent-scientific-advice-according-germany-uk>; Madureira Lima, Joana, and Sandro Galea, 'Corporate Practices and Health: A Framework and Mechanisms' (2108) 14 (1) Globalization and Health 21 <https://globalizationand-health.biomedcentral.com/track/pdf/10.1186/s12992-018-0336-y?site=globalization-andhealth.biomedcentral.com> accessed 6 July 2020.

5 See for instance, Sheila Jasanoff, *The Fifth Branch: Science Advisers as Policymakers* (Harvard University Press 1990); Christian Joerges, Karl-Heinz Ladeur and Ellen Vos (eds), *Integrating Scientific Expertise into Regulatory Decision-making. National Experiences and European Innovations* (Nomos 1997); Sheila Jasanoff, *Designs on Nature: Science and Democracy in Europe and the United States* (Princeton University Press 2005); Justus Lentsch and Peter Weingart (eds), *The Politics of Science Advice: Institutional Design for Quality Assurance* (CUP 2011), and in particular Sheila Jasanoff, 'Quality Control and Peer Review in Advisory Science' in Justus Lentsch and Peter Weingart (eds), *The Politics of Scientific Advice: Institutional Design for Quality Assurance* (CUP 2011) 19–35; Monika Ambrus and others, *The Role of 'Experts' in International and European Decision-Making Processes* (CUP 2014); Cathrine Holst, 'What Is Epistocracy?' in Simen Andersen Øyen, Tone Lund-Olsen and Nora Sørensen Vaage (eds), *Sacred Science?* (Wageningen Academic Publishers 2012) 41–54.

6 For works discussing issues related to the accountability of experts, see Peter Weingart and Sabine Maasen (eds), *Democratization of Expertise? Exploring Novel Forms of Scientific Advice in Political Decision-Making* (Springer 2005); Alessandra Arcuri and Marta Simoncini, 'Scientists and Legal Accountability: Lessons from the L'Aquila Case' (2015) EUI Department of Law Research Paper No. 2015/17 <http://ssrn.com/abstract=2600406> accessed 30 April 2020; Elena Madalina Busuioc, 'Blurred Areas of Responsibility European Agencies' Scientific "Opinions" under Scrutiny' in Ambrus and others (eds) (n 5) 383–402; Madalina Busuioc, *European Agencies. Law and Practices of Accountability* (OUP 2013); Sean Gailmard and Patty John, *Learning While Governing. Expertise and Accountability in the Executive Branch* (University of Chicago Press 2012); Cathrine Holst and Anders Molander, 'Public Deliberation and The Fact of Expertise: Making Experts Accountable' (2017) 31 Social Epistemology 235; contributions by Anchrit Wille, 'The European Commission's Accountability Paradox', Gijs Jan Brandsma, 'Accountable Comitology?' and Madalina Busuioc, 'European Agencies: Pockets of Accountability' in Mark Bovens, Deirdre Curtin, and Paul 't Hart (eds), *The Real World of EU Accountability. What Deficit?* (OUP 2010); Giandomenico Majone, 'Delegation of Regulatory Powers in a Mixed Polity' (2002) 8(3) European Law Journal 319.

side-lining of accountability as a central theme of technocratic governance may be related to the haunting past, where scientists have been publicly prosecuted for their 'perilous' knowledge, the trial of Galileo being one of the most spectacular examples. With such (in-)famous trials in the back of our mind, it is wise to handle the idea of expert accountability with care. At the same time, it would be a mistake to transform this awareness into a taboo. Breaking what we may call the 'Galileo taboo', this book tackles the urgent questions of whether and how experts and/or expert bodies *are* and *can be* held accountable. But, what does accountability mean and how could it be meaningful vis-à-vis expertise? Before cracking this question, it is worth spending few words on the concept of experts employed in this book.

1 Policy-making in a world of experts

The book rests on a broad conceptualization of experts and it draws on the idea of 'regulatory science', which refers to the body of knowledge that serves policy-making.[7] Such experts typically work for or with institutions, which exercise epistemic and legal authority concomitantly.[8] A variety of regulatory bodies, including regulatory agencies and authorities, *ad hoc* technical expert bodies, subsidiary bodies of international organizations, private-public regulatory partnerships and other regulatory networks are the natural habitat for contemporary regulatory expertise.

Examples can be found in virtually all fields of law, from food and safety regulation to the economic realm and criminal law. Think for instance of food safety. In many countries, an agency with dedicated experts is entrusted with the task of assessing the safety of various substances that could pose a risk to the consumer. This is also true at the global level, where the scientific bodies of the Codex Alimentarius Commission are entrusted with the assessment of the safety of a wide variety of compounds related to food, from pesticides to additives.[9] The advice of experts is typically followed by decision-making bodies. As for food safety, this is true for many other fields. International climate change policy, for once, is closely linked

7 Sheila Jasanoff, 'Contested Boundaries in Policy-Relevant Science' (1987) 17(2) Social Studies of Science 195; Jasanoff, *The Fifth Branch: Science Advisers as Policymakers* (n 5); Jasanoff, *Designs on Nature: Science and Democracy in Europe and the United States* (n 5).

8 Oren Perez, 'The Hybrid Legal-Scientific Dynamic of Transnational Scientific Institutions' (2015) 26 European Journal of International Law 391; for a similar conceptualization, see also Alessandra Arcuri, 'Three Dimensions of Accountability for Global Technocracy' (Chapter 3 in this volume). In relation to the term 'legal authority' we draw on the broad approach towards public authority developed by Armin Von Bogdandy, Philipp Dann and Matthias Goldmann, 'Developing the Publicness of Public International Law: Towards a Legal Framework for Global Governance Activities' in Armin Von Bogdandy and others (eds), *The Exercise of Public Authority by International Institutions: Advancing International Institutional Law* (Springer 2010) 3–32.

9 Alessandra Arcuri, 'Global Food Safety Standards: The Evolving Regulatory Epistemology at the Intersection of the SPS Agreement and the Codex Alimentarius Commission' in Panagiotis Delimatsis (ed), *The Law, Economics and Politics of International Standardisation* (CUP 2015) 79–103.

to the reports of the UN Intergovernmental Panel on Climate Change (IPCC). Similarly, the International Standardization Organization (ISO) regulates the most disparate items from robot to nanotechnologies, through a plethora of committees mainly composed by experts. Turning to European Union's (EU) monetary policy, we discover a different kind of expertise, of economic and financial nature, embodied in the European Central Bank (ECB). In a different EU policy field, the Serious and Organised Crime Threat Assessment (SOCTA) compiled by Europol's data analysts provides an EU-wide situational awareness and recommendations concerning serious and organized cross-border crime, thereby representing arguably the backbone of policy priority setting in this area; similarly, Europol's Internet Organised Crime Threat Assessment (IOCTA) provides key findings on emerging threats and developments in cybercrime, and recommendations to tackle cybercrime.[10] Also, in the EU context, one may mention the role of the discreet European Network and Information Security Agency (ENISA) in advising the European Commission and the Member States in the area of network information security, and providing guidelines on cybersecurity.[11] But can we pull such variegated expertise, ranging from traditional 'hard' science (e.g. biologists and physicists) to other types of sciences (e.g. economic and financial expertise, forensic investigation techniques, crime-related information/intelligence processing and analysis, computer science), in one category?

Arguably yes. While legal-economic experts acting in the Brexit or the Euro crisis are of a different kind than toxicologists, they contribute to the decision-making process in comparable ways. Take for instance the Greek crisis. The estimates made by economists at the International Monetary Fund (IMF) and by ECB experts were instrumental for giving Greece the financial assistance. When a scientific committee of the European Food Safety Agency (EFSA) or of the Codex Alimentarius Commission concludes that a substance is safe, such expert report is instrumental for the legal decision to allow that substance (e.g. a food additive) on the EU market.[12] In both cases, the expert opinion is contestable and yet hard to contest, because only a select group of individuals, who have acquired the specific competences to master the field and some official qualifications, are arguably knowledgeable. In short, technocratic economic governance depends on and is intertwined with economic experts in similar, albeit distinct, ways as food regulation is with scientific experts. In a nutshell, a common denominator of the operation of experts is their influence on policy-making, irrespective of their field of expertise. Given their unquestionable influence on the policy-making process,

10 See the chapter by Florin Coman-Kund, 'Holding Europol Accountable: The Promise and Challenges of (Hybrid) Multilevel Accountability' (Chapter 12 in this volume).

11 See the chapter by W. Gregory Voss, 'The Concept of Accountability in the Context of the Evolving Role of ENISA in Data Protection, ePrivacy and Cybersecurity' (Chapter 11 in this volume).

12 Arcuri (n 9).

it is of crucial importance to better understand in what ways experts are (and can) be held to account. Against this background, we are confident that a broad conception of experts will enable us to engage with a more sophisticated understanding of diverse instances of expert-based decision-making in which accountability is at issue.

2 Policymakers and experts: A complex relation

One dimension that deserves particular attention is the complex relationship between expertise and politics. Expertise and politics meet both in formal and informal venues within the regulatory process, in the context of evidence/scientifically based decision-making or when policy formulation and implementation requires specialized knowledge (e.g. conducting monetary policy or ensuring compliance with data protection legal standards). The relationship is complex because politics is typically seen to rest on values and normative judgements, whereas technical knowledge or science in a very broad sense is seen to rely on positive analysis and 'disinterestedness'. The complex relationship between expertise and policy-making is a vexed one and several scholars in the field of sociology of knowledge and science and technology studies have shed light on how values can and do legitimately permeate the sphere of science.[13] One important insight from this scholarship is that the way questions are framed, the choice between different plausible analytical models or the methods to deal with uncertainty are all points where value judgements enter the realm of science. In some regulatory ambits, such as risk regulation in the United States, the relationship between policymakers and experts has been institutionalized by establishing an iterative process whereby scientists and policymakers have to be in a continuous dialogue with one another.[14] Such relation should enable the policymaker to better appreciate value judgements in science and, symmetrically, it should enable experts to take into some consideration the normative questions key to policy-making. Despite some attempts to regulate the relationship between the sphere of policy-making and the sphere of knowledge production, such relation remains

13 Maasen and Weingart (n 6); Helga Nowotny, Peter Scott and Michael Gibbons, *Re-thing Science: Knowledge and the Public in an Age of Uncertainty* (Wiley 2001); Bruno Latour and Steve Woolgar, *Laboratory Life: The Construction of Scientific Facts* (Princeton University Press 1986); Heather Douglas, 'Inserting the Public into Science' in Maasen and Weingart (eds) (n 6) 153–169.

14 National Research Council, 'Risk Assessment in the Federal Government: Managing The Process' (National Academy Press 1983); important Reports for the evolution of these debate are: National Research Council, 'Science and Judgment in Risk Assessment' (National Academy Press 1994); Paul C. Stern and Harvey V. Fineberg (eds), *Understanding Risk: Informing Decisions in a Democratic Society* (National Academy Press 1996) and Royal Commission on Environmental Pollution, 'Setting Environmental Standards' (21st Report 1998). For an overview and an analysis, see Elizabeth Fisher, 'Framing Risk Regulation: A Critical Reflection' (2013) 4 European Journal of Risk Regulation 125.

dense and tense. An insightful way to look at this question is through the lenses of philosophy of science, as shown in chapters 3 and 10 in this volume.[15]

The relationship between politics and expert decision-making is also closely related to the legitimacy deficits of expert-based decision-making. As well captured by the words of Wouter Werner: 'A (...) factor that helps to explain the decrease in the legitimacy of experts is the increasing realization that translating scientific knowledge into legal and political decision-making is not a neutral enterprise, but involves a politics of framing and defining'.[16] It should also be noted that the contestation of experts can be partly ascribed to the mistrust caused by the sometimes too 'cosy' relation between experts and power.[17] When experts are seen to serve vested interests, instead of pursuing the public interest through an allegedly neutral analysis of facts, they lose legitimacy. In view of this, questions relating to the accountability of experts are important also for the very legitimacy of expert-based decision-making.

3 Grasping accountability

A systematic analysis of the accountability of experts requires few preliminary words on the concept of accountability. The notion of accountability is, in fact, protean. On the one hand, it is regarded as one of the 'golden concepts' of modern governance.[18] On the other hand, accountability has become 'the victim of its own success' turning into an 'umbrella concept'[19] that carries out 'most of the major burdens of "democratic governance"'.[20] Accountability has acquired

15 See Alessandra Arcuri, 'Three Dimensions of Accountability for Global Technocracy' (Chapter 3 in this volume) and Osman Caglar Dede, 'The Value Free Ideal of Science and Non-Epistemic Values in Regulatory Toxicology' (Chapter 10 in this volume).

16 Wouter Werner, 'The Politics of Expertise' in Ambrus and others (eds) (n 5) 48.

17 See, for example, Naomi Oreskes and Erik M Conway, *Merchants of Doubt, How a Handful of Scientists Obscured the Truth on Issues from Tobacco Smoke to Global Warming* (Bloomsbury Press 2010); Fiona Godlee, 'Conflict of Interests and Pandemic Flu' (2010) 340 British Medical Journal 1256; Emily A. Bruemmer and Allyn L. Taylor, 'Institutional Transparency in Global Health Law-Making: The World Health Organization and the Implementation of the International Health Regulations' in Andrea Bianchi and Anne Peters (eds), *Transparency in International Law* (CUP 2013).

18 Mark Bovens, Thomas Schillemans and Paul 't Hart, 'Does Accountability Work? An Assessment Tool' (2008) 86 Public Administration 225. For leading monographic studies on accountability, see Mark Bovens, *The Quest for Responsibility: Accountability and Citizenship in Complex Organisations* (CUP 1998); Richard Mulgan, *Holding Power to Account. Accountability in Modern Democracies* (Palgrave Macmillan 2003); Mark Bovens, Deirdre Curtin and Paul 't Hart (eds), *The Real World of EU Accountability. What Deficit?* (OUP 2010); Mark Bovens, Robert E. Goodin and Thomas Schillemans (eds), *The Oxford Handbook of Public Accountability* (OUP 2014).

19 Madalina Busuioc, *The Accountability of European Agencies. Legal Provisions and Ongoing Practices* (PhD dissertation, Eburon 2010) 31.

20 Richard Mulgan, 'Accountability: An Ever-Expanding Concept?' (2000) 78 Public Administration 555.

various meanings over time, some narrow, others broad, and it has been used interchangeably with concepts like transparency, responsibility, responsiveness and control.[21] This led Schillemans to conclude that conceptually, 'accountability is one of these alluring concepts that are like fine old wine: they are full of depth and complexity, they have a "good feel", yet they are very difficult to define in a conclusive way'.[22] To capture its polyhedral meaning, Flinder has christened accountability as 'the *über*-concept of the twenty-first century'.[23]

In one of the most well-known definitions put forward by Bovens, accountability has been characterized as a 'relationship between an actor and a forum, in which the actor has the obligation to explain and justify his or her conduct, the forum can pose questions and pass judgment, and the actor might face consequences'.[24] From this perspective, accountability is concerned with *ex post* oversight, it determines whether the actor acted within the limits of its mandate and discretion,[25] and it is operationalized through three mains steps (informing, debating and the possibility for facing consequences). Yet, both in policy/institutional practice and in academia, accountability is often employed beyond Bovens's conceptualization. In broad terms, accountability encompasses different values and has numerous ramifications: the sense of responsibility and concern for the public interest expected from public servants ('professional' and 'personal' accountability); the various institutional checks and balances to control public powers (accountability as 'control'); the extent to which public power responds to the needs of their citizens (accountability as 'responsiveness') or the public discussion between actors and citizens as a feature of deliberative democracy (accountability as 'dialogue').[26]

Variations in accountability relationships occur also depending on how (accountability mechanism or regime), for what (the conduct for which the actor is held accountable) and to whom (the type of forum) accountability is rendered. Also, various forms of accountability have been devised ranging from managerial

21 Colin Scott, 'Accountability in the Regulatory State' (2000) 27 Journal of Law and Society 38; Busuioc (n 19) 31–32; Mira Scholten, Michiel Luchtman and Elmar Schmidt, 'The Proliferation of EU Enforcement Authorities: a New Development in Law Enforcement in the EU' in Mira Scholten and Michiel Luchtman (eds), *Law Enforcement by EU Authorities. Implications for Political and Judicial Accountability* (Eduard Elgar Publishing 2017) 7; see also Florin Coman-Kund, 'Holding Europol Accountable: The Promise and Challenges of (Hybrid) Multilevel Accountability' (Chapter 12 in this volume).

22 Thomas Schillemans, 'Horizontal Accountability. A Partial Remedy for the Accountability Deficit of EU Agencies' (paper presented at 5th Transatlantic Dialogue 'The Future Governance', Washington DC, 11–13 June 2009), 3 [quote taken from Madalina Busuioc (n 19) 32].

23 Matthew Flinders, 'The Future and Relevance of Accountability Studies', in Bovens, Goodin, and Schillemans (eds), *The Oxford Handbook of Public Accountability* (n 18) 661.

24 Mark Bovens, 'Analysing and Assessing Public Accountability. A Conceptual Framework' (2007) 13 European Law Journal 450; Mark Bovens, 'Two Concepts of Accountability: Accountability as a Virtue and as a Mechanism' (2010) 33 West European Politics 946.

25 Busuioc (n 19) 35.

26 See Mulgan (n 20) 556.

and professional accountability to public, political and legal accountability.[27] In the context of this book, professional accountability, understood as 'a system marked by deference to expertise where reliance must be placed on the technical knowledge of experts',[28] bears particular relevance. Salient issues here are to devise the appropriate standards and mechanisms to ensure accountability of experts and to operationalize and reconcile multiple channels of accountability, ranging from systems of professional peer review to broader democratic accountability to the public and public representatives.[29]

In the European and international law context, accountability has often been construed broadly, in light of the aims it serves and the setting within which it operates.[30] In this respect, besides the more specific aim of securing control of public power, accountability may serve far-reaching goals, including 'enhancing the legitimacy of international and European law as such'[31] and inducing public power to reflect and learn from its successes and failures.[32] In the EU context, Van Gerven maintained that the ultimate objective of the process of accountable government in the European Union 'is about making the Union's structure more democratic and the Union's decision-making process more legitimate'.[33] This broader function accountability fulfils on the EU and international levels entails that accountability in this context is not only a retrospective process (*ex post*) but often also a prospective one (*ex ante*) 'potentially embracing issues such as participation and standard setting'.[34] In this respect, also Bovens admits that in practice '[t]he line between retrospective accounting and proactive policy-making can be thin' as accountability 'is not only about control' but 'also

27 Ruth W. Grant and Robert O. Keohane, 'Accountability and Abuses of Power in World Politics' (2005) 99 American Political Science Review 29; Mark Bovens, 'Analysing and Assessing Public Accountability. A Conceptual Framework' (2006) European Governance Papers (EUROGOV) No. C-06-01, 22 <http://edoc.vifapol.de/opus/volltexte/2011/2459/pdf/egp_connex_C_06_01.pdf> accessed 22 May 2020; see also, Busuioc (n 19) 41.

28 Barbara S. Romzek and Melvin J. Dubnick, 'Accountability in the Public Sector: Lessons from the Challenger Tragedy' (1987) 47 Public Administration Review 227, 229.

29 See Mulgan (n 20) 558–560.

30 For a framework conceptualizing accountability including both prospective and retrospective mechanisms, see Deirdre Curtin and Andre Nollkaemper, 'Conceptualizing Accountability in International and European Law' in *Netherlands Yearbook of International Law* (vol 36, CUP 2005) 3–20.

31 Ibid 9–10; Walter Van Gerven, 'Which Form of Accountable Government for the European Union?' In *Netherlands Yearbook of International Law* (vol 36, CUP 2005) 227–258.

32 Bovens, 'Analysing and Assessing Public Accountability. A Conceptual Framework' (n 24) 463–464.

33 Van Gerven (n 31) 228.

34 Curtin and Nollkaemper (n 30) 8; see for similar views, Anne Davies, *Accountability: A Public Law Analysis of Government by Contract* (OUP 2001) 81; Carol Harlow, *Accountability in the European Union* (OUP 2002) 10; Elizabeth Fisher, 'The European Union in the Age of Accountability' (2004) 24(3) Oxford Journal of Legal Studies 495, 510.

about prevention'.[35] Accountability thus can be seen as a continuous process that entails informing and explaining, inquiring and debating, and passing judgement both over past and future conduct. This vision, encompassing both prospective and retrospective dimensions, well aligns with the characterization of accountability advanced by the International Law Association, whereby transparency, participation, reason-giving and review mechanisms are listed as key elements of accountability.[36] This book embraces such broader conceptualization of accountability, acknowledging that different dimensions of accountability can serve different functions and that in different contexts some mechanisms could be more apt than others. Aware of the perils of a too broad understanding of accountability,[37] our conceptual choice is justified by the need to best reflect the current dynamics of regulatory decision-making and to grasp various manifestations of accountability both in international and EU legal orders. The different contributions in the book will further elaborate on why certain forms of accountability could best serve the regime studied.

4 Accountability in multilevel law and governance

While accountability has been studied in various domains, this book focuses on expertise situated in multilevel law and governance, with an emphasis on European and international law. The fact that powers are exercised across national, European and international levels by multiple public and (quasi-public) actors embedded in complex procedures poses significant challenges from an accountability perspective as this phenomenon tends to blur lines of control and channels of accountability. In multilevel and polyarchic regulatory regimes, the contribution of each participant to the decision-making is often obscured, leading to the so-called problem of many hands.[38] Such dispersion of authority between national, European and international layers puts existing legal frameworks under strain, thereby posing challenges to the rule of law and rendering accountability difficult. Arguably, the propagation of decision-making towards European and global levels is not (always) matched by a corresponding development of legal frameworks and safeguards, which may obfuscate accountability. In this context, multilevel governance poses specific risks such as the multiplication and (potential) redundancy of accountability mechanisms and fora or, on the

35 Bovens 'Analysing and Assessing Public Accountability. A Conceptual Framework' (2006) (n 27) 13; see also Florin Coman-Kund, 'Holding Europol Accountable: The Promise and Challenges of (Hybrid) Multilevel Accountability' (Chapter 12 in this volume).

36 International Law Association (ILA), 'Report of the International Law Association Berlin Conference on the Accountability of International Organizations', reprinted in [2004] *1(1)* International Organizations Law Review 221.

37 See on this, Bovens, 'Analysing and Assessing Public Accountability. A Conceptual Framework' (2007) (n 24) 449–450.

38 See, for instance, Andre Nollkaemper, 'The Problem of Many Hands in International Law' (2015) Amsterdam Law School Legal Studies research paper, No. 2015-35; Bovens, *The Quest for Responsibility: Accountability and Citizenship in Complex Organizations* (n 18) 46.

contrary, the insufficiency or inappropriateness of existing accountability frameworks to cover vertically and/or horizontally diffused decision-making. Hence, from a conceptual point of view, accountability should be flexible enough to encompass various actors (or assemblages of actors), diverse (sometimes unconventional) accountability fora and varied (often creative) accountability mechanisms.[39] Against this background, it may be advanced that the best match for multilevel governance should be multilevel accountability, prompting questions as regards the interplay between accountability mechanisms at different levels, 'how accountability mechanisms at one level can supplement and fill gaps that arise at other levels'[40] or the prospects for designing hybrid or integrated accountability tools for pooled or composite multilevel regulatory processes.[41]

Taking stock of the burgeoning scholarship on accountability, this book holds to the core of the concept of accountability as an eminently ***relational ideal***, whereby actors exercising public authority are ultimately held to account by those subjected to power. As mentioned above, the dimensions to realize this relationship can be manifolds, encompassing ***both ex ante and ex post mechanisms***. Accordingly, for the purpose of this book, accountability of expert-based decision-making in multilevel governance encompasses checks and balances, procedural safeguards, participation, openness and transparency, legal and quasi-legal review mechanisms, and it resonates with input/throughput/output legitimacy perspectives.[42] In view of the diversity characterizing expert-based decision-making processes in the EU and global context, we prefer viewing accountability as a widespread net, which can intercept and possibly mitigate abuses of power, rather than an instrument for performing a high-precision surgery.[43]

39 Curtin and Nollkaemper (n 30) 10–11 and 13.

40 Ibid; see also Eyal Benvenisti and Gearge W. Downs, 'National Courts Review of Transnational Private Regulation' (2011) Tel Aviv University Law Faculty Papers, Working Paper 125, available at <http://law.bepress.com/taulwps/art125> accessed 7 July 2020; Ayelet Berman, 'The Role of Domestic Administrative Law in the Accountability of Informal International Lawmaking: The Case of the ICH' in Joost Pauwelyn, Ramses Wessel and Jan Wouters (eds), *Informal International Lawmaking* (OUP 2012) 468.

41 See for the conceptualization and application of 'hybrid (fluid) multilevel accountability' with regard to European Union agencies, Florin Coman-Kund, 'Holding Europol Accountable: The Promise and Challenges of (Hybrid) Multilevel Accountability' (Chapter 12 in this volume).

42 Vivien A. Schmidt, 'Democracy and Legitimacy in the European Union Revisited: Output, Input and Throughput' (2010) KFG Working Paper Series, No. 21 <https://www.polsoz.fu-berlin.de/en/v/transformeurope/publications/working_paper/wp/wp21/index.html> accessed 7 July 2020.

43 For attempts to operationalize and measure public accountability with some degree of precision, see David and Keith Dixon 'The Public Accountability Index: Crafting a Parametric Disclosure Index for Annual Reports' (2004) 36(1) The British Accounting Review 79; Fabian Amtenbrink, 'Towards an Index of Accountability for Informal International Lawmakers?' in Joost Pauwelyn, Ramses Wessel and Jan Wouters (eds) *Informal International Lawmaking* (OUP 2012) 337–356; Mark Bovens and Anchrit Wille, 'Indexing Watchdog Accountability Powers a Framework for Assessing the Accountability Capacity of Independent Oversight Institutions' (2020) Regulation & Governance 1-21 available at <https://onlinelibrary.wiley.com/doi/full/10.1111/rego.12316> accessed 6 July 2020.

5 The challenges of experts' accountability and the 'nobody problem'

One limit inherent to holding experts accountable is precisely their expertise, which raises questions about the level of expertise someone should master in order to evaluate experts' performance and, more generally, about the feasibility of public (democratic) accountability of experts. As accountability entails a relationship (giving account), it is crucial that the actors engaged in the accountability relationship can talk the same language. The problem though is that resort to experts is necessary precisely because of the unique knowledge they possess and because, in a certain sense, experts speak different languages than the layman and the policymaker. Take, for instance, scientific expertise in health and safety regulation. Both at the domestic and international levels, new institutions have been created to let the experts (e.g. toxicologists) provide an answer to scientific/technical questions (e.g. are residues of pesticide x, in quantity y, carcinogenic for humans?). In this context, accountability fora (be they political bodies or courts) face obvious difficulties to grapple with the 'knowledge asymmetry' hurdle. This leads to a paradox where formal accountability mechanisms and processes in place may have a limited potential to enable effective accountability.[44] This challenge is amplified when expert-based decision-making is exercised away from public eye and without appropriate transparency safeguards.[45]

The particular regulatory setting in which many experts operate gives rise to another glitch, which we call the 'nobody' problem. In the book of Odyssey, Homerus narrates the story of Ulysses in the land of the Cyclopes. To escape the terrible giant Polyphemus, Ulysses tells him that his name is 'Nobody'. When blinded by Ulysses, Polyphemus calls his fellow giants for help, shouting that 'Nobody' had blinded him. This trick ensures safe escape to Ulysses and his fellow travellers. Drawing on the myth, we ask: Are experts involved in decision-making also 'nobodies'? Albeit remaining part and parcel of the decision-making process, their atypical nature may render these actors 'nobodies' in the legal field as they are often devoid of formal decision-making powers. Notwithstanding the increasing, if scattered, evidence as to their capacity of exercising public authority, it could be difficult to trigger their accountability because we lack the legal vocabulary to call them. In short, expert-based decision-making may escape accountability because of what we term the 'nobody' problem. Few examples may be illustrative of the phenomenon. Think,

44 On an early work focusing on how non-expert bodies could hold experts to account, see Patricia Day and Rudolf Klein, *Accountabilities: Five Public Services* (Tavistock 1987). Arguably, this accountability 'paradox' can be mitigated to some extent if the accountability forum relies on the support of independent experts in the relevant field as a means to effectively scrutinise the performance of the actor.

45 See with regard specifically to the ECB, Deirdre Curtin, 'Accountable Independence of the European Central Bank: Seeing the Logics of Transparency' (2017) 23 European Law Journal 28; Agustin José Menéndez, 'Democracy, Translucidity and Accountability: The Eurozone vs. The Democratic Right to Know' (2017) 23 European Law Journal 2.

for instance, of the role of the 'Troika' in the Greek crisis.[46] While it is evident that many legally relevant decisions matured within this body, legal avenues to challenge these decisions were foreclosed because *legally* the Troika is 'nobody'. Or consider the work of various rather informal international standard-setting bodies (ISSBs), for instance the non-binding global regulatory standards for capital requirements adopted by the quasi-formal Basel Committee on Banking Supervision (BCSB), incorporated by the European Union through EU secondary legislation, and implemented by the European Banking Authority (EBA)[47] and the Single Supervisory Mechanism (SSM), bringing together the European Central Bank (ECB) and the banking supervisory authorities of the Member States. The experts instrumental to adopt these standards are invisible and can hardly be challenged. In a rather different context, one can recall Europol's Serious and Organised Crime Threat Assessments (SOCTA) informing the EU Policy Cycle for Serious and Organised Crime;[48] again this EU agency is not formally involved in the adoption of the final EU policy priorities in the field of police cooperation and organized crime, thereby remaining some sort of 'nobody' in the decision-making process.

In other instances, expert bodies enjoy formal decision-making powers but they are equipped with such a marge of discretion and degree of independence that the triggering of accountability may become 'mission impossible'. Take, for instance, the role of the expert-driven ECB in Union's monetary policy, including ECB's involvement in more controversial crisis-related measures and tools such as the European Stability Mechanism (ESM), the Outright Market Transactions (OMT) programme or the Public Sector Purchase Programme (PSPP). In the latter cases, the CJEU already confirmed that EU institutions making 'choices of a technical nature' and undertaking 'forecasts and complex assessments' should enjoy broad discretion.[49] More generally, expert institutions have allegedly been established to de-politicize certain processes (e.g. the ECB managing the euro), and for this reason they should be granted in principle a certain level of independence and safeguards to ensure that they are relatively insulated from policy/political influences. By creating accountability mechanisms, the risk might be to force experts to develop sensitivities towards politics, thereby affecting their independence and neutrality. At the same time, completely lacking oversight over powerful technocratic institutions like the ECB entails the risk of serious abuses of power being committed and left unpunished. While admittedly independence

46 'Troika' is the vernacular term referring to the informal cooperation between the three EU and international institutions (i.e. the European Commission, the European Central Bank and the International Monetary Fund) involved in bailing out Greece and other EU Member States facing financial difficulties in the wake of the financial crisis in 2007–2008.

47 See Maurizia de Bellis, 'Global Financial Standards and Networks: The Global Administrative Law Perspective' (2013) 30 Revista de Derecho Publico 5.

48 Alexandra de Moor and Gert Vermeulen, 'The Europol Council Decision: Transforming Europol into an Agency of the European Union' (2010) 47 CML Rev 1089, 1111–1112.

49 See *Peter Gauweiler v Deutscher Bundestag*, Case C-62/14 EU:C:2015:400, para 68; see also Case C-493/17 *Heinrich Weiss and Others* EU:C:2018:1000, para 91.

should not exclude *per se* accountability,[50] the real challenge is how to design and devise accountability keeping technocratic bodies in check without endangering the functional independence experts need in order to fulfil their tasks.

Another tension lies in the very rationale for involving experts in policy and decision-making – that is enhancing the effectiveness and efficiency of the regulatory process and policy implementation. In this context, a recurring concern in scholarly literature in particular with regards to agencies and other expert bodies has been that accountability overload or simply misconceived accountability mechanisms may actually be seen as undoing the benefits of expert-based decision-making.[51] Thus, for instance, excessive accountability would run the risk of paralyzing the activities of expert bodies and, in the extreme case, to deter experts from entering any form of regulatory science. Arguably, the intermingling and complex interactions between policy-making and expertise, including the hybrid (both experts and policymakers) nature of certain actors (e.g. the European Commission or the ECB), make it difficult to identify a one-size-fit-all suitable conceptual framework or tailored parameters for accountability in expert-based decision-making. The 'nobody' problem, then, can be seen to come in at least two different guises. Under the first, experts become invisible regulators – hence totally unaccountable. Misconceived accountability in this context could among others result in gaps regarding scrutiny of expert-based decision-making and the possibility to adopt corrective actions to remedy problems and increase effectiveness. Under the second, experts would be driven out the regulatory process because of fears of negative consequences associated with their possible mistakes. With fears of extreme sanctions for possible mistakes, *nobody* may be willing to act as 'expert' in a regulatory process.[52]

Against this background, the contributors to this volume engage in different ways with a common pool of core questions:

- How is accountability understood and what are the various accountability frameworks and arrangements in place regarding expert-based decision-making in multilevel governance?
- What are or should be the normative parameters for holding experts accountable (focus on input, process, output or a combination thereof)?
- To whom (policymakers, political representatives, peers, various stakeholders, courts and other supervisory authorities) should experts be accountable

50 See Busuioc (n 19) 38.

51 See, for instance, Madalina Busuioc and Martijn Groenleer, 'The Theory and Practice of EU Agency Autonomy and Accountability: Early Day Expectations, Today's Realities and Future Perspectives' in Michelle Everson, Cosimo Monda and Ellen Vos (eds), *European Agencies in-between Institutions and Member States* (Kluwer Law Publishing 2014) 175–200; Bovens, Schillemans and 't Hart, 'Does Accountability Work? An Assessment Tool' (n 18); see also Mark E. Warren, 'Accountability and Democracy' in Bovens, Goodin and Schillemans (eds), *The Oxford Handbook of Public Accountability* (n 18) 39–54, warning against the risks that over-accountability erodes trust in society.

52 Busuioc and Groenleer (n 51) 197–200.

and how should accountability be designed for different accountability fora? When there are multiple accountability fora, how are they linked to each other?
- In how far should accountability be shared between the expert and the policy/decision-maker formally responsible for the final decision? Does it make a difference whether the policy/decision-maker merely 'rubber stamps' expert's draft decision, or whether, on the contrary, she largely disregards the expert advice?
- Are there accountability overloads or deficits, and how could these be addressed?
- And, above all, is accountability a meaningful paradigm for tackling the problems and limits of technocracy in a multilevel setting?

In tackling these questions, this volume aims to bridge theoretical perspectives regarding accountability of experts in multilevel governance with case studies concerning thematic areas that feature remarkable developments in terms of technocratic governance. The case studies make a specific contribution to the literature on EU and global technocracy, by dissecting specific challenges in the areas of economic and financial governance, environmental/health and safety governance, and the governance of digitization and data protection in the area of cybersecurity and police cooperation in cross-border crime. Examining these areas transversally enables a comparative outlook, with insights into the potential commonalities and the different ways in which accountability of experts is designed and works (or does not).

6 Accountability of experts: Mission impossible?

Part I of this volume (**Perspectives on expertise and accountability in multilevel law and governance**) is opened with a thought-provoking contribution by Jan Klabbers, who boldly questions the plausibility of traditional accountability frameworks for experts. The elusive and fluid concepts of experts, accountability and governance are unlikely to be 'solidified' and managed by a traditional framework of accountability. Reflecting on the 'Eichmann problem' – that is the paradox of having to fault experts for being 'overly zealous' – Klabbers exposes one of the key weaknesses of traditional accountability frameworks: the neglect of 'the temporal element and the context in which political action is embedded'. Against this background, and despite his initial claim that 'the accountability of experts is, properly conceived, all but impossible', Klabbers paves new ways for thinking about accountability of experts. He suggests that a virtue-ethical framework is likely to be more meaningful for holding experts accountable. To those who may be sceptics of virtue ethics, especially in relation to its vagueness, Klabbers responds that legal systems often rely on principles (e.g. good faith), resonating with virtues. This change in register for thinking about accountability may be particularly helpful for placing expertise 'in context', adding nuances and tolerating mistakes, which are physiological to the life of an expert. The 'sense of propriety' of experts' actions would become a new centre of gravity for accountability under a virtue-ethics framework. What remains more challenging is the operationalization of such a framework. Some of the contributions in this volume could be read to offer insights on how to tackle this challenge.

In chapter 2, Sanne Taekema rethinks accountability of transnational experts through the rule of law prism. Taekema rests on a teleological conception of the rule of law, whose core is seeking to reduce the arbitrary exercise of power. To appreciate the relevance of the rule of law paradigm, Taekema first identifies the type of authority exercised by experts. Drawing on a rich body of legal theory, she convincingly portrays experts' authority as hybrid, liquid and relative. It is hybrid in the sense that it encompasses both epistemic and practical authority; it is liquid, as it is hard to pin down to specific sites and actions and it is difficult to distinguish from legitimacy; and it is relative because is often exercised in relation to and conjunction with other bodies, being more accurately characterized as 'inter-authority'. The latter dimension is particularly problematic, as accountability may be confined only to the relations between authorities. However, Taekema argues that '[t]he rule of law (...) requires an outward accountability beyond the interactions between authorities, to the people who are subject to these authorities'. For Taekema, it is key that experts can meaningfully give account of their practical authority to those (in-)directly affected by them. The practices and standards that could realize this outward dimension of experts' accountability are an important site where the functional and the normative meet.

A third perspective on the conceptualization of accountability of experts concludes the first part of the book. Similarly to Taekema, Alessandra Arcuri conceptualizes accountability as part and parcel of a teleological understanding of the rule of law and of a public law approach. In her chapter (3), accountability is 'conceived as a constellation of mechanisms aimed not only at realizing the public interest, but also as means for the perpetual search of what the public interest is in the global regulatory space'. Drawing on both international legal scholarship and Science and Technology Studies (STS), Arcuri identifies and discusses three dimensions along which the accountability of global regulatory scientific bodies can be operationalized.

The first dimension enlists the overarching values that an accountability framework strives to protect. While science and expertise are typically portrayed as value-free, Arcuri notes that embedding expert reasoning in some values is not only acceptable but also desirable. In this context, she distinguishes illegitimate from legitimate values. To the extent that a value is illegitimate (e.g. protecting vested interests), accountability should strive to assert disinterestedness (in line with the Mertonian vision of science). Yet, when ethical values could be part of a legitimate scientific process, accountability can be useful to clarify which values have shaped experts' reasoning. For example, the guidelines on risk assessment by the Codex Alimentarius Commission are predicated on precaution (normative value). In such context, an expert may give account on how the methodology used resonates with precaution (e.g. minimizes false negatives in toxicological studies). The function of a legal framework for accountability of global regulatory experts is thus two-fold. 'On the one hand, it should aim at maintaining disinterestedness – that is exclude considerations of personal gains or ideology from the regulatory scientific process. On the other hand, accountability mechanisms rather than denying interestedness should distinguish legitimate from illegitimate interests'. The second dimension of the triangle delineates the scope of accountability by identifying the levels of regulatory science relevant for the accountability relationship in global technocracy. In this context, it is important to distinguish at which level regulatory science comes into play. Can first hand-science be even considered in an accountability relation? The third dimension concerns the mechanisms that are (or could be) employed to operationalize the accountability relations. These include a variety of *ex ante* (procedural) mechanisms, such as conflict of interest rules and rules to determine acceptability of scientific studies in the regulatory process (e.g. studies following the Organisation for Economic Co-operation and Development (OECD) Good Laboratory Practices), to *ex post* mechanisms (ranging from legal to quasi-legal scrutiny). These three dimensions are all important for the analysis of the accountability relationship, as no single one can do justice to its complexity. The chapter is enriched by a constellation of examples, which shows how in concrete these dimensions work.

All in all, the first three chapters enhance our legal vocabulary and the conceptual-analytical tools for better understanding the challenges and complexities of accountability in technocratic multilevel governance. They offer rich perspectives and angles for tackling accountability in regulatory and technocratic processes, and set the scene for the more tailored discussions in the subsequent chapters regarding the accountability of experts embedded in various areas and policy-institutional frameworks.

In Part II of the volume (**Expertise and accountability in economic and financial law and governance**), Marijn van der Sluis examines from a predominantly constitutional perspective the different ways in which ECB's technical decision-making can be challenged (chapter 4). His main underlying premise is that the institutional relations of ECB differ from those of other central banks in a way that emphasizes law as the primary tool to organize the review of technical decision-making. The division of powers between the EU and the Member States in economic and monetary policy leaves the ECB without an authoritative counterbalance to its expertise. Since its institutional position and independence are entrenched in the EU Treaties, the ECB can be said to enjoy privileged protection regarding its objective of monetary policy and thereby also its expertise. As a result, the author argues, the relations between the ECB and other EU institutions are primarily mediated through law. Hence, there is little room for outside experts to challenge the substantive analyses of the ECB in the formulation of its policies, this being visible both within the 'monetary dialogue' between the ECB and the European Parliament (EP), and in the context of the judicial review exercised by the Court of Justice of the European Union (CJEU). While the author conveys that the expansion of ECB's powers during the euro crisis has increased the opportunities for other EU institutions to challenge its expertise, he remains cautious as to the prospects of widespread contestation of ECB's decisions. Similar to Klabbers, the author dismisses accountability as a meaningful path for assessing ECB's expertise, and proposes instead an alternative approach based on the distribution of competences and the balance of powers between EU institutions and bodies, as a way to understanding the institutional relations of the ECB.

In chapter 5, Sebastian Heidebrecht focuses both normatively and empirically on ECB's democratic accountability framework, namely the accountability relationship between the EP and the ECB. The chapter explores the underlying rationale for delegating decision-making powers over monetary policy and banking supervision to economic experts and the characteristics of their expert knowledge, before delving into the institutional aspects of the framework to hold ECB's experts to account, as well as the actual application of accountability mechanisms by Members of the European Parliament (MEPs). Its empirical argument is, in line with the analysis of van der Sluis, that although the ECB became more important especially in the period following the euro crisis, its accountability framework has been sparsely adjusted. As a result, economic experts in independent central banks have more powers but not more substantial accountability obligations, which, in the author's view, is problematic from the perspective of democratic legitimacy. While pointing at differences between the democratic accountability frameworks of ECB in its monetary policy function and as a banking supervisor within the Single Supervisory Mechanism (SSM), the author emphasizes the lack of sufficient information and clear benchmarks as common problems of parliamentary scrutiny. He therefore concludes that ECB's accountability framework should be revised given the increasing powers of economic experts in the very independent central bank. He warns, however, that such a revision 'should take into account the dangers of politicising central banking by intergovernmental interests and reflect therefore the supranational European level of monetary policy'. In his view, a reform of ECB's accountability framework 'should contribute to a more appropriate relationship between central banks, the public and the economy' and 'by avoiding political backlashes', it could also support ECB's independence, credibility and effective monetary policy.

In chapter 6, Nathanael Tilahun examines the accountability of experts on the global level, namely in the area of international anti-money laundering and counter-terrorism financing. He takes the Financial Action Task Force (FATF), the foremost global standard-setting body on matters of money laundering and terrorism financing, as a case study and shows, by relying on international relations scholarship, the ways in which the granting of international legal personality to global standard-setting bodies could both enhance and foreclose the accountability of their experts. The FATF represents an excellent illustration of a 'nobody' who might become 'somebody' by acquiring a formal international legal status. Yet according to the author, becoming legally 'somebody' does not automatically address all accountability problems raised by informal expert bodies. He thus challenges the belief that 'unambiguously placing expert bodies under the constraining regime of an increasingly constitutionalized international legal order enhances their accountability'. His chapter reveals specific institutional dynamics under which granting international legal personality to FATF could both enhance and curtail accountability, conceptualized in the context of global governance. As such, the legal status of global expert bodies does not guarantee *per se* full success, but is just one of the ingredients in the recipe for effective accountability.

Part III (**Expertise and accountability in environment, health and (food) safety law and governance**) focuses on the area within which the experts *par excellence* – 'hard scientists' – are enlisted by regulatory authorities. The first two chapters by Robert Howse and Machiko Kanetake engage with same events and risks: the Fukushima Daiichi Nuclear Power Plant accident of 2011 and the related risks from exposure to ionizing radiation. In chapter 7, Robert Howse focuses on food safety and discusses a supposedly unusual site of accountability: the World Trade Organization (WTO). After the nuclear accident, concerns were raised on the safety of seafood products, and Korea (as well as other states) imposed an import ban on fish products originating from the area of the accident. The controversy is clearly related to the role of experts in regulatory affairs (most particularly in the area of the food safety). What is often obscured in debates about such technical issues is that safety is a concept engaging not only science but also a number of socio-economic and cultural considerations relating to perceptions of risk.[53] What is remarkable in this case is how the WTO Appellate Body was able to discern how risk assessments are intertwined to democratic governance. Assessing the risks from exposure of certain food with radiation level depends on the 'politics of framing' and thus on the decision of the questions to ask: can long-term consequences of low-dose radiation exposure be considered in the analysis? Would governmental deception on the risk be legitimate factors to consider in risk analysis? The Appellate Body has displayed a nuanced and constructive approach, distinguishing the technical from the political, and 'insisting that WTO adjudicators must conduct more holistic analyses, which bring into play, alongside scientific expertise, perspectives of governments and citizens, including concerns about trust in and accountability of experts in particular contexts'. Above all, when considerations of 'the integrity of risk regulation processes and procedures' are legitimate, the WTO can turn out to be a site to enhance transnational frameworks of expert accountability. Howse convincingly concludes that the Fukushima dispute between Japan and Korea 'does suggest that global governance can have a positive impact in enhancing accountability for expertise-based risk decisions (as opposed to abandoning democratic accountability for rule by scientists)'.

In chapter 8, Machiko Kanetake lucidly pins down the accountability deficits of standards adopted domestically, but set transnationally. Transnational science-based standards are typically enacted in hybrid transnational fora, where experts and other groups of society (e.g. industry groups, government

53 Paul Slovic, 'Perception of Risk' (1987) 236 Science 280.

representatives) interact. One such body is the International Commission on Radiological Protection (ICRP), a formally non-governmental and non-profit expert committee. The standards adopted by the ICRP have been particularly salient in the aftermath of the Fukushima nuclear accident. In fact, the reliance of Japan on the ICRP standards, particularly fixating on the safety of the level of 20 millisieverts for school buildings and playgrounds, provoked public outcry. Kanetake analysis persuasively illustrates that a key vulnerability of the use of transnational science-based standards in domestic context is the suppression of legitimate politics. In noting how 'the ICRP itself openly acknowledges, the setting of permissible dose limits involves value judgment', Kanetake criticizes the way in which the Japanese government has relied on ICPR, excluding wider domestic political deliberation. The imposition of standards, which could be oblivious to the interests of domestic constituencies, has problematic implications for accountable governance.

Another rich case for the understanding of accountability in technocratic governance is the one relating to the re-authorization of glyphosate in Europe. Glyphosate is the most widely used pesticide compound in the world. In March 2015, the International Agency for Research on Cancer (IARC) classified glyphosate as 'probably carcinogenic to humans'.[54] After this classification, several domestic authorities have reviewed the safety of glyphosate. In Europe, two regulatory agencies, the European Food Safety Authority (EFSA) and the European Chemicals Agency (ECHA), concluded that glyphosate is not carcinogenic. These different assessments generated a crisis of EU politics, with many citizens and non-governmental organizations (NGOs) contesting the authorization of glyphosate, and they provide an excellent illustration of the blurred relation between law, policy and expertise.[55] In chapter 9, Marta Morvillo craftily dissects the mechanisms of accountability and the challenges in disentangling accountability of scientists and of decision-makers in the EU. On the basis of a painstaking study of the EU context, Morvillo distinguishes at least three types of accountability mechanisms: political, legal and quasi-legal. Political accountability was realized through two distinct initiatives: European Citizens' Initiative (ECI) to ban glyphosate and the establishment by the European Parliament of a special committee (PEST committee), with a broad mandate to assess the conformity of the European Commission's decisions vis-à-vis relevant regulations as well as 'to address broader issues of transparency and accountability of EU pesticides governance'. Legal accountability took the form of several court cases, where citizens and parliamentarians took issue with the secrecy over some scientific studies that were part of the institutional risk assessment conducted by EFSA. These court

54 IARC Monograph 112 <http://monographs.iarc.fr/ENG/Monographs/vol112/> accessed 7 July 2020.

55 Alessandra Arcuri, 'Glyphosate' in Jessie Homan and Daniel Joyce (eds) *Objects of International Law* (OUP 2018) 234–246.

cases were complemented by cases before the EU Ombudsman relating, among others, to EFSA's and ECHA's practices with regard to public consultations and access to documents. All these accountability mechanisms have already led to some remarkable reforms of EU risk regulation (e.g. new EU General Food Law), which for once enhances the transparency of risk assessment procedures. Morvillo concludes that 'the glyphosate case helps us understand and characterize the ways in which the adoption of expert-based measures can be held to account, while respecting the essentially different and closely intertwined roles of political institutions and regulatory expertise'. Above all, Morvillo's analysis shows that accountability of expert decision-making is not only possible; it is already developing in interesting and variegated forms.

The case studies in this part of the book are complemented by insights from the philosophy of science. Engaging with lawyers and political scientists, Osman Çağlar Dede sets out to answer the following questions: 'Should scientific experts be held responsible for not taking the relevant non-scientific considerations into account in reaching policy-relevant conclusions? How should scientific experts include non-epistemic values into their practice while leaving the cogency and objectivity of their evaluations intact? How and in how far should ordinary citizens participate in the evaluations of evidence-based policies'? This chapter (10) offers a review of the debate on the value-free ideal and the status of non-epistemic values in science. It provides the reader with philosophical insights into how these compelling problems might be dealt with in practice, with special reference to the regulation of agricultural pesticides based on toxicological assessments, which is particularly relevant for the field of safety and environmental regulation. More specifically, Dede considers 'different ways in which scientific experts can be permissibly expected to let non-epistemic value judgments to influence their assessments' and concludes that 'the contemporary philosophical debates on the role of values in science urge us to consider ways in which values may play roles in regulatory scientists' analysis, but within certain limits that keep the reliability of scientific experts as authoritative epistemic agents so that the cogency of expert-based policy-making can be sustained'.

In Part IV (**Expertise and accountability in digitization and data protection governance**), the two chapters by W. Gregory Voss and Florin Coman-Kund look at the accountability of two technocratic European Union agencies possessing specific expertise in the area of digitization. In chapter 11, W. Gregory Voss examines the accountability framework of the European Union Agency for Network and Information Security (ENISA), one of the Union's expert agencies in the area of cybersecurity whose expertise has come to light recently with various incidents of 'hacking' and the exposure of vulnerabilities of computer networks and systems. He approaches ENISA's accountability framework comprehensively and in connection to the nature of the mandate, powers and evolution of the Agency. Premised on the view that intensity and extensiveness of accountability should be commensurate with the powers of the agency, after a thorough analysis, the author finds accountability of ENISA not being very problematic in view of its light advisory and information-related tasks. In this respect, he argues that the 'one size fits all' approach to the accountability of EU Agencies based on the 2012 EU Common Approach on EU Agencies actually resulted in (administrative) accountability overloads for ENISA due to its limited mission and small budget and staff. However, the author indicates a trend of growing ENISA's mandate that is likely to continue in the near future, rendering the question of Agency's accountability related to the 'expertification of decision-making' all the more important. In this context, he also reflects on the need for a process for review beyond mere formal and budgetary considerations, where Agency's expertise-based actions may not easily be evaluated by non-expert European Union institutions.

In chapter 12, Florin Coman-Kund looks into the accountability of 'Europe's police agency' by examining in particular two types of accountability recently redesigned by Europol's legal framework, namely democratic accountability and specialized administrative personal data processing accountability. Similarly to ENISA, the added value of Europol in the fight against serious cross-border crime lies mainly with its information-related tasks; Europol's core expertise is thus located in the field of criminal and forensic investigation techniques in combination with information/intelligence processing and analysis in the area of cross-border serious crime. Acknowledging EU as a complex *sui generis* transnational governance system and the hybrid (supranational and intergovernmental) nature of Europol and of its expertise, the conceptual underpinnings guiding the analysis are coined by the term 'hybrid multilevel accountability', whereby both EU-level institutions and Member States are involved in holding the Agency accountable. In line with the understanding of accountability in this volume, the author regards accountability from a fluid/dynamic perspective, as a continuous process encompassing both *ex post* evaluation of Europol's past conduct and a forward-looking perspective aimed at shaping Agency's future behaviour. With regards to the two types of accountability examined, the author reveals the complex interplay between EU level and national actors in holding Europol accountable, featuring as a distinctive element the creation of mixed coordination bodies (i.e. the Joint Parliamentary Scrutiny Group and the Europol Cooperation Board) bringing EU level and national accountability holders together. He identifies a complementary and supportive relationship between Europol's parliamentary scrutiny and personal data scrutiny partly addressing the 'knowledge/information asymmetry' hurdle between the accountability fora and Europol, thereby offering the prospect of a more meaningful democratic accountability of the Agency. The author concludes that on paper, the general impression is that both parliamentary scrutiny and personal data supervision of Europol's activities have been significantly enhanced, but identifies a number of challenges to the actual functioning and interplay between the new accountability tools in holding the Agency effectively accountable. He draws more general implications from this case study, suggesting that hybrid (fluid) multilevel accountability is a hallmark of the current degree of EU administrative integration, being applicable to virtually all EU agencies and technocratic bodies whose design and operation feature a pooling of EU and national resources and powers.

7 In lieu of a conclusion: Accountability as empowerment?

As we are finalizing this book, the Covid-19 pandemic has taken hold of the world, with experts unquestionably playing a role in the management of the crisis. It would go beyond the scope of this book to undertake an analysis of their role and possible accountability mechanisms at play in this crisis. It is worth noting in passing that, just like other crises, the Covid-19 crisis revealed the weaknesses of transboundary or multilevel expert decision-making processes, entailing, both within the EU and globally, piecemeal approaches, disparate decisions and solutions, or simply lack of reaction in tackling the pandemic. Though partly understandable, this was matched by a general feeling of defective accountability in times of crisis, with very limited political steering and accountability via parliaments, suboptimal reporting and information to judge performance, and with peer expert accountability remaining elusive in situations involving a large measure of scientific uncertainty (i.e. how to deal with a new virus). Another feature of the COVID-19 crisis is the uncertainty regarding the kind of expertise that is needed (e.g. medical, economic, social, management, policy expertise) and in particular how different types of expertise should be intertwined in effectively managing a complex crisis situation, like a pandemic. Precisely delineating the role and responsibilities of different experts is of course very relevant for the 'accountable for what'? question.

There is at least one remarkable development, which is worth discussing to bring to light a neglected function of accountability. We opened this introduction with a portrayal of so-called populists, particularly in the context of Brexit, as harsh critics of expertise. Since the outburst of Covid-19, there was abundant contestation of experts, including social attacks on politically and/or economically undesirable expertise.[56] Yet, in a strange twist of history, Boris Johnson, the paladin of Brexit who used to bash experts, made a U-turn, apparently embracing expertise. In the words of Matthew Flinder, '[t]he sight of Boris Johnson, and now various other ministers, flanked at their daily press conferences by various scientific advisers is a strategic performative act of blame-sharing and blame-displacement'.[57]

While the Covid-19 crisis may be an extreme case, the risk of experts being enlisted for blame-displacement is not implausible in more prosaic areas and cases. If there is one common insight resulting from virtually all the chapters in

56 A good illustration is provided by the case of Christian Drosten, Germany's leading COVID-19 expert, Laura Spinney, Germany's Covid-19 expert: 'For Many, I'm the Evil Guy Crippling the Economy' *The Guardian* (26 April 2020) <https://www.theguardian.com/world/2020/apr/26/virologist-christian-drosten-germany-coronavirus-expert-interview> accessed 7 July 2020.

57 Matthew Flinder, Coronavirus Blame Games – Who Really Benefits? The Conversation, April 3, 2020, available at: <https://theconversation.com/coronavirus-blame-games-who-really-benefits-135470> accessed 7 July 2020.

this book, it is that the disentanglement between politics and expertise is central for the conceptualization, operationalization and well-functioning of accountability. This disentanglement should not lead to the subjugation of politics to expertise or *vice versa*. To the contrary, it should entail a clarification of the relation between epistemic and legal authority. For accountability to exist, when experts' analysis rests on value judgements (and we argued that it usually does), such judgements should be me made explicit and contestable. The fundamental problem with technocracy is that it often tends to morph expertise into 'politics-by-other-means', excluding the voices and interests of those further away from power. In this context, it is important to establish accountability mechanisms by which experts will be answerable not to power but to those affected by power. If accountability serves the goal of curbing the arbitrary exercise of power (as several authors in this book contend), then accountability of experts should be designed so that they can resist the desiderata of entrenched powers. The chapters in this book present insights on a variety of ways in which accountability of expertise is taking shape, from accountability through parliaments, courts and other expert bodies, to indirect accountability through international organizations (e.g. WTO). Yet, more research is necessary to further explore different contexts and mechanisms through which accountability regimes of experts are and can be realized in meaningful ways. Arguably, under well-designed accountability frameworks, experts may become more nuanced in their findings, acknowledging the limits of their expertise, and in so doing, forcing the politics to take back some of its responsibility and avoid blame displacement.

Against this background, accountability of experts can be seen as a shield for the role of expertise in public decision-making (rather than its opposite). Meaningful accountability frameworks can avoid abuse of power, realized through the 'abuse of expertise'. By giving experts the duty and right to be answerable, they could more easily (and dialogically) reflect on and gain awareness of 'the sense of propriety' of their actions, their virtues.

Part I

Perspectives on expertise and accountability in multilevel law and governance

1 Conceptualizing expert accountability

Towards virtue

Jan Klabbers

1 Introduction

Possibly, the most outstanding characteristic of contemporary politics, at whatever level, is the abdication of political responsibility. In some cases, parliamentary majorities toeing the party line do their best to protect their fellow ideologues from being held accountable, and in some cases, politicians plan to escape any form of accountability by refusing to take decisions. Instead, they organize referenda, such as the ill-considered and ill-fated Brexit referendum held in the UK in 2016.[1] This is disturbing enough in its own right, and a perversion of democracy, but more serious still are those occasions where democratic decision-making has little or no traction left, either because decisions are taken elsewhere (think of how the US and the EU radiate their legislation outwards, with others having little choice but to accept), or because it is unclear who takes the decisions.[2]

The abdication of political responsibility is related, no doubt, to the economic mindset. Economists in the neoclassical tradition have long since figured out that when producers are confronted with unexpected costs, they try to shift these on to their consumers or, as the case may be, their suppliers. Those suppliers will try to do the same, and pass on the costs to their (other) consumers or suppliers, and from each individual perspective, doing so makes sense. An important point to note is that it makes sense because the underlying assumption is that companies as well as consumers are interested in maximizing their profits. In politics, this same underlying assumption now seems to have been adopted, with politicians no longer terribly interested in serving the nation, the common good or the public, but more interested in maximizing their own profit, i.e. their careers in

1 Jan Klabbers, 'The Passion and the Spirit: Albert Camus as Moral Politician' (2016) 1 European Papers 13.

2 See the brief observations by Friedrich Kratochwil, 'Of Maps, Law, and Politics: An Inquiry into the Changing Meaning of Territoriality' in Harry D. Gould (ed), *The Art of World-making: Nicholas Greenwood Onuf and His Critics* (Routledge 2017) 213.

politics, either as proper careers or as stepping stones to a lucrative post-political career writing their memoirs and touring the lecturing circuit.[3]

The standard model of political authority, in vogue since the American and French revolutions, is no longer an accurate depiction of how political decision-making takes place. This model suggests (top-down) decisions by responsible political leaders, elected for that purpose, and ultimately under control (bottom-up) from the electorate.[4] If the political leaders would not deliver on their promises, so the model suggested, the voters would reconsider matters and might end up voting for someone else. The result was a coherent and (more or less) legitimate picture, based around the idea of democratic accountability and serving the public good (however precisely defined), but without the troubling fiction that elected politicians should simply carry out the people's will – the latter is a populist conceit of fairly recent origin,[5] and marred by the awkward circumstance that 'the people' itself is, politically, a hopelessly elusive concept.[6] Democracy then is best seen as being about controlling the government rather than issuing binding instructions to the government.

This model has lost whatever accuracy it may once have possessed – and there are reasons to suppose that it never was very accurate to begin with, in that the model never properly captured the role of special interests, pressure groups, lobbyists, et cetera. Even so, it has been replaced by a different style of politics or rather, a different style of governing, which pays tremendous amounts of lip service to such things as democracy, transparency and participation, but which does not rely on formal mechanisms and procedures and, in the end, bears little resemblance to the ideas about what politics is all about that have been transmitted through Aristotle and his followers,[7] ranging from Arendt to MacIntyre and Villa.[8] Instead, it relies more than ever on the power of words, of concepts, of measures and indicators, and knowledge. Democratic governance has by and large been displaced by epistemic governance;[9] and deliberative democracy, not

3 By way of example, former UK Prime Minister David Cameron, the genius responsible for the Brexit referendum, reportedly received a whopping 800 000 British Pounds as an advance on his to-be-written memoirs. See Esther Addley, 'So what is David Cameron really doing now?' *The Guardian* (London, 17 January 2019).

4 Maarten Hajer, *Authoritative Governance: Policy-making in the Age of Mediatization* (OUP 2009).

5 Very useful on this point is Philip Pettit, *Republicanism: A Theory of Freedom and Government* (OUP 1997).

6 Margaret Canovan, *The People* (Polity 2005).

7 Aristotle, *The Politics* (Sinclair transl., Penguin 1992).

8 Hannah Arendt, *The Human Condition* (University of Chicago Press 1958); Alasdair MacIntyre, *After Virtue: A Study in Moral Theory* (2nd edn, Duckworth 1985); Dana R. Villa, *Arendt and Heidegger: The Fate of the Political* (Princeton University Press 1996).

9 Pertti Alasuutari and Ali Qadir, 'Epistemic Governance: An Approach to the Politics of Policy-making' (2014) 1 European Journal of Cultural and Political Sociology 67.

so long ago enthusiastically embraced as the answer to democracy's deficits with even a possible application on a global scale,[10] seems to have little traction left.

It is against this background that the much-maligned governance by experts must be situated and assessed. Over the last two decades or so, many have been the explorations of governance by experts. Arguably, social scientists were the first to note that much politically relevant decision-making takes place by groups of people not necessarily elected or appointed to politically relevant decision-making positions. Like all groups of people, experts within a particular office or organization (at whatever level) develop their own cultures, their own habits, their own mechanisms of inclusion and exclusion and even their own forms of resistance to hierarchy,[11] and these bureaucratic cultures tend to have an impact on political decision-making.[12] The insight as such is by no means novel,[13] but it took a while before well-read international lawyers picked it up and alerted the international law community that all this could have a bearing on international law as well and might be worth studying.[14] Part of the 'mystery of global governance' may well be that governance is exercised by experts, and that it turns out to be difficult to hold them to account.[15]

In this chapter, I will argue that aiming to establish the accountability of experts is, properly conceived, all but impossible, for a variety of reasons. One is that the notion of accountability is itself too unstable to be of much use; another is that the notion of expert defies easy definition and application; but the major reason is that it is precisely the point of governance by experts to be unaccountable. If accountability would be considered desirable, it could possibly (though not unproblematically) be established. But desired it is not: it is precisely the point of what has been called authoritative governance to remain elusive, unaccountable – Aristotle's classic division into governance by the one, the few or the many needs to be supplemented by a fourth category: governance by no one in particular, or at least no one identifiable (sometimes referred to as 'the nobody problem')[16]. It is only once this epistemological hurdle is overcome that

10 John S. Dryzek, *Deliberative Global Politics* (Polity 2006).

11 See, for instance, Remco Ensel, *Alleen Tijdens Kantooruren: Kleine Cultuurgeschiedenis van het Kantoorleven* (Vantilt 2008).

12 Insightful is Michael Barnett and Martha Finnemore, *Rules for the World: International Organizations in Global Politics* (Cornell University Press 2004); John Mathiason, *Invisible Governance: International Secretariats in Global Politics* (Kumarian Press 2007).

13 See, for instance, Marilyn Strathern (ed), *Audit Cultures: Anthropological Studies in Accountability, Ethics and the Academy* (Routledge 2000).

14 What may have added to the attraction is that a focus on experts can be seen as helpful in overcoming the classic 'agent versus structure' problem: experts appear as agents working as structure, and thus, it may have been thought, phenomenologically helpful.

15 David Kennedy, *A World of Struggle: How Power, Law, and Expertise Shape Global Political Economy* (Princeton University Press 2016); Erin Hannah, James Scott and Silke Trommer (eds), *Expert Knowledge in Global Trade* (Routledge 2015).

16 See Alessandra Arcuri and Florin Coman-Kund, 'Introduction: Breaking Taboos, Talking Accountability' (in this volume).

lawyers and social scientists can even begin to think about holding experts to account. In the meantime, the best that can be hoped for is that experts behave decently.[17]

2 The notion of governance

Some time ago, the political theorist John Gray astutely confessed that he had no idea who was exercising what was then the relatively novel phenomenon of global governance.[18] Clearly, he felt, global governance was not really exercised by individual states, nor was it immediately obvious that it was the sole province of international organizations. And tempting as it may have been to attribute global governance to multinational corporations, Gray clearly was not convinced, observing that many of them just acted in conformity with what they thought the market expected from them. As a consequence (although it is not certain Gray followed his own thought to the ultimate conclusion), it transpired that global governance was the work of no one in particular, since no one can control how markets operate and what they demand from market actors. Indeed, markets have constantly developed without much formal political steering.[19] It is no doubt true, on the one hand, that markets owe much to governmental regulation and governments and international organizations can facilitate what goes on.[20] On the other hand, markets also develop spontaneously and, one is tempted to say, organically; they defy steering by identifiable individuals or organs beyond a bare minimum, even if embedded in legal rules and institutions.[21]

Gray may have been on to something: in a globalizing world, few things remain that are controllable in any meaningful sense. Markets operate on their own accord, and scarily, many things have been commodified to such an extent that markets are everywhere, and have taken over many tasks that used to be the province of deliberate (if not deliberative) governance.[22] States have lost control of things such as transportation or education: whether intentional or not, all over the world such tasks have been privatized, with the result that the public idea behind education has given way to concerns about efficiency and profit margins. Market mechanisms have been introduced left, right and centre, resulting in the end of the once-heralded 'primacy of politics'; this has

17 Avishai Margalit, *The Decent Society* (Goldblum transl., Harvard University Press 1996); Jan Klabbers, Maria Varaki and Guilherme Vasconcelos Vilaça (eds), *Towards Responsible Global Governance* (University of Helsinki 2018).
18 John Gray, *False Dawn: The Delusions of Global Capitalism* (Granta 1998).
19 On the development of market thinking in terms of political theory, see Eric MacGilvray, *The Invention of Market Freedom* (CUP 2011).
20 Craig Murphy, *International Organization and Industrial Organization: Global Governance since 1850* (Polity 1994).
21 Quinn Slobodian, *Globalists: The End of Empire and the Birth of Neoliberalism* (Harvard University Press 2018).
22 See already John Dewey, *The Public and its Problems* (first published 1927, Swallow Press 1954).

been displaced by the 'primacy of the bottom line', often in the name of 'the taxpayer'.[23] And on the few topics where governments have aimed to prevent commodification, grey or underground markets have appeared. Prostitution may often officially be taboo, but is nonetheless ubiquitous and resilient; where governments aim to limit migration, a private market has occurred both above ground (companies selling help in document processing or offering relocation services for a fee) and underground, with enterprising individuals promising to smuggle people for a fee.[24]

Of course, while governments have lost much of what was once under their control, they can still oppress their citizens, and block their population's access to internet (but typically not access to internet commerce), or aim to influence elections elsewhere, or make blustering claims about blocking immigration.[25] And this, in turn, helps to make politicians as well as other persons in positions of leadership reluctant to accept any degree of responsibility: if they cannot control things, so the thought proceeds, then they should not be held accountable either. Instead, those who are in control should be held accountable, and those in control are always elsewhere: faceless international organizations, anonymous market forces, unelected experts.

3 The notion of accountability

Accountability is a complex, multifaceted phenomenon, carrying both descriptive and normative loads.[26] As a term, it is usually connected to what goes on in politics.[27] It would be odd to suggest that a company should be held 'accountable' for putting a flawed product on the market – t-shirts falling apart at the seams, or mobile phones whose batteries run empty in cold weather. In such a case, we would usually say that the company should be held responsible or liable for any damage and injury that may result (unlikely in the case of t-shirts or mobile phones), but we would not, usually, think in terms of accountability. That is not to say markets and accountability do not mix, for they do: there is nothing odd about claiming in a more abstract sense that a company is eventually accountable to its clients or customers.

23 Who used to be referred to as 'the citizen', a notion that entails a broader set of concerns than the dismal reduction of individuals to taxpayers.

24 Jan Klabbers, 'Notes on the Ideology of International Organizations Law: The International Organization for Migration, State-making, and the Market for Migration' (2019) 32 Leiden Journal of International Law 383.

25 Indeed, the rise of anti-immigrant rhetoric might owe much to the frustrations of politicians and citizens alike that few processes can be controlled: the one thing left, up to a point, is the physical movement of persons – so politicians aiming to depict themselves as being 'in charge' have few options but to resort to control of migration.

26 Descriptively, we tend to say that A is accountable to B; normatively, we usually think this is a good thing.

27 Conceptually, the following draws on Judith Gruber, *Controlling Bureaucracies: Dilemmas in Democratic Governance* (University of California Press 1987).

Still, often when we talk of accountability, our talk refers to relations involving political power. A member of government may be accountable to parliament; a parliamentarian may be accountable to her constituency; an international organization may be accountable to its member states, and a government agency may be accountable to the government. None of this is carved in stone, and accountability relations need not be exclusive, although the dominance of delegation theory often makes it look exclusive, with agents being mostly thought to be accountable to their principals.[28] Still, a strong case can be made that the international organization may be accountable not only to its member states but also to the people it is supposed to serve, and the parliamentarian may be accountable not only to her constituency but also to her political party.[29] If this is accurate, then it would seem that accountability is typically reserved for the political arena, while noting that the political arena is itself a broad concept: in much the same way as the international organization is accountable to its member states, so the local table tennis club and the local bird watching society are accountable to their respective members, if not for their transactions with others than at least for the policies they adopt and implement and the ways in which they relate to their members. For surely a table tennis club or bird watching society that discriminates between male and female members, or refuses to allow members of certain races or religions, is engaged in a political activity.

Accountability is never (or rather can never really be) a purely abstract phenomenon: it presupposes the existence of standards against which the entity or individual concerned is to be held accountable.[30] Typically, in most cases involving some kind of delegation of tasks, those standards will be related to those tasks: the task may not be accomplished, or may be accomplished in unpalatable manner. The local table tennis club may be given the task of securing promotion to a higher division. Failure to accomplish this may mean the members hold the club or its officials to account, but even success may be questionable: surely, securing promotion should not be accomplished through bribery of officials or through blackmailing members of competing table tennis clubs. And perhaps even aesthetic arguments may play a role: it is often said of Dutch football teams (soccer, for American readers), that they prefer playing attractively and losing to playing boringly yet winning. Accountability may affect both ends and means,

28 On delegation theory, see Darren G. Hawkins et al. (eds), *Delegation and Agency in International Organizations* (CUP 2006). For a discussion on how this influences the law relating to international organizations, see Jan Klabbers, 'The EJIL Foreword: The Transformation of International Organizations Law' (2015) 26 European Journal of International Law 9.

29 Useful on international affairs is Ruth W. Grant and Robert O. Keohane, 'Accountability and Abuses of Power in World Politics' (2005) 99 American Political Science Review 29.

30 It is no coincidence that some conceptualize accountability as a 'subset' of Foucauldian 'governmentality': see Edward Weisband and Alnoor Ebrahim, 'Introduction: Forging Global Accountabilities' in Alnoor Ebrahim and Edward Weisband (eds), *Global Accountabilities: Participation, Pluralism, and Public Ethics* (CUP 2007) 15.

but the crucial point for present purposes is the relevance of some kind of standard: one cannot be held to account in a vacuum. One cannot be held to account without there being something to be accountable for: a missed target, a failure to perform the mandate,[31] a violation of some rule or other, no matter how opaque.[32] Whether those standards are legal standards or not is not all that relevant: the table tennis chairperson who secures promotion through a love affair with the chairperson of a competing club breaks no laws, but nonetheless acts in inappropriate manner – or so many would hold.

It would seem then that holding experts to account (experts acting as such, that is, rather than experts appointed to political positions – see below) implies that experts can be seen as standing in some political relationship to someone, and that their work is subject to accountability standards. Experts may be appointed by politicians, or their authority may be politically approved and recognized,[33] and they are supposed to work in accordance with some standards, usually various standards at the same time. Neither of these two conditions is easily met, although the second will prove harder than the first.

4 The notion of expert

If accountability is a complex and under-conceptualized notion, it is likewise by no means self-evident what makes an expert. On one level, there needs to be some kind of expertise (whatever that may mean), but leaving it at this is casting the net rather too wide perhaps. There are at least two other factors at issue: the kind of expertise someone possesses, and whether that person occupies some kind of particular role in the exercise of governance.

For the notion of expert to have some analytical traction, it seems important not to conflate it with the notion of politician, in whatever function. Thus, President Trump, whatever else he may or may not be, is not best seen as an expert for purposes of exercising authority;[34] neither are prime ministers, foreign ministers or other government ministers, members of parliament, et cetera. All of these occupy a specific, more or less well-defined position in governance processes and, in the normal course of events and within liberal democracies, with those positions come specific accountability mechanisms. They may possess

31 On this, see Jan Klabbers, 'Reflections on Role Responsibility: The Responsibility of International Organizations for Failing to Act' (2017) 28 European Journal of International Law 1133.

32 See, for instance, Peter Cane, *Responsibility in Law and Morality* (Hart 2002).

33 One example among many is how the work of the Codex Alimentarius Commission is recognized in several World Trade Organization agreements.

34 To make things more complicated still, he may be an expert in related and supporting matters or activities. Trump might be an expert tweeter, and while this has no bearing on his substantive advice, it may have a bearing on how his policies are communicated. His predecessor Ronald Reagan, lest it be forgotten, was often seen as a great communicator, even if his command of policy matters was often deemed a little sketchy.

expertise in spades (and often enough it is considered helpful if a government member or parliamentarian has some expertise on the topics in her portfolio), but their role is not that of the expert.

In similar ways, it would be odd to speak of the military as an expert body, although it is not immediately obvious why that is the case; perhaps an answer resides in the circumstance that for the military too, in western democracies at any rate, there exist particular accountability mechanisms, with the military typically being controlled by political leadership. Here, it gets tricky though for two reasons. One is, that this suggests, *a contrario*, that experts are those who are not accountable – which strikes at the very least as an eccentric way to conceptualize expert governance. Second, the military does not merely act on political instruction, but engages in a two-way process: it also advises political leadership, the same political leadership to which it, typically, is accountable.[35]

So what then is an expert, for purposes of solving the 'mystery of global governance'? Koppl has suggested that an expert is everyone who has an opinion and is paid to express it, but this surely must be too broad. Such a conception would have to include the types of news commentator who comments on current events or concrete policy proposals from the sidelines, the 'Monday morning quarterbacks', without bearing any factual responsibility for them. This is not to deny that such commentators may play an influential role in politics (the people at Fox News may serve as a reminder), but it would seem that their role is not best captured by the 'expert' label, if only because they might actually not possess much relevant expertise – merely opinions.[36]

Perhaps it is wiser to focus on experts actively involved in policy-making.[37] This might involve different classes of 'expert', and at least four different categories are identifiable of experts who are more or less directly involved in governance processes. This excludes those whose influence on governance processes is mostly indirect, e.g. as authors of academic works, or teachers at institutions of higher education. That they play an important role cannot be gainsaid, and someone like Keynes was extremely well aware of his potential influence,[38] but

35 This is briefly discussed in Antonia Handler Chayes, *Borderless Wars: Civil Military Disorder and Legal Uncertainty* (CUP 2015).

36 Roger Koppl, *Expert Failure* (CUP 2018). For the record and at the risk of stating the superfluous, Koppl is of the view that those who are paid to express an opinion must be considered 'experts' – it is this view that I contest here.

37 The literature is growing fast; insightful contributions include Ole Jacob Sending, *The Politics of Expertise: Competing for Authority in Global Governance* (University of Michigan Press 2017), and Annabelle Littoz-Monnet (ed), *The Politics of Expertise in International Organizations: How International Bureaucracies Produce and Mobilize Knowledge* (Routledge 2017).

38 He dedicated his analysis of the Versailles settlement to the self-conscious 'formation of the general opinion of the future', knowing fully well that the future depends less on the acts of statesmen than it does on 'instruction and imagination'. See John Maynard Keynes, *The Economic Consequences of the Peace* (MacMillan 1920) 279, 278, respectively.

such influence is likely to be mostly indirect.[39] Their teachings, findings and concepts must first be absorbed by their audiences, who can then effectuate them if and when they come to occupy an expert position.[40] Hence, an important element of expert governance resides in the particular position occupied by individuals.

The first of these expert governors, and perhaps the group most often thought of when thinking about governance by experts, are the policy advisors, whose tasks are foremost to help develop or formulate policies or, most likely, both. In global governance, this refers to the economists at the World Bank or the European Investment Bank, the finance experts at the Basel Committee, the doctors working for the World Health Organization (WHO), the chemists employed by the Organisation for the Prohibition of Chemical Weapons (OPCW), but also the lawyers working at those agencies. It may cover the economic policy advisors at the International Monetary Fund (IMF), or the fisheries experts at one of the many regional intergovernmental fisheries organizations, or the environmental engineers at the United Nations Environment Programme (UNEP).

And the question that arises in this context, broadly, is this: what if the advice rendered by those experts goes wrong? What if it fails to accomplish what it is supposed to achieve, or what if it meets its targets but at the expense of other concerns? Examples are not hard to find, although sometimes difficult to generalize: the IMF has been criticized for deepening financial crises during the 1980s and 1990s, implying that the expert advice clearly did not work.[41] The WHO promulgated a swine flu pandemic in 2009, and did so rather too soon, according to some, in the process leading to huge profits for those pharmaceutical companies that had their vaccines ready, while disadvantaging the companies who were still producing them.[42] In such a setting, can the experts be blamed for being early or even too early, and if so, what is the yardstick here? And just as relevant, what if they would have waited and several dozens of people would have died as a result?

A second group of experts are those working within bureaucracies not so much with a view to advising on policy, but with a view to implementing policy. Here, the individuals concerned may include logistics experts charged with finding the proper way to transport sensitive vaccines through tropical areas, or tasked with ensuring that military equipment reaches the sites of peacekeeping.

39 In Keynes' case, of course, some of it was also directly exercised: he was influential in designing the Bretton Woods institutions. A different example is discussed in Jan Klabbers, 'Governance by Academics: The Invention of Memoranda of Understanding' (2020) 80 Zeitschrift für ausländisches öffentliches Recht und Völkerrecht 35.

40 For further discussion, see Jan Klabbers, 'Bureaucrats in the Classroom? Epistemic Governance and the Expert Legal Scholar', in Emilia Korkea-Aho and Päivi Leino-Sandberg (eds), *Law, Legal Expertise, and EU Policy Making* (CUP forthcoming).

41 Joseph E. Stiglitz, *Globalization and Its Discontents* (Penguin 2002).

42 For brief discussion of some of the links between the World Health Organization and the corporate sector, see Abigail C. Deshman, 'Horizontal Review between International Organizations: Why, How and Who Cares about Corporate Regulatory Capture' (2011) 22 European Journal of International Law 1089.

It may include those who run or oversee waste management near refugee camps or peacekeeping missions.

A third broad group are those working behind the scenes not so much in advising on policy or implementing policy, but working on the creation of instruments that are themselves supposed to support policies. Statisticians for instance developing surveys on a wider variety of topics may be covered by this category;[43] demographers surveying populations or specific characteristics are part of this group; so too are the education specialists designing the questionnaires on which the Programme of International Student Assessment (PISA) rankings of the Organisation for Economic Co-operation and Development (OECD) are based, and even the early designers of the Nansen passport for refugees can probably be included in this category.

And a fourth group, finally, are those experts who are given an explicitly political role. This group includes the 'special rapporteurs' and 'independent experts' enlisted by the United Nations (UN) to report on a specific topic, whether gender violence, extreme poverty, human rights in the fight against terrorism, or sovereign debts and human rights. Their task is based on their expertise, but not limited to the merely technical application of that expertise. In much the same way as the International Law Commission is a body of experts charged with both the codification of international law (seemingly a technical task) and the overtly political task of stimulating the progressive development of international law, so too special rapporteurs and independent experts are tasked with a mixture of (seemingly) technical and political tasks.[44] After all, to discuss the role of the World Bank in extreme poverty is to take a political stand, whether intentionally or not; discussing torture is impossible to do in a merely technical way, as any state accused of torture will acknowledge. And special rapporteurs might feel that a political role is expected from them, precisely because of their expertise: the proper expert not only knows what is going on but also has the intellectual tools, so it might be thought, to pay attention to new horizons and add depth to a topic.

5 The Eichmann problem

As the above suggest, holding experts to account in governance will be ever-problematic: it is unclear what we mean by accountability; it is unclear who qualifies as an expert and on what basis; and it is even unclear what we mean by governance. It seems highly doubtful that all these issues could be 'solved' or 'solidified'. Perhaps at some point in time crystallized and generally accepted

43 See Sally Engle Merry, *The Seductions of Quantification: Measuring Human Rights, Gender Violence, and Sex Trafficking* (University of Chicago Press 2016). A measured endorsement of the use of indicators and similar instruments by a Dutch public administration scholar is Hans de Bruijn, *Prestatiemeting in de Publieke Sector: Tussen professie en verantwoording* (2nd edn, Lemma 2006).

44 Much the same may apply to committees of 'wise men' (usually also 'white men'), sometimes set up in reference to specific incidents or episodes.

notions of 'expert', 'governance' and 'accountability' will emerge, allowing for the design, rational or otherwise, of some kind of regime.

Should that ever happen (it might be wise not to hold our breath though), then a problem of a different nature emerges. The expert typically follows some sort of instruction – she is embedded in a deontological framework, carrying out duties assigned to her by her superiors or following a legally prescribed mandate. The UN special rapporteur will typically follow instructions set by the UN General Assembly or whichever precise organ appoints her; the Central Bank governor may have to follow a mandate laid down in the law establishing the Central Bank, while the chairperson of the table tennis club will have to abide by the by-laws of the table tennis club.

This has one sobering consequence: they cannot, normally speaking, be held accountable for acting as mandated or instructed – doing so would be highly unfair. Put differently: while embedded in a deontological logic and acting in accordance with their task, they can only be held accountable for the consequences of their acts.[45] The obligations resting on them are obligations of result, not obligations of effort or intention or even duty, and the result, to make matters worse, in politics and public life might be 'too good', so to speak. And this is also, eventually (if not earlier), where any analogy between business life and public life must falter: what counts as success in business may spell gross failure in public life.

For the manager of a big company, the result to be achieved is typically financial: the share price must be kept high, making allowance for the need to develop new products, explore new markets, rectify mistakes by predecessors, et cetera. Generally speaking, the higher the company's share price, the better the businessman has performed, and vice versa – there is, at any rate, under normal circumstances no such thing as too much success. Our businessman is likely to meet with criticism if profits remain limited and share prices drop, but will be heralded if profits are abundant and share prices high. Our businessman knows what to do, and knows how his performance will be measured. As long as no laws are broken (legal or even otherwise), he knows what is expected of him.[46]

Here, things differ with the policy expert. It is clear that her work needs to be successful, but is unclear what qualifies as success. The World Bank economist who successfully manages a big development project in Pakistan may nonetheless meet with criticism if her success entails the displacement of thousands of people, or comes with considerable environmental costs. The UN special rapporteur who includes domestic abuse in his definition of torture may well meet with

45 This presupposes that the expert does not cut corners, manipulate data or otherwise act in defiance of the many standards applicable to her. The hard case is not the fraudulent expert, but the sincere and conscientious expert.

46 Which is not to say accountability is without problems: see Robert Jackal, *Moral Mazes: The World of Corporate Managers* (first published 1988, OUP 2010).

approval in some circles, but strong disapproval in other circles, where he may be accused of 'stretching' existing legal categories. The Central Bank manager who manages to keep inflation under control may be criticized for the effects of austerity measures. Et cetera.

In an extreme form, the problem can be summarized as the Eichmann problem. As is well-known ever since Hannah Arendt published her report on the banality of evil, in Nazi-Germany, Adolf Eichmann was responsible for authorizing the transfers of Jews to extermination camps. On trial in Jerusalem, he denied responsibility, not so much because he only had been following superior orders (his was not the classic 'superior order' defence), but rather more that he had only been doing his job to the best of his ability. He was expected to handle logistics, and handle logistics he did. He had merely been extremely diligent and good at his job, and surely there was nothing wrong with that?[47]

The problem therewith transpired, *pace* Arendt, that Eichmann's actions defied the traditional categories of criminal law. His crimes had not sprung from greed or lust or maliciousness, as is usually the case. Instead, she reached the conclusion that his main 'crime' had been thoughtlessness – he had implemented his tasks without giving them much thought, and without exercising any kind of judgment or discretion. It was his thoughtlessness, his utter incapacity to think for himself and spout anything other than clichés, that Arendt found so offensive, and in the end, she agreed that no penalty was really appropriate for a man who had so thoughtlessly sent so many others to their graves – this was beyond anything the criminal law could handle, and therefore he deserved to die.[48]

In a sense, the Eichmann problem is probably too extreme. It is clear that he was overly zealous, overly diligent, but at the same it is difficult to imagine him doing anything else without attracting opprobrium – other than not signing any transport documents. Put differently, it is estimated that he sent hundreds of thousands of people to the camps,[49] and while that certainly qualifies as overzealous, it is difficult to think of any number that would not qualify as such. The enormity of his crime was not so much that he did his job really beyond the call of duty, but rather that he did his job at all. Reducing the number of his victims by half would not make him look much better; indeed, reducing it by 99% would not do so. Some things are just plain wrong, although a mitigating factor might be that in those heady days, others might have done much the same for a while – it may have taken

47 Hannah Arendt, *Eichmann in Jerusalem: A Report on the Banality of Evil* (Penguin 1963). Arendt's analysis has itself been much discussed – a useful collection is Stephen E. Ascheim (ed), *Hannah Arendt in Jerusalem* (University of California Press 2001).

48 The remedy against thoughtlessness and 'extensive evil' may be, accordingly, to place a premium on education and thinking: see Elizabeth Minnich, *The Evil of Banality: On the Life and Death Importance of Thinking* (Rowman and Littlefield 2017).

49 I derive the figure somewhat randomly from Harry Mulisch, *De zaak 40/61: Een Reportage* (Bezige Bij 1961).

some time to realize that faithfully executing the *Führer*'s wishes was a terrible idea.[50]

This factor then distinguishes Eichmann's situation from that of most experts active in global governance – or does it? Colloquially put, there was no excuse for Eichmann, while many others are caught on the horns of dilemma and thus might have an excuse available. Or do they? Much here depends on the normative pull of possibly differing demands, as well as the precise consequentialist calculus adopted. The proverbial World Bank economist might provide a useful example. It may well be assumed that managing a large-scale development project is in itself justifiable (but remember, the same applies in principle to managing railway logistics) and thus, all else remaining equal, there is nothing wrong with what our World Bank economist is doing.[51] Instead, much may be right with our economist's work: the project may lead to a better energy supply, thus possibly stimulating economic development and raising the welfare and life expectancy of the entire country. So, in principle, a good project.

But then the question of costs enters the picture. If the project means people die, is it still justified? And does it matter how many die? If the project does not result in deaths but in massive displacements; if it provokes riots which are forcefully suppressed resulting not in death but with some people ending up in wheelchairs and on crutches; if it entails massive environmental degradation, or even simply leads to the area becoming less populated – if any of these obtain, is it still a good project?

The point is that it is well-nigh impossible to make those calculations in advance, for there is simply far too much to calculate, and far too many factors that can enter the equation – what if the riots are artificially stimulated by *agents provocateurs* with an interest not in stopping the project but in seeing the government brought down? Or what if the environmental effects only become obvious a decade or more after the project's completion? Unlike the Eichmann case, where Eichmann could reasonably have been expected to realize that he was doing something wrong, our World Bank economist can perhaps be forgiven for not immediately reaching that conclusion. This, in turn, is an important consideration: often, in the real world of expert governance, the consequences of normal action only become visible with a serious time delay. *Ex post* assessment may be possible; *ex ante* assessment is almost by definition excluded, precisely because even the most cautious and detailed calculation cannot calculate everything and anything that might come to be of relevance.[52]

50 Others were perhaps quicker to realize as much, such as Josef Hartinger, the Munich-based prosecutor portrayed in Timothy Ryback, *Hitler's First Victims: The Quest for Justice* (Knopf 2014).

51 It has been observed though that in the time-honoured manner of bureaucracy, bringing in and managing large projects has become its own measure of success, rather independent from implementation or effects in the real world. See, for instance, Galit A. Sarfaty, *Values in Translation: Human Rights and the Culture of the World Bank* (Stanford University Press 2012).

52 As a general proposition, moreover, governance usually takes place without full information and under time pressure. See generally Friedrich Kratochwil, *Praxis: On Acting and Knowing* (CUP 2018).

The dilemma will be clear. It is impossible to exercise full *ex ante* scrutiny and make a reasonable judgement of what might or might not come to pass. This in turn entails that our expert ends up, to some extent, blindfolded: she will just have to wait and see what the consequences of her recommendations and suggestions are, and hope that no dramatically intervening variables present themselves.

6 Virtuous experts?

Establishing accountability for experts along deontological lines proves nigh-on impossible: as long as experts do their job, it will be difficult to find fault with them.[53] Establishing accountability along consequentialist lines will prove equally difficult, as it is nigh-on impossible to calculate in advance what factors should be included in the equation, and the consequences of any action may not reveal themselves until long after an action has taken place. And this is not even considering other factors that might intervene, such as path dependencies: once a policy has been initiated and initial costs have been incurred, it is more difficult to change course.[54] And even if one could (hypothetically) create something of an accountability framework along either deontological or consequentialist lines, such a framework would remain structurally vulnerable for opposing critiques: a deontological argument can typically be met by a consequentialist response, and vice versa. As MacIntyre not unreasonably summarizes it, post-Enlightenment moral debates 'can find no terminus'.[55]

Against this background, it might be helpful to resort to Aristotelian ethics broadly conceived,[56] and resort to the virtues.[57] Deontologists and consequentialists alike usually quickly dismiss the virtues by suggesting that a virtue ethics approach is not very good at providing precise guidelines for how to act, and they are right in their criticism: the virtue ethicist can usually not go much further than to implore the listener to 'do what a virtuous person would do'. But

53 And this regardless of the general critique of rules, well-accepted in jurisprudence and elsewhere, to the effect that rules are indeterminate, and tend to be both over- and under-inclusive. See generally Frederick Schauer, *Playing by the Rules: A Philosophical Examination of Rule-Based Decision-Making in Law and in Life* (Clarendon 1991). Moreover, as Hursthouse reminds us, rules can always be manipulated: 'The Devil, after all, can quote scripture to serve his own purposes; one can conform to the letter of a rule while violating its spirit'. See Rosalind Hursthouse, *On Virtue Ethics* (OUP 1991) 40.

54 Noted philosopher Onora O'Neill advocates for 'intelligent accountability': Onora O'Neill, *A Question of Trust* (CUP 2002).

55 MacIntyre (n 8) 6. I explore some consequences for international organizations law in Jan Klabbers, 'Interminable Disagreement: Reflections on the Autonomy of International Organisations' (2019) 88 Nordic Journal of International Law 111.

56 Aristotle, *Ethics* (Penguin 1976, Thomson transl.).

57 This builds on Jan Klabbers, 'The Virtues of Expertise', in Monika Ambrus et al. (eds), *The Role of 'Experts' in International and European Decision-making Processes: Advisors, Decision Makers or Irrelevant Actors?* (CUP 2014) 82.

unlike what the critique suggests, 'doing what a virtuous person would do' is not a vacuous concept – quite the contrary.[58] Moreover, both deontologists and consequentialists are in need of a doctrine of the virtues. It is no good having a strong principle on how to act without being able to recognize the sort of situation that demands application of the principle, and it is no good focusing on consequences unless one has some inkling as to how best to achieve those consequences. Both of these demand practical wisdom (*phronesis*) – the paragon virtue in accordance with Aristotelian doctrine. Hence, it is no coincidence that even Kant, Hume and Smith all included ideas about practical wisdom and how best to achieve it in their work.[59]

An insistence on the virtues demands that experts, in whatever precise capacity, are at a minimum honest, courageous, temperate and humble. While there is discussion on what exactly the virtues are, some candidates must be dismissed: for instance, the proclamation of selfishness as a virtue is decidedly un-Aristotelian.[60] Other candidate virtues are perhaps best seen as related to virtue, but not themselves a virtue: trust, for instance, appears essentially a relational concept, and thus difficult to envisage in a virtue ethics framework, despite valiant attempts to do so.[61] And some virtues are contested, with empathy being a prime example: some hold that empathy necessarily entails bias and would thus not be properly virtuous.[62] Whether this holds is open to question though: the circumstance that people may often practice empathy leading to bias, does not entail that empathy necessarily leads to bias.[63]

Be that as it may, operationalizing the virtues, even only a few of them, would entail that experts do not inflate their expectations; have the courage to withstand their political taskmasters; remain aware that even when they do their work properly, they may nonetheless be mistaken, or unable to assess all consequences in advance; and realize that their expert advice comes to affect real people of flesh and blood, people moreover who might be in a vulnerable position to begin with.

And there are epistemological virtues, which might be all the more relevant precisely when expert governance is concerned, for much expert governance

58 See, for instance, Hursthouse (n 53); Christine Swanton, *Virtue Ethics: A Pluralistic View* (OUP 2003); Linda T. Zagzebski, *Exemplarist Moral Theory* (OUP 2017).

59 The most surprising of these may be Adam Smith, whose reliance on the virtues is spelled out in Adam Smith, *The Theory of Moral Sentiments* (first published 1759, Penguin 2009). For authoritative discussion, see Ryan Patrick Hanley, *Adam Smith and the Character of Virtue* (CUP 2009).

60 One of Ayn Rand's works is titled *The Virtue of Selfishness* (Signet 1964).

61 The ostensible virtue of trust plays an important role in Michael Ignatieff, *The Ordinary Virtues: Moral Order in a Divided World* (Harvard University Press 2017). On trust, see Marek Kohn, *Trust: Self-Interest and the Common Good* (OUP 2008).

62 Paul Bloom, *Against Empathy: The Case for Rational Compassion* (Penguin 2016).

63 Elsewhere I mobilize empathy as an important aspect of judicial reasoning: see Jan Klabbers, 'Doing Justice: Bureaucracy, the Rule of Law and Virtue Ethics' (2017) 6 Rivista di Filosofia del Diritto 27.

taps into the epistemic authority of the experts.[64] Here too, the virtue ethics framework may translate into fairly concrete guidance: clearly, it would be counterproductive (not to mention unjust) for an expert or group of experts working on projects involving indigenous people to dismiss indigenous knowledge as not relevant, or less relevant than the knowledge acquired at Harvard's Kennedy School of Government, the Economics Department at the University of Chicago, or the Massachusetts Institute of Technology.

7 By way of conclusion

Insisting on virtuous experts is unlikely to reveal all mysteries of global governance and solve all that troubles it, and if conceived as a like-for-like replacement for accountability frameworks, then only disappointment can result. But perhaps the problem is not so much with the virtues, but rather with our contemporary notions of accountability, which thinks too much in terms of individual action and punishment. Accountability frames often lose track of collective agency (the popularity of the International Criminal Court and its insistence on individual responsibility for collective crimes suggests as much) and usually ignore the temporal element and the context in which political action is embedded. This is no surprise: popular culture does much the same, as perhaps best embodied in the 'reality' TV-show *Cheaters*.[65] The show thrives on dis-embedding individuals in their personal lives focusing solely on the act of cheating on their spouses. This makes for dramatic television perhaps, but completely ignores whether the spouses treated each other badly or whether their relationship had already degenerated, and is even less likely to pay any attention to socio-economic circumstances and the effects of poverty or relative poverty on human relationships.

A proper[66] virtue-ethical framework for accountability, on the other hand, will enable the assessor (be it a judge or someone else) to place acts in their relevant context, and appraise them with empathy and courage. A proper virtue-ethical framework will remind the assessor to be humble and honest, both intellectually and otherwise, and appropriately temperate when it comes to expressing condemnation.[67]

64 For excellent discussion, see Miranda Fricker, *Epistemic Injustice: Power and the Ethics of Knowing* (OUP 2007).

65 Cheaters TV Show, <https://www.cheaters.com/> accessed 21 January 2020.

66 It goes without saying that the virtues can be abused and manipulated; some might suggest that the Chinese communist party's invocations of the teachings of Confucius taps into Confucian ethics without actually engaging with it properly. Without making this point, very useful on Confucianism is Stephen C. Angle, *Contemporary Confucian Political Philosophy: Toward Progressive Confucianism* (Polity 2012).

67 This owes something to Colin Farrelly and Lawrence B. Solum (eds), *Virtue Jurisprudence* (Palgrave MacMillan 2008), and in different ways also to Iris van Domselaar, *The Fragility of Rightness: Adjudication and the Primacy of Practice* (DPhil thesis, University of Amsterdam 2014).

In this light, a virtue ethics approach to holding experts to account might not be worse than, and possibly be preferable to, a more traditional accountability framework.[68] And if this should sound a little *Weltfremd*, it is well worth remembering that law generally tends to recognize doctrines about abuse of rights,[69] or that Canadian courts have developed a doctrine relying on the 'honour of the Crown' so as to come to terms with aboriginal rights and colonial justice.[70] Moreover, law generally, and international law in particular, is infused with notions such as good faith – indeed, an appeal to general principles, in any legal system, is a thinly disguised appeal to the virtues.

To sum up: 'governance', 'accountability' and 'expert' are all fluid and ill-defined notions; this factor alone makes it highly unlikely to develop an accountability framework for expert governance along more or less traditional lines, whether deontological or consequentialist. Indeed, both of these general approaches are unsuitable for expert accountability, and tend to lapse into each other at any rate; and the combination of unstable concepts and unbalanced ethical approaches might help explain some of the attractions of expert governance for those in power. If all this is plausible, it would seem to be the case that the only possible escape is to change register completely and appeal not to the duties of those who govern us, and not to the desirability or otherwise of the consequence their actions may bring, but appeal rather to their sense of propriety, their virtues.

68 Some of the links between law and virtue are explored in Amalia Amaya and Ho Hock Lai (eds), *Law, Virtue and Justice* (Hart 2013).

69 Useful is Rupert Klaus Neuhaus, *Das Rechtsmissbrauchsverbot im Heutigen Völkerrecht* (Duncker and Humblot 1984).

70 Discussed in Mariana Valverde, *Chronotopes of Law: Jurisdiction, Scale and Governance* (Routledge 2015) 125–153.

2 Expert accountability and the rule of law

Intertwinement of normative and functional standards?

Sanne Taekema

1 Introducing the problem

Expert knowledge is present in legal decision-making in various ways. In some policy areas, such as migration or criminal justice, public discussions are often conducted in terms of politics or popular legitimacy. In other areas, such as environmental or economic policy, expert knowledge is central. The recent climate change debate has forefronted the need for sound knowledge as input for sustainable climate policies and regulations to reduce CO_2. However, as the other parts of this book show, expert knowledge informs regulation and law at all levels of governance in ways that are not all visible but all the more influential. The quality of legal decision-making often crucially depends on expert knowledge, although the quality of that knowledge may be contested.

An example. In sports, a strict gender division is used to ensure fair competition. However, athletes use their natural advantages in height and muscle development to excel. Sometimes this means that competitors in women's competitions are at an advantage if they display features that are associated with a male physique. There is a need for a clear boundary, but how to construct that boundary is difficult. Current attempts to do so base it on biological knowledge: what are natural features for male or female bodies, and what is the range of natural variation? Unfortunately for regulators, the range of variation is great in various dimensions: chromosomes combined with hormone levels and visible features do not lead to a clear male/female division applicable to every individual. In middle distance running, this has now led to the decision to focus on testosterone levels, which are said by experts to give an unfair advantage to women with levels much higher than average.[1] Some women have naturally high testosterone levels as part of a condition called 'hyperandrogenism'. For one athlete, Caster Semenya, the limit on testosterone levels severely affects her life and career. As a result of losing her

1 Emma Eklund and others, 'Serum Androgen Profile and Physical Performance in Women Olympic Athletes' (2017) 51 British Journal of Sports Medicine 1301; Stephane Bermon and Pierre-Yves Garnier, 'Serum Androgen Levels and Their Relation to Performance in Track and Field: Mass Spectrometry Results from 2127 Observations in Male and Female Elite Athletes' (2017) 51 British Journal of Sports Medicine 1309.

appeal to the Court of Arbitration for Sport (CAS), she is required to take medication to bring the level down artificially in order to compete.[2] The expert decision thus has serious consequences, but it is not at all clear whether testosterone is the only factor; other experts see this singling out as a debatable choice.[3] The expert opinion that is endorsed by the International Association of Athletics Federations (IAAF)[4] and CAS, in practice determines the notion of fair competition.

I give this example because it clearly shows the problematics of expert knowledge in decision-making. Expertise does not just generate knowledge; it determines legal and policy decisions. Such decisions affect the lives and interests of the people subject to them. If that expert knowledge is contested, and given the serious consequences, it raises the question whether contestation and accountability for the decision should be restricted to legal actors. By legal actors I refer to actors that are established by legal frameworks or make decisions based on such frameworks.[5] This is, therefore, how I interpret the central problem of this book: the consequences of reliance on expert knowledge give a prima facie reason to extend accountability to experts. This leads to a range of further questions, out of which I focus on the framing of transnational expert accountability. My point of departure is a legal notion of accountability as part of a rule of law framework. The core purpose of the rule of law is the limiting of arbitrary exercise of power of legal authorities. Accountability in the sense of giving account, being called upon by a forum to explain and be judged,[6] can be seen as part of being governed by the rule of law in order to limit arbitrary conduct. In order for that framework to be applicable, an actor needs to be in a position of authority, being able to exercise power legitimately. With regard to experts, the primary question is whether this requirement is applicable at all. More precisely, this leads to the main questions of this chapter. In what sense are experts authorities to which rule of law standards can be applied? And, following this, in what way do rule of

2 *Mokgadi Caster Semenya v. International Association of Athletics Federations* [2018] CAS /O/5794 and *Athletics Federation South-Africa v. International Association of Athletics Federations* [2018] CAS O/5798.

3 Roger Pielke, Ross Tucker and Erik Boye, 'Scientific Integrity and the IAAF Testosterone Regulations' (2019) 19 International Sports Law Journal 18; Katrina Karkazis and others, 'Out of Bounds? A Critique of the New Policies on Hyperandrogenism in Elite Female Athletes' (2012) 12 American Journal of Bioethics 3; Peter Sonksen and others, 'Medical and Ethical Concerns Regarding Women with Hyperandrogenism and Elite Sports (2015) 100 Journal of Clinical Endocrinology & Metabolism 825.

4 IAAF is now known as World Athletics. Because the name change occurred in late 2019, after the case discussed here, I refer to IAAF in the text.

5 Standard legal actors include national governments, courts and international actors that set up and implement legal frameworks (e.g. the UN Security Council). In the context of this book, the term legal actor is ambiguous, because the cases and regimes discussed are at the boundaries between law, policy and expertise. See further Alessandra Arcuri and Florin Coman-Kund, 'Introduction: Breaking Taboos, Talking Accountability' (in this volume).

6 Mark Bovens, 'Analysing and Assessing Public Accountability. A Conceptual Framework' (2007) 13 European Law Journal 447, 450.

law standards need to be adapted to make sense in the functional domain of the expert bodies in question?

To complicate matters, we are not just considering experts in law, such as expert witnesses in criminal proceedings. The expert bodies at issue here are situated in various transnational legal settings. Examples such as the experts involved in the International Panel on Climate Change (IPCC),[7] the experts consulted by the IAAF,[8] the experts monitoring implementation of Forest Stewardship Council standards,[9] the experts setting safety standards in the International Commission on Radiation Protection,[10] all involve committees, groups or bodies working outside of national legal orders but with influence on international and national policy and lawmaking. The transnational dimension complicates matters because the legal character of such expert bodies is often unclear, and the influence of expert advice may be diffused over different legal systems and levels. The interactions within specific areas of multilevel governance are not my concern here,[11] but these do raise the question of how the authority of expert bodies is to be understood in a context of multiple authorities.

My argument here proceeds along the following steps. First, in Section 2, I characterize expert authority by situating it in the broader theoretical debate on authority. Rather than use a narrowly formal definition of legal authority, I draw on the distinction between theoretical and practical authority to argue that expert authority can be understood as a form of practical authority. To explain this, I use the theory of Joseph Raz.[12] More importantly, I use the more specific concepts of hybrid, liquid and relative authority to understand how expert authority may be a legitimate form of authority.[13] In Section 3, I link the notion of practical authority to the applicability of the rule of law and argue for a specific understanding of rule of law standards that is suitable for a transnational context. In Section 4, I argue that variations in the functional domain of expertise require contextualization of rule of law standards and suggest that institutionalization of such standards is a promising way to safeguard rule of law conformity.

7 Oren Perez, 'The Hybrid Legal-Scientific Dynamic of Transnational Scientific Institutions' (2015) 26 European Journal of International Law 391.

8 World Athletics, 'IAAF to introduce eligibility rules for females with hyperandrogenism'. Available at: <https://www.worldathletics.org/news/iaaf-news/iaaf-to-introduce-eligibility-rules-for-femal-1> last accessed 10 March 2021.

9 Olga Maletz and Maria Tysiachniouk, 'The Effects of Expertise on the Quality of Forest Standards Implementation: The Case of FSC Certification in Russia' (2009) Forest Policy and Economics 422.

10 Machiko Kanetake, 'The Dual Vulnerability of Transnational, Science-based Standards in the National Legal Order' (2016) 7 Transnational Legal Theory 470.

11 See the examples and exposition in Arcuri and Coman-Kund, 'Introduction' in this volume.

12 Joseph Raz, *The Morality of Freedom* (Clarendon 1986) 23–69; Joseph Raz, 'Authority, Law, and Morality', in *Ethics in the Public Domain. Essays in the Morality of Law and Politics* (Clarendon Press 1995) 210–237.

13 I use the concepts of hybrid, liquid and relative authority as explained by Oren Perez, Nico Krisch and Nicole Roughan, respectively. See references below in Section 2.

2 Experts as authorities

It is possible to define legal authorities in a formal way, as being instituted by legal norms. The definition given by Bogdandy and others is of this kind: 'the legal capacity to *determine* others and to reduce their freedom, i.e. to unilaterally shape their legal or factual situation'.[14] In the context of this chapter, however, this definition is not helpful, for two reasons. First, it defines legal authority as 'legal capacity', which means that the question of what makes it legal is pushed forward. This is problematic because the question regarding experts is exactly to determine whether and to what extent they can be authorities to which legal, rule of law, standards apply.[15] Second, it also postpones the question of legitimacy because it is defined in terms of legal power; it is an open question whether a legal authority is legitimate.[16] Philosophically, however, the concept of authority implies a claim to legitimacy.[17] Authority is distinguished from raw power by the claim that it deserves to be followed. The philosophical discussion concerns the normative question whether and when a purported authority has legitimate authority. Although the philosophical normative conceptions of authority will be the main sources for this section, I should say upfront that this perspective cannot be completely sustained. It is helpful to distinguish a normative account of authority from a sociological account which is descriptive and tries to map different existing forms of authority not in terms of what can be claimed for them but in terms of their social role and factual recognition.[18] Both are different from the legal account, which forefronts the formal conditions. All three conceptions are necessary to understand the idea of expert authority.

If we want to understand experts' normative authority, it is helpful to start with the standard distinction between epistemic (or theoretical) and practical authority.[19] Following the influential theory of Joseph Raz, the distinction between the two can be summarized in terms of the reasons applying to subjects to authority.[20] Whereas theoretical or epistemic authority provides someone

14 Von Bogdandy and others (eds), *The Exercise of Public Authority by International Institutions. Advancing International Institutional Law* (Springer 2010).
15 See also the discussion of Krisch and liquid authority below.
16 Here too, I suspect that the 'legal' element does the work: by packing the legal conditions for the capacity with standards legitimacy can be generated. As will be clear from the following argument I follow the legal philosophy route of seeing legal authority as a form of practical authority.
17 Raz, *Morality of Freedom* (n 12) 23–28; Scott Shapiro, 'Authority' in Jules Coleman and Scott Shapiro (eds) *The Oxford Handbook of Jurisprudence and Philosophy of Law* (OUP 2002).
18 Sociological accounts often refer back to Weber's theory of authority: Max Weber, *The Theory of Social and Economic Organization* (Talcott Parsons ed., The Free Press 1947) 324–423. That particular theoretical background is not decisive here; it is about the empirical orientation.
19 Tom Christiano, 'Authority', *Stanford Encyclopedia of Philosophy* 2013 (Spring 2013 edn) <https://plato.stanford.edu/archives/spr2013/entries/authority/> accessed 26 January 2020.
20 Raz, *Morality of Freedom* (n 12) 29.

with a reason to change a belief, practical authority gives a person a reason for action. In a sense, experts are the prime example of epistemic authorities: they are a reason to change your belief, not a reason to act differently. You go to the doctor to get a diagnosis, and as a result you will believe that your pain has a certain cause. This does not directly change your reasons for action, although indirectly it may be reason for treatment. A policeman diverting traffic is a practical authority, giving you a direct reason to change your route. One way to think of the expert authority problem is as a mixing of epistemic and practical authority: it is because expert decisions have direct influence on action-related, i.e. practical, authority that they become problematic. If experts would purely advise other authorities, who independently decide what to do, there would not be a problem. However, the work of experts is often much more than free advice; it points in a direction to change action. Thus, it makes sense to see their authority as hybrid: partly epistemic and partly practical.

Hybrid authority is a term coined by Oren Perez. He describes regulatory scientific institutions (RSIs), such as the IPCC, as follows: 'the authority of RSIs has a hybrid legal-political-epistemic nature'.[21] Although Perez does not use the term practical authority, the way he subsumes legal and political authority under normative authority is similar.[22] The institutions Perez discusses are hybrid in their institutional set-up: they combine expert committees with legal or political decision-making bodies. They are hybrid not only in the authority they exercise, but also institutionally. This need not be the case everywhere. Importantly, some expert bodies are instituted to generate advice only, but in practice determine practical decisions. The example of IAAF is a case in point. In the context of athletics, the IAAF itself is the primary practical authority: it decides on the rules and policies that apply to athletes, and makes decisions based on those rules, such as judging an athlete eligible to compete. In the case of hyperandrogenism or differences in sexual development (hereafter: DSD), the IAAF regulation, adopted by the IAAF Council, was explicitly based on 'broad medical and scientific consensus, supported by peer-reviewed evidence and data from the field'.[23] As Pielke, Tucker and Boye show, the regulation mainly draws on one 2017 study, which was performed by IAAF commissioned researchers and funded by IAAF.[24] The content of the regulation, setting the limit of testosterone at which this is supposed to yield unfair competitive advantage, is based directly on this study. Moreover, the determination whether a particular athlete is subject to the conditions set in the DSD regulation is made by a panel

21 Perez (n 7) 392.

22 Perez contrasts normative and epistemic authority rather that practical and theoretical as is customary in the philosophical debate, see Christiano (n 19).

23 World Athletics, 'C 3.6 Eligibility Regulations Regarding the Female Classification', version 1 November 2019, <https://www.worldathletics.org/about-iaaf/documents/book-of-rules> accessed 14 January 2020, commonly referred to as the DSD regulation.

24 Pielke, Tucker and Boye (n 3) 20, about Bermon and Garnier, 'Serum androgen levels and their relation to performance in track and field'.

of IAAF appointed medical experts. In effect, therefore, the medical experts determine the practical consequences of this regulation. One could argue that the regulations are an IAAF policy or regulatory decision, based on the epistemic authority of medical experts, and therefore a distinction between expert epistemic authority and IAAF practical authority is possible. The same cannot be said of the application of the regulation: the concrete decision to ban an athlete from competition made by a medical panel is a direct exercise of practical authority. And even in the context of the regulation, the content of the rule is so directly based on the medical evidence that it is hard to argue that the rule is an exercise of legitimate authority by IAAF itself: its legitimacy depends on the medical support completely.[25]

The hybridity of expert authorities as epistemic and practical is well-supported as an empirical matter: we can point to many expert bodies or mixed institutions that display such hybridity. What is more difficult is how to approach the question of legitimacy of hybrid authorities.[26] In the philosophical discussions of practical authority, primarily in relation to the work of Joseph Raz, the distinction between de facto authority and legitimate authority is the starting point. According to Raz, the two concepts are interdependent. An actor who has de facto authority, necessarily claims legitimate authority (a claim which can be false). Legitimacy may be provided by procedure – like Parliament having democratic legitimacy – or substantively – leading to a better decision.[27] Vice versa, only if an actor has de facto authority, meaning that they are effective in being generally followed, can they also have legitimate authority.[28] The condition of effectiveness is not very strict: it is sufficient if there is general acceptance of the authority's decisions and rules. Without the factual base of effectiveness, the legitimacy question does not arise. This might generate a problem in regard to expert authorities, because it is not always clear to what extent they are followed directly or whether other decision-making authorities make their own deliberations on the basis of the expert advice. This is why the sociological account of authority cannot be missed: we need to establish the factual influence of the authority in order to assess whether it can meaningfully be said to exercise practical authority. Raz applies his framework to traditional political-legal authority, that of state institutions and law, which is why his attention is on the legitimacy

25 I return the legitimacy point at the end of Section 3.

26 Perez (n 7), 392; he argues that this is a (difficult) question of scientific legitimacy versus political-legal legitimacy for RSIs. I agree with his analysis to a large extent, but would like to broaden the discussion beyond science-based expertise.

27 Raz has a specific theory of legitimate authority, the 'service conception', that I don't follow here, see in particular: Joseph Raz, *Between Authority and Interpretation: On the Theory of Law and Practical Reason* (OUP 2009) 134–142. It seems sufficient to distinguish procedural and substantive aspects of authority, compare below Roughan (n 28) 27–42.

28 Raz, *Morality of Freedom* (n 12) 26; Nicole Roughan, *Authorities: Conflicts, Cooperation and Transnational Legal Theory* (OUP 2013) 30.

and effectiveness of practical authority. Although similar issues of legitimacy and effectiveness can be raised regarding epistemic authority, he sees it as a less relevant category in the context of politics and law. Applying his framework of de facto and legitimate authority to expert authorities may well present a different picture. It raises the question of whether the expert is a legitimate epistemic authority, meaning that the expert opinion provides a good reason to change our beliefs. With regard to epistemic authority, it seems legitimacy is more central than effectiveness: the judgement that an expert opinion deserves to be followed does not depend on de facto acceptance of the opinion. Thus, the strength of the condition of de facto authority may be challenged, when it comes to less conspicuous forms of authority than the authority of state institutions. This seems particularly relevant to expert bodies with hybrid authority. One might argue that a legitimate authority deserves to be followed, even if it is not in fact followed in practice. For instance, such an argument can be made in cases where climate change scepticism determines state policy. The condition of effectiveness may be too strong, especially when the authority is (partially) epistemic rather than practical. Moreover, the condition of effectiveness may not be stable: even when it concerns traditional legal institutions, such as governments or courts, it is clear that their de facto authority may change, as it does in volatile political situations such as Venezuela or Afghanistan.

Here, a second conception of authority, applicable to experts, becomes important: the idea of liquid authority advanced by Nico Krisch.[29] Krisch draws attention to the impact of 'soft' forms of governance, many of them involving expertise, and rightly points out that the focus on 'bureaucratic' or 'traditional' forms of authority obscures the real influence that these other forms of governance have.[30] Like the notion of hybrid authority, liquid authority is a sociological notion, as Krisch himself notes. It is useful here, because it enables me to track authority that is not easily categorized in traditional political or legal terms. Liquidity refers to the informal and dynamic character of transnational authorities:[31] they do not necessarily have formal legal recognition and their authority may change over time. These are two characteristics that are helpful to understand expert authorities: experts get involved in practical decision-making because of the need to include expert knowledge, which is an informal involvement (at least at the start); their role may very well change over time, depending on the importance of the knowledge they offer or on the political changes

29 Nico Krisch, 'Authority, Solid and Liquid, in Postnational Governance', in Roger Cotterrell and Maksymilian Del Mar (eds), ***Authority in Transnational Legal Theory. Theorizing Across Disciplines*** (Edward Elgar 2016) 25–48; Nico Krisch, 'Liquid Authority in Global Governance' (2017) 9 International Theory 237.

30 Krisch, 'Authority, Solid and Liquid' (n 29) 26.

31 Ibid 27. He also includes multiplicity of actors and substantive rather than formal grounding, but I take these two as specific for liquidity. Substantiveness is already absorbed in hybrid authority (because epistemic authority is substantively grounded). Multiplicity (as plurality) is key to relative authority, to which I will turn shortly.

of the decision-making context. For instance, transnational expert bodies have been prominent in development of European Union regulation, but their influence and importance varies over time and policy area.[32] Thus, the informality and dynamism introduced by liquid authority are useful to understand expert authorities. However, this is not enough.

One thing shown by the informal and dynamic aspects of liquidity is the intertwinement of factual authority in a sociological sense with the dimension of legitimacy. Although it is important sociologically to see the shift away from formality as an empirical phenomenon, to understand it fully it needs to be made part of a normative account.[33] If we grant that expert authority in an empirical sense depends on the informal substantive reasoning that makes the authority practically worth following, we should not turn away from a normative argument on why and when practical authority of experts is legitimate. The normative account of authority that accords with hybrid and liquid authority best is the relative authority theory of Nicole Roughan.[34]

The idea of relative authority is that legitimate authority is interdependent and that the conditions for legitimacy include a relativity condition. Roughan builds on earlier authority theories by specifying procedural and substantive grounds for legitimacy.[35] Procedural grounds include institutional rules that give standing to an authority, such as the democratic system legitimizing parliaments. Substantive grounds include the notion, also defended by Raz, that the authority should help its subjects to improve their practical reasoning. For instance, it is important for citizens to pay for the upkeep of collective goods, such as infrastructure. A legitimate authority, such as well-ordered tax department, enables citizens to do so by following its orders. Such an authority has procedural legitimacy (if it is set up with adequate procedures) and substantive legitimacy. Roughan sees the relativity condition as a necessary addition because authorities are plural and the subjects of their authority overlap or interact. The relativity condition means that: '(…) in circumstances of plurality of prima facie authorities, the justification of authority depends upon a justified inter-authority relationship'.[36] She applies it to legal pluralism within the state and to multilevel legal orders such the EU: these are both cases in which individuals are subject to overlapping authorities. This account of authority gives a normative account for situations of plural authorities, and focusses attention on the inter-authority relationship between the authorities themselves. The normative account implies that both subjects and authorities themselves need to attend to the legitimacy of

32 Burkard Eberlein and Edgar Grande, 'Beyond Delegation. Transnational Regulatory Regimes and the EU Regulatory State' (2005) 12 Journal of European Public Policy 89.

33 Compare Nicole Roughan, 'From Authority to Authorities: Bridging the Social/Normative Divide', in Roger Cotterrell and Maksymilian Del Mar (eds), *Authority in Transnational Legal Theory. Theorizing Across Disciplines* (Edward Elgar 2016) 280–299.

34 Ibid.

35 Ibid 134.

36 Ibid 138.

the inter-authority relationship: in some situations, this relationship may require that one of the authorities involved defers to the other, while in other situations it may call for cooperation between authorities. The aspect of inter-authority relationships is especially important for expert authorities because these typically do not depend on direct following of their authority by subjects (the individuals whose reasons for action change). The dynamics of expert authority tend to arise from the relationships to other authorities. An expert body may at first be engaged by a government for a limited task, such as a scientific advisory report. If the report serves the government's need, the government may implement policies to give it practical effect. In the context of those policies, experts may be given different responsibilities.

There are two other aspects of Roughan's account that are worth highlighting. First, she emphasizes the domain of authority.[37] One of the reasons why plurality of authorities is such a visible phenomenon in transnational law is that each authority has a particular domain of application and an ensuing limited reach in terms of subjects. Inter-authority relationships then arise because domains of application overlap.[38] One of the drawbacks of traditional theories of authority is that they tend to focus on comprehensive territory-based authorities, which makes them less applicable to transnational plurality of authority. Finally, Roughan rightly criticizes views of authority which see authorities as independent.[39] Although the view of an authority as independent of others may make sense at the level of nation states, it does not if we consider intra-state authorities, even the state institutions of legislature and judiciary, or international or transnational authorities.

The main value of the relative authority account for transnational expert authority lies in the inclusion of the relativity condition in legitimacy: only if authorities take the right approach to other authorities can they be seen as legitimate. This enables a critical discussion of the stance experts take towards the authorities they collaborate with: do they defer to political or legal decision-makers when they should?[40] It also enables a discussion of the quality of the institutional setting of experts: does the way they are required to operate and relate to other authorities enable legitimacy of decision-making? These critical questions also link to the main framework providing legitimacy in a legal context: the rule of law.

37 Ibid 46: 'Same-domain plurality exists when more than one person/body is authoritative for the same subjects in relation to the same field of activity. (…) Interactive-domain plurality, in contrast, exists where the domains of the authorities are separate but come into contact, either through the interaction of their respective subjects or the interconnectedness of the activities they seek to regulate'.

38 A well-known example, discussed by Roughan (n 33) 202–203 is the Kadi case which concerned overlap between the UN Security Council and the European Union.

39 Ibid 81.

40 In some situations, it may be difficult to disentangle expertise and legal powers: legal expertise, for instance on highly technical regulations, can also be a relevant category. It is often, but not necessarily, combined with decision-making power. A good example is the expertise of the European Commission and its bureaucracy. (Thanks to Florin Coman-Kund, who suggested this to me.)

3 Relative rule of law

Especially in the Anglo-American context, the rule of law is often taken to have a narrow meaning: attaching to the quality of formal legal rules, which are to be clear, stable, prospective and general.[41] However, if one asks what the point of the rule of law is, a broader account of it comes into view. Such a purposive or teleological conception of the rule of law sees it as aiming to reduce arbitrary exercise of power.[42] Generally, theories of the rule of law focus on constraining independent political authorities; more particularly, the observance of rule of law standards is taken to provide legitimacy (in a normative sense) to the state. The rule of law sets limits, and observance of those limits contributes to legitimate government. In a way that parallels the theoretical debate of authority, rule of law theorizing has paid little attention to the rule of law as a guiding purpose for non-state institutions. Although rule of law constraints are discussed in terms of state authority, many of them are in principle applicable more broadly. For instance, procedural safeguards usually provided by an independent judiciary can translate into more informal complaint and review mechanisms.[43] Some have argued for an international rule of law or an internationalized rule of law, which includes both international organizations and national states as addressees.[44] However, the rule of law in this line of theorizing remains a matter of clearly public institutions. Discussions of a transnational rule of law are mainly concerned with the way other institutions, such as the European Union or international courts, can support the rule of law at the national level. This is an important way of extending the reach of the rule of law, but it does not explore the application of the rule of law framework to other kinds of authorities, hybrid, liquid or relative.

If it is granted that transnational expert bodies may exert a form of relative authority, and that this authority needs to be legitimate, exploring how the rule

41 I leave aside the standard debate about the nature of the rule of law as formal, substantive or procedural. See Paul P. Craig, 'Formal and Substantive Conceptions of the Rule of Law: An Analytical Framework' [2017] Public Law 467; Brian Z. Tamanaha, *On the Rule of Law. History, Politics, Theory* (CUP 2004) 91–113; Jeremy Waldron, 'The Concept and the Rule of Law', (2008) 43 Georgia Law Review 1; Jeremy Waldron, 'The Rule of Law and the Importance of Procedure' in James E. Fleming (ed), *Getting to the Rule of Law* (New York University Press 2011) 3.

42 The term 'teleological' comes from the work of Krygier, one of the main proponents of this approach. See Martin Krygier, 'Four Puzzles about the Rule of Law: Why, What, Where? And Who Cares?' in James E. Fleming (ed), *Getting to the Rule of Law* (New York University Press 2011) 64, 75; Martin Krygier, 'The Rule of Law: Legality, Teleology, Sociology' in Gianluigi Palombella and Neil Walker (eds), *Re-locating the Rule of Law* (Hart 2009) 45.

43 E.g. the World Bank Inspection Panel, see e.g. Andria N. Fourie, *World Bank Accountability – In Theory and in Practice* (Eleven International Publishing 2016).

44 Simon Chesterman, 'An International Rule of Law?' (2008) 56 American Journal of Comparative Law 331; André Nollkaemper, 'The Internationalized Rule of Law' (2009) 1 Hague Journal on the Rule of Law 74.

of law can be involved in providing such legitimacy seems worth considering. The teleological view of the rule of law offers a good starting point, because it is agnostic about the characteristics of the actor exercising power.[45] The question to ask therefore is whether the activities of expert bodies are such that they may amount to exercise of power which is potentially arbitrary. If the activities of experts influence practical legal-political decision-making, as I argued above, this seems likely. In an important sense, the worries over legitimate authority and abiding by the rule of law converge: both are centred on the relationship between an actor wielding power and the subjects to that power. Rule of law concerns one specific aspect of that relationship, arbitrariness, while legitimate authority concerns the broader issue of following directives or decisions for good reasons. To return to Roughan's account of authority, it is possible to connect the rule of law standards to the procedural justification of authority. Roughan sees that procedural justification as concerned with the question of who has standing as an authority, and thus focuses on the procedure by which an actor acquires authority.[46] The question of how to exercise authority is treated as a different question and a matter of substantive justification.[47] The rule of law, however, does not fall on one side of this divide: avoiding arbitrary exercise of power is both a matter of proper procedures which circumscribe an actor's authority and of constraints upon the actual exercise of an actor's powers. Still, the rule of law does not concern the full range of substantive reasons that underpin legitimate authority. To understand in what way it is less extensive, the idea of arbitrariness needs to be explained further.[48]

Arbitrariness means being subject to another's unconstrained will; it implies being subjected to the whims of another person. Thus, it means insecurity: not knowing what might happen. However, it is not only insecurity, it also means that the person acting upon a whim will not explain why they act this way. In addition to insecurity, it implies incomprehension, a lack of understandable reasons. As a mirror image, the attempt to act non-arbitrarily implies minimizing unpredictability and justifying one's actions. We can see this in the concern of rule of law with reasoned decision-making, with predictable actions based on

45 Krygier, 'Four Puzzles about the Rule of Law' (n 42) 88: 'There are many ways in which power can be exercised, used, and abused without the intervention of law, even by the state, unless by definition everything the state does is counted as done by law. The rule of law is intended to exclude all those other ways from the start'.

46 Roughan (n 33) 126–127.

47 Ibid 134: the exercise is a separate condition for justifying authority. This does not mean that having authority and exercising it are unrelated: together they determine its legitimacy.

48 Almost parallel to drafting this paper, I have worked on a companion piece, 'Commitment to the rule of law: From a political to an organizational ideal' to appear in Guilherme Vilaca & Maria Varaki (eds), *Ethical Leadership in International Organizations* (forthcoming, CUP 2021). The same ideas on arbitrariness also play a large role in that piece. Both accounts build on the first articulation of the idea in Elaine Mak and Sanne Taekema, 'The European Union's Rule of Law Agenda: Identifying Its Core and Contextualizing Its Application', (2016) 8 Hague Journal on the Rule of Law 25.

norms, with fairness in the context of concrete decisions, and with accountability to those who are affected by the actions.[49] The overarching value of the rule of law as non-arbitrariness can thus be specified through its constitutive values of rationality, predictability, fairness and accountability. None of these values are what most would call substantive values, although, with the exception of predictability, they are not merely formal or procedural. The point here is that the rule of law is relevant to legitimacy of authorities, both in relation to the procedures of giving them standing and in relation to the actual exercise of authority. To apply the rule of law to a particular form of authority, such as expert authority, requires contextualizing these values for that particular setting.[50]

In order to combine the arguments made above that expert authority is best understood normatively as a form of relative authority, and that rule of law is a relevant framework to legitimate authority, the question is how the rule of law may apply to relative authority as exercised by experts. It is possible to reformulate the rule of law for plural, relative authorities by considering what relativity means to the purpose of reducing arbitrariness. One of the key aspects of the relative authority account is that legitimacy of authority requires both legitimate relations to subjects of authority and to other authorities. The rule of law ideal, in a similar way as legitimate authority, derives its core meaning from the vertical relationship between ruler and subject: ultimately, it is the consequences for the people affected by power that count. However, the situation of plurality of authority affects that subjection to power in interesting ways: arbitrariness in an authority's decision-making may also mean ignoring the relevant decisions of another authority, or an authority choosing to acknowledge one particular other authority rather than another without justification. Thus, in the interests of the subjects of authority and power, non-arbitrary relationships between authorities are important. We may therefore say that, under conditions of pluralism, the rule of law ideal demands that authorities acknowledge the relevance of other authorities. Does this mean that the application of the rule of law collapses into a relative authority account after all? I do not believe it does: the rule of law makes specific demands as to the quality of the relationship, either between authority and subject or between authorities in the interest of subjects, that need to be part of the broader analysis of relative authority. In a sense, the rule of law's constitutive values require more than passing the procedural and substantive tests of relative authority: they require quality of decision-making processes that may go further than the judgement that an authority is legitimate, i.e. deserves following of its decisions. The rule of law impacts the exercise of authority itself: it requires assessing how a decision is made, whether it fairly considered relevant interests, whether it is justified in terms that are understandable for those affected. Even if an authority is procedurally and substantively legitimate, its

49 Mak and Taekema (n 48) 29.

50 Compare Philip Selznick, '"Law in Context" Revisited' (2003) 30 Journal of Law and Society 177.

decisions and procedures can be scrutinized for rule of law conformity. The rule of law is an open-ended ideal in a way legitimate authority is not.[51] However, because the meaning of the values of rule of law is so open, the application of the rule of law to transnational experts still needs further consideration. To apply these rule of law values to experts, a shift in emphasis may be necessary. If we think of the exercise of expert authority, some of these values are more directly applicable than others. Taking up the example of IAAF's DSD regulation may clarify this. In the context of the regulation itself, predictability of application is certainly an issue, but one in which a combined effort of experts and the regulatory authority of the IAAF Council is necessary. The purported role of the experts was that of providing a scientifically robust definition of a relevant testosterone level for unfair advantage, one that could be applied in a medical test. As we have seen, the scientific ground on which this definition was based was shaky.[52] In terms of rule of law values, this simplified definition enhanced predictability but could not be seen as sufficiently rational – lacking firm scientific support, nor as procedurally fair – subjecting professional athletes to degrading medical testing. Although there is a form of accountability for the decision in the possibility to appeal to CAS, this is an appeal against the IAAF decision, in which the medical experts are not challenged directly. In this example, the rule of law value of predictability matters less than rationality and fairness.

4 The functional context of expert authority and accountability

So far, I have argued that transnational experts exercise a form of hybrid, liquid and relative authority and that, because such authority needs to be legitimate, rule of law values are applicable in order to make the exercise of authority less arbitrary. The combined characteristics of hybridity, liquidity and relativity have consequences for the way in which rule of law values may be applied. Moreover, these characteristics take on a particular meaning if they are connected to the functional tasks of experts.

As noted in Section 2, the hybridity of expert authority concerns the combination of epistemic and practical authority: experts have a role in practical decision-making that is justified by their epistemic authority, their claim to better knowledge. The assessment of their role in terms of exercise of power thus also depends on this key functional attribute: that they have relevant knowledge that other authorities or the subjects to those authorities lack. As Perez points out with regard to scientific knowledge used for policy purposes – a point

51 This open-endedness can be linked to the formulation of the ideal of rule of law as 'progressively to reduce the degree of arbitrariness in positive law and its administration' by Philip Selznick (with P. Nonet and H. Vollmer), *Law, Society and Industrial Justice* (Russell Sage 1969) 12, and Philip Selznick, 'Sociology and Natural Law' (1961) 6 Natural Law Forum 84, 94.

52 Pielke, Tucker and Boye (n 3).

generalizable to expertise beyond science – the problematic issue is the warrant or support for that knowledge: this is caught between scientific and legal-political logics.[53] It is worth connecting the problem of the warrant for expert knowledge to the liquidity of authority: the informality and dynamics of providing a warrant for expertise mean that the authority of experts over subjects shifts. Empirically, one can observe dynamics in how contestation of expertise can undermine the authority of the expert in question.[54] This can be countered by embedding the expert authority in a structure of practical (legal-political) authorities, but, as Perez shows, this may have the consequence that the expert authority's decisions are justified on the basis of practical legitimacy rather than epistemic. This is where the notion of arbitrary exercise of power may come in: in the functional context of expert decisions it may indeed be arbitrary to supplant a procedural justification for a knowledge-based one. One crucial danger of hybrid and liquid expert authority that is highlighted by such a rule of law approach is the spill-over of authority: limited expert authority may be used for more far-reaching practical authority decisions, and vice versa, expert authorities may borrow support from practical procedure. The example about athletics from the introduction may illustrate the first spill-over effect: even though the determinativeness of testosterone for performance is debatable, testosterone's role in hyperandrogenism is treated practically as the sole biological indicator of unfair enhanced athletic performance of women.[55] The IAAF and CAS as practical authorities use the medical expertise as determinative of their practical decision, despite the controversy. Vice versa, an expert body may use the fact of practical implementation or the following of legal or policy procedures as justifying their expert report. For instance, in the context of court proceedings, experts may point to the fact that they are registered in an official system to support the legitimacy of their report. Such legal recognition may be taken as a reason to minimize the need to justify their contribution in scientific terms.[56] The lens

53 Perez (n 7) 402–408.

54 A good example is the debate on vaccination, in which the authority of mainstream medical experts is no longer widely accepted and vaccination rates decline, see e.g. Julie A. Boom and Rachel H. Cunningham, *Understanding and Managing Vaccine Concerns* (Springer 2014).

55 Supporting the IAAF point of view: Martin Ritzén and others, 'The Regulations about Eligibility for Women with Hyperandrogenism to Compete in Women's Category are Well Founded. A Rebuttal to the Conclusions by Healy et al.' (2014) 82 Clinical Endocrinology 307; questioning it: Peter H. Sönksen and others, 'Hyperandrogenism Controversy in Elite Women's Sport: An Examination and Critique of Recent Evidence' (2017) 52 British Journal of Sports Medicine 1481–1482. On the history of gender tests in athletics, see Marion Müller, 'Constructing Gender Incommensurability in Competitive Sport: Sex/Gender Testing and the New Regulations on Female Hyperandrogenism' (2015) 39 Human Studies 405, 416–419.

56 This is what may happen through the institutionalization of expert involvement in court procedures in the form of public registers of experts. Such a register exists in The Netherlands, see <www.nrgd.nl>; for a European overview, see <https://e-justice.europa.eu/content_find_a_forensic_expert-550-en.do> accessed 21 January 2020.

of rule of law may show that relative authority harbours dangers. Rather than being relative authorities enhancing each other's legitimacy, actors may use each other's purported legitimacy to hide behind.

In the case of expert authority which intertwines with legal-political practical authority, it seems important to institutionalize not just relative authority, but hybrid relative authority. By this I mean that the hybridity needs to be acknowledged in the institutional relationships between authorities. To use these relationships for improving the rule of law quality of relative authorities, the reciprocal dependence needs to be specified: while the expert authority's decision needs to be justified on epistemic grounds towards the legal authority, the legal authority needs to justify its own decision on the basis of legal-political grounds. Although sociologically expert and regulatory decisions have become fused into hybrid bodies, from a rule of law point of view it is important to disentangle the justifications for decisions. Again, the IAAF example is useful. Although there may be epistemic reasons to conclude that testosterone levels are the only viable option to test for hyperandrogenism, the justification of the expertise towards the practical authority of IAAF and CAS should include discussion of the degree of uncertainty and contestation. Here more is probably claimed in terms of scientific certainty than warranted.[57] Additionally, the legal and political authorities need to justify their decisions by considering broader values. Of course, in this respect the functional domain of sports plays a crucial role: the notion of fair play is central but also unclear. However, as practical authorities decision-makers need to address other, moral and legal, considerations, also to embed the epistemic authority in the political and legal context. Most importantly, this entails considering the consequences for the human beings subjected to this regime, and the moral problem of forcing medication on healthy individuals.[58] From a rule of law perspective, then, the value of rationality or reasoned decision-making requires a structure that disentangles hybridity of justification, and makes clear that there are differences between the epistemic and the practical judgment. The institutions in which expertise is employed need to be such that this disentanglement is possible. Hybrid relativity of authorities should include acknowledgement of the functional limitations of each authority. An important question then is to what extent disentanglement of epistemic and practical judgments can be achieved in practice. Of course, the existence of hybrid bodies is in itself an indication that they serve a practical need. It does not seem feasible to abolish these altogether. However, I would like to make two suggestions for clarifying the distinction between epistemic and practical judgment. First, it may be possible to make more explicit what the role and strength of the (scientific) expertise are in the process of decision-making, as a transparency requirement. This would include making it possible to contest the expertise in that process. In the context of the IAAF example, the crucial claim

57 Pielke, Tucker and Boyle (n 3).
58 Karkazis and others (n 3) 12.

of scientific consensus for the content of the testosterone norm should not have been made. Second, practical judgments should involve broader legal and moral considerations. I do not suggest separating expert knowledge and practical judgment, but there should be guarantees that practical judgment is not reduced to following the scientific assessment. In the IAAF example, this means that the decision to ban athletes needs be based on more than medical evidence, most crucially, also on ethical and human rights considerations.

A second important aspect of applying the rule of law ideal to expert authority is the problematic of accountability. Within the rule of law framework, the idea of accountability serves to mitigate or redress arbitrary consequences of the subjects of authoritative decision-making. This may be achieved by participation in the decision-making process, or more importantly, by the possibility to voice complaints about the decisions.[59] One of the drawbacks of expert authorities as interdependent relative authorities is that such interdependence may lead to inter-authority accountability only. The rule of law, however, requires an outward accountability beyond the interactions between authorities, to the people who are subject to these authorities. Inter-authority accountability mechanisms are important because, from the point of view of power structures, they are potentially effective. However, although the other authority involved may have the means to enforce or threaten, it may also have a narrow view focussing on the functional tasks of the authorities towards each other only. This does not necessarily do much to reduce arbitrary consequences for the people affected by the complex of decisions made by the authorities. For instance, authorities may demand a form of justification of decisions from each other that is not understandable for the subjects of authority, who may need more explanation. The main difficulty of achieving accountability when multiple authorities are involved is how to hold accountable the authority that matters most for the decision-making. Because of the tendency of practical authorities to rely heavily on the outcomes of expert decision-making, it may be necessary to hold the experts to account directly.[60]

Here too, the rule of law perspective shows the difficulties of relative authorities. If their decision-making processes are intertwined, knowing who is responsible for which part of the complex of decisions may be hard to find out. Knowing to whom and how to voice grievances is possibly too complicated for affected individuals. In traditional legal contexts, this problem is solved by giving individuals one entry point for accountability: a court procedure. Expert decisions can usually be challenged within those procedures. This puts the main burden of determining accountability on a legal authority, including the task to disentangle the responsibilities of the various authorities involved. We can see this process at work in the IAAF example: in the arbitration procedure before the

59 Waldron (n 41).

60 Alessandra Arcuri and Marta Simoncini, 'Scientists and Legal Accountability: Lessons from the L'Aquila Case', EUI Working Paper Law 2015/17.

CAS, both the expertise and the moral and legal framework used by the IAAF are contested. However important the expertise has been, a legal authority such as the CAS has difficulty holding the experts to account. This is due to the familiar problems of the need for expertise to judge expertise, and of the battle of experts.[61] From a rule of law point of view, this seems to call for procedures that give genuine opportunities for those affected to put forward their problems and that require genuine responses from the different authorities involved. It is not, however, evident that mimicking the formal procedures of national courts in the context of transnational expert authorities is necessarily the best way forward. The formal rules of evidence, of rights to be heard, of legal representation, may not always serve to enhance accountability; they may also create new, legal, barriers for genuine engagement. For instance, Kate Macdonald and Terry Macdonald argue that both public accountability and 'pragmatic experimentalism' may be good responses to liquid authority in the transnational context.[62] Pragmatic experimentalism refers to institutional mechanisms that are less formal, more open-ended and more collective, whereas public accountability is a more traditional standards-based procedure. This is not to say that they should always be literally experimental, in the sense of tailor-made mechanisms for one case. The aim should still be to provide a recognizable route to address grievances. In a legal context, it may be hard to imagine how a pragmatic alternative might work, although mediation processes can be seen as an example.[63] The collective, collaborative dimension of pragmatic experimentalism is at first sight at odds with a rule of law ideal, which seems to call for standards, but there may well be contexts in which knowledge and practical standards are in development, where this may provide a way to reduce the arbitrary nature of authoritative decision-making.

5 Conclusion

Transnational experts exercise authority in a way that can be captured through the concepts of hybrid, liquid and relative authority. Their decisions straddle the divide between epistemic and practical authority – hybridity; the extent of their authority and its legitimacy is changeable and hard to pin down – liquidity; and the legitimacy of their authority depends on inter-authority relations – relativity. I have argued that an authority approach needs to be supplemented by the closely related but different perspective of the rule of law. A rule of law approach zooms in on the potentially arbitrary nature of authoritative decision-making

61 Herbert M. Kritzer, 'The Arts of Persuasion in Science and Law: Conflicting Norms in the Courtroom' (2009) 72 Law and Contemporary Problems 41, 60–61.

62 Kate Macdonald and Terry Macdonald, 'Liquid Authority and Political Legitimacy in Transnational Governance' (2017) 9 International Theory 329, 336.

63 This is also what Macdonald and Macdonald seem to have in mind. Their prime example is the International Finance Corporation Compliance Advisor Ombudsman of the World Bank, whose procedures are a form of mediation, ibid 340.

and prompts questions on how to curb arbitrariness. In my interpretation of the rule of law ideal applied to experts, reduction of arbitrariness can in part be achieved by providing institutional clarity on the differences between experts and legal-political authorities and the interaction between epistemic and practical justifications. This is only a small part of a rule of law approach, however, because it needs to be critically examined in light of the consequences for the ultimate subjects of authority, the people whose interests are affected. Doing justice to their interests in the functional domains involved may sometimes mean that an informal procedure in which different authorities and subject interact to achieve a collective decision may be necessary. If such a procedure gives sufficient weight to reducing adverse consequences for subjects, that may be in line with a rule of law approach. However, the precariousness of such a pragmatic approach needs to be acknowledged. Working towards clear standards and formal institutionalized procedures, while not always providing substantive solutions, may often be the best way to achieve an acceptable reduction of arbitrary exercise of authority in a complex context.

Acknowledgment

Many thanks to the participants in STeM section seminar in Rotterdam in January 2019 and the LSA panel in Washington DC in June 2019 for their comments and suggestions. Thanks to Lieske Bottema and Alma Besic for research assistance, and to Alessandra Arcuri and Florin Coman-Kund for their comments on the first draft.

3 Three dimensions of accountability for global technocracy

Alessandra Arcuri

1 Introduction

International standards in the fields of health, safety and environmental regulation are often produced by standard setting bodies, cooperating and/or relying on the work of scientific and quasi-scientific bodies. These bodies are henceforth referred to as Global Regulatory Scientific Institutions (GRSIs). Examples of GRSIs include the scientific advisory bodies producing reports for the Codex Alimentarius Commission (Codex), the International Commission on Non-Ionizing Radiation Protection (ICNIRP), a non-governmental organization (NGO) in official relations with the World Health Organization (WHO), the International Agency for Research on Cancer (IARC), which is the specialized cancer agency of the WHO, the numerous expert committees embedded in the WHO, which are instrumental in decisions relating to the global governance of health,[1] as well as the International Organization for Standardization (ISO) and the International Electrotechnical Commission (IEC) committees working on nanotechnologies. These institutions deserve special attention because of their capacity to exercise regulatory authority by greatly influencing the production of international and transnational standards. Placing at the centre of analysis the institutionalization of *technê* in the form of GRSIs is critical in order to deepen our knowledge of global governance 'understood as an essentially technocratic process'.[2]

In spite of their exercise of regulatory authority, GRSIs remain often backgrounded in the study of global technocracy and go unnoticed by broader publics. The fact that GRSIs are obscure and yet influential raises the question of how they are being held accountable. While studies on accountability of global

1 J Benton Heath, 'SARS, the "Swine Flu" Crisis and Emergency Procedures in the WHO. States and Global Administrations in Context' (2012) Institute for Research on Public Administration 147; J Benton Heath, 'Global Emergency Power in the Age of Ebola' (2015) 57 Harvard International Law Journal 1.

2 Armin Von Bogdandy, Philipp Dann and Matthias Goldmann, 'Developing the Publicness of Public International Law: Towards a Legal Framework for Global Governance Activities' in Armin Von Bogdandy and others (eds), *The Exercise of Public Authority by International Institutions: Advancing International Institutional Law* (Springer 2010) 3.

governance institutions have proliferated, no systematic study of the accountability of GRSIs has been conducted so far. This chapter aims at filling the gap in existing scholarship by conceptualizing the accountability for GRSIs. Investigating the accountability of GRSIs is urgent as it goes to the core of the process of global governance. This chapter offers a first conceptualization of the dimensions that ought to be considered when studying and designing accountability frameworks for regulatory scientific institutions and, more generally, of global technocracy.

This analysis proceeds in three steps. In the next section, a portrait of the way authority is exercised by GRSIs is sketched. It is beyond the scope of this essay to provide an exhaustive list of the numerous GRSIs populating the emerging global administrative arena, though few examples are illuminating. The main aim of this section is to illustrate ways in which authority is exercised. Section 3 presents a bird's eye on the literature on accountability in global law, that is, the main body of legal scholarship interested in the question of accountability of global institutions. It further suggests that accountability is best understood through the prism of public law. Within the body of scholarship on accountability, the question of regulatory scientific institutions remained under-explored. To fill this gap, in Section 4, the chapter identifies and discusses three dimensions along which the accountability of GRSIs can be conceptualized and further operationalized.

2 Regulatory science in global governance and the need for accountability

Scientific advisory bodies are key actors not only in domestic contexts but also in international and transnational legal processes. Slightly revising the jargon used by Perez,[3] I employ the term GRSIs to refer to institutions embedding scientific expertise into both international and transnational decision-making processes. Through GRSIs, regulatory science is institutionalized at the global level.[4]

Three major features can be ascribed to GRSIs. Firstly, the authority exercised by these institutions is felt globally; secondly, the authority 'is often non-hierarchical, dynamic, difficult to locate and hard to grasp', a type of authority labelled as liquid by Krisch;[5] and thirdly, GRSIs exercise contextually ***epistemic*** and ***legal*** authority. GRSIs can be embedded in private and in public bodies. Example of the former is the ISO, which establishes a wide range of standards

3 Oren Perez, 'The Hybrid Legal-Scientific Dynamic of Transnational Scientific Institutions' (2015) 26 (2) European Journal of International Law 391.

4 Sheila Jasanoff, 'What is the Regulatory Science? Concept and History in United States and in Japan: Interview with Professor Sheila Jasanoff – translated by C Kurihara and Saio T' (2011) 39(1) Clinical Evaluation 80; Sheila Jasanoff, *The Fifth Branch: Science Advisers as Policymakers* (Harvard University Press 1990).

5 Nico Krisch, 'The Structure of Postnational Authority' (2015), available at SSRN: <http://ssrn.com/abstract=2564579.> accessed 5 July 2020.

regulating the production and use of disparate things, from robots to nanotech. Examples of the GRSIs embedded in public bodies are the committees of the Codex, the international standard setting body in the field of food safety.[6] Even if the scientific opinions of GRSIs most often go through a process of political ratification (e.g. at Codex standards are commonly adopted by consensus by Member States), GRSIs remain key actors in the standard setting process. They are, in short, an instance of 'new global rulers'.[7]

2.1 *GRSIs and Regulatory Authority*

GRSIs exercise regulatory authority in at least two ways: (a) creating non-binding standards that are nevertheless widely followed and (b) de facto influencing the production of standards by, for example, lending cognitive legitimacy to certain policies/standards. Few examples are used to illustrate how regulatory authority is exercised *in concreto*.

(A) Authority through non-binding standards

An example of the first type of authority is provided by the standards established by the ICNIRP. The ICNIRP is arguably the most important transnational regulatory scientific institution for setting health and safety standards of electromagnetic fields.[8] ICNIRP is a private non-profit organization, registered in Germany. It was officially established in 1992 by a decision of the International Radiation Protection Association (IRPA), but its roots date back to 1974 when the IRPA had already decided to engage in studying the risks related to non-ionizing radiation and established a working group to this end.[9] The main objective of the ICNIRP set up in the 1992 Charter is to advance 'Non-Ionizing Radiation Protection for the benefit of the people and of the environment and in particular to provide guidance and recommendations on protection from NIR exposure'.[10]

ICNIRP is composed only by scientists and organized in a main Commission and several scientific expert groups, with no affiliation to international organizations or national regulators. Its founding Charter provides that the ICNIRP

6 Marielle D Masson-Matthee, 'The Codex Alimentarius Commission and Its Standards' (2007) Food and Agriculture Organization (FAO).

7 Tim Büthe and Walter Mattli, *The New Global Rulers: The Privatization of Regulation in the World Economy* (Princeton University Press 2011).

8 Perez (n 3) 2.

9 Pascual, 'Not Entirely Reliable: Private Scientific Organizations and Risk Regulation – The Case of Electromagnetic Fields' (2013) 4(1) European Journal of Risk Regulation 29. For a more detailed history of the ICNIRP, see the official webpage <http://www.icnirp.de/what.htm>.

10 ICNIRP, *Charter adopted by the General Assembly of the International Radiation Protection Association*, 20 May 1992; the Charter can be downloaded at <https://www.icnirp.org/en/activities/collaboration/details/irpa.html>.

shall maintain a 'close liaison' with IRPA, by submitting to it its recommendations for comments. IRPA's Executive Council is also involved in the selection procedure for the members of the ICNIRP Commission. Apart from this, ICNIRP remains totally independent from IRPA.

In spite of the lack of any legal normativity, ICNIRP's standards have been widely taken up by regulators across the globe. In 1996, the WHO launched the International Project on Electric and Magnetic Fields (EMF Project) to assess the health and environmental effects of exposure to electric and magnetic fields and its partners include the ICNIRP, as well as the IARC, and the International Telecommunications Union (ITU, the United Nations agency for information and communication technology issues) and the International Labour Organization (ILO). Instead of issuing specific standards for EMF, the WHO has endorsed the ICNIRP standards.[11]

(B) De facto influencing the production of standards

The scientific bodies embedded in the Codex provide a powerful example of GRSIs indirectly influencing the production of standards. Codex is made up of several political committees, composed by representatives of the Members and covering different issue areas (ranging from commodity committees, such as the Codex Committee on Milk and Milk Products, to general subject committees, such as the Codex Committee on Food Additives and Contaminants). Codex' decision-making process greatly relies on the scientific meta-analysis conducted by its expert advisory bodies, such as the Joint WHO/FAO Expert Committee on Food Additives (JECFA) (which in fact preceded Codex, having been established in 1955), the Joint FAO/WHO Expert Meetings on Microbiological Risk Assessment (JEMRA) and the Joint WHO/FAO Expert Meeting on Pesticide Residues (JMPR). It is interesting to note that the birth of some of the scientific bodies operating within the Codex framework preceded the establishment of the Committee where the standards are negotiated. For example, the JMPR was established before the Codex Committee on Pesticide Residues (CCPR), which means that its terms of references are broader than those of the CCPR.[12]

Codex scientific bodies have no power to adopt standards. Standards are proposed by a non-scientific Committee or a Member and submitted for adoption to the Codex Commission, where all the Members are represented. In step 2 of an eight-step procedure, scientific bodies are called to give a non-binding recommendation on a draft text (e.g. JECFA could recommend the adoption

11 WHO, 'Framework for developing health-based EMF standards' (2006) <http://www.who.int/peh-emf/standards/EMF_standards_framework%5B1%5D.pdf?ua=1> accessed 5 July 2020.

12 Liora Salter, William Leiss and Edwin Levy, *Mandated Science, Science and Scientists in the Making of Standards* (Kluwer 1988).

of Acceptable Daily Intakes (ADI) and/or Maximum Residue Levels). Yet, experts' recommendations are typically endorsed in the final standards. It has also been noted that in relation to certain substances, such as flavouring, the opinions of the scientific body (in this case JECFA) directly translate into standards.[13]

This means that, in the end, global standards are greatly influenced by a limited number of scientists, even if only indirectly. The centrality of few scientists in the production of global food safety standards is well-captured by the words of one of them:

> Huge buildings, isn't it? FAO and WHO are huge buildings, but if you go somewhere inside the FAO building you see [nom X anonymisé] and [nom Y anonymisé] and their secretary. That's it. That's it. If you go to Geneva you see [noms Z, V et W anonymisés]. That's it. This is nothing. Two great big names, WHO, FAO, but food safety is five people. If they're all in the same car and it's in a traffic accident, food safety in the world is finished (Expert JEMRA).[14]

Other interesting cases include the UN Intergovernmental Panel on Climate Change (IPCC), as a good illustration of how a GRSI may play a pivotal role in the negotiations of an international agreement by lending cognitive legitimacy to certain policies and rules;[15] the Technical Panels and Expert Working Groups within the FAO International Plant Protection Convention; the Specialists Commissions (e.g. Scientific Commission for Animal Diseases) and Reference Centres of the World Organization for Animal Health (OIE); and so on and so forth. These examples are illustrative of how scientific advisory bodies are part and parcel of international and transnational decision-making. The proliferation of GRSIs can be partly explained by the consolidation of science-based regulation as a regulatory paradigm in contemporary systems of global governance.[16]

13 See Antoine Debure, 'Crédibiliser pour expertiser: Le Codex Alimentarius et les comités d'experts FAO-OMS dans la production réglementaire internationale de sécurité sanitaire des aliments' (DPhil thesis, EHESS 2012) <http://www6.jouy.inra.fr/metarisk/Productions/Defended-Ph.D.-Thesis/Ph.D.-Thesis-Antoine-Debure>, where he quotes a delegate explaining the status of JECFA opinion on flavours: 'It's interesting the way Codex is handling flavours compared to food additives. Codex is taking the approach in terms of management perspective: simply to refer to the JECFA's evaluation. JECFA has evaluated it and, therefore, it's acceptable for Codex. And Codex is not maintaining its own list of flavours. Codex has defined the different definition. But at the substance level, if JECFA has said that there is no safety concern with the use of this level of flavour it's ok, it has standing within Codex' (CCFA, Délégation des USA, CAC-05) at 163.

14 This quote is taken from an interview conducted by Antoine Debure, ibid, 157.

15 Timothy Meyer, 'Epistemic Institutions and Epistemic Cooperation in International Environmental Governance' (2013) 2(1) Transnational Environmental Law 15.

16 Jacqueline Peel, *Science and Risk Regulation in International Law* (CUP 2010).

2.2 *Accountability gaps*

As reliance on scientific advisory bodies became widespread, so has scepticism. Science's authority and objectivity are put into question partly because of suspicions of conflicts of interest and partly because of conflicting opinions among scientific advisory bodies of various regions and sectors.

An illustrative example of the possible conflict of interests playing out in GRSIs is the high-profile case about the pressures exercised on science by the tobacco industry, painstakingly documented in a 2000 Report commissioned by the WHO.[17] This example offers enough evidence of the seriousness of the risk of capture for global regulatory science. The 2000 Report addresses how one WHO scientific advisory body may have been subjected to the influence of the tobacco industry when deciding about a pesticide used for tobacco products. The Report indicates that one scientist, Gaston Vettorazzi, was heavily funded by the tobacco industry to provide a favourable assessment of ethylene bisdithiocarbamate, a pesticide used on tobacco and other crops for fungi and moulds. Vettorazzi had served both on the scientific body on pesticide residues (JMPR) and on the scientific panel for food additive (JEFCA). While at the time of the pesticide assessment he had already retired from the WHO, he was allowed to participate in the JMPR meetings. At that time, he was hired by the Cooperation Centre for Scientific Research Relative to Tobacco (CORESTA), an institution financed by the tobacco industry. However, while sitting on the JMPR committee, he did not disclose his ties with the industry.[18] In the end, the pesticide was judged safe by the JMPR and the influence of Vettorazzi on this process remains unclear (note that the US Environmental Protection Agency found the pesticide to be carcinogenic). In the words of the authors of the WHO report, 'the case study demonstrates the ability of tobacco companies to fund a consultant within a UN standard-setting activity, all the while concealing the manufacturers' role'.[19]

Another case highlighting possible conflicts of interest concerns the allegations that improper influence was exerted by the pharmaceutical industry on the WHO Expert Committee dealing with the 2009 A(H1N1) avian influenza.[20] When in 2009 an outbreak of avian influenza erupted, the WHO

17 WHO, 'Report of the Committee of Experts on Tobacco Industry Documents' (2000) <http://www.who.int/tobacco/en/who_inquiry.pdf> accessed 5 July 2020.

18 Ibid 156 et seq.

19 Ibid at 156.

20 Emily A Bruemmer and Allyn L Taylor, 'Institutional Transparency in Global Health Law-Making: The World Health Organization and the Implementation of the International Health Regulations' in Andrea Bianchi and Anne Peters (eds), *Transparency in International Law* (CUP 2013) 269; Deborah Cohen and Philip Carter, 'WHO and the Pandemic Flu "Conspiracies"' (2010) 340 British Medical Journal 1274; Council of Europe, Resolution 1749, 24 June 2010; and Recommendation 1929, 24 June 2010; Fiona Godlee, 'Conflict of Interests and Pandemic Flu' (2010) 340 British Medical Journal 1256.

established an Emergency Committee in order to evaluate the risks. Following the Committee's advice, Margaret Chan, then WHO Director-General, declared the pandemic. The WHO has been criticized for having chosen scientists with ties to the pharmaceutical industry, particularly to the firms that later greatly benefited from selling the vaccines.[21] The policy of supporting widespread vaccinations and stockpiling of drugs was in fact adopted following the advice of the WHO Emergency Committee to declare the flu a pandemic.

Even one of the most sophisticated scientific advisory bodies in the field of international environmental law, the IPCC, has not escaped its own credibility crisis. In 2009 the IPCC, which is the UN scientific advisory body established in 1988 to advise on issues related to global warming, was charged with accusations of fraud in what has been labelled by the popular media the 'climategate'.[22] In spite of the conclusions of eight enquiry committees that no fraud occurred, the IPPC has reformed its procedural guidelines to enhance the transparency of the drafting of Reports.[23]

At the time of writing, another case is unfolding. The re-evaluation of glyphosate – the most widely used active substance for pesticides worldwide – has raised acrimonious controversies on the credibility of regulatory science. In 2015, the IARC has classified glyphosate as potentially carcinogenic. By contrast, agencies around the world concluded that the substance is safe. The diversity of conclusions among domestic, transnational and international regulatory scientific institutions has led to a crisis of the science-based paradigm. In Europe, for example, the EFSA judged the substance safe. Yet, the European Parliament and several Member States did not want to re-authorize the substance for an extended period and have been critical of the risk assessment conducted by the EU authorities.[24] A political compromise has been reached where the substance has been re-approved for only 5 years, when legally the approval should be for 15 years. Once again possible conflicts of interests have fraught this process. Also known as the 'Monsanto papers', several investigations show that Monsanto may

21 Council of Europe (n 20); Godlee (n 20) 6.

22 Christopher Booker, 'Climate Change: This Is the Worst Scientific Scandal of Our Generation', *The Telegraph* (London, 28 November 2009) <http://www.telegraph.co.uk/comment/columnists/christopherbooker/6679082/Climate-change-this-is-the-worst-scientific-scandal-of-our-generation.html> accessed 5 July 2020; James Delingpole, 'Climategate: The Final Nail in the Coffin of "Anthropogenic Global Warming"?' *The Telegraph* (London, 20 November 2009) <http://climaterealists.com/index.php?id=4406> accessed 5 July 2020.

23 Bernd Siebenhüner, 'Changing Demands at the Science-Policy Interface: Organizational Learning in the IPCC' in Monika Ambrus and others (eds), *The Role of 'Experts' in International Decision-Making: Advisors, Decision-Makers or Irrelevant?* (CUP 2014).

24 EP Resolution of 24 October 2017 on the draft commission implementing regulation renewing the approval of the active substance glyphosate in accordance with Regulation (EC) No 1107/2009 of the European Parliament and the Council concerning the placing of plant protection products on the market, and amending the Annex to Implementing Regulation (EU) No 540/2011.

have shaped the science on the safety of the pesticide and could have influenced some of the scientists involved in regulatory scientific committees.[25] The glyphosate case is also interesting because it has contributed to re-politicize the field of transnational risk assessment by bringing certain political choices, typically back-staged in science-based regulatory processes, to the front.[26]

These cases, which in some instances led to reforms of procedures for expert bodies, suggest that GRSIs may be captured, absent accountability mechanisms. Some general features of regulatory science may underlie the potential for GRSIs capture. One of the key problems of scientific studies conducted for regulatory purposes is their level of malleability. Scientific endeavours to appraise the safety of chemicals, food, pharmaceuticals and environment are particularly prone to this risk. Science can be shaped by 'multiple layers of micro-biases', which are 'difficult to identify, even with vigorous scrutiny by sophisticated peers'.[27] The evidence that science is being strategically bent to pursue private interests is overwhelming.[28] For example, one study published in *Nature* in 2005 has found that approximately one-third of scientists, on a 3000+ sample, had either 'changed the design, methodology or results of a study in response to pressure from a funding source' or used flawed data and, in a minority of cases, committed fraud.[29] Multiple reviews have also shown positive correlation between research outcomes and the interests of the funder, causing what has been termed the 'funding effect'.[30] The fact that in several science-based regulatory processes, the

25 Stéphane Foucart, 'Ce que les "Monsanto Papers" Révèlent du Roundup', *Le Monde* (Paris, 18 March 2017) <http://www.lemonde.fr/planete/article/2017/03/18/ce-que-les-monsanto-papers-revelent-du-roundup_5096602_3244.html> accessed 5 July 2020; see also, Stéphane Foucart, '"Monsanto Papers": Des Eurodéputés Veulent la Révision de l'Expertise du Glyphosate', *Le Monde* (Paris, 24 March 2017) <http://www.lemonde.fr/planete/article/2017/03/24/monsanto-papers-des-eurodeputes-veulent-la-revision-de-l-expertise-du-glyphosate_5100479_3244.html> accessed 5 July 2020; conflict of interests were also allegedly found in the composition of one WHO/FAO Panel, see Arthur Neslen, 'UN/WHO Panel in Conflict of Interest Row Over Glyphosate Cancer Risk' *The Guardian* (London, 17 May 2016) <https://www.theguardian.com/environment/2016/may/17/unwho-panel-in-conflict-of-interest-row-over-glyphosates-cancer-risk> accessed 5 July 2020.

26 See Marta Morvillo, 'From Contestation to Accountability in EU Pesticides Regulation? The Case of Glyphosate' (chapter 9 in this Volume); see also, Alessandra Arcuri, 'Glyphosate' in Jessie Homan and Daniel Joyce (eds), *International Law's Objects* (OUP 2018); Alessandra Arcuri and Yogi Hendlin, 'The Chemical Anthropocene: Glyphosate as a Case Study of Pesticide Exposures' (2019) 30(2) King's Law Journal 234–253, available at: https://www.tandfonline.com/doi/full/10.1080/09615768.2019.1645436

27 Thomas O McGarity and Wendy E Wagner, *Bending Science: How Special Interests Corrupt Public Health Research* (Harvard University Press 2008) 65.

28 McGarity and Wagner, *ibid*, at 7; Wendy E Wagner and Rena Steinzor (eds), *Rescuing Science from Politics: Regulation and the Distortion of Scientific Research* (CUP 2006).

29 Meredith Wadman, 'One in Three Scientists Confesses to Having Sinned' (2005) 435 Nature 718.

30 Sheldon Krimsky, 'Do Financial Conflicts of Interest Bias Research? An Inquiry into the "Funding Effect" Hypothesis' (2013) 38(4) Science, Technology & Human Values 566.

information is mainly supplied by the industry may also lead to titling the outcome of decisions towards industry interests, a phenomenon termed as 'information capture'.[31] Finally, uncertainty, which invariably characterizes areas subject to regulatory science, has often been used strategically to downplay the negative effects of certain products/technologies.[32]

Against this wealth of evidence, the need to design accountability mechanisms capable of mitigating the problems of capture becomes apparent. One of the difficult challenges in articulating frameworks for accountability of global regulatory science stems from the fact that standards for credibility in science and in law differ. GRSIs can be safely considered as 'boundary bodies' mediating between the realms of science and politics.[33] Given the interstitial space where these bodies operate, it is not easy to subject these actors to familiar forms of legal accountability. Before proceeding to articulate the accountability questions specific to GRSIs, the next section offers a concise overview of how the discourse on accountability has gained traction within the international legal scholarship and how some insights can be helpful for a conceptualization of accountability for regulatory experts.

3 Conceptualizing accountability in global governance

One challenge for studying accountability is to circumscribe its meaning, which has been elusive and ever-changing.[34] Amidst different conceptualizations of accountability, most adhere to a *relational* definition, by which actors have to account for their behaviour before a forum, and may be subject to sanctions for misconduct.[35] Normatively, accountability is relevant for (1) controlling public powers (democratic perspective), (2) limiting abuse of power (constitutional perspective) and (3) developing learning (learning perspective).[36]

31 Ayelet Berman, 'Industry, Regulatory Capture and Transnational Standard Setting' (2017) 111 AJIL Unbound 112.

32 David Michaels (ed), *Doubt Is Their Product* (OUP 2008).

33 Sheila Jasanoff, 'Contested Boundaries in Policy-Relevant Science' (1987) 17(2) Social Studies of Science 195; David H Guston, 'Stabilizing the Boundary Between Politics and Science: The Role of the Office of Technology Transfer as a Boundary Organization' (1999) 29 Social Studies of Science 87; David H Guston, 'Boundary Organizations in Environmental Policy and Science: An Introduction' (2000) 26(4) Science Technology and Human Values 299.

34 Mark Bovens, Thomas Schillemans and Robert E Goodin, 'Public Accountability' in Mark Bovens, Thomas Schillemans and Robert E Goodin (eds), *The Oxford Handbook of Public Accountability* (OUP 2014) 1; Richard Mulgan, '"Accountability": An Ever-Expanding Concept?' (2000) 78(3) Public Administration 555.

35 Mark Bovens, 'Analysing and Assessing Public Accountability. A Conceptual Framework' (2007) 13(4) European Law Journal 447; Mark Bovens, 'Two Concepts of Accountability: Accountability as a Virtue and as a Mechanism' (2010) 33(5) West European Politics 946; Ruth W Grant and Robert O Keohane, 'Accountability and Abuses of Power in World Politics' (2005) 99(1) American Political Science Review 29.

36 Mark Bovens, 'Analysing and Assessing Public Accountability' (n 35) 463.

Questions of accountability in the international and transnational legal order are central to the field of Global Administrative Law (GAL), which refers to 'the mechanisms, principles, practices, and supporting social understandings that promote or otherwise affect the accountability of global administrative bodies'.[37] The centrality that accountability plays in the GAL project begets ambiguity. On the one hand, accountability seems to be an end in itself; on the other hand, it is referred to as a means for attaining the goal of achieving global administrative law.[38] GAL scholarship is contiguous to the wide variety of scholarship that has focused on accountability questions in the international and transnational arena, ranging from the renewed interests of public international lawyers[39] to the Informal International Law Project (IN-LAW)[40] and the International Public Authority Project (IPA).[41] These three clusters of international legal scholarship intersect with the work of political scientists and international relations scholars.[42]

The great merit of this body of scholarship is to have studied contextually the emergence of *new forms of authority* in the global legal space[43] and the related *accountability regimes* (or lack thereof). This scholarship shed light on the role of non-traditional actors, such as hybrid public-private networks,[44] and addressed how frameworks for thinking about accountability, typically conceptualized at the domestic level,[45] can be re-conceptualized in a meaningful way

37 See Sabino Cassese and others (eds), *Global Administrative Law: Cases, Material, Issues* (IRPA – IILJ 2nd ed., 2008); Benedict Kingsbury and others, 'The Emergence of Global Administrative Law' (2005) 68 Law and Contemporary Problems 15–62.

38 Philipp Dann and Marie von Engelhardt, 'Legal Approaches to Global Governance and Accountability' in Armin Von Bogdandy and others (eds), *The Exercise of Public Authority by International Institutions: Advancing International Institutional Law* (Springer 2010), 107, at 117.

39 Deirdre Curtin, 'Holding (Quasi-) Autonomous EU Administrative Actors to Public Account' (2007) 13(4) European Law Journal 523; André Nollkaemper and Deirdre Curtin, 'Conceptualizing Accountability in International and European Law' (2007) 36 Netherlands Yearbook of International Law 3.

40 Joost Pauwelyn, Ramses Wessel and Jan Wouters (eds), *Informal International Lawmaking* (OUP 2012).

41 Armin Von Bogdandy and others (eds), *The Exercise of Public Authority by International Institutions: Advancing International Institutional Law* (Springer 2010).

42 Mark Bovens, 'Analysing and Assessing Public Accountability. A Conceptual Framework' and 'Two Concepts of Accountability: Accountability as a Virtue and as a Mechanism' (n 35) 8; Allen Buchanan and Robert O Keohane, 'The Legitimacy of Global Governance Institutions' (2006) 20(4) Ethics & International Affairs 405; Grant and Keahone (n 35) 8; Ngaire Woods and Amrita Narlikar, 'Governance and the limits of accountability: the WTO, the IMF and the World Bank' (2001) 53(170) International Social Science Journal 569.

43 Pawuelyn et al (n 40) 8; Von Bogdandy et al (n 2) 3–32.

44 Anne-Marie Slaughter, *A New World Order* (Princeton University Press 2004).

45 Colin Scott, 'Accountability in the Regulatory State' (2000) 27(1) Journal of Law and Society 38; Mulgan (n 34).

for international and transnational institutions.[46] The seminal work by Grant and Kehoane[47] has been useful to identify seven types of different accountability mechanisms constraining abuse of powers in global world politics, including hierarchical, financial, legal and peer accountability. Next to mechanisms implemented on a global level, domestic institutions have been considered as capable, albeit in a limited way, to hold international and transnational bodies accountable.[48] Accountability has been studied in a variety of different domains of global governance, ranging from global regulation of banking to pharmaceuticals (see the case studies in the referenced projects).[49]

Traditional conceptualizations of accountability have circumscribed accountability to ex post or retrospective mechanisms.[50] Yet, broader conceptualizations of accountability, whereby both prospective and retrospective mechanisms fall within its scope, have become widespread in international (and European) legal scholarship. An inclusive conceptualization of accountability is meaningful because it allows to study complementarities and synergies between *ex ante* and *ex post* mechanisms.[51] This broader framing is also reflected in the conceptualization of accountability endorsed by the International Law Association, where transparency, participation, reason-giving and review mechanisms all have been considered important elements for accountability.[52]

Many studies of accountability rely on principal-agent theory. However, in the EU evolving legal system and, more generally in multi-level and global governance, the principal-agent framing has been considered analytically inadequate.[53] In these contexts, the chains of delegation are fragmented, possibly with a multitude of principals. Likewise, when authority is 'liquid' – that is not grounded in formal and

46 Eyal Benvenisti and George W Downs, 'National Courts Review of Transnational Private Regulation' (2011) Tel Aviv University Law Faculty Papers, Working Paper 125, <http://law.bepress.com/taulwps/art125> accessed 5 July 2020; Ayelet Berman, 'The Role of Domestic Administrative Law in the Accountability of Informal International Lawmaking: The Case of the ICH' in Joost Pauwelyn, Ramses Wessel and Jan Wouters (eds), *Informal International Lawmaking* (OUP 2012) 468.

47 Grant and Keohane (n 35) 8.

48 Benvenisti and Downs (n 46) 9; Berman (n 31) 9.

49 Von Bogdandy et al (n 2); see Cassese et al (n 37); Pauwelyn et al (n 40) 8.

50 Bovens, 'Analysing and Assessing Public Accountability. A Conceptual Framework' (n35); Grant and Keohane (n 35).

51 Berman (n 46) 9; Nollkaemper and Curtin (n 39) 8.

52 International Law Association (ILA), 'Report of the International Law Association Berlin Conference on the Accountability of International Organizations', reprinted in (2004) 1(1) International Organizations Law Review 221.

53 Curtin (n 39) 8; Yannis Papadopoulos, 'Problems of Democratic Accountability in Network and Multilevel Governance' (2007) 13 European Law Journal 469; Yannis Papadopoulos, 'Accountability and Multi-Level Governance' in Mark Bovens, Robert E Goodin and Thomas Schillemans (eds), *The Oxford Handbook of Public Accountability* (OUP 2014) 1. For a view proposing 'hybrid (fluid) multilevel accountability' as a solution to remedy the accountability problems of agencies and technocratic bodies whose design and operation feature a pooling of EU and national resources and powers, see Florin Coman-Kund, 'Holding Europol Accountable: The Promise and Challenges of (Hybrid) Multilevel Accountability' (Chapter 12 in this volume).

binding sources – mere delegatory frames for articulating accountability relations are unconvincing.[54] The accountability problems related to fragmented chains of delegation are exacerbated in the global regulatory arena, because of the systematic lack of accountability mechanisms in global governance.[55] Take, for instance, judicial (e.g. administrative courts) and quasi-judicial (e.g. ombudsman) review of administrative laws and procedures. These types of review mechanisms, generally entrenched in domestic legal systems, are not common at the international level. Accountability gaps are thus generated by the mismatch between the global harmonization of administrative laws and the fragmentation of accountability regimes.[56] Moreover, it has been convincingly argued that the risk of 'regulatory capture' – that is the phenomenon by which regulators are captured by vested interests[57] – is higher in the realm of global governance than at the domestic level.[58]

The question of accountability in global governance is also intertwined with its much-lamented democratic deficits. Problems of democratic representation are inherent to international and transnational bodies. Accountability in the global regulatory space can, therefore, be seen as a complementary forum for realizing democracy. Here, it can be argued that by creating space for relations between power wielders and those affected by their decisions, accountability is a site for re-distributing power. Hence, part and parcel of democracy (as power to the demos).

Last but not least, accountability comes with its own set of problems. Besides the obvious costs that any accountability process may have, over-accountability could contribute to erode trust in social institutions. In the words of one scholar: 'Finally, any society in which accountability relationships are both pervasive and always acted upon would not be a very good society from the standpoint of commitments, trust, freedom, and solidarity. Any system of accountability will have inflection points at which accountability degenerates into mutual suspicion and intrusive surveillance, undermining the very agent capacities that would be held to account. Trust—which is not only efficient but essential to most working social relationships—can be crowded out by accountability. *Thus we should think of good accountability systems as backstopping rather replacing trust, so that accountability costs are assumed only when trust fails*'.[59] Good accountability systems will make actors internalize the potential check and balances and review mechanisms so that in practice, there will be less need to deploy them.

54 Krisch (n 5) 2.
55 Von Bogdandy et al (n 2) 1.
56 Daphne Barak-Erez and Oren Perez, 'Whose Administrative Law Is It Anyway? How Global Norms Reshape the Administrative State' (2013) 46(3) Cornell International Law Journal 455.
57 George J Stigler, 'The Theory of Economic Regulation' (1971) 2(1) The Bell Journal of Economics and Management Science 3.
58 Eyal Benvenisti, 'Exit and Voice in the Age of Globalization' (1999) 98(1) Michigan Law Review 167.Eyal Benvenisti, 'Toward a Typology of Informal International Lawmaking: Mechanisms and their Distinct Accountability Gaps' in Joost Pauwelyn, Ramses Wessel and Jan Wouters (eds), *Informal International Lawmaking* (OUP 2012) 297.
59 Mark E Warren, 'Accountability and Democracy' in Mark Bovens, Robert E Goodin and Thomas Schillemans (eds), *The Oxford Handbook of Public Accountability* (OUP 2014) 7.

In a reflection on GAL, Dyzenhaus[60] considers '*publicity*' as the red thread of public administration, an emphasis further echoed in the IPA project,[61] as well as in the work by one of the originators of GAL.[62] In this context, three dimensions of publicity have been articulated: 'the public delegation of authority, the justification in public of the exercise of authority, and the fact that the decision thus justified has to represent a reasonable interpretation of the public interest', corresponding to 'constitutive', 'procedural' and 'substantive' administrative law.[63] These elements are intimately woven and normatively bound to the overarching public interest ideal.

Building on this approach, the conceptualization of accountability taken in this chapter defies the subordination of substance to procedure. Accountability is here taken to be part and parcel of a public law approach as well as of a teleological rule of law paradigm, where limiting abuse of power features as its central tenet.[64] In the global space, where interests and (legal) cultures differ, the triangulation between the constitutive, procedural and substantive elements of GAL becomes even more salient as it enables contestation and mutual controls in a heterarchical system of constitutive powers. Articulating accountability along the constitutive/substantive/procedural triad befits with the tradition of constitutional pluralists.[65] Against this background, accountability necessarily encompasses both prospective and retrospective mechanisms. Accountability is here conceived as a constellation of mechanisms aimed not only at realizing the public interest but also as means for the perpetual search of what the public interest is in the global regulatory space.

60 David Dyzenhaus, 'Accountability and the Concept of (Global) Administrative Law' (2008) IILJ Working Paper 2008/7, Global Administrative Law Series.

61 Von Bogdandy et al (n 2).

62 Benedict Kingsbury, 'The Concept of "Law" in Global Administrative Law' (2009) 20 European Journal of International Law 23.

63 Dyzenhaus (n 60) 21.

64 Martin Krygier, 'The Rule of Law: Legality, Teleology, Sociology', in Gianluigi Palombella and Neil Walker (eds), *Re-Locating the Rule of Law* (Hart Publishers 2008) <https://ssrn.com/abstract=1218982> accessed 5 July 2020. See also Sanne Taekema, 'Expert Accountability and the Rule of Law: Intertwinement of Normative and Functional Standards?' (Chapter 2 in this volume).

65 Neil Walker, 'The Idea of Constitutional Pluralism' (2002) 65 MLR 317; Mattias Kumm, 'The Cosmopolitan Turn in Constitutionalism: On the Relationship between Constitutionalism in and beyond the State' in Jeffrey L Dunoff and Joel P Trachtman (eds), *Ruling the World? Constitutionalism, International Law and Global Governance* (CUP 2009); Miguel P Maduro, 'Courts and Pluralism: Essay on a Theory of Judicial Adjudication in the Context of Legal and Constitutional Pluralism', in Jeffrey L Dunoff and Joel P Trachtman (eds), *Ruling the World? Constitutionalism, International Law and Global Governance* (CUP 2009); Alec S Sweet, 'A Cosmopolitan Legal Order: Constitutional Pluralism and Rights Adjudication in Europe' (2012) 1 J Global Constitutionalism 53; Nico Krisch, *Beyond Constitutionalism: The Pluralist Structure of Postnational Law* (OUP 2010). Clustering this scholarship under the rubric of constitutional pluralism resonates with the analysis of Shaffer 2012, who writes in terms of a framework of common constitutional principles, functions, and other attributes, see Gregory Shaffer, 'A Transnational Take on Krisch's Pluralist Structure of Postnational Law' (2012) 23 (2) European Journal of International Law, 565, see particularly at p. 573.

4 Operationalizing accountability for Global Regulatory Scientific Institutions

> Yet the tendency of government agencies to defer to expert opinion, and the parallel habit of experts to deny that they are making the decisions, threaten to leave democracies in a perpetual state of *organized irresponsibility*, in which no one can be assigned full and final accountability for informed action.[66]
>
> Sheila Jasanoff

The main quest for accountability of (global) regulatory science comes from the observation of its co-constitutive powers in standard setting and other policy-making endeavours. That the man of knowledge is one of power is not a new idea. In his 1513 book – *The Prince* – Niccolò Machiavelli already implied that the 'holder of the God's-eye view of the entire state is neither the King, who looks down at the people from the top of the hierarchy, nor the people, who see the King at the top of from their lower state. It is a person like himself, a "man of knowledge"'.[67] At the same time, the delegation of powers to (regulatory) scientists arguably originates in the calls for more rational and accountable regulatory governance. For example, since at least the seventies, risk assessment has emerged as a benchmark for testing the rationality of risk regulation.[68] Techniques of technocratic regulatory governance, such as cost-benefit analysis in the United States[69] and regulatory impact analysis in Europe,[70] have emerged as checks and balances on regulators. The turn to technocratic governance as a

66 Sheila Jasanoff, 'Quality Control and Peer Review in Advisory Science' in Justus Lentsch and Peter Weingart, *The Politics of Scientific Advice: Institutional Design for Quality Assurance* (CUP 2011) 26.

67 Yaron Ezrahi, *Encyclopedia of the Social & Behavioral Sciences*, originally edited by Neil Smelser and Paul Baltes, 26 Vols (Elsevier 2015), 13657.

68 Alessandra Arcuri, 'Risk Regulation' in Regulation and Economics' in Alessio M Pacces and Roger J. Van den Bergh (eds), *Encyclopedia of Law and Economics* (Edward Elgar 2012) 303. See also Brian D Israel, 'An Environmental Justice Critique of Risk Assessment' (1995) (3) New York University Environmental Law Journal 469.

69 Richard H Pildes and Cass R Sunstein, 'Reinventing the Regulatory State' (1995) 62 (1) The University of Chicago Law Review 1; John F Morrall, 'An Assessment of the Us Regulatory Impact Analysis Program' in Rex Deighton-Smith and Scott H Jacobs (eds), *Regulatory Impact Analysis: Best Practices in OECD Countries* (OECD 1997); Arrow and others, 'Is there a role for Cost-Benefit Analysis in Environmental, Health and Safety Regulation?' (2006) (272) Science 221; Robert W Hahn and Cass R Sunstein, 'A New Executive Order for Improving Federal Regulation? Deeper and Wider Cost-Benefit Analysis' (2002) 150 (5) University of Pennsylvania Law Review 1489.

70 Andrea Renda and others, 'Assessing the Costs and Benefits of Regulation', Study for the European Commission delivered on 10 December 2013 <http://ec.europa.eu/smart-regulation/impact/commission_guidelines/docs/131210_cba_study_sg_final.pdf> accessed 5 July 2020; Claudio M Radaelli and Fabrizio De Francesco, 'Regulatory Impact Assessment' in Martin Cave, Robert Baldwin and Martin Lodge (eds), *The Oxford Handbook of Regulation* (OUP 2010).

means to control abuse of power is visible also in the international trade regime. Since the establishment of the World Trade Organization (WTO), the illegality of trade measures is increasingly ascertained on the basis of techno-scientific knowledge.[71] Science can then be seen as a means to hold domestic regulators accountable in relation to possible protectionist behaviour (e.g. science can help scrutinizing whether a health measure is sound or protectionist).

The circularity discernible in the quest for accountability for regulatory science – which in itself can be a mechanism of accountability – echoes the blurred boundaries between the conceptual categories of authority and accountability. From this vantage point, accountability can be seen as a way to redistribute authority among different actors (e.g. policymakers and scientists). This nexus hints also at the possible dangers when shifting authority from politics to the scientific realm. Science can easily become a pretext to elude political responsibility,[72] and possibly to curb democracy. In those cases, accountability of regulatory science can function to minimize such illiberal tendencies.

As mentioned earlier, one of the major challenges for studying GRSIs is that the legal and scientific worlds are governed by different (and at times conflicting) logics.[73] Science and Technology Studies (STS) scholars, as well as a number of socio-legal scholars, have long engaged with the hybridity of regulatory science.[74] In considering the thorny issue of the quality of scientific advice to policy-making, social scientists have enlisted a dual reference system: regulatory science should be *epistemically* and *politically robust*.[75] This double norm

71 Andrew Lang, 'Neoliberalism and the Formal-Technical Turn' in Andrew Lang (ed), *World Trade Law After Neoliberalism: Re-Imagining the Global Economic Order* (OUP 2011) 221.

72 Wendy E Wagner, 'The Science Charade in Toxic Risk Regulation' (1995) (95) Columbia Law Review 1613.

73 Bruno Latour, 'Scientific objects and legal objectivity' in Alain Pottage and Martha Mundy (eds), *Law, Anthropology, and the Constitution of the Social: Making Persons and Things* (CUP 2004) 73.

74 Salter et al (n 12); David Demortain, 'Standardising through Concepts: The Power of Scientific Experts in International Standard-Setting' (2008) 35(6) Science and Public Policy 391; David Demortain, *Scientists and the Regulation of Risk: Standardising Control* (Edward Elgar 2011); David Demortain, 'The Tools of Globalization: Ways of Regulating and the Structure of the International Regime for Pharmaceuticals' (2015) 7 Review of International Political Economy 1; David H Guston, 'Boundary Organizations in Environmental Policy and Science: An Introduction' (2001) 26(4) Science Technology and Human Values 299; Jasanoff (n 33) 7; Sheila Jasanoff, *Designs on Nature: Science and Democracy in Europe and the United States* (Princeton University Press 2005); Jasanoff, *The Fifth Branch: Science Advisers as Policymakers* (n 4) 2; Meyer (n 15); Perez (n 3) 2; David E Winickoff and Douglas M Bushey, 'Science and Power in Global Food Regulation: The Rise of the Codex Alimentarius' (2010) 35 Science, Technology, & Human Values 356; Alessandra Arcuri, 'Global Food Safety Standards: The Evolving Regulatory Epistemology at the Intersection of the SPS Agreement and the Codex Alimentarius Commission' in Panagiotis Delimatsis (ed), *The Law, Economics and Politics of International Standardisation* (CUP 2015) 79; Arcuri (n 26) 6.

75 Justus Lentsch and Peter Weingart, *The Politics of Scientific Advice: Institutional Design for Quality Assurance* (CUP 2011) 7–8.

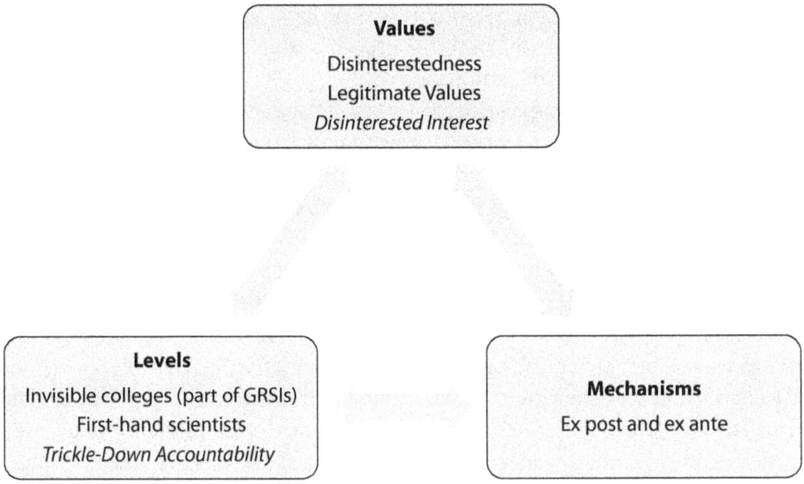

Figure 3.1 The three dimensions of accountability.

could find expression in at least **three dimensions of accountability** for GRSIs (see Figure 3.1). The first enlists the overarching **values** that an accountability framework strives to protect. The second dimension delineates the scope of accountability by identifying the **levels** of regulatory science relevant for the accountability relationship. The third dimension concerns the **mechanisms** that could be employed to operationalize the accountability relation. These three dimensions are all important for the analysis of the accountability relationship, as no single one can do justice to its complexity.

4.1 *Values*

A critical value for achieving epistemically robust science is 'disinterestedness'. Disinterestedness features prominently among the Mertonian canons for credibility for science. '"Disinterestedness" implies that scientists apply their methods of inquiry … without consideration of personal gain, ideology, or fidelity to any cause other than pursuit of truth. Scientists may not be disinterested … They must, however, behave *as if* they were disinterested by allowing the data to determine the fate of their hunch'.[76] This criterion underwrites the idea that credible science should be epistemically robust, as scientists ought to be respectful of the raw data and of the widely shared norms of scientific research. In practical terms, this implies that scientists should not manipulate data to obtain results that could enhance their (or other groups') private gains. The criterion of disinterestedness

76 Sheldon Krimsky, 'Publication Bias, Data Ownership, and the Funding Effect in Science: Threats to Integrity of Biomedical Research' in Wendy E Wagner and Rena Steinzor, *Rescuing Science from Politics: Regulation and the Distortion of Scientific Research* (CUP 2006).

also echoes the function that various forms of legal accountability perform in controlling regulatory capture. In this sense, this overarching criterion poses no conflict between the scientific and legal realm.

If disinterestedness is unquestionably a key principle for the credibility of science, it is also important to acknowledge that science is enmeshed with value judgments and that a certain degree of 'interest' is normal in science. Policy-relevant science is influenced by values and the awareness of its potential social consequences.[77] Scientific work is understood as evolving within social institutions such as regulatory institutions.[78] There are several entry points for ethical values into a scientific process: making a decision about the research design and/or the framing questions; deciding about methodology; deciding what types of errors to minimize, etc. Different assumptions underlying scientific assessment methods, such as epidemiology, animal bioassay and extrapolations models, may lead to different results.[79] Such choices entail both epistemic and value judgments. In the presence of uncertainties, the ethical choices are likely to play a salient role. As put by Heather Douglas '[b]ecause much of the science needed to make policy falls into … developing areas of science rife with contention among scientists, such science is also rife with the need for scientists' judgments'.[80]

The idea that public values are and should be included in regulatory science is grounded in philosophy of science.[81] Recognizing that interest is part of a normal regulatory scientific process stands in no conflict with the value of 'disinterestedness'. The point is simple: disinterestedness strives for an eradication of certain vested interests from the knowledge production process; by contrast, ethical values can be part of a legitimate scientific process. Against this background, '*disinterested interest*' becomes a meaningful oxymoron for regulatory science. The function of a legal framework for accountability of GRSIs is thus two-fold. On the one hand, it should aim at maintaining disinterestedness – that is exclude considerations of personal gains or ideology from the regulatory scientific process. On the other hand, accountability mechanisms rather than denying interestedness should distinguish legitimate from illegitimate interests.

Juggling interest with disinterest, in other words, translates in the challenge of dissecting legitimate values for regulatory science. In the global regulatory

77 Sabine Maasen and Peter Weingart (eds), *Democratization of Expertise? Exploring Novel Forms of Scientific Advice in Political Decision-Making* 24 Vols (Springer 2005).

78 Helga Nowotny, Peter Scott and Michael Gibbons, *Re-thing Science: Knowledge and the Public in an Age of Uncertainty* (Polity 2001); Bruno Latour and Stephen Woolgar, *Laboratory Life: The Construction of Scientific Facts* (Princeton University Press 1986).

79 Alon Rosenthal, George M Gray and John D Graham, 'Legislating Acceptable Cancer Risk from Exposure to Toxic Chemicals' (1992) 19(2) Ecology Law Quarterly 269.

80 Heather Douglas, 'Inserting The Public Into Science' in Sabine Maasen and Peter Weingart (eds), *Democratization of expertise? Exploring Novel Forms of Scientific Advice in Political Decision-Making* 24 Vols (Springer 2005) 155.

81 Heather Douglas, 'Inductive Risk and Values in Science' (2000) 67(4) Philosophy of Science 559; see also Osman Çağlar, 'The Value Free Ideal of Science and Non-epistemic Values in Regulatory Toxicology' (Chapter 10 in this volume).

arena, the challenge may appear daunting because standards are to serve diverse constituencies across the globe. Yet, the challenge may be less daunting when we consider that the system of global governance is grounded, at least to some extent, on constitutional norms. Many international organizations (IOs), within which the work of several GRSIs is nested, aim at protecting global public values. Permissible ethical values can hence be discerned from the constitutive instruments of the regime within which a particular GRSI is operating. Consider, for example, the ethical values that a GRSI operating within the realm of international food safety may apply in the process of risk analysis. In this context, the Codex has adopted a set of principles for risk analysis, recognizing among other issues that '[p]recaution is an inherent element of risk analysis' (Codex 2007, para. 12).[82] This means that the experts conducting the meta-analysis, when in doubt, may make methodological choices that would minimize risks of under-detecting hazards in food (e.g. giving weight to studies showing risks, in spite of confounding factors; privilege the minimization of false negative vis-à-vis false positive).

Next to the identification of shared values as legitimate ethical criteria for shaping regulatory science, criteria that allow for a plurality of views to be expressed in the process are needed. This is because of the different constituencies which are part of the global arena. Plurality has also been recognized as one principle for good advice in regulatory science.[83] Hence, ***pluralism*** could be an important dimension of the institutional set-up of the GRSIs.

Understanding the mutual interplay between the values of disinterest and interest in regulatory science is intimately bound up with one of the classical questions underpinning the accountability discourse, that is 'accountable to whom'. The GRSIs are accountable to both the scientific epistemic community where they come from and the global publics they are serving. It is here contended that the existence of multiple addressees does not pose threats to the integrity of science; rather, it qualifies the nature of the enterprise. In fact, scientists are normally operating within multiple spheres of responsibility, where different values are to be accommodated.[84] In delivering 'serviceable truths',[85] global regulatory scientists should be able to respond to global publics, whose interests are often reflected in the constitutive instruments of the organizations within which they operate. One of the most lamented problems of the relationship between science and law is the hiding of political decisions in technocratic processes. The explicit consideration of legitimate values that scientists can resort to in accountability frameworks may contribute to rebalance the thorny relationship between science and law.

82 Codex Alimentarius Commission, Working Principles for Risk Analysis for Food Safety for Application By Governments (2007), *CAC/GL 62-2007.*

83 Lentsch and Weingart (n 75) 13.

84 Heather Douglas, 'The Moral Terrain of Science' (2014) 79 Erkenntnis 1.

85 Sheila Jasanoff, 'Serviceable Truths: Science for Action in Law and Policy' (2015) 93(7) Texas Law Review 1723.

4.2 *Levels of regulatory expertise*

Within the GRSIs, at least two levels of regulatory science are implicated. On the one hand, there are 'invisible colleges' of experts[86] directly operating within the specialized committee or body; on the other hand, there are first-hand scientific studies produced for a regulatory purpose by scientists not directly involved in the regulatory process. Examples of the former are toxicologists working as experts in the Codex scientific committees, IPCC, ICNIRP etc. Examples of the latter are scientists conducting research for studies that can be submitted for evaluation to the GRSIs (e.g. toxicology studies performed by public or private laboratories to test the carcinogenicity of certain substances). The invisible colleges typically conduct meta-analysis of first-hand research and, in certain circumstances, co-produce the rules for assessing those studies.

The concerns that first-hand regulatory science may not be disinterested are particularly serious, in light of recent studies in the emerging field of economics of science. Mirowski and Sent,[87] among the few economists pioneering this field, have distinguished three phases of the organization and funding of science from the beginning of the twentieth century to today. They distinguish a Protoindustrial Regime, the Cold War regime and Globalized Privatization Regime. Under the first regime (spanning from early twentieth century to the early forties), major corporate players influenced the organization of science by exporting practices and protocols and directly funding academic research. The Cold War regime (from World War II until the eighties) witnessed a process by which scientists gained independence because of substantial funding of research by the government. This process is reversed under the last regime, complicit shrinking public budgets. As academic researchers became under-funded, universities looked for funds elsewhere. It is at this juncture that the university-corporation alliance is concluded. This in turn implies that corporate interests influence the research planning.[88] Other studies have also presented data on the intensifying relation between scientific research and industry, and more generally have argued that science is increasingly organized to serve a neoliberist agenda.[89] While these studies tend to focus on the United States, they are relevant for our purposes because they exemplify possible macro trends of how

86 Demortain, *Scientists and the Regulation of Risk: Standardising Control* (n 74) 12.

87 Philip Mirowski and Esther-Mirjam Sent (eds), *Science Bought and Sold: Essays in the Economics of Science* (University of Chicago Press 2002); Esther-Mirjam Sent, 'The Economics of Science in Historical and Disciplinary Perspective' (2013) 7(1) Spontaneous Generations: A Journal for the History and Philosophy of Science 6.

88 Sent and Mirowski offers as an example an agreement between the University of California-Berkley and Novartis establishing that Novartis has veto power in decisions of the research committee of the university's departments of plant and microbial biology (n 87) 32.

89 Kelly Moore and others, 'Science and Neoliberal Globalization: A Political Sociological Approach' (2011) 40(5) Theory and Society 505.

science is funded and organized.[90] This macro-perspective may challenge more fundamentally the role of science-driven international institutions and shed more light on the need for accountability mechanisms in the regulatory science underpinning much of the regimes shaped by GRSIs.

While it may appear overambitious to include accountability mechanisms for first-hand science in the discourse of accountability for GRSIs, it is disingenuous not do so. The point is simple. Given the problems of the malleability of regulatory science, accountability should address not only the questions directly related to the experts working for GRSIs, but should also ***trickle-down*** to the first-hand regulatory science. Let us now turn to the analysis of the mechanisms, where attention will be paid both to the values that each mechanism can protect and to the levels of regulatory science falling under the scope of the accountability relationship.

4.3 *Mechanisms*

The aim of this section is to map the main typologies of potential accountability mechanisms for GRSIs. Even if domestic institutions can work as indirect mechanisms to hold global administrative bodies accountable, such vertical forms of accountability are limited.[91] Hence, the focus will mainly be on accountability mechanisms at the global level. As explained above, accountability is here conceptualized to include ex ante and ex post mechanisms.

Through ex ante mechanisms, global regulatory scientists are asked to give account of their credibility before the actions demanded of them are performed. These mechanisms may be particularly useful when the activity to be performed is complex and when it is costly to assess its quality ex post. This is clearly the case for regulatory science, given the malleability of science discussed above, as well as the cost of re-assessing scientific evidence.

4.3.1 *Ex ante mechanisms*

Some ex ante mechanisms are instrumental for realizing the principle of epistemic robustness. In this respect, most GRSIs select the experts on the basis of their scientific qualities (e.g. excellent toxicologist). Next to epistemic robustness, ex ante mechanisms can also aim at political robustness. Selection criteria, for example, can refer to parameter such as gender, geographical representation (e.g. developed and developing countries) and representation of different theories, methods and approaches. Several GRSIs have already internalized criteria for pluralism, which in turn could facilitate the respect of legitimate interest in the regulatory scientific process. Yet, there is no (systematic) study of how

90 Sent argues that while her analysis appears mainly focused on the US, Europe displays similar characteristics; see Sent (n 87) 7–8.

91 Benvenisti and Downs (n 46) 9.

these norms are implemented. More systematic studies of the process by which decision-making is taking place within GRSIs could also generate new ideas on how to improve the quality the scientific assessments and lead to much needed imaginative reforms. Think, for instance, of the practice of 'designated dissenter'.[92] In group-decision-making, a person is given the role to 'skilfully' disagree. This form of institutionalized disagreement tends to enhance the quality of the decisions, as it can overcome some of the deficiencies of groupthink. Would it be fruitful to embrace practices inspired by the 'designated dissenter' within GRSIs?[93]

Ex ante criteria are also useful to detect and minimize the pursuit of private interest in regulatory science from the outset. The ex ante mechanisms *par excellence* in regulatory science are Conflict of Interest (COI) rules. The Codes of conducts of many GRSIs, especially those nested in IOs refer to such rules. Including COI rules in the criteria to select the scientists for the advisory bodies could be seen as a means to ensure 'disinterestedness', as defined above. However, much will depend on how COI rules are framed in practice. Are scientists with a COI excluded from the committee? Are there checks on the self-declarations of scientists? And how broad or narrow is a COI rule? What are the consequences for a performed risk assessment, when a Member has had a conflict of interest, which was not detected at the time of selection? In areas, where GRSIs are prone to serious risk of regulatory-science capture, the way COI rules are designed may be crucial. While several GRSIs have COI policies,[94] it remains to be appraised on a case-by-case basis whether such mechanisms are working well to protect disinterestedness.

Take for example the GRSIs operating within the context of Codex, which is subject to the WHO 'Regulations for Expert Advisory Panels and Committees' (Regulations), a text adopted by the WHO Assembly[95] as well as by some FAO

92 Thanks to Brian Tamanaha for drawing my attention to the idea of the 'designated dissenter'. See Jonah Berger, *Invisible Influence: The Hidden Forces that Shape Behavior* (Simon and Schuster 2016).

93 William Kaplan has taken issue with the utility of designated dissenter, arguing that dissent should be 'authentic', as manufactured dissent may not have the credibility of a genuine dissenting voice; see William Kaplan, *Why Dissent Matters: Because Some People See Things the Rest of Us Miss* (McGill Queen's Press 2017) 302.

94 See ICNIRP, Statute Article 6(2); IPCC CONFLICT OF INTEREST POLICY, Approved at the Thirty-Fourth Session (Kampala, Uganda, 18–19 November 2011); amended at the Fortieth Session (Copenhagen, Denmark, 27–31 October 2014); and the Forty-Fourth Session (Decision IPCC/XLIV-3, Bangkok, Thailand, 17–20 October 2016).

95 Text available at: <http://apps.who.int/gb/bd/PDF/bd47/EN/regu-for-expert-en.pdf> accessed 5 July 2020. The text of the regulation was adopted by the Thirty-fifth World Health Assembly (resolution WHA35.10), in replacement of the regulations adopted by the Fourth World Health Assembly. Amendments were adopted at the Forty-fifth, Forty-ninth, Fifty-third and Fifty-fifth World Health Assemblies (decision WHA45(10), resolution WHA49.29, resolution WHA53.8 and resolution HA55.24, respectively.

general principles.[96] Once selected by FAO and WHO Director-Generals, experts have to declare potential conflict of interests.[97] Both the general regulations and specific procedural guidelines contain a rather general obligation of disclosure of possible conflict of interests, but do not specify what the circumstances that could lead to such a conflict are. If a conflict of interest is disclosed, it remains up to the discretion of the Committee to decide whether the scientists may participate in the risk assessment of a particular substance.[98] No clear-cut criterion is established to exclude experts with potential conflicts of interests and no external review mechanism is put into place to challenge the decisions to appoint certain experts or to sanction these experts, should they be violating the rules (e.g. not declaring industry funding, etc.).

The question, then, is whether these COI rules can sufficiently ensure disinterestedness. For example, in the case of glyphosate discussed earlier, the Codex scientific advisory body on pesticides (JMPR) has been criticized for conflict of interests.[99] The Chair and Co-chair of the JMPR had institutional affiliations with the ILSI, an industry think tank, sponsored among others by Monsanto, the main producer of glyphosate. In Europe, affiliation with ILSI constitutes conflict of interest and, in 2011, the person who was Co-Chair of the JMPR had to resign from the pesticide EFSA Panel after the same conflict of interest emerged.[100] At best, this case shows how rules on conflict of interest may vary and the need for more research on this ex ante mechanisms to ensure disinterestedness in regulatory science. At worst, it shows how the FAO/WHO COI rules for its scientific advisory bodies are insufficient to rule out conflicts of interest.

The ex ante mechanisms listed so far address only the questions related to the qualities of the regulatory scientists operating within the global committees and to the quality of the decision-making process. Yet, given the many ways in which a study can be shaped, and the difficulties in detecting manipulations, it appears naïve to focus the attention only on the experts embedded in scientific

96 Masson-Matthee (n 6) 2, 44–46. Next to the Regulations, specific guidelines for each of these committees have been developed by both FAO and WHO. Given the similarities of the rules for JECFA, JMPR and JEMRA committees, I rely on these rules interchangeably.

97 The Regulations provide that 'they [the experts] shall disclose all circumstances that could give rise to a potential conflict of interest as a result of their membership of an expert committee, in accordance with the mechanisms established by the Director-General for that purpose'.

98 Sect. 3 of the JECFA procedural Guidelines reads: 'Both Members and FAO Consultants are required to disclose in writing all circumstances that could lead to potential conflicts of interest. When an interest is declared on a particular substance, the Committee will discuss and adopt a decision whether the scientist may participate in the evaluation of this substance'. FAO, *Procedural Guidelines for the Joint FAO/WHO Expert Committee on Food Additives Food Additives and Food Contaminants* (FAO, February 2003) 3.

99 Helmut Burtscher-Schaden and others, *Glyphosate and Cancer: Buying Science How Industry Strategized (and Regulators Colluded) in an Attempt to Save the World's Most Widely Used Herbicide from a Ban* (Austria Global2000 2017).

100 Nelsen (n 25).

committees and on the design of the decision-making process at the trans- and international level. Ex ante mechanisms that trickle down to the first-hand regulatory science could also be devised.

Some of these strategies are already in place. For instance, in certain areas such as food safety, privately funded studies have to respect publicly devised guidelines or protocols (e.g. OECD Good Laboratory Practices), to be accepted by the reviewing body. Yet, given the mounting – albeit not systematic – evidence of influence of vested interests in first-hand regulatory science,[101] more powerful mechanisms could be imagined. Embryonic ideas on such mechanisms include the establishment of criteria to weigh privately funded research in meta-analysis differently than research conducted in the public interest. Likewise, studies partly or fully funded by vested interests could be accepted for evaluation by GRSIs only if they followed best practices aimed at preserving 'disinterestedness'. For example, it could be asked that when scientists perform work for a private party, they should do so under contracts that would allow them to disseminate information potentially damaging for the funder. These mechanisms, while adopted at the global level, trickle down in the sense that first-hand regulatory scientists would gain awareness of the necessity to respect certain norms for their studies to be accepted in the global regulatory process. More attention to trickle down mechanisms and some institutional imagination could increase the epistemic and politically robustness of the decision-making.

4.3.2 *Ex post mechanisms*

Compared with ex ante mechanisms, ex post accountability mechanisms are less available, at the global level.[102] The review mechanisms typical of the domestic level, such as courts or non-judicial review bodies (e.g. ombudsman) do not exist at the global level. In fact, there is no court or ombudsman that could review the conduct of specific GRSIs as such. Take the example of glyphosate again. On December 2017, several legal suits have been launched before domestic courts against alleged misconduct of the experts of EFSA.[103] In particular, it has been argued that the report assessing the safety of glyphosate was in great parts plagiarized from studies by Monsanto.[104] It is yet unclear whether these cases will

101 McGarity and Wagner (n 27) 7; Wagner and Steinzor (n 28) 7.

102 This section mainly focuses on legal accountability and does not address issues of political, democratic and financial accountability, as they do not seem particularly meaningful for (global) regulatory scientists. Reputational accountability is briefly discussed, but also considered as not very powerful in this area.

103 Global2000, 'Complaint Filed Against EU Authorities after Glyphosate Approval' <https://www.global2000.at/en/node/5346> accessed 5 July 2020.

104 Stephan Weber, 'Expert opinion on adherence to the rules of good scientific practice in the subsections "B.6.4.8 Published data (released since 2000)", "B.6.5.3 Published data on carcinogenicity (released since 2000)" and "B.6.6.12 Published data (released since 2000)" in the report "Final addendum to the Renewal Assessment Report. Risk assessment […] for the active substance GLYPHOSATE […]"' (2017) Report for Global2000, October 2015, 4322 pages, <https://www.global2000.at/en/node/5346> accessed 5 July 2020.

be granted jurisdiction at the domestic level, given that the misconduct to be reviewed is of a European body.[105] It is clear, though, that the same challenges could not have been launched against the respective global scientific advisory committee (in this case, the JMPR).

The examples discussed in Section 2 offer evidence that, in the absence of courts, ad hoc forms of ex post review are in place at the global level. In the case of the A(H1N1) avian influenza pandemic, the Council of Europe issued a resolution which reviewed the case ex post (Council of Europe 2010); in the case of the influence of the tobacco industry on the WHO, it was a WHO internal report.[106] These forms of ex post review have no binding force and there is no systematic study of their effects on GRSIs. Future research may shed light on the potential impacts of these ad hoc reviews on the functioning of GRSIs.

Ex post reviews can focus both on procedural and substantive issues. In the examples discussed above, the issues reviewed related almost exclusively to conflicts of interest, thus implicating procedural questions. In light of the malleability and uncertainty of regulatory science, it may be difficult for (quasi-)legal reviewers to focus on substantive questions. Yet, given the key role of scientific experts in decision-making, it may be desirable that, at least in serious cases, decisions of GRSIs be substantively reviewed by courts or quasi-courts.[107] At the domestic level, tort liability or criminal trials have been useful to unveil major problems with decisions resting on science[108] and adversarial science has proved useful in bringing to light important scientific information.[109]

At the international level, while scrutiny of the type conducted at domestic level is not possible, several courts could indirectly engage in review related to substantive questions. For example, the Appellate Body of the WTO, when confronted with the findings of one GRSI, could consider alternative scientific studies as equally valid and thus legitimize (or should we say legalize?) policies not in line with international standards. In this context, it has been argued that the Appellate Body could provide some scrutiny of the work of the Codex by 'disqualifying' standards that have been

105 Reuters reports that the ECJ has told that it would not be possible to take EFSA before a national court; Shadia Nasralla, 'Environmentalists Say They'll Try to Sue German, EU Authorities Over Glyphosate' *Reuters* (London, 4 December 2017) <https://www.reuters.com/article/us-eu-health-glyphosate-lawsuit/environmentalists-say-they-ll-try-to-sue-german-eu-authorities-over-glyphosate-idUSKBN1DY1QT> accessed 5 July 2020.

106 WHO (n 17) 5.

107 Alessandra Arcuri and Marta Simoncini, 'Scientists and Legal Accountability: Lessons from the L'Aquila Case' (2015) EUI Department of Law Research Paper No. 2015/17 <http://ssrn.com/abstract=2600406> accessed 5 July 2020; Madalina Busuioc, 'Blurred Areas of Responsibility European Agencies' Scientific "Opinions" under Scrutiny' in Monika Ambrus and others (eds), *The Role of 'Experts' in International and European Decision-Making: Advisors, Decision Makers or Irrelevant Actors?* (CUP 2014).

108 For a discussion of these cases see McGarity and Wagner (n 27) 285–286.

109 Sanne H Knudsen, 'Adversarial Science' (2014) 100 Iowa Law Review 1503.

adopted in controversial circumstances and without consensus;[110] as such, this indirect review could influence the scientific advisory bodies, albeit in a rather loose way. Such indirect reviews can also help to scrutinize what (legitimate) values have played a role in the scientific assessment. An adjudicatory body, like the WTO Appellate Body, could for example try to understand whether the assumptions made were conservative, whether certain studies were given more credit for certain reasons, etc. While this would not amount to a review *stricto sensu*, it would entail the possibility of bringing to light-sensitive questions including the role of uncertainty. Most importantly, it would add transparency to the process and raise awareness among the scientists that they may be called upon to justify their reasoning more extensively. Such awareness can also enable the scientists to resist the pressures of politicians or vested interests. In this sense, accountability could be seen as empowering rather than constraining science.

Another means through which ex post substantive review of GRSIs can occur is through peer review. GRSIs with overlapping competences could peer review each other's work. The case of glyphosate offers an illustration of the potential for inter-institutional peer review between different bodies, where two bodies (JMPR and IARC) have been looking at the carcinogenic properties of two substances. The possibility of inter-institutional peer review at the international level has remained under-explored in the literature on regulatory science.

Finally, it could also be argued that reputational accountability is at work in the field of regulatory science and renders other legal or quasi-legal accountability mechanisms redundant. If reputation generally plays a role for scientists, the uncertainties pervading regulatory scientific questions make it difficult to detect misconduct. Only the extreme cases, where serious frauds are committed, are likely to be caught in the net and possibly cause reputational damages to scientists. From this vantage point, the existence of legal and quasi-legal review mechanisms may still be deemed desirable.

The three dimensions presented above could be used to frame future research and, in particular, the study of specific regulatory regimes (e.g. food safety, pesticide regulation, biotechnologies, etc.). They can be used to assess empirically what type of accountability mechanisms exist in different domains. For example, for each regime, one could ask: what are the ex ante and ex post review mechanisms to check for disinterestedness? Are there legitimate values in the constitutive documents of the organization within which the GRSI operate? (How) Can these values be taken into account in the assessment? What levels of regulatory science fall under the accountability regime? Etc.

110 Michael A Livermore, 'Authority and Legitimacy in Global Governance: Deliberation, Institutional Differentiation, and the Codex Alimentarius' (2006) 81 New York University Law Review 766. See also, Robert Howse, 'Expertise, Trust and Accountability in Food Safety: The Evolving Role of the World Trade Organization' (Chapter 7 in this volume)

5 Conclusion

Recourse to scientific experts is key to global governance. Technical issues such as those dealt with in the areas of health, safety and environmental regulation cannot be decided without insights and the understanding of the underpinning scientific questions. Institutions that have embedded regulatory scientists in the decision-making chain have mushroomed in the past decades. Given the key roles of scientific regulatory bodies in global law and governance as well as the serious and documented threats to their credibility, it is of high importance to establish well-designed accountability institutions. While the risks of accountability overload should not be neglected, shying away from a serious debate on the accountability of global regulatory science is unwise.

This chapter has identified and described three dimensions along which accountability for GRSIs can be conceptualized and operationalized. Much work remains to be done to empirically understand what type of accountability mechanisms are already operational in the global arena and whether, in certain areas, there are more pronounced accountability gaps than in others. The three dimensions outlined in this essay can guide future work in this field at the intersection of law and science. The risk of unaccountable global technocratic bodies is not only poor decision-making. Uncritical reliance on scientific experts leads to a technocratic model of global governance that hampers democracy. Such a system can backlash. Unaccountable global technocracy may favour mistrust in science and attacks on the global legal order. Enhancing the accountability of GRSIs is thus crucial not only to improve the quality of decision-making at the global level but also to enhance its very legitimacy.

Acknowledgment

The author would like to thank Sanne Taekema, Wibren Van der Burg, David Demortain, Jan Klabbers, Rob Howse, Federica Violi and the participants of the International Conference *Unpacking the 'Accountability Paradox' in Expert-Based Decision-Making*, Erasmus University Rotterdam, 1 December 2017. The author also thanks Marta Morvillo, Brian Tamanaha, and the other participants to the EUI Colloquium on Regulatory Governance, European University Institute, Florence, 22 May 2018. An EUR Fellowship by Erasmus University Rotterdam is gratefully acknowledged.

Part II

Expertise and accountability in economic and financial law and governance

4 Contesting the monetary policies of the European Central Bank

Marijn van der Sluis

1 Introduction[1]

The euro crisis has highlighted the pivotal role of the European Central Bank (ECB) in the governance of the European Union. As described in countless academic papers, newspaper articles and, finally, personal memoirs, the decisions of the ECB were a key component of the response to the euro crisis. It depends on one's views on the causes of the euro crisis, the responsibility for its duration and also the overall view of European integration, whether the actions by the ECB are viewed favourably or not. Some see in the ECB a tool of Northern European domination, with the ECB being (partially) responsible for austerity, particularly in relation to Member States (MS) that received financial assistance.[2] Others see the ECB as going beyond its mandate by having adopted other goals for its unconventional policies.[3] The policies of the ECB have also been challenged before the Courts from both sides. Meanwhile, the ECB repeats its mantras of central bank independence and price stability.

As the independence and competences of the ECB are enshrined in the 'constitutional charter' of the European Union, direct challenges to the authority of the ECB are infrequent. However, this does not mean that the expertise and authority of the ECB are unassailable. This chapter examines how the authority and expertise of the ECB are constructed in the relation with other actors in the EU, and how the avenues through which they can be challenged have evolved over time. This research adopts a structural perspective, and is concerned foremost with the manner in which the ECB is embedded in the institutional environment of the EU through the organization of competences. This approach is based on the understanding that the interactions between the ECB and the Union institutions, as

1 This contribution was finalized as the ECB had started taking measures against the negative economic consequences of the actions against the coronavirus. It therefore does not discuss in depth such measures as the Pandemic Emergency Purchase Programme. It also preceded the controversial judgement of the German Constitutional Court of 5 May 2020 on the proportionality of the Public Sector Purchases Programme of the ECB.

2 See, e.g. the controversial account of former Greek Minister of Finance: Yanis Varoufakis, *Adults in the Room: My Battle with Europe's Deep Establishment* (Farrar, Straus and Giroux 2017).

3 See, e.g. Hans-Werner Sinn, *The Euro Trap – On Bursting Bubbles, Budgets, and Beliefs* (OUP 2014) ch 8.

organized explicitly by EU law, matter less for how the expertise of the ECB can be challenged than the power dynamics that result from the distribution and organization of competences.[4] In other words, a necessary condition to effectively question the authority of the ECB is that an entity can influence the context in which the ECB exercises its monetary policy. For example, expansive fiscal policies may counteract tight monetary policies and vice versa. Hence, the fiscal policymaker and the monetary policymaker have an incentive to coordinate their policies. It is through examining (the changes in) the power-relations in Economic and Monetary Union (EMU) that the ways in which the expertise and authority of the ECB can be challenged become apparent. This approach thus departs from a traditional accountability-approach to studying the institutional relations of the ECB. In part, this is due to the large number of contributions that already exists on this topic.[5] Moreover, accountability-studies generally disregard the underlying balance of powers in their analysis of institutional relations in the EU. It is argued here that the distribution of competences, which shapes the balance of powers, is in fact key to understanding the institutional relations of the ECB.

The setup of the chapter follows the creation and evolution of the ECB within the EU before (Section 2) and during the euro crisis (Section 3). The reason for taking this perspective, rather than focusing solely on the ECB as it stands today, is that the conflicts and ideas that shaped the ECB in the past are still relevant today. Although the inter-institutional dynamics concerning the decision-making in the ECB are different today than they were before the crisis, EMU has not been completely overhauled.[6]

The focus of this chapter is on the monetary policy expertise of the ECB, even though the ECB has also acquired tasks of banking supervision during the crisis. The connections between supervision and monetary policy are complex and evolving. Although the focus will be on the monetary policy powers of the ECB, banking supervision will be taken into account insofar it can be seen as a route to challenge monetary policy. This will be discussed in the final sections.

2 The ECB as a constitutional central bank in an asymmetric monetary union (1998–2009)

The ECB was created in June 1998, a couple of months before the exchange rates of 11 EU MS would be irreversibly locked and the euro would see the light of day. The founding rules of the ECB had lain dormant for a few years, after the entry into force of the Maastricht Treaty.

4 For recent discussions on the legal forms of the institutional connections of the ECB through the perspective of accountability, see the contributions in the recent special issue (vol. 26, no. 1) of the *Maastricht Journal of European and Comparative Law*.

5 Ibid. See also Sebastian Heidebrecht, 'Technocratic Governance at the Centre of the European Economic and Monetary Union – Exploring the Accountability of Expert-based Decision-making in the European Central Bank' (Chapter 5 in this volume).

6 Bruno De Witte, 'Euro Crisis Responses and the EU Legal Order: Increased Institutional Variation or Constitutional Mutation?' (2015) 11 European Constitutional Law Review 434.

The predecessor of the ECB, the European Monetary Institute (EMI), had already done the preparatory work for the new central bank, but the transition from EMI to ECB was of high symbolic importance. The start of the second phase of EMU in 1994 (the introduction of the euro in 1999 was the third stage) had not dispelled the fears that the euro would not be created. Despite the clear political statement of the Maastricht Treaty, turmoil in the European Monetary System and difficulties with convergence had led to doubts about the final step to a European single currency.[7] If the ECB had been created at the start of the second stage, these doubts about the start of the third stage might have damaged the reputation of the new central bank. Hence, the EMI was created in 1994 and dissolved in 1997, to allow the ECB a grand entrance.

This origin-story of the ECB shows the concern and difficulties of the drafters of the Maastricht Treaty for a strong central bank.[8] Whereas the central bank on which the ECB was modelled, the German Bundesbank, had developed its fierce reputation for independence over several decades,[9] the ECB would have to develop such a reputation over time. What made this task especially difficult was that the credibility, i.e. its reputation, of a central bank had become crucial for its effectiveness. Lacking a long history, the ECB would have to build its reputation from scratch.

The ECB had one advantage in this regard: it was based on a set of rules that in substance resembled the German Bundesbank. From its decentralized structure to its mandate, the text of the Statute of the European System of Central Banks and of the European Central Bank (ESCB/ECB Statute), mirrored the text of the *Bundesbankgesetz*.[10] This gave the impression that the ECB would continue the traditions and policy-orientations of the Bundesbank. However, the resemblance of the ECB to the Bundesbank is only a small part of the story, especially insofar it concerned the institutional relations of the ECB. Central to the creation of the ECB was that it would function in a 'political and social vacuum'.[11] Two aspects in particular determined the institutional context in which the ECB would function: the lack of a fully-fledged government on the European level with which the ECB could interact, and the constitutional foundations of the ECB.[12]

7 Jean Pisani-Ferry, *The Euro Crisis and Its Aftermath* (OUP 2014) 39.

8 See Harold James, *Making the European Monetary Union: The Role of the Committee of Central Bank Governors and the Origins of the European Central Bank* (Harvard University Press 2012).

9 See for a critical analysis of the reputation surrounding the Bundesbank, Jeremy Leaman, *The Bundesbank Myth: Towards a Critique of Central Bank Independence* (Palgrave Macmillan 2001).

10 See for an extensive comparison, Fabian Amtenbrink, *The Democratic Accountability of Central Banks: A Comparative Study of the European Central Bank* (Hart 1999).

11 Giandomenico Majone, 'Rethinking European Integration after the Debt Crisis' (2012) 3 University College London Working Paper 14. Also see Amy Verdun, 'The Institutional Design of EMU: A Democratic Deficit?' (1998) 18 Journal of Public Policy 107; Marijn Van der Sluis, 'Maastricht Revisited: Economic Constitutionalism, the ECB and the Bundesbank' in Maurice Adams, Federico Fabbrini and Pierre Larouche (eds), *The Constitutionalization of European Budgetary Constraints* (Hart Publishing 2014).

12 Majone (n 11) 14.

The constitutional foundations of the ECB can, of course, be traced back to the Maastricht Treaty, which extensively regulated the new central bank. As the Court of Justice of the European Union (CJEU) noted in 1988, the EEC Treaty was the constitutional charter of the Community.[13] From a comparative perspective, the ECB is therefore an outlier amongst central banks. Even if central banks are mentioned in a national constitution, it is usually in very general terms.[14] In the history of European (monetary) integration, there have also been other proposals for a single currency that would not be regulated in detail in the Treaties. The most prominent example is the *Spinelli Draft Treaty* from 1984, which only briefly dealt with monetary integration and allowed wide discretion to the European legislator regarding the overall setup of the euro.[15]

The benefit of using an extensive Treaty-revision to regulate the stages towards monetary union, the institutional setup of the ECB and the fiscal rules is that it brought together two strands of thought about deepening European integration.[16] Using an EU Treaty meant that the MS would be collectively in charge over the future of the euro.[17] Substantial changes to the text of the Treaty would require joint action of all MS. At the same time, using Treaty rules to regulate the ECB and MS finances conformed to a set of popular economic ideas at the time that economic governance should be based on specific rules, removed from the whims of everyday politics.[18]

For the ECB, this meant that the rules on its independence (Article 130 TFEU[19]), its mandate (Article 127(1) TFEU), its tasks (Article 127(2)-(4) TFEU), its decision making bodies (Article 10-11 ESCB/ECB Statute), its decentralized structure (Article 14 ESCB/ECB Statute), and financial affairs (Articles 27-31 ESCB/ECB Statute) would be part of EU primary law and amendable in most cases only through EU Treaty revision. Only in specific instances determined by the Treaty, either the Council alone or together with the European Parliament (EP) can adopt rules that amend the Treaty or which transfer new tasks to the ECB.[20] During the euro crisis, for example, the Council gave the ECB tasks in banking supervision.

13 Case C-294/83, *Parti écologiste 'Les Verts'* v. *European Parliament*, [1986] EU:C:1986:166, para 23.
14 See for short descriptions of the legal bases of the central banks in France, Germany, the Netherlands, the United States and New Zealand, Amtenbrink (n 10).
15 Draft Treaty establishing the European Union, Bulletin of the European Communities, February 1984, No. 2, p. 8–26.
16 Marijn Van der Sluis, *In Law We Trust: The Role of EU Constitutional Law in European Monetary Integration* (PhD, European University Institute 2017).
17 The concept of the collectivity of Member States is set forth in Luuk Van Middelaar, *The Passage to Europe: How a Continent Became a Union* (Yale University Press 2014).
18 For fiscal policy see George Kopits and Steven Symansky, 'Fiscal Policy Rules' (IMF 1998) Occasional Paper 162.
19 Consolidated Version of the Treaty on the Functioning of the European Union [2012] OJ C 326/47.
20 Article 40 ESCB/ECB Statute.

2.1 *The ECB and the EP*

The Treaty-based nature of the rules of the ECB limits the ability of the EP and, to a lesser extent, the Council, to challenge the expertise of the ECB. Firstly, the institutions are formally prohibited from trying to influence the decision-makers of the ECB under Article 130 TFEU. In comparison, the independence of the Bundesbank (before the euro) was directed only towards the Government. Secondly, the EP, as part of the European legislator, cannot credibly threaten to revoke or amend many of the foundational elements of the ECB through EU legislation.

Despite these legal provisions restricting the interaction between the EP and the ECB, the EP is widely studied as the most appropriate venue through which to exercise democratic oversight over the ECB. This is a result of Article 284(3) TFEU, which requires the ECB to submit an annual report to the EP and holds that the President of the ECB may be heard by the EP. A practice has emerged where the ECB also responds to written questions by individual members of the EP. The questions by the MEPs are generally short and the answers of the ECB rarely span more than two pages.

The main avenue for public scrutiny of the ECB therefore became the so-called monetary dialogue, whereby the President of the ECB appears before the EP four times a year and engages in discussion with the Members of the Economic and Monetary Atab;leffairs Committee. From the side of the EP, these meetings are prepared by short notes from academics and experts in the field of monetary policy. These briefings offer a critical background for MEPs to examine the decisions of the ECB. The monetary dialogue has attracted attention from scholars as to whether the EP was able to effectively hold the ECB to account. Research on the early years of the euro suggests that the EP has not found the ECB too willing to substantively engage with the concerns it raised. According to Amtenbrink and Van Duin in 2009: 'the debate on the objectives of the ECB and calls for more attention to growth and employment have arguably increasingly taken on the characteristics of a ritual dance'.[21]

One of the difficulties for the EP in this regard is the construction of the mandate of the ECB, which consists of two parts. The primary objective of the ECB is to maintain price stability. As a secondary goal, the ECB is to support

21 Fabian Amtenbrink and Kees Van Duin, 'The European Central Bank before the European Parliament: Theory and Practice after Ten Years of Monetary Dialogue' (2009) 34 European Law Review 561, 577. A more positive assessment of the influence of the EP is given by Sylvester CW Eijffinger and Edin Mujagic, 'An Assessment of the Effectiveness of the Monetary Dialogue on the ECB's Accountability and Transparency: A Qualitative Approach' (2004) Intereconomics 190. For an evaluation of the monetary dialogue during the euro crisis, see Stefan Collignon and Sebastian Diessner, 'The ECB's Monetary Dialogue with the European Parliament: Efficiency and Accountability during the Euro Crisis?' (2016) 54 Journal of Common Market Studies 1296. They conclude (p. 1309) that 'MEPs [Members of the European Parliament] correctly feel that the dialogue did not make a big difference for the management of the euro crisis'.

the general economic policies in the Union, but this is without prejudice to the primary goal of price stability. Whilst this focus on price stability gives the EP on the one hand a good benchmark to assess the actions of the ECB, it limits the ability of the EP on the other hand to redirect the attention of the ECB to other concerns.[22] Where the EP would itself be able to set the goal of monetary policy, the independence of the ECB would be less problematic. However, as the mandate is part of the Treaties, the members of the EP have no influence over the standard to which they should hold the ECB to account. Moreover, the mandate is inherently forward looking and therefore difficult to use ex-post to assess the actions of the ECB.[23] Whilst the ECB can be blamed for not having achieved its self-imposed goal of a level of inflation close to, but below 2%, whether other or different actions are warranted in the present, remains an assessment to be made by the ECB. The conclusion is that, at least prior to the crisis, the EP was not well-positioned to challenge the expertise of the ECB in the conduct of its monetary policy, due to the constitutionally enshrined independence and mandate of the ECB.

2.2 *The ECB and the Council/Eurogroup*

The institutional context in which the ECB would conduct its monetary policies before the euro crisis was shaped by the asymmetrical design of the euro. This meant that whereas the monetary policy was centralized and transferred to a powerful and independent institution, fiscal and economic policies remained largely in the hands of the MS. The EU Treaties imposed some limits on the discretion of the MS in this regard, most famously through the instruction for MS to avoid excessive deficits.[24] The interpretation of what would constitute an excessive deficit and the imposition of sanctions was tightly regulated by the Excessive Deficit Procedure, which in turn guaranteed the discretion of the Council to make the necessary economic evaluations.[25]

The economic effects of this imbalance between economic and monetary integration have been extensively studied.[26] For this chapter, it is important to observe how the imbalance also affected the institutional position of the ECB. In short, it meant that the ECB was missing a natural counterparty for its monetary policies in the form of a Minister of Finance.[27] On the national level, central banks operate in highly crowded fields of economic governance, mostly dominated by ministries of finance and economics. It is in the interaction between

22 Mark Dawson, Ana Bobić and Adina Maricut-Akbik, 'Reconciling Independence and Accountability at the European Central Bank: The False Promise of Proceduralism' (2019) 25 European Law Journal 77–80.
23 Van der Sluis (n 16) 118–119.
24 Article 126(1) TFEU.
25 Article 126(6) TFEU.
26 Joseph Stiglitz, *The Euro: And Its Threat to the Future of Europe* (Allen Lane 2016), part II.
27 Van der Sluis (n 16).

these ministries and the central banks that the expertise of central banks is challenged most directly.

On the national level, monetary policy would interact with a range of economic and fiscal policies. The effectiveness of monetary policy could be strengthened or weakened by fiscal policies and vice-versa.[28] This meant that the decision makers in both areas had an incentive to coordinate, challenge and sometimes confront each other, even if the central bank was independent. Moreover, in most cases, both independent central banks and ministries of finance have an incentive to minimize public disagreements.[29] Public criticism from a Minister of Finance about monetary policy might force a central bank to assert its independence. Public criticism by a central bank can easily backfire, as it could be seen as un-democratic. Hence, the interaction occurred mostly behind closed doors, and revolved, in part at least, on the quality of the arguments.

These dynamics changed with the creation of the euro. Even though fiscal and economic policies still shape the context in which monetary policy is executed, and vice-versa, they are decided on different levels. Monetary policy would be decided centrally and for the Eurozone as a whole; fiscal policies remained largely decentralized. As a result, monetary policy would be made in light of first 11, now 19, different economic and fiscal policies. The coordination game changed from one-on-one to one-vs-many. Individual ministers of finance no longer had an incentive to adjust their policies in order to assuage the central bank. Of course, the interactions between the different policies still meant that both sides had an incentive to remain well informed about the others policies and also to shape them; there were simply fewer credible tools to do so. In the (somewhat blunt) words of former ECB President Duisenberg about his interactions with fiscal policymakers: 'I hear, but I do not listen'.[30]

The imbalance in integration thus led to an isolation of the ECB. Padoa-Schioppa wrote in this regard about the 'institutional loneliness' of the ECB.[31] This should not solely be interpreted as having strengthened the independence of the ECB. As noted also by Louis, the absence of a decision maker on the European level also makes the ECB vulnerable.[32] As the only European actor

28 On the national level, another important factor contributing to the inter-dependence between central banks and the government, in particular the Minister of Finance, was the regulation of international monetary cooperation. See especially David Marsh, *The Bundesbank: The Bank That Rules Europe* (Heinemann 1992).

29 ibid.

30 Duisenberg, '*Introductory statement Willem F. Duisenberg, President of the European Central Bank*', 11 April 2001, available at <https://www.ecb.europa.eu/press/pressconf/2001/html/is010411.en.html>.

31 Tommaso Padoa-Schioppa, 'An Institutional Glossary of the Eurosystem' [2000] Zentrum für Europäische Integrationsforschung Center for European Integration Studies Working Papers.

32 Jean-Victor Louis, 'The Euro-Group and Economic Policy-Coordination' in Jean-Victor Louis (ed), *The Euro in the National Context* (British Institute of International and Comparative Law 2002) 365–366.

able to influence economic conditions across the Eurozone, the ECB may be held solely responsible for economic downturns.

Although the organization of EMU led to a change in dynamics between fiscal and monetary policymakers, the separation between them was not absolute. Two developments in the early years of the euro illustrate this: the adoption of the Stability and Growth Pact (SGP) and the creation of the Eurogroup. The SGP intensified the coordination amongst the MS of the surveillance of each other's economic and fiscal policies. Although the legal relevance of the SGP is easily overstated, its symbolic meaning was significant: the MS restated their commitment to pursue economic policies that would keep government deficits within 3% of GDP.[33] Whereas the SGP resulted mostly from German demands, the Eurogroup flowed from French ideas about an 'gouvernement economique'.[34] When it was created, the Eurogroup was an informal meeting of the Ministers of Finance of the Euro area, joined by a member of the Commission and, upon invitation, the President of the ECB. Since the Lisbon Treaty, the Eurogroup is recognized in the Treaties, but still not able to take formal decisions. Its aim was thus to offer a forum for the economic policymakers of the Euro area to meet.[35] Although the Eurogroup grew in importance during the euro crisis, its task-description and purpose in the first years was not altogether clear. Given the lack of tools for economic policy on the European level, the creation of the Eurogroup did not significantly alter the institutional dynamics in EMU. There were few open political questions in the governance of EMU for the Eurogroup to answer, at least until the start of the euro crisis.

2.3 *The ECB and the CJEU*

The combination of the two aforementioned characteristics, the constitutional foundations of the euro and the asymmetry of the EMU, meant that conflicts between the ECB and other EU institutions and bodies could not easily be resolved through informal mechanisms. Whereas on the national level, independent central banks rarely appeared before a court over conflicts relating to its monetary policies or independence, the institutional position of the ECB relied, in part, on the strength of law.[36] The judicialization of monetary policy in the Euro area, although a break with constitutional traditions in the MS, also

33 Matthieu Segers and Femke Van Esch, 'Behind the Veil of Budgetary Discipline: The Political Logic of the Budgetary Rules in EMU and the SGP' (2007) 45 Journal of Common Market Studies 1089.

34 David Howarth, 'Making and Breaking the Rules: French Policy on EU "Gouvernement Économique"' (2007) 14 Journal of European Public Policy 1061.

35 Uwe Puetter, *The Eurogroup: How a Secretive Circle of Finance Ministers Share European Economic Governance* (Manchester University Press 2006) ch 2.

36 Marijn Van der Sluis, 'Similar, Therefore Different: Judicial Review of Another Unconventional Monetary Policy in Weiss (C-493/17)' (2019) 46 Legal Issues of Economic Integration 263.

flowed from the logic of the Maastricht Treaty. When the Maastricht Treaty was adopted, the process of integration was already characterized by a high level of judicialization. For a rules-based euro to become part of a legal order characterized by a high level of judicialization, the involvement in the Court in the construction of the institutional position of the ECB could not come as a surprise.[37]

Nevertheless, the judicialization of monetary policy was a process with a rather slow start, due to an unwillingness of the CJEU to engage deeply with the first cases on EMU presented to it. The first case on the ECB appeared before the CJEU in 2000, as the European Commission challenged an ECB decision of October 1999 in a dispute over the scope of application of a regulation on fraud prevention. The ECB had wanted to escape its scope of application and had adopted a competing set of rules, which the Commission challenged.[38] At the heart of the matter was the question whether the EU legislator could adopt rules for EU bodies and agencies that would apply to the ECB. The Court avoided theorizing on the precise legal position of the ECB in the EU, rejecting only implicitly some extravagant theories that held that the ECB was an independent specialized organization of Community law over which the institutions held little legislative authority.[39] The legislation on fraud prevention could therefore apply to the ECB, as it was not considered to endanger the independence of the ECB.

The Court's refusal to develop the theoretical foundations of EMU was repeated in the case on the other side of EMU in 2004, on the application of the Excessive Deficit Procedure against France and Germany.[40] In that case, the Court equated the effectiveness of the procedure with procedural integrity, in order to avoid having to specify the purpose and nature of the rules on EMU. Hence, in the first decade of EMU, judicialization was limited to two high-profile cases. As the Court applied a rather straightforward textual reading of the Treaties in both cases, the Court acknowledged the crucial role of law for EMU and its own role in enforcing those rules, whilst refusing to become a policy innovator.[41] The role of the Court in EMU was thus markedly different from its role in the internal market, where it was a 'motor of integration'.[42]

37 See, however exceptionally, Paul Craig, 'EMU, the European Central Bank and Judicial Review' in Paul R Beaumont and Neil Walker (eds), *Legal Framework of the Single European Currency* (Hart 1999).

38 Case C-11/00, *Commission* v. *ECB*, [2003] EU:C:2003:395. Roger J Goebel, 'Court of Justice Oversight Over the European Central Bank: Delimiting the ECB's Constitutional Autonomy and Independence in the OLAF Judgment' (2006) 29 Fordham International Law Journal 610.

39 For example, see Chiara Zilioli and Martin Selmayr, 'The European Central Bank: An Independent Specialized Organization of Community Law' (2000) 37 Common Market Law Review 591. See the academic debate on their position in: Ramon Torrent, 'Whom Is the European Central Bank the Central Bank Of? Reaction to Zilioli and Selmayr' (1999) 36 Common Market Law Review 1229.

40 Case C-27/04, *Commission* v. *Council*, [2004] EU:C:2004:436.

41 Van der Sluis (n 36).

42 The seminal work on the role of the court in the development of European integration is Joseph H. H. Weiler, 'The Transformation of Europe' (1991) 100 Yale Law Journal 2403.

3 The ECB in the euro crisis

The euro crisis has tested the robustness of the euro and led to a significant overhaul of its substantive rules.[43] MS in financial difficulties can now apply for financial assistance from an international organization, the European Stability Mechanism (ESM), although the assistance comes with strict conditionality.[44] Economic governance has intensified with new procedures, e.g. on macro-economic imbalances, and fewer obstacles for enforcement. The ECB has moreover incorporated the survival of the euro within its mandate and adopted several unconventional monetary policies. The creation of the Banking Union also awarded the ECB tasks in banking supervision. The extent of these reforms on the overall functioning of EMU, is, however, often overstated. The way in which the euro is governed has not fundamentally changed, even though the substantive rules have been changed.[45] This means that the MS remain in charge over the future of the euro, through the ESM Treaty and the EU Treaties, whilst the institutions have some discretion on how they implement their tasks.[46]

The institutional position of the ECB has also evolved, to a limited extent, as a result of (the responses to) the euro crisis and so have the opportunities to challenge the expertise of the ECB. These changes are described here as exceptions to the key characteristics of the institutional position of the ECB, as developed above.

3.1 *A more symmetrical EMU*

The euro-crisis has led to a more symmetrical EMU in two ways: through a limited localization of monetary policy and a limited Europeanization of fiscal policy. The correction of the asymmetry has thus come from two directions. Firstly, the localization of monetary policy has meant that in the exercise of its overall task of setting monetary policy for the Euro area as a whole, the ECB has found itself in a position in which it had to make decisions that affect individual MS or groups of MS. Hence, the coordination game between fiscal and monetary policy entered a new phase.

One way in which monetary policy has become localized is through Emergency Liquidity Assistance (ELA). In 1999, the ECB noted that ELA was a national competence, exercised by national central banks (NCBs).[47] Under Article 14 of

43 For overviews, see Kaarlo Tuori and Klaus Tuori, *The Eurozone Crisis: A Constitutional Analysis* (CUP 2014); Alicia Hinarejos, *The Euro Area Crisis in Constitutional Perspective* (OUP 2015); René Smits, 'The Crisis Response in Europe's Economic and Monetary Union: Overview of Legal Developments' (2015) 38 Fordham International Law Journal 1135.

44 Article 136(3) TFEU.

45 De Witte (n 6).

46 Van der Sluis (n 36)

47 ECB, *Annual Report 1999*, 98–99 <https://www.ecb.europa.eu/pub/pdf/annrep/ar1999en.pdf?94f617e383ca3cf41a839372bf8c8bb3> accessed 18 May 2020.

the ESCB/ECB Statute, the ECB can limit the exercise of other tasks exercised by NCBs when they interfere with the objectives and tasks of the ESCB. During the euro crisis, NCBs started to provide significant amounts of ELA to banks in the run-up to agreements on financial assistance.[48] Although NCBs are supposed to only offer ELA for appropriate collateral, during a crisis this is notably difficult to check.[49] As a result, when the ECB stepped in on several occasions in the middle of negotiations on financial assistance with the announcement that it would restrict the provision of ELA by the NCB, it was perceived as threat meant to push MS to agree to the conditionality attached to the financial assistance.[50] Although the ECB maintained that it used Article 14 of the ESCB/ECB Statute to protect the integrity of the monetary policy of the Eurozone as whole, it was undoubtedly the case that those decisions affected specific MS in particular. Rather than take decisions that (only) affect the Euro area as a whole, the ECB now took decisions that specifically affected some MS.

Other examples where ECB policies particularly affected a single MS or a small group of MS are the changes in collateral policy, for example exempting Greek government bonds from the general requirements that central banks may only lend against collateral of a certain quality,[51] and the purchase of government bonds of only certain MS under the Securities Markets Programme (SMP).[52] Obviously, these measures have been highly contentious. What matters here is that they brought about a new dynamic between MS and the ECB. Suddenly, the behaviour of a single MS was relevant for the behaviour of the ECB and vice versa, opening new avenues to scrutinize and challenge the expertise of the ECB. For example, a parliamentary investigation of the crisis in Ireland brought to light letters sent by ECB President Trichet in 2010 to the Irish Minister of Finance, outlining the conditions under which ELA could continue.[53] Although Trichet subsequently testified before the Irish Parliament in his

48 Thomas Beukers, 'The New ECB and Its Relationship with the Eurozone Member States: Between Central Bank Independence and Central Bank Intervention' (2013) 50 Common Market Law Review 1593.

49 The requirements for providing ELA are now set out in the Governing Council 'Agreement on emergency liquidity Assistance' of 17 May 2017.

50 Beukers (n 48). Also see the account provided by Transparency International of the ELA provided in Greece in 2015: Benjamin Braun, 'Two Sides of the Same Coin? Independence and Accountability of the European Central Bank' (2017) Transparency International.

51 Tuori and Tuori (n 43) 102–103.

52 Peter Sester, 'The ECB's Controversial Securities Market Programme (SMP) and Its Role in Relation to the Modified EFSF and the Future ESM' (2012) 9 European Company and Financial Law Review 156. Under another unconventional monetary policy, the Public Sector Purchases Programme (PSPP), the NCB's buy government bonds on the secondary market. The reason for letting the NCB's make (most) of these purchases, instead of the ECB, is that in case of default, the losses remain local, due to the lack of risk sharing. This controversial aspect of PSPP can be seen as a response to the difficult situations that arose from other localized monetary policies.

53 Vincent Boland and Peter Spiegel, 'ECB Threatened to End Funding Unless Ireland Sought Bailout', *Financial Times* (London, 6 November 2014).

capacity as ex-President in 2015, the ECB as such, represented by a member of the Executive Board, refused to appear before the parliamentary enquiry.[54] This 'localization' of monetary policy in the Eurozone has been irregular in form and intensity through the euro crisis. Rather than a sustained relationship developing between a monetary and an economic/fiscal policymaker, this has resulted in highly politicized and tense interactions, often drawn out in public.

Secondly, a counterpart to the limited localization of monetary policy in the Eurozone has been the limited Europeanization of economic and fiscal policies. Whereas before the crisis the EU lacked the opportunity to shape the fiscal and economic conditions in which the monetary policies of the ECB would take effect, the crisis led to several instances where European entities had a decisive influence over economic and fiscal policies in the Eurozone.[55] The main example of this development has been the creation and use of financial assistance mechanisms. As the financial assistance that is offered to MS in economic troubles comes with strict conditionality, the negotiations over the size, scope and timing of the bailout packages constitute a crucial form of European policy-making for the euro-area.[56] Where the ECB interacted on the one hand with MS through the localization of its monetary policy, it interacted with a European policymaker on the other hand as a result of a limited Europeanization of economic and fiscal policies. The primary interlocutor for the ECB has been the Eurogroup, who had discovered its relevance during the crisis.[57] Whereas the Eurogroup had been in search for a task prior to the crisis, the creation of several instruments both within and outside the EU legal order required political coordination amongst Euro area MS. Hence, it was in the Eurogroup meetings that a more familiar dynamic between monetary and economic/fiscal policymakers was re-established.

The dependence of the ECB on this new form of European policy-making is perhaps best visible in the decision in 2012 to include a condition in the Outright Monetary Transactions (OMT) programme that a financial assistance programme is concluded for the MS whose bonds the ECB plans to buy.[58] This decision has the effect that it limited the exposure of the ECB to the national politics of a MS in trouble. It allows the ECB to redirect invitations for support from MS to the ESM (de facto to the Eurogroup). The political negotiations over the bailout packages are therefore between the Eurogroup and the MS. As part of the Troika, the ECB

54 Draghi did eventually appear before the Irish Parliament in 2018, as part of a tour of several parliaments of Eurozone Member States, see Tobias Tesche, 'Instrumentalizing EMU's Democratic Deficit: The ECB's Unconventional Accountability Measures during the Eurozone Crisis' (2018) Journal of European Integration 447.

55 Pierre Schlosser, *Europe's New Fiscal Union* (Palgrave Macmillan 2019) ch 4.

56 Although the bailout packages are agreed with a single recipient Member State, the policies included therein have European effects.

57 Paul Craig, 'The Eurogroup, Power and Accountability' (2017) 23 European Law Journal 236.

58 ECB, 'Technical features of Outright Monetary Transactions' press release (6 September 2012).

plays a role in the negotiations and implementation of those packages, but since its formal role is 'advisory', the political responsibility on the European level lies with the ESM/Eurogroup.[59] The ECB has thus found its political 'shield' on the European level. At the same time, this dependence on the Eurogroup exposes the ECB to scrutiny from the Eurogroup.[60] Through the explicit intertwinement of their tasks, the Eurogroup and the ECB are mutually dependent, inviting both to closely monitor and act strategically in relation to each other.[61]

Another aspect of the limited Europeanization of economic and fiscal policies has been the growth of European economic governance through the so-called 'six-pack' and 'two-pack'.[62] Together, these eight pieces of legislation created new procedures for the correction of macro-economic imbalances and the monitoring of national budgets, and tightened existing procedures by making it easier to impose sanctions. The relative institutional 'winner' of these reforms, however, is the Commission.[63] The Eurogroup has certainly seen an increase in its capacity to influence the overall economic direction in the Eurozone, but so far has spent its attention more towards its relation with the Commission than towards the ECB.[64]

The intensification of the relation between the ECB and the Eurogroup has increased the opportunities to effectively challenge ECB policies. Whether and to what extent the Eurogroup has made use of these opportunities is difficult for an outsider to ascertain, as the workings of the Eurogroup are notoriously opaque.[65] One indication that the ECB has an interest in the discussions in the

59 But see Opinion of AG Cruz Villalón, Case C-62/14, *Gauweiler* [2015] EU:C:2015:7.

60 An interesting saga has been the interaction between the ECB and the Council/Eurogroup on the competence to regulate Central Counterparties (CCP's). The ECB had requested a treaty change to expand its regulatory competences, but was refuted by the MS. See Jim Brunsden and Claire Jones, 'ECB Scraps Clearing Powers Request in Feud with European Capitals' *Financial Times* (London, 20 March 2019).

61 For one account of the strategic behavior of the ECB, see Jonathan Yiangou, Mícheál O'Keeffe and Gabriel Glöckler, '"Tough Love": How the ECB's Monetary Financing Prohibition Pushes Deeper Euro Area Integration' (2013) 35 Journal of European Integration 223.

62 Schlosser (n 55) ch 3. See for a discussion of these pieces of legislation De Streel, 'The Evolution of the EU Economic Governance Since the Treaty of Maastricht: An Unfinished Task' (2013) 20 Maastricht Journal of European and Comparative Law 336; Rainer Palmstorfer, 'The Reverse Majority Voting under the "Six Pack": A Bad Turn for the Union?' (2013) European law Journal 186; Sergio De la Parra, 'The Two Pack on Economic Governance: An Initial Analysis' (2013) March 2013 ETUI Background analysis.

63 Michael W Bauer and Stefan Becker, 'The Unexpected Winner of the Crisis: The European Commission's Strengthened Role in Economic Governance' (2014) 36 Journal of European Integration 213.

64 See, e.g. the political maneuvering in the Council leading up to the decision to cancel the fines for Spain and Portugal in the Excessive Deficit Procedure. Council Implementing Decision 2017/2351 on imposing a fine on Spain for failure to take effective action to address an excessive deficit [2017] OJ L 336/27.

65 Transparency International, 'Vanishing Act: The Eurogroup's Accountability' (2019) 29–32 <http://transparency.eu/eurogroup/>.

Eurogroup is that it has broken with the tradition of restricting its parliamentary engagements to the EP. Since 2015, the President of the ECB has visited the parliaments of several of the MS.[66] Not coincidentally, Draghi has mostly visited those MS that are either seen as having a powerful voice in the Eurogroup and/or resistant to further integration in EMU.

3.2 *EMU and secondary legislation*

Although the euro crisis has led to substantial changes in the legal framework of the euro, these changes were not enacted through primary law. Their legal origins instead lay in international law, ECB acts and, crucially, EU legislative acts, often adopted through the ordinary legislative procedure.[67] As confirmed by the *OLAF*-case, discussed above, EU secondary legislation may not affect the independent exercise of monetary policy competences of the ECB. However, secondary legislation can nonetheless significantly impact the context in which monetary policy is decided and the involvement of the EP in the adoption (and future amendment) of several of these pieces of legislation has given it a modicum of leverage with regard to the ECB.

The most important set of EU legislative acts in this regard has been the Banking Union, which concerns the supervision and resolution of European banks. In accordance with Article 127(6) TFEU, the Council conferred on the ECB the task of supervising significant banks in the Eurozone through the Single Supervisory Regulation (SSM Regulation). The SSM Regulation organizes amongst other things the internal position of the Supervisory Board within the ECB and (re-)affirms the independence of the ECB in supervision. The SSM Regulation also formally instructs the ECB to be accountable towards the EP and the Council.[68] However, the Regulation offers no tools to the EP to sanction the ECB.[69] Whilst the ECB must respond to questions of the EP, the SSM Regulation itself offers no incentives for the ECB to engage in depth with such questions. More relevant therefore for the relation between the ECB and the EP is that the rules the ECB applies in banking supervision spring from the 'Single Rulebook', as laid down by the EP and the Council. It is through the influence over these pieces of legislation, which in light of the quickly changing circumstances of financial globalization may have to be

66 Tesche (n 54).

67 On the use of international law, see Bruno De Witte, 'Using International Law in the Euro Crisis: Causes and Consequences' (2013) No 4 June 2013 ARENA Working Paper.

68 Article 20 Council Regulation 1024/2013 conferring specific tasks on the European Central Bank concerning policies relating to the prudential supervision of credit institutions [2013] OJ L 287/63.

69 Fromage and Ibrido argue that the Regulation allows for 'accountability of a special kind', Diane Fromage and Renato Ibrido, 'The "Banking Dialogue" as a Model to Improve Parliamentary Involvement in the Monetary Dialogue?' (2018) 40 Journal of European Integration 295.

updated and amended regularly, that the EP has (finally) gotten some leverage over the ECB.[70]

3.3 *A judicial dialogue on the boundaries of monetary policy*

Throughout the euro crisis, the ECB has experimented with several new monetary policy tools to counteract centrifugal economic forces in the Eurozone and to stimulate economic growth. The ECB has always maintained to have acted within its mandate, and argued that its unconventional measures were prompted by unconventional circumstances. Draghi's famous words that 'the ECB is ready to do whatever it takes to preserve the euro', were indeed preceded by the reassurance: 'within our mandate'.[71] The extraordinary measures have nonetheless led to several judicial challenges.

The approach of the CJEU to these challenges has so far been cautious; even though it examined whether the ECB overstepped its mandate, and thus engaged with the core challenge to the unconventional monetary policies, it has by-and-large accepted the underlying claims of the ECB as to the interpretation and necessity of the policies. The Court has thereby continued its minimal role in EMU.[72] Whilst in the pre-crisis era, the Court emphasized the procedural and institutional limits of the Treaty through a rather plain reading of the Treaties, the role of the Court in the euro crisis was to emphasize the respective areas within which the MS (collectively) and the institutions could take responsibility over the future of the euro.

The hesitance of the CJEU to challenge the expertise of the ECB stands in stark contrast with the approach of the German Constitutional Court (GCC).[73] Monetary integration has featured heavily in the GCC's jurisprudence on European integration, and it can therefore not be seen as a surprise that the reforms of the euro have been examined in detail by the GCC. (Legal) opposition to the bailouts and to the unconventional monetary policies has also been mobilized through these constitutional debates.

The judicial dialogue on the legality of the actions of the ECB between the GCC and the CJEU took the form of two references for a preliminary question in constitutional complaints submitted by groups of individuals. The admissibility of these questions by the GCC was disputed, not in the least because they

70 See for the strategies applied by the EP in the negotiation over several pieces of EMU legislation vis-à-vis the MS, see Magnus Schoeller and Adrienne Héritier, 'Driving Informal Institutional Change: The European Parliament and the Reform of the Economic and Monetary Union' (2019) 41 Journal of European Integration 277.

71 Speech by Mario Draghi, President of the European Central Bank at the Global Investment Conference in London, 26 July 2012.

72 Van der Sluis (n 36).

73 Mark Dawson and Ana Bobić, 'Quantitative Easing at the Court of Justice – Doing Whatever It Takes to Save the Euro: Weiss and Others' (2019) 56 Common Market Law Review 1005.

appeared to offer individuals a new way to challenge Union acts, circumventing the Union's system for legal protection.[74] Perhaps due to the political sensitivity of the case and the fact that this was the first ever reference from the GCC, the CJEU chose to nevertheless engage with the substance of the questions.

The first reference of the GCC concerned the implementation of Draghi's promise to do 'whatever it takes to save the euro', through OMT. Under this programme, the ECB promised to help MS in financial difficulties by buying their government bonds on the secondary markets, thereby reducing the (excessive) interest rates that markets imposed out of fear of a break-up of the euro. The GCC challenged the legality of OMT, because it supposedly violated the mandate of the ECB.[75] As OMT has so far not been employed, the discussion necessarily focused on the overall legal construction of the mandate of the ECB. Nevertheless, the Bundesbank submitted a 29-page brief to the GCC, outlining its opposition to OMT.[76] This supported the GCC's rather aggressive position towards the CJEU and the ECB, as it had its own source of expertise.

In its response, the CJEU accepted the reinterpretation of the mandate of the ECB to also aim to maintain the integrity of the Eurozone and laid out a structure for the review of the legality of monetary policy decisions of the ECB.[77] First, the Court tested whether the programme should be classified as monetary or economic policy, looking at the goal and instruments of the policy. Second, the Court tested the proportionality of the measure, and third, tested the conformity of the measure to the prohibition of monetary financing. OMT was approved in all three tests. One criticism of the judgement was that it gave the ECB too much discretion to interpret its own action: the *stated* objective of OMT was crucial for all three steps, and not seriously challenged by the Court.[78] Nevertheless, the Court also set economic indicators for the legality of monetary policy measures, for example that the measure would lead to a harmonization of interest rates of the MS, regardless of their economic and budgetary situation.[79] This would allow economic debate before the CJEU, thus opening a venue to challenge the expertise of the ECB.

74 Case C-62/14, *Gauweiler*, (n 59), para. 18–31. Also see Jacopo Alberti, 'Challenging the Evolution of the EMU: The Justiciability of Soft Law Measures Enacted by the ECB against the Financial Crisis before the European Courts' (2018) 37 Yearbook of European Law 626.

75 Mattias Kumm, 'Rebel Without a Good Cause: Karlsruhe's Misguided Attempt to Draw the CJEU into a Game of "Chicken" and What the CJEU Might Do About It' (2014) 15 German Law Journal 203.

76 Deutsche Bundesbank, 'Statement to the Federal Constitutional Court, with a particular focus on the OMT programme and the matter of TARGET2 balances', 21 December 2012, available at: <https://www.bundesbank.de/resource/blob/799688/a6e46b-9d71e86f076c2aa07e1cd24b7a/mL/2012-12-21-omt-data.pdf>.

77 Case C-62/14, *Gauweiler*, (n 59) para. 48.

78 Christian Joerges, 'Pereat Iustitia, Fiat Mundus: What Is Left of the European Economic Constitution after the Gauweiler Litigation?' (2016) 23 Maastricht Journal of European and Comparative Law 99, 106–107.

79 Case C-62/14, *Gauweiler*, (n 59) para. 113.

Although the GCC accepted the judgement of the CJEU on the legality of OMT, it referred another question to the CJEU on the legality of the Public Sector Purchases Programme (PSPP).[80] PSPP has been somewhat less controversial, as it has the more traditional monetary policy goal of staving off deflation and follows the example of other high-profile central banks, such as the U.S. Federal Reserve, the Bank of England and the Bank of Japan. In its reference, the GCC challenged the method used by the CJEU to ascertain the objective of a disputed measure of the ECB. The GCC argued that the economic effects of a measure could be used to disprove the *stated* objective, even if it did not offer specific evidence that the PSPP had such effects. The CJEU refuted the GCC again and even reduced the importance of economic arguments in its reasoning.

The challenges by the GCC to the authority of the ECB and the CJEU are only one part of the broader trend of judicialization of EMU through the euro crisis. Many cases either directly or indirectly involved the ECB. In general, the CJEU has been rather dismissive of these challenges, for example by refusing applicants standing or by stating that no challengeable acts were adopted.[81] This meant, among other things, that the ECB's participation in the negotiations of financial assistance packages,[82] as well as its decisions to restrict ELA,[83] have escaped extensive scrutiny. Nevertheless, these cases highlight the increased interest to use legal tools to challenge the ECB, and in some instances they do affect the ECB, even if the claim is ultimately dismissed. In the *Accorinti*-case, for example, the General Court found that the ECB was allowed to participate in a swap agreement with the Greek Government in order to avoid losses that might end up endangering the functioning of the ECB.[84] Although the Court generally embraced the reasoning of the ECB, the fact that it recognized the ECB's position about the necessity to avoid losses can prevent a change in attitude by the ECB in the future.

4 Conclusion

The ECB has a unique place within the EU's institutional framework, which can be explained by looking at the historical process of European monetary integration. The primary concern in the design of the ECB was the reproduction of a strong, fiercely independent institution in the tradition of the German Bundesbank. However, by emulating the German example through the Maastricht Treaty, the ECB perhaps more closely resembles the ideal-type of an independent central bank than the Bundesbank ever did.

The institutional relations between the ECB and the other EU institutions and the MS as established by the Treaties thus only tell part of the story of how

80 Van der Sluis (n 36).
81 Case T-492/12, *Von Storch and Others* v. *ECB* [2013] EU:T:2013:702.
82 Case T-786/14, *Bourdouvali*, [2018] EU:T:2018:487, para. 83.
83 Case T-368/15, *Alcimos* v. *ECB*, [2016] EU:T:2016:438.
84 Case T-79/13, *Accorinti* v. *ECB*, [2015] EU:T:2015:756.

the ECB is politically embedded in the EU. That story must be complemented by an analysis, firstly, of the peculiar legal nature of those rules. The ECB is a *constitutional central bank*, in the sense that its foundational rules are enshrined in rules that have a higher level of rigidity and which are supreme over ordinary rules. This means, among other things, that the ECB is less susceptible to (legislative) threats to its mandate or independence. Moreover, the ECB is a central bank in an *asymmetrical* monetary union, in which fiscal and economic policy are largely determined on the national level. The ECB is lacking a fiscal/economic policy partner that can take responsibility for the economic situation in the Eurozone. Together, these features largely prevented other actors in the EU to challenge the monetary policies of the ECB.

The euro crisis has resulted in some changes in the institutional position of the ECB. A limited localization of monetary and a limited Europeanization of economic policy have brought relief for the 'institutional loneliness' of the ECB. Although the institutional position of the ECB remains quite distinct from the national environments in which Eurozone national central banks used to operate, the changes have led to increased opportunities to challenge the ECB's expertise. The crisis has also deepened the use of judicial review.

The analysis presented in this chapter holds one lesson for the ongoing reforms of the Eurozone, namely that concerns of democratic legitimacy, or accountability, should not *follow* the transfer or allocation of competences to European bodies. The common refrain is that (new) European powers should be accompanied by proper forms of accountability. This chapter aimed to show that what matters is the balance of powers between institutions and bodies, rather than the explicit organization of specific connections between entities through law. Democratic legitimacy and countervailing powers should be at the centre of the re-design of the euro, rather than something that can be organized at the end of the reform process.

5 Technocratic governance at the centre of the European Economic and Monetary Union

Exploring the accountability of expert-based decision-making in the European Central Bank

Sebastian Heidebrecht

1 Introduction

The European Central Bank (ECB) is clearly one of the most important institutions of the European Economic and Monetary Union (EMU), while it is also the European Union's (EU) technocratic institution par excellence. The area of monetary policy is one of the policy area in which the delegation of authority over policy is most substantially, namely exclusively, delegated from the level of member states to the level of the EU. In case of the ECB, very independent experts are appointed to make far-reaching decisions on monetary policy, without interference of politically more representative and more accountable actors or institutions like for instance the European Parliament (EP). Furthermore, in the period following the euro crisis, the powers of the independent experts in the ECB increased substantially. Through its far-reaching policy decisions, the ECB became in the eyes of most observers a *de facto* lender of last resort for governments in the Eurozone (thereby expanding substantially its original mandate to maintain price stability), it received important authority over financial stability with the introduction of the European Banking Union, and it took on new responsibilities by acting as a government adviser during the euro crisis.[1] However, while the powers of the ECB have increased significantly, its accountability and transparency framework is only poorly adjusted. This results in a comprehensive strengthening of technocratic decision-making at the centre of the EMU, exercised by independent experts in the ECB.

The political and institutional developments over the last decade increased the role of expert-based decision-making and the ECB as an especially important case. However, the technocratic concept of expert-based decision-making in independent central banks is not unchallenged. For instance shows today's populist politics tendencies to politicize central banking. US President Donald Trump asks publicly about his power to dismiss Federal Reserve Chairman

1 See on a discussion of ECB's role as a government adviser, Michele Chang, 'The Creeping Competence of the European Central Bank During the Euro Crisis' (2018) 51 Credit and Capital Markets 41.

Jerome Powell.[2] A more political though less populist trend is also observable in the EU, where two former politicians, Christine Lagarde and Luis de Guindos, became President and Vice President of the ECB in 2018 and 2019. More generally, the appropriate design and degree of central bank independence is and always has been controversial. Different approaches to central banking are possible. In contrast to the ECB, the US Federal Reserve focuses on price stability and (maximum) employment, without formally privileging one of these goals over the other.[3] The UK Treasury sets the Bank of England's inflation target. In the EU, already at the beginning of the euro project, scholars like Buiter argued prominently that the ECB's 'paternalistic' approach to central banking is not appropriate for a contemporary democratic society, and asked for more accountability and especially an EP that can both bark and bite.[4]

To reflect on the special case of accountability of expert-based decision-making in the ECB, this chapter proceeds by discussing the specific concept of central bank independence and the particularities of expert-based decision-making in the ECB, as the world's most independent central bank (Section 2).[5] While the subsequent section explores the characteristics of the educational and occupational experience of the independent experts that are selected for the top of the ECB (Section 3), the two following sections explore the increasing importance of its accountability framework (Section 4) and its actual application (Section 5). They highlight that although the ECB's accountability framework has become more important, desirable democratic reforms are missing. The last section concludes.

2 Central bank independence and the special case of the European Central Bank

The ECB is a very independent and by design quite conservative central bank. The Treaty on the Functioning of the European Union (TFEU) defines a relatively narrow mandate of the ECB: to maintain price stability as its primary objective. Article 127 (1) TFEU defines that only 'without prejudice to the objective of price stability', shall the ECB 'support the general economic policies in the Union with a view to contributing to the achievement of the objectives of the Union'. These include *inter alia* 'full employment' and 'balanced economic growth' (Article 3 (3) TEU). In line with economic reasoning during the time of negotiating the Maastricht Treaty, European policy makers established the ECB as an outstanding institution – typically regarded as the most independent

2 Kevin Liptak, 'Trump Asking Adviser If He Can Legally Fire Fed Chief' (*CNN politics*, 22 December 2018) < edition.cnn.com/2018/12/22/politics/trump-jerome-powell-fire-interest-rate-hike/index.html> accessed 22 March 2020.

3 Sebastian Heidebrecht, 'Wie Transparent Ist Die Europäische Zentralbank: Eine International Vergleichende Betrachtung vor dem Hintergrund Weitreichender Neuerungen zum Januar 2015' (2015) 25 Zeitschrift für Politikwissenschaft 501.

4 Willem Buiter, 'Alice in Euroland' (1999) 37 Journal of Common Market Studies 181, 187.

5 Nergiz Dincer and Barry Eichengreen, 'Central Bank Transparency and Independence: Updates and New Measures' (2014) 10 International Journal of Central Banking 189.

central bank in the world.[6] Article 130 TFEU explicitly shields the ECB from any kind of political influence. Further, as the only supranational central bank in the world, changing the ECB's legal statute would require unanimity of all EU Member States because the ECB's legal independence is enshrined in the EU-Treaties. In order to prevent political demands, the ECB is legally prohibited from monetary financing (Article 123 TFEU). The independence of independent experts in the ECB is also accompanied by fiscal policy restrictions in the EMU, like the so-called 'no bailout clause' (Article 125 TFEU) and rigid fiscal measures like the so-called Fiscal Compact. Overall, this regime of 'sound (public) finances'[7] was designed to ensure macroeconomic stability and the prevention of a necessity of central bank intervention.

The principle of central bank independence, namely the delegation of monetary policy exclusively to central banks that are independent of political interference, shall sustain inflation rates on a low level.[8] Until the most recent financial meltdown, there was a wide consensus – especially among economists – stating that monetary policy performs best when delegated to economic experts in independent central banks out of reach of politicians and given the legal obligation to maintain price stability.[9] The assumption that central bank independence is necessary to counteract inflationary biases rests on a number of theoretical explanations. The core argument is that politicians are likely to have incentives to use monetary policy to stimulate the economy and boost output in the short run for electoral reasons, regardless of whether these policies are likely to produce economic trouble in the longer run. This is probable because macroeconomics assumes a relation in terms of a trade-off between inflation and unemployment.[10] Accordingly, politicians may be confronted with demands to use monetary policy instruments to stimulate the economy which increases inflation but might reduce unemployment.[11] Because such alleged short-sighted

6 Ibid. See also Marijn van der Sluis, 'Contesting the Monetary Policies of the European Central Bank' (Chapter 4 in this volume).

7 Commission of the European Communities, 'Stable Money – Sound Finances, Community Public Finances in the Perspective of EMU' (1993) European Economy 53; Jonathan Yianghou, Mícheál O'Keeffe and Gabriel Glöckler 'Tough Love: How the ECB's Monetary Financing Prohibition Pushes Deeper Euro Area Integration' (2013) 35 Journal of European Integration 223.

8 See on a more detailed discussion of the economic idea of central bank independence Sebastian Heidebrecht, 'Central Bank Independence: Economic Common Sense and Economic Device' (2018) 19 Economic Sociology – The European Electronic Newsletter 25; see on the economic reasoning of central bank independence, e.g. Alan S. Blinder, *Central Banking in Theory and Practice* (Cambridge/London, 2nd ed., MIT Press 1999) 53 et seq.

9 Alex Cukiermann, 'Monetary Policy and Institutions Before, During and After the Global Financial Crisis' (2013) 9 Journal of Financial Stability 373, 374.

10 Paul Samuelson and Robert Solow, 'Analytical Aspects of Anti-inflation Policy' (1960) 50 American Economic Review 177.

11 Alberto Alesina and Guido Tabellini, 'Bureaucrats or Politicians: Part I Single Task' (2007) 97 American Economic Review 169; Alberto Alesina and Guido Tabellini, 'Bureaucrats or Politicians? Part II: Multiple Tasks' (2008) 92 Journal of Public Economics 426.

political attempts to stimulate the economy by monetary stimulus is considered to result in both high unemployment and high inflation in the long run, economic common sense recommends that decision-making powers over monetary policy should be transferred to economic experts in independent central banks. Therefore, the ECB, as a newly established and supranational central bank, became the most independent central bank in the world.

3 European central bankers and their expertise

More generally, experts in public institutions are increasingly trained in economics,[12] which as a discipline offers measurement techniques claiming to provide decision-making criteria for most conceivable areas of public policy and social life.[13] However, expert advice can differ, not only because of different assumptions about causal relations between policy instruments and desired outcomes, but also because of what is actually considered the problem and what should be the goal in the first place. Such paradigmatic opposing views are prominently discussed in context of the conversion from Keynesianism to Monetarism in the 1970s and 1980s.[14] This development suggests that the policy relevance of expert knowledge and expert advice is not just a question of academic superiority, but is also more political in tone and requires politicians to reach judgements on which group of experts to regard as 'authoritative'. It is for instance not unusual that different interest groups (like labour unions and employer associations) have their own economic experts with different economic models and policy recommendations. This indicates that changes of macroeconomic expert advice are – as Peter Hall puts it – 'more sociological than scientific'.[15] In the EMU, among the most such influential economic experts are European central bankers, whose importance in expert bodies like the Delors Committee allowed them to transfer their economic perspective to the design of the EMU.[16] Afterwards, they became the experts responsible to decide on EU's monetary policy in the ECB, independent of more political bodies.

With regard to characteristics of European central bankers, one of the most recent studies,[17] notably conducted before the appointment of Christine Lagarde,

12 See on a more comprehensive discussion of central banker expertise the discussion in Sebastian Heidebrecht, 'Solidifying Consensus. An Inquiry into the Expertise of European Monetary Policy Makers' (2018) 51 Credit and Capital Markets 127.

13 Marion Fourcade, *Economists and Societies* (Princeton University Press 2009).

14 Mark Blyth, *Great Transformations. Economic Ideas and Institutional Change in the Twentieth Century* (CUP 2002).

15 Peter Hall, 'Policy Paradigms, Social Learning, and the State: The Case of Economic Policymaking in Britain' (1993) 25 Comparative Politics 275.

16 Amy Verdun, 'The Role of the Delors Committee in the Creation of EMU: An Epistemic Community?' (1999) 6 Journal of European Public Policy 308; Stefan de Rynck, 'Banking on a Union: The Politics of Changing Eurozone Banking Supervision' (2016) 23 Journal of European Public Policy 119.

17 See for a comprehensive discussion of the following data especially, Heidebrecht (n 12).

found European central banking to be a male business (with only four women having served on the ECB's Governing Council out of more than 70 persons). More than 80% of them hold their highest degree in economics (when counting the French École nationale d'administration), followed by degrees in law especially among central bankers from Germany and Austria. Close to 50% even have PhDs in economics. On average, European central bankers have one-third of their career experience in non-policy making positions within central banks, approximately 20% of their career experience in national finance ministries, and 17% of career experience in academic faculties of economics. Less than 10% of their career experience is, on average, in finance (7%) and business (1%), with literally no experience in labour organizations, but about 8% in international or European supranational organizations, like especially the International Monetary Fund (IMF) and the World Bank, as well as the European Commission (Figures 5.1 and 5.2).

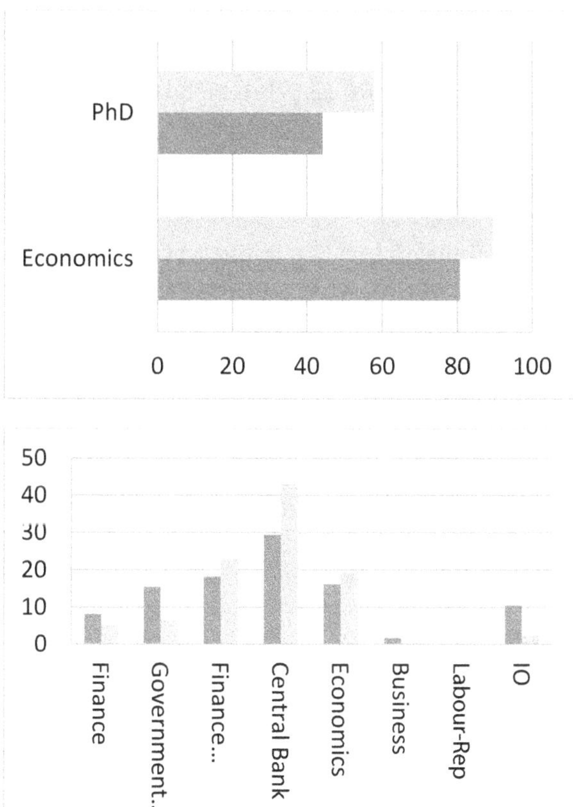

Figures 5.1 and 5.2 Data on Central Banker Expertise, scaled in percentage points (grey for ECB Executive Board and dark grey bars for ECB Governing Council, 1999–2018).

Source: Own data and presentation.

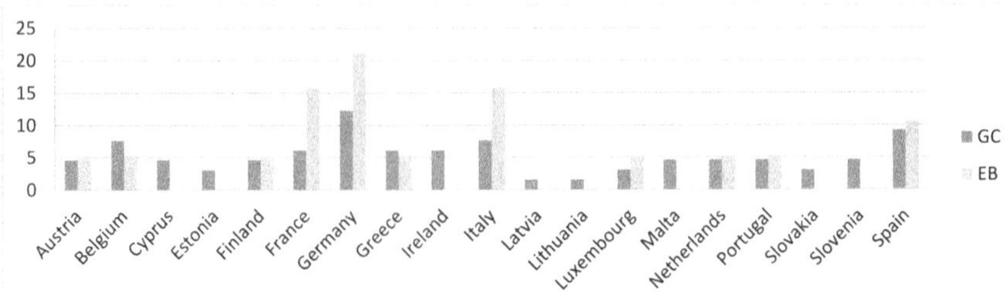

Figure 5.3 Data on Central Banker Nationality, scaled in percentage points (grey bars for ECB Executive Board (EB) and dark grey bars for ECB Governing Council (GC), 1999–2018).

Source: Own data and presentation.

At first sight, these patterns seem in line with today's economic common sense, which states that central banks should be independent institutions run exclusively by qualified economic experts. Article 283 TFEU therefore states that the appointment of central bankers shall be based exclusively on technical (economic) expertise. However, biographical data on the career paths of leading central bankers reveal issues of revolving doors with the private and the political sector. They raise doubts on the application of the technical selection principle and suggest the relevance of other or additional criteria. While relations of ECB officials with the financial sector are often publicly discussed,[18] data on career experience do not indicate on average – compared to other experience – strong or increasing importance of career backgrounds in the financial sector. More important and equally conflicting with principles of expertise-based selection criteria are revolving doors that involve career backgrounds in professional politics, including central bankers that served as member of national parliaments, hold positions as pivotal as that of Minister or even Prime Minister. The appointment of Christine Lagarde and Luis de Guindos as President and Vice President of the ECB are among the most prominent recent examples of more political appointments, but more than 20% of ECB Governing Council members have been professional politicians. This quite political trend is underlined by national representation patterns (Figure 5.3). There is a clear dominance of larger Member States on the ECB's Governing Council compared with a relatively modest representation of the smaller and newer Member States. Top ECB appointments clearly reflect an informal consensus among the four largest EMU Member States (France, Germany, Italy and Spain) to permanently maintain one national representative on ECB's Executive Board.[19] It shows that appointments

18 Benjamin Braun, 'Two Sides of the Same Coin? Independence and Accountability of the European Central Bank' (2017) Report for Transparency International EU.

19 David Howarth and Peter Loedel, *The European Central Bank: The New European Leviathan?* (Palgrave Macmillan 2004); Jean Pisani-Ferry, 'There is Room for Improvement in the Appointment of ECB Executive Board Members' (2006) Bruegel Policy Contribution.

are not exclusively based on technical economic expertise, but that they are also driven by European politics. This observation raises further doubts about the acclaimed comprehensive political independence of the ECB.

4 The increasing importance of the European Central Bank's accountability

The transfer of expert knowledge into policy involves politics (e.g. in the selection of experts or the design of institutions with expert authority), and technocratic institutions like the ECB require accountability to secure legitimacy.[20] Even independent central banks should be perceived as legitimate by the people. This is especially important for the ECB, whose legitimacy rests foremost on its accountability with the EP. The ECB cannot ignore its perceived legitimacy by the people because shrinking public support can trigger political backlashes, which can involve in the EU also international conflicts. This could also endanger its capacity to effectively maintain price stability.[21] Legitimacy is commonly thought of as a multidimensional concept that can be analytically distinguished into three types. Building on Scharpf's canonical distinction between the input and output dimension of legitimacy,[22] Schmidt adds a third analytical category, namely throughput legitimacy.[23] In a nutshell, input legitimacy depends on citizens expressing demands institutionally and deliberatively through representative politics. These should respect their sense of identity and community and allow for constructive support of the citizens. In the intergovernmental model, input legitimacy rests typically on Member State parliaments, whereas in the supranational model, like the one of the ECB, input legitimacy rests on the EP.[24] Output legitimacy mainly requires policies to work effectively. In case of the ECB, output legitimacy rests on its ability to reach effectively its key goal of maintaining price stability (Article 127(1) TFEU). Throughput legitimacy relates to the institutional and governance processes of the EU. According to Schmidt,[25] it 'encompasses the myriad ways in which the policy-making processes work both institutionally and constructively to ensure the efficacy of EU governance, the accountability of those engaged in making the

20 See on the concepts discussed in Section 4 also the discussion in Sebastian Heidebrecht, 'Balancing Independence and Legitimacy: How the European Parliament Holds the European Central Bank to Account' (2019) 29 Zeitschrift für Politikwissenschaft 393.

21 Erik Jones, 'Output Legitimacy and the Global Financial Crisis: Perceptions Matter' (2009) 47 Journal of Common Market Studies 1085; Francisco Torres, 'The EMU's Legitimacy and the ECB as a Strategic Political Player in the Crisis Context' (2013) 35 Journal of European Integration 287.

22 Fritz W. Scharpf, *Governing Europe* (OUP 1999).

23 Vivien A. Schmidt, 'Democracy and Legitimacy in the European Union Revisited: Input, Output and "Throughput"' (2013) 61 Political Studies 2.

24 European Central Bank, Monthly Bulletin (2002) November; European Central Bank, Economic Bulletin (2018) No 5; Ben Crum, 'Parliamentary Accountability in Multilevel Governance: What Role for Parliaments in Postcrisis EU Economic Governance?' (2018) 25 Journal of European Public Policy 268, 270.

25 Schmidt (n 23) 7.

decisions, the transparency of the information and the inclusiveness and openness to "civil society"'. This links the important throughput dimension especially to the accountability framework in place between the ECB and the EP.

The important point of these different legitimacy dimensions is that while the input and output dimension have been especially important until the euro crisis, the ECB relies especially on its throughput legitimacy and therefore on accountability in the subsequent period. In a first phase, the ECB could rely on input legitimacy that the institution received from the signing and ratification of the Maastricht Treaty by Member States in accordance with their constitutional requirements, which laid out the framework for the prospective ECB. As a very independent central bank, its public support rested until the euro crisis especially on the central bank's output legitimacy. As Högenauer and Howarth show,[26] this kind of legitimacy of the ECB was defended by its proponents, including Majone and Moravcsik,[27] especially by three elements, namely (1) the presence of (and adherence to) a clear mandate assigned by national governments, (2) the absence of (highly visible) redistributive effects and (3) the low political salience of ECB policies. Compliance with all three of these elements is a prerequisite for the ECB to enjoy reliance on its output legitimacy. However, in the period after the euro crisis, the ECB no longer complies with the three prerequisites of its output legitimacy. Political decisions for institutional expansion and the Central Bank's unconventional monetary policy blur the lines between monetary and fiscal policy.[28] Its new tasks as a *de facto* lender of last resort and its political role as government adviser indicate an expansion of its clear and narrow mandate.[29] Meanwhile, the political salience of the ECB's policies increased,[30] while the rate of people reporting distrust in the Central Bank increased from 24% in 1999 to 42% in late 2018.[31] In sum, these developments undermine the prerequisites of

26 Anna-Lena Högenauer and David Howarth, 'The Democratic Deficit and European Central Bank Crisis Monetary Policies' (2019) 26 Maastricht Journal of European and Comparative Law 82.

27 Giandomenico Majone, 'Europe's "Democratic Deficit": The Question of Standards' (1998) 4 European Law Journal 5; Andrew Moravcsik, 'Reassessing Legitimacy in the European Union' (2002) 40 Journal of Common Market Studies 603.

28 Clement Fontan, Francois Claveau and Peter Dietsch, 'Central Banking and Inequalities: Taking Off the Blinders' (2016) 15 Politics, Philosophy & Economics 319; Anna-Lena Högenauer and David Howarth, 'Unconventional Monetary Policies and the European Central Bank's Problematic Democratic Legitimacy' (2016) 71 Zeitschrift für öffentliches Recht 81; Högenauer and Howarth (n 26), 6 et seq.

29 Willem Buiter and Ebrahim Rahbari, 'The European Central Bank as Lender of Last Resort for Sovereigns in the Eurozone' (2012) 50 Journal of Common Market Studies 6; Paul De Grauwe and Yuemei Yi, 'Correcting for Eurozone Design Failures: The Role of the ECB' (2015) 37 Journal of European Integration 739; Chang (n 1).

30 Tobias Tesche, 'Instrumentalizing EMU's Democratic Deficit: The ECB's Unconventional Accountability Measures During the Eurozone Crisis' (2019) 4 Journal of European Integration 447, 5 et seq.

31 European Commission, Standard Eurobarometer of November 2018 <ec.europa.eu/commfrontoffice/publicopinion/index.cfm/Chart/getChart/themeKy/7/groupKy/14> accessed 20 March 2020.

ECB's output legitimacy for effectively maintaining price stability. Accordingly, in the period after the euro crisis, the ECB's legitimacy relies increasingly on throughput by means of its accountability to the EP.

Accountability itself is a multidimensional concept. It can be defined, in accordance with Bovens,[32] as a relationship between an actor and a forum, in which the actor is obliged to explain and justify his conduct, whereas the forum can pose questions; pass judgement, and the actor may face consequences. Assessments of the appropriateness of central bank accountability have to respect that the concept combines normative and functional dimensions.[33] More precisely, on the one hand, the idea to delegate monetary policy to economic experts in independent central banks follows a functional logic of effectiveness and requires appropriate accountability to avoid political backlashes against its independent mandate.[34] On the other hand, a normative understanding in terms of democratic legitimacy requires the representation of the people affected by decisions, and assesses appropriate central bank accountability in terms of its responsiveness to citizen concerns.[35] The challenge for the ECB's accountability framework is that it has to balance the requirements of central bank independence (to secure its output legitimacy) and demands of democratic legitimacy (allowing for citizen representation and responsiveness). The problem is that while central bank independence and central bank legitimacy are mutually dependent on each other, their underlying logics (effectiveness and democratic legitimacy) are sometimes conflictive. The accountability framework has to balance this trade-off between effectiveness and democratic legitimacy; both too strong and too weak accountability endanger central bank independence. If too weak, accountability increases the probability of political backlashes against the Central Bank's independent mandate, because the people may feel that their democratic interests are not adequately represented. If too strong, accountability risks politicising monetary policy, so that politicians get more influence. This could be problematic for the legal prohibition of political influence (Article 130 TFEU), and challenge core principles of central bank independence.

5 Accountability between the European Central Bank and the European Parliament

The ECB's accountability rests especially on its relationship with the EP.[36] Despite its increasing importance, the legal framework has not been expanded. Article 284(3) TFEU and Article 15.3 of the Statute of the European System of Central Banks and of the European Central Bank (ESCB/ECB Statute) define explicit accountability obligations. These legal obligations imply special rights for the

32 Mark Bovens, 'Analysing and Assessing Accountability: A Conceptual Framework' (2007) 13 European Law Journal 447.

33 Mark Bovens, 'Two Concepts of Accountability: Accountability as a Virtue and as a Mechanism' (2010) 33 West European Politics 946.

34 Jones (n 21).

35 Torres (n 21).

36 See on the data presented in Section 5 also the discussion in Heidebrecht (n 20).

President of the Council and the European Commission, while the ECB is in the eyes of most observers (including the ECB itself) 'primarily', or 'first and foremost' accountable to the EP in its role as direct representation of the European citizens.[37] The interpretation of the ECB's primary accountability to the EP is in line with legal and political arguments, namely that the transfer of executive powers to independent experts on the supranational level requires new sources of (input) legitimacy, provided by the supranational EP.[38] As Torres argues,[39] the EP is the logical supranational choice as it is *a priori* less affected by domestic (debt-biased) vested interests and political business cycles than the Council. Oppositions to national governments are also represented in the EP and may well have different opinions on the central bank policy issue under discussion. This can allow a broader representation of perspectives and preferences in the ECB's key accountability forum.

The accountability framework of the ECB can be divided into *formal* and *informal* accountability channels.[40] *Informal* channels comprise especially reporting and information practices, allowing the ECB to explain and justify its conduct. They are not legally formalised, such as press conferences, the publication of its 'Economic Bulletin', weekly financial statements, accounts of the ECB's monetary policy meetings, and other communication with the public through articles, interviews and speeches. The *formal* accountability channels are foremost outlined in the TFEU and the ESCB/ECB Statute. The actual practice of accountability between the two institutions has evolved since the establishment of EMU and is partly codified in the Rules of Procedure (RoP) of the 9th EP.[41] The *formal* accountability framework comprises three accountability channels, namely hearings and exchanges of views, written questions from Members of the European Parliament (MEPs) to the ECB, and the presentation of the ECB's annual report in the EP. A fourth channel, though not formally considered part of the central bank's accountability, is the EP's role in the appointment process of central bankers.[42] The first two channels have in common that they are basically of an informative nature, while the latter two involve the drafting of a report by the EP. Because of these common features, I discuss in the following their characteristics broken down into the two sets of formalised accountability channels in place between the ECB and the EP. See Table 5.1 for an overview.

37 European Central Bank 2002 (n 24) 51; Jean Claude Trichet, 'Introductory Statement. Hearing at the Committee on Economic and Monetary, Affairs of the European Parliament' Brussels 4 October 2011; European Central Bank 2018 (n 24) 49.

38 Crum (n 24) 270.

39 Torres (n 21) 296.

40 See for a recent presentation European Central Bank 2018 (n 24).

41 European Parliament 2019–2024, Rules of Procedure 9th parliamentary term, December 2019.

42 See on this point also Michele Chang, 'The Constraints of Central Bank Independence: The European Central Bank's Unconventional Monetary Policy and Incremental Accountability in the Euro Crisis' (2019) 15 Journal of Contemporary European Research 143, 156.

Table 5.1 Overview of key ECB accountability channels

Key Accountability Channels of ECB Monetary Policy	
Formal Accountability Channels (and formal arrangements)	*Additional Accountability Channels (Mostly of informational nature allowing the ECB to explain its conduct)*
Hearings and exchanges of views *(Article 284(3) TFEU; Rule 135 of EP's RoP)*	Press conferences
Written questions *(Rule 140 and 141 of EP's RoP, and Annex III RoP)*	Economic Bulletin
Annual Report *(Article 284(3) TFEU; Rule 135 of EP's RoP; Article 15(3) of the ESCB/ECB Statute)*	Weekly financial statements *(Article 15(2) of the ESCB/ECB Statute)*
EP Opinion on Appointments *(Article 283 TFEU; Rule 130 of EP's RoP)*	Accounts of monetary policy meetings
	Articles, interviews and speeches

5.1 *Exchanges of views and written questions*

According to Article 284(3) TFEU, the President of the ECB and the other members of the Executive Board have to participate in hearings and exchanges of views with the EP. The details of this framework are further defined in Rule 135 of EP's RoP. Accordingly, the ECB's President participates in quarterly hearings before the Committee on Economic and Monetary Affairs (ECON), which is often referred to as the 'monetary dialogue'.[43] Other Executive Board members also participate in ECON Committee hearings and explain ECB's reasoning and decisions on specific topics. In the context of the monetary dialogues, debates in ECON are led by the committee's chair and usually last approximately two hours.[44] During these meetings, approximately twenty MEPs ask questions. To gain additional information, every MEP can also submit questions to the ECB for written answer. This arrangement was created in the early 2000s by mutual agreement between the ECB and the EP and is currently formalised in Rule 140 of the 9th Parliament's RoP. Accordingly, the number of written questions is restricted to six questions per month per individual MEP. In accordance with Annex III of the EP's RoP, the written questions have to comply with specific criteria, *inter alia* not to exceeding 200 words; questions and answers provided by the ECB are published on the institutions' websites.[45]

43 Stefan Collignon and Sebastian Diessner, 'The ECB's Monetary Dialogue with the European Parliament: Efficiency and Accountability During the Euro Crisis?' (2016) 54 Journal of Common Market Studies 1296.

44 Ibid.

45 Written questions and answers are available online on the EP's website under the following link: <https://www.europarl.europa.eu/committees/en/econ/documents/search; and on the website of the ECB under the following link: https://www.ecb.europa.eu/pub/pub/intco/html/index.en.html> accessed 3 May 2020.

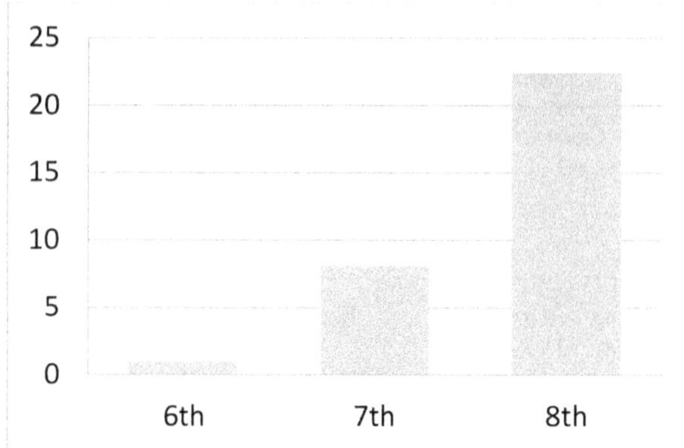

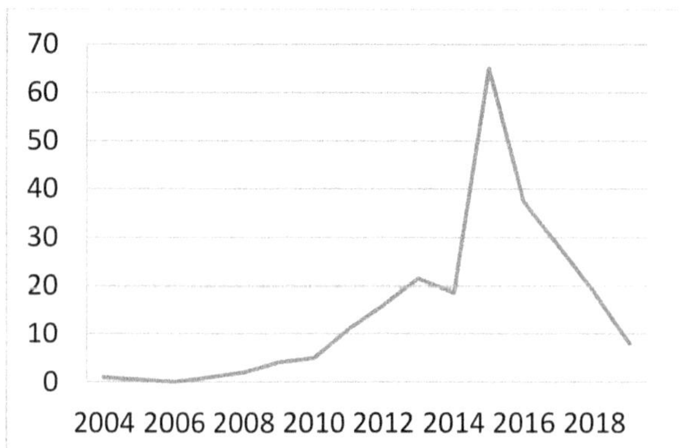

Figures 5.4 and 5.5 Relative frequency of MEP's written questions to the ECB.

Source: Own presentation and data. Note that the numbers are normalised to 6th term = 1 and 2004 = 1, respectively.

Generally, the frequency and usage of both channels increased, with a special importance around the peak of the financial crisis. Because the formal rules of the monetary dialogue are not significantly changed since its establishment, the frequencies of quarterly hearings and oral questions raised by MEPs have been approximately stable over time. However, especially in the context of important crisis related events between 2011 and 2015, more than ten extraordinary meetings with ECB Executive Board members (including its President) took place, and exchanges of views at staff level happen more frequently.[46] The usage of written questions also increased substantially over the last two parliamentary terms. A first significant increase can be reported for the 7th parliamentary term and especially for the period subsequent to the euro crisis (see Figures 5.4 and 5.5).

46 European Central Bank, Annual Report of 2011, 145 et seq.; European Central Bank, Annual Report of 2012, 148; European Central Bank, Annual Report of 2013, 164; European Central Bank, Annual Report of 2014, 95; European Central Bank, Annual Report of 2015, 90.

However, the amount of written questions peaked in 2015, and decreased afterwards. This might reflect a shift of MEP priorities before the end of the legislative term (e.g. to be more present in campaigning or to finalize pressing reports), a generally decline of importance of this accountability channel because the euro crisis felt less pressing, or both.

The content of the exchanges of views and written questions follows topics on the political agenda. Before meetings in the context of the monetary dialogue, the EP asks an expert panel of mostly economists and political scientists to provide briefing papers on one or two specific topics.[47] These papers are also published on EP's website shortly before the meeting and it is common practice that the ECB addresses these topics in the ECON Committee debate. Recent data provided by the ECB reveal that MEPs tend to seek expert advice on reform proposals under discussion.[48] Consequently, they asked for advice on institutional and financial sector policies in the 7th term during the negotiations about the so-called Banking Union, or European financial assistance programmes in the aftermath of the financial crisis. The content of written questions follows a similar trend. While the largest number of questions relate to monetary policy (41% in the 8th term), questions about the Banking Union and related matters (like institutional or financial policies) were especially prominent in the 7th term. In the 8th term, MEPs became increasingly interested in the ECB's role in the Greece assistance programme (an increase from 12% to 23% from the 7th to the 8th term). Questions addressed *inter alia* controversial aspects like the precise functioning and rationale for the eligibility rules applied to Greek bonds used as collateral in Eurosystem monetary policy operations.[49]

Political factors like partisanship and nationality can help to explain the usage of accountability channels by MEPs. Smaller party groups from the far left and right political spectrum are especially active in submitting written questions to the ECB (see Figure 5.6). This is especially true for GUE/NGL group, the Non-Inscrits (NI) in the 7th term, and the ENF group that was formed in the 8th term and comprises many of the former NIs, as well as to a smaller extent also for the EFDD group. The other side of this coin is that the larger party groups, especially the S&D in the 7th and the EPP group in the 8th term are relatively strongly underrepresented. These patterns reflect in part the fact that smaller party groups receive less time for questions in the monetary dialogue, so they seek to compensate by written questions (also because they might want to gain information that is otherwise available only to party groups represented in national governments).[50] Further, ideologically more left or right party groups might be more critical about business as usual and therefore and request

47 Collignon and Diessner (n 43).

48 European Central Bank 2018 (n 24).

49 Ibid 68.

50 See on this point for instance Christian Jensen, Sven-Oliver Proksch and Jonathan B Slapin, 'Parliamentary Questions, Oversight, and National Opposition Status in the European Parliament' (2013) 38 Legislative Studies Quarterly 259.

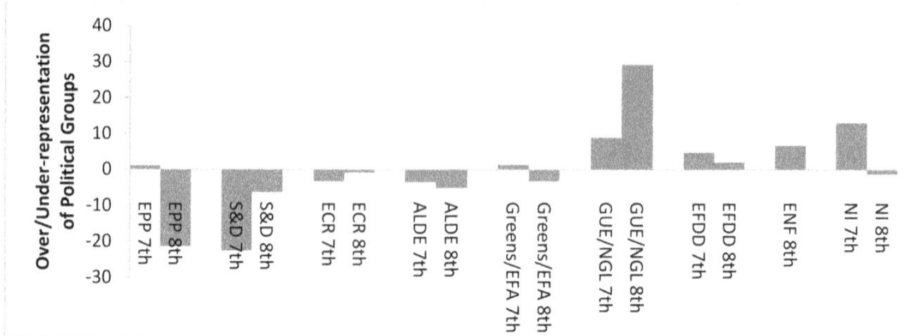

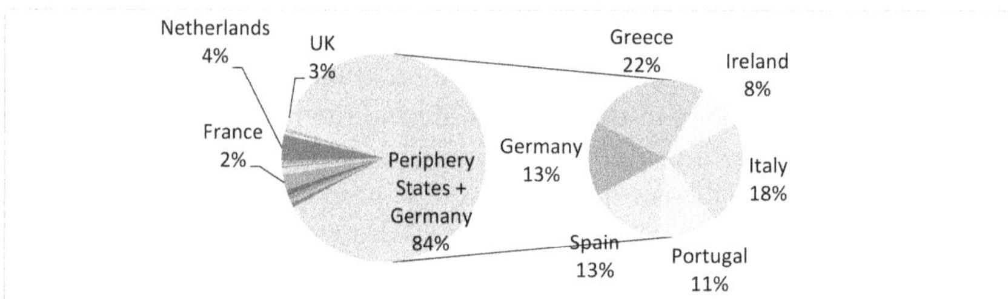

Figures 5.6 and 5.7 Over/Under-representation of political groups in the EP (± percentage points for 7th and 8th term) and distribution of written questions by nationality of MEPs (1st until 8th term).

Source: Own presentation and data. Note: Only member states with a share bigger than 2% are displayed in Figure 5.7.

information on practices they find controversial, like for instance the ECB's role in financial assistance programmes.

The nationality of the MEPs plays a clear role in the patterns of usage of accountability channels. The distribution of questions with regard to nationality shows that 84% are from MEPs of just six countries: Germany, Greece, Ireland, Italy, Portugal and Spain (see Figure 5.7). This shows that MEPs from programme countries in particular make use of this accountability mechanism. This pattern holds when controlled for total representation in Parliament. Also, German MEPs are among the most active (but not over proportionally active in relation to their total group size). The German case indicates also the ambiguity and political dynamics of written questions. Especially in context of the crisis, ECB policy was very controversially discussed in Germany. On the one hand, a relatively large share of questions (20%) was submitted by MEPs of the ECR group (especially former German Eurosceptic AfD members) criticizing the ECB for expanding or overstepping its narrow mandate of maintaining price stability. On the other hand, the majority of questions were submitted by MEPs from Greens/EFA (28%) and the GUE/NGL group (38%), demanding more transparency and accountability and criticizing the ECB for more or less the exact opposite, namely for being too hawkish. The usage of exchanges of views and written questions highlights the political demand for increased central bank accountability. It also shows that the ECB may be confronted with more ideological, partisan and national interests, so that it is important for its accountability framework to mediate these dimensions without impairing its independence.

5.2 *Drafting of reports on ECB's annual report and on the appointment of central bankers*

While the herarings and written questions mainly encourage informative exchange between the two institutions, appointments and the presentation of ECB's annual report imply drafting of and voting on reports in the EP. It drafts a report on the occasion of the presentation of the ECB's annual report and the appointment process of central bankers. Article 284(3) TFEU and Article 15(3) of the ESCB/ECB Statute oblige the ECB to report on its activities and monetary policy in an annual report to the EP. The details of this framework in the EP are further defined in Rule 135 of its RoP. The report is presented each year in the EP by the Vice-President of the ECB in a dedicated session of the ECON Committee and by the ECB President on the occasion of a plenary debate. Prior to the debate on the presentation of the annual report by the ECB's President, ECON drafts a report following the own-initiative procedure and the EP adopts a resolution. The President of the ECB can address the report in his introductory speech, which shall allow for a more substantial dialogue of the two institutions.

The EP has only a consultative role in the process of appointments for ECB's Executive Board, including its President and Vice-President. The appointment procedure is defined in Article 283(2) TFEU. Accordingly, the ECB's Executive Board is appointed by the European Council, which acts by a qualified majority, on a recommendation of the Council, after it has consulted the EP and the Governing Council of the ECB. Within the EP, in accordance with Rule 130 of its RoP, it is the ECON that drafts a proposal for an EP decision on the Council's recommendation as a non-legislative enactment. It is common practice that the ECON chair drafts the proposal and that the candidate nominated by the Council for the Executive Board of the ECB appears in ECON to make a statement and answer questions of ECON members. After approval in the ECON Committee, the EP's full plenary votes on the report. While it could be argued that the EP has a mere decorative role, the procedure allows the EP to comment on appointments, scrutinize candidates in hearings and thereby also articulate own political opinions.

The application of these mechanisms allows the EP to act in its role as the ECB's accountability forum and to articulate policy preferences as the representation of the European citizens. Drafting of reports on the ECB's annual reports and on appointments allows for bargaining within the EP and for contestation of ECB's activities along political dimensions such as partisanship. Although the resolutions are non-binding, the processes involve formal debates and votes in committee and full plenary. The amendment process allows MEPs to discuss and vote on broad issues around central banking and the ECB's role in economic

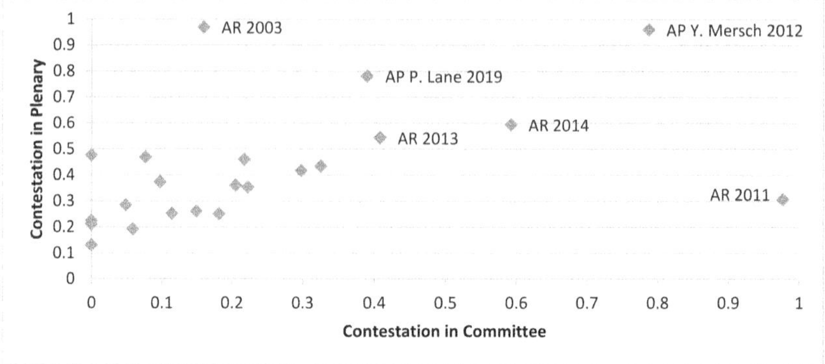

Figure 5.8 Contestation of ECB in accountability reports in committee and plenary.

Source: Own data and calculation. The index presents the ratio of Yes- to No-Votes in committee and plenary, following $C = 1 - (\Upsilon(x) - N(x))/(\Upsilon(x) + N(x))$, where '$C$' denotes contestation, 'Υ' and 'N' the number of yes or no votes respectively. Note: Only the most pronounced cases are labelled. 'AR' refers to EP's reports on ECB Annual Reports; 'AP' refers to Reports on Appointments. Higher numbers indicate more contestation.

and monetary governance in the EMU. This is especially the case for reports on the ECB's annual report, whose relevance for MEPs is *inter alia* reflected in the number of tabled amendments. For the EP reports on ECB's annual reports, on average the figures more than tripled since 2010 (from around 75 to around 240 tabled amendments), excluding a peak of amendments in 2016 (568 amendments). With regard to appointments, amendments were only tabled for the report on the process concerning Yves Mersch in 2012 (5 amendments).[51] However, an index-based comparison of the voting patterns on the two kinds of reports reveals that one is not per se more contested than the other, nor that the reports are more contested over time (see Figure 5.8).

The voting patterns in the EP reveal the importance of political factors like partisanship, ideological tone of the respective report (e.g. more keynesian or more monetarist) and the political salience of the topic under discussion. Given their relatively comprehensive coverage, especially the reports on the ECB's annual report allow MEPs to express opinions on ECB activities and evaluate past behaviour. Therefore, they can be considered as the most important accountability mechanism available to the EP.[52] *Inter alia*, this takes the form of political debates about more general questions such as whether European relative economic weakness was caused by a lack of structural reforms or a lack of aggregate demand (as in case of the debate around the ECB's annual

51 Heidebrecht (n 20).

52 See on this point also Stanislas Jourdan and Sebastian Diessner, 'From Dialogue to Scrutiny: Strengthening the Parliamentary Oversight of the European Central Bank' (2019) Report of Positive Money Europe.

report of 2003). Throughout the euro crisis, debates included questions about potentially positive and negative effects of unconventional monetary policy and the ECB's role in EMU's economic governance regime (as in case of the debate about ECB's annual report of 2011). Opinion on these aspects often varies with MEPs' position on the political left-right spectrum. For instance, the three most controversial reports (according to our index, see above) on the ECB's annual reports (for 2003, 2011 and 2014) are the ones not drafted by an MEP from the centre Grand Coalition of the European People's Party (EPP), the Progressive Alliance of Socialists and Democrats (S&D) and the Liberal Group (in 2003 by a member of Greens–European Free Alliance, 2011 by a member of European United Left–Nordic Green Left and 2014 by a member of the European Conservatives and Reformists Group). Since 2010, the reports have always been written by a MEP from programme countries (namely: Greece 1, Italy 1, Portugal 1 and Spain 5), indicating special national interests.

The debates about EP's reports on appointments are less driven by partisanship and ideological tone and more concerned instead with questions of gender of the candidate in particular, because female underrepresentation is a key issue. The gender question made the appointment of Yves Mersch the most controversial report, which eventually led to a – though non-binding – rejection of the candidate by the EP. However, Mersch's appointment was only delayed and the European Council subsequently still approved it. This, once again, highlights the absence of enforceable consequences on the side of the EP, and thereby its relatively weak powers in the appointment process. Eventually, female representation remains a key concern, and the EP complains that the European Council has not taken this issue seriously.[53] Further, the EP scrutinises the political independence of the candidates, and raises concerns for instance in the case of Luis de Guindos, appointed as ECB Vice-President in 2018, asking about his political independence because he was serving Minister of Economy in Spain.[54]

To sum up, EP's accountability channels do not allow to impose any consequences on the ECB (thereby respecting the principle of central bank independence). However, the drafting of reports on ECB's annual report and on appointments do allow MEPs to argue about appropriate central bank policy, and to bargain for specific aspects when drafting and voting on the report on ECB's annual report. Especially the appointment process suffers from EP's weak position and the practice of the European Council to present only one candidate to the EP, which even reduces its non-binding position even further to a mere yes-no answer. Accordingly, especially the process of drafting a report on ECB's annual report allows MEPs to discuss central bank policy and can be a relatively important accountability channel that allows the EP to criticise the ECB and to articulate own policy positions.

53 European Parliament, European Central Bank: appointment of a member of the Executive Board 2019/0801(NLE).

54 European Parliament, European Central Bank: appointment of Vice-President, 2018/0804(NLE).

5.3 *The ECB's accountability in the Banking Union*

The competences of the ECB expanded after the euro crisis and comprise now also new tasks for financial supervision in context of the European Banking Union. Especially the problems of several Euro area periphery countries and their banking systems in the years after 2009 revealed the weakness of the European System of Financial Supervision (ESFS) to address the sovereign debt-bank 'doom-loop'. Due to the euro crisis, increasing levels of sovereign debt stressed financial stability of national banking systems because they were closely linked to Member States' ability to servicing debt at sustainable interest rates. When financial markets demanded higher interest rates as a consequence of the crisis, cross-border spillover effects further threatened financial stability of the entire Eurozone because the single currency had enforced financial integration and increased cross-border banking.[55] The resulting euro crisis made policy makers aware of the absence of a credible European architecture of financial supervision, the non-existence of a European fiscal capacity and the lack of a normal central bank to act as Lender of Last Resort. In other words, the euro crisis revealed a mismatch between the European scope of banking and national responsibility for financial stability.[56] The resulting reforms empowered the ECB and call for adjustments of its accountability framework with national parliaments and the EP.

ECB empowerment started in June 2012, when the European Council agreed to the creation of the Banking Union and the European Commission launched a number of initiatives to institutionalise a single supervisory mechanism (SSM), single resolution mechanism and the single rulebook. A common deposit insurance scheme is by time of writing still under discussion. The choice of the ECB at the centre of the SSM was the most straightforward in that it could be based on Article 127 (6) TFEU and therefore would not require an EU-Treaty change.[57] Accordingly, European financial supervision, the SSM, was delegated through the SSM Regulation (hereafter SSM-R) to the ECB.[58] Now, the ECB acts as the European financial supervisor in cooperation with national supervisory authorities and directly supervises the largest and most important banks of the Euro area since 2014. However, the delegation of supervisory authority to the ECB implies potential conflicts of interest between its monetary and supervisory powers, because the newly assigned tasks turn the ECB into a supervisor

55 David Howarth and Lucia Quaglia, 'The Steep Road to European Banking Union: Constructing the Single Resolution Mechanism' (2014) 52 Journal of Common Market Studies 125, 128.

56 Shawn Donnelly, 'Power Politics and the Undersupply of Financial Stability in Europe' (2011) 21(4) Review of International Political Economy 980.

57 Gabriel Glöckler, Johannes Lindner and Marion Salines, 'Explaining the Sudden Creation of a Banking Supervisor for the Euro Area' (2017) 24 Journal of European Public Policy 1135.

58 Council Regulation 1024/2013 of 15 October 2013 conferring specific tasks on the European Central Bank concerning policies relating to the prudential supervision of credit institutions [2013] OJ L 287/63.

with access to central bank liquidity. This can be problematic because its knowledge acquired through its supervisory tasks about weaknesses in banks' balance sheets could force the central bank to relax its monetary policy in order to save banks in the short run. This could then turn into more financial instability in the longer run, generate inflationary bias and impair its monetary policy credibility. Therefore, in line with Article 19(3) SSM-R, the ECB has to ensure the separation of supervisory and monetary policy tasks, which are carried out independently, in order to avoid conflicts of interest. The ECB's decision-making bodies have to discuss monetary policy and supervisory issues in separate meetings and staff members who directly contribute to monetary policy are organisationally separated from those contributing to financial supervision.

The establishment of the Banking Union is certainly among the most significant steps in European economic integration since the introduction of the Euro. Thus, policymakers were aware that the institutionalization of the SSM under the auspices of the ECB requires the set-up of a complex accountability mechanism. The SSM-R explicitly demands that 'any shift of supervisory powers from the Member States to the Union level should be balanced by appropriate transparency and accountability requirements' (Recital 55 SSM-R). The accountability framework has to allow for effective banking supervision that is separated from ECB's monetary policy tasks. It has further to take into account the stronger participation of Member States (whose supervisory authorities are involved in the supervisory operations) and to balance these demands with the must to secure ECB's independence. The challenge for an appropriate accountability framework is that financial supervision was delegated from the national to an independent European institution, while strong independence is typical for monetary policy but not an automatic impulse for financial supervision.[59]

The solution was that the ECB's accountability in the Banking Union resembles its accountability framework in the area of monetary policy, with two main differences. First, the SSM's Supervisory Board is accountable to a larger range of actors, including the Eurogroup and national parliaments. While ECB's annual report is sent to the EP, the European Commission, the Council and the European Council, the SSM's annual report is also sent to the Eurogroup and national parliaments of Euro area Member States (Articles 20-21 SSM-R). In reaction, national parliaments may address their 'reasoned observations' to that report, and may request the ECB to reply in writing to any observations or questions submitted by them, and they can request face-to-face exchanges of view with the Chair or a member of the Supervisory Board in relation to the supervision of credit institutions in their jurisdiction.[60] The EP can request

59 Michele Chang, 'The Constraints of Central Bank Independence: The European Central Bank's Unconventional Monetary Policy and Incremental Accountability in the Euro Crisis' (2019) 15(2) Journal of Contemporary European Research 143, 156.

60 Article 21 SSM-R; see also Diane Fromage and Renato Ibrido, 'The "Banking Dialogue" as a Model to Improve Parliamentary Involvement in the Monetary Dialogue?' (2018) 40 Journal of European Integration 295.

additional meetings as well.[61] Second, while the EP has for the appointments of the ECB's President only a consultive (and thus non-binding) role, the EP received confirmatory powers for the appointments for the SSM chair and vice-chair (Article 26(3) SSM-R). Noteworthy, it is common practice that the ECB provides the EP with a shortlist of candidates,[62] so that the EP's deliberation on appointments can go substantially beyond a mere 'yes or no' question, which is the case in the area of monetary policy. This constitutes an improvement of the democratic quality of the appointment procedure of the independent experts that are responsible for financial supervision. However, a problem of accountability in the area of banking supervision is that it is difficult for outsiders to assess the performance of the experts in the SSM, because they lack a clear benchmark and might require access to confidential information on private banks' operations for their assessments. In order to improve transparency and accountability of banking supervision, the EP could therefore seek to establish policy or regulatory audit by external experts and secure access to such information on a confidential basis.[63]

6 Conclusion: Politics and technocratic governance

While the powers of the ECB have increased significantly, its legal accountability and transparency framework are not reformed correspondingly. This reveals a mismatch of increased technocratic powers and democratic accountability. On the other hand, data on exchange of views and written questions in the EP document their potential contribution to the informative accountability of the independent experts in the ECB. They allow for transparency and access to information and they provide channels for inter-institutional arguing and exchanges between the two institutions.[64] The EP's reports on the ECB's annual report and on appointments can be (especially the former) constructive channels contributing to the ECB's accountability. However, respecting the principles of central bank independence, they only allow for argumentative dialogue between the two institutions, articulation of criticism of the ECB and political bargaining within the EP. Reports in both areas involve debates, amendments processes and votes at committee and full plenary level. As data on their usage show, especially the EP's reports on the ECB's annual report allow the EP to address a broad set of topics and enable political bargaining between party groups. The EP makes increasing political usage of this channel as it is reflected by the increasing number of tabled amendments and the inclusion of broader concerns of civil society (such as the relationship between climate and finance or concerns about inequalities). To date, the reports on appointments lead to less debates about

61 Chang (n 59).
62 Jourdan and Diessner (n 52).
63 Phedon Nicolaides, 'Accountability of the ECB's Supervisory Activities (SSM): Evolving and Responsive' (2019) 26 Maastricht Journal of European and Comparative Law 136.
64 Heidebrecht (n 20).

policies than those on ECB's annual reports. This is also because of the practice of the Council to submit only one candidate to the EP. The decision on the report takes then the form of a simple and non-binding 'yes or no' question. However, while the EP's decisions are non-binding in both areas, the voting on reports can enhance the substance of the argumentative dialogue with the ECB. The presence of the ECB President in the plenary for the debate about the ECB's annual reports underlines the symbolic weight of this process and can, in principle, allow for a more direct and responsive process of arguing between the experts in the ECB and the MEPs.

The empowerment of technocratic experts in the independent central bank might be effective but it can also be a problematic governance strategy. This is because technocratic empowerment contradicts the logic of democratic legitimacy and can endanger political and in effect also monetary and financial stability. In reaction to this, policy recommendations for increased accountability have been presented by several authors and institutions over the last years. With some variation, they tend to demand a stronger role of the EP in the existing formal accountability framework, call for more transparency and recommend a more important role of the EP in the appointment process of central bankers.[65] With EU-Treaties reform being very unlikely at this moment, recommendations to increase accountability focus more pragmatically on efforts within the EP and unilateral and voluntary efforts of the ECB. While recommendations for the former – notably its Committee of Economic Affairs – include the building-up of own central bank expertise, for instance by establishing a sub-committee on central bank matters, the latter is asked to provide more transparency. Increasing accountability and transparency is even more difficult in context of banking supervision. [66] The quality of supervisory practices cannot reasonably be assessed without access to confidential information on private banks' operations. Holding the ECB to account for its SSM activities might therefore require the set-up of a policy or regulatory audit by external experts who can access such information on a confidential basis.[67]

Overall, from a democratic perspective, a key concern is that the ECB's powers increased significantly without corresponding reforms of its transparency and accountability frameworks. As a reaction to this mismatch, a general recommendation is that the accountability framework of the ECB should be revised. Such a revision process should allow the participation of broader societal groups that are affected by ECB powers (for instance labour representatives). Some more democratic practices, like confirmatory powers of the EP in the appointment process and the expanded participation of parliaments are already exercised in context of the SSM and can therefore inform the reform debate of

65 See on this point for instance Braun (n 18); Jourdan and Diessner (n 52).

66 See for an analysis of ECB's transparency regime within SSM, Florin Coman-Kund, Anastasia Karatzia and Fabian Amtenbrink, 'The Transparency of the European Central Bank in the Single Supervisory Mechanism' (2018) 51 Credit and Capital Markets 51, 55–72.

67 Nicolaides (n 63).

ECB accountability more generally. However, a revision has to take into account the dangers of politicizing central banking by intergovernmental dynamics and acknowledge the special supranational characteristic of monetary policy in a multilevel European polity. Generally, most agree that a revision should contribute to a less hierarchical relationship between central banks, the public and the economy. Such a more democratic accountability framework could also help to avoid political backlashes, and thereby also support ECB's independence, its credibility and eventually also effective monetary policy.

6 The re-organization of the FATF as an international legal person and the promises and limits to accountability

Nathanael Tilahun

1 Introduction

The international anti-money laundering and counter-terrorism financing (AML/CTF) regulatory regime, spearheaded by the Paris-based Financial Action Task Force (FATF), increasingly impacts individuals, corporations and states across the world.[1] States are required to make deep-cutting reforms in their criminal justice, tax, finance, security and intelligence systems, among others. Corporations are forced to commit substantial resources and effort in undertaking what could be characterized as delegated intelligence and enforcement roles for states – undertaking financial intelligence, identifying threats of criminal or terrorist abuse, assessing risk, collecting and passing information on their customers and executing sanctions on designated targets. Individuals, situated at the receiving end of this regime, become affected through targeted action or as inadvertent collateral victims. The typical harm individuals face is the denial of financial services, once they are designated as 'high risk' customers by hyper-cautious financial institutions. There are reports that this 'de-risking' trend has led to significant disruption of access to financial services and foreign currency in several states in Africa, the Caribbean, Central Asia and in the Pacific.[2]

The FATF sits at the center of a global constellation of AML/CTF rule making and monitoring bodies.[3] Like most of these bodies, the FATF is a club-like institution dominated by a select group of like-minded states (37 member states

1 On the general state of confusion regarding what precisely the harm is that AML seeks to address, see Peter Alldridge, *What Went Wrong with Money Laundering Law?* (Palgrave Macmillan 2016).

2 Official surveys quoted by Christine Lagarde, IMF Managing Director, 'Working Together to Fight Money Laundering and Terrorism Financing' (Address to the FATF Plenary Meeting, Valencia, June 2017); IMF, 'Recent Trends in Correspondent Banking Relationships: Further Considerations' (2017) IMF Policy Paper.

3 The broader constellation includes 9 FATF-style regional bodies, the World Bank, the International Monetary Fund (IMF), G20, Global Counterterrorism Forum and others. For more information, see: FATF, 'Members and Observers' <https://www.fatf-gafi.org/about/membersandobservers/> accessed 17 April 2020.

and 2 regional organizations) networking at a ministerial level.[4] Established in 1990 as an anti-money laundering body, the FATF has significantly grown institutionally in the post-9/11 years by adding the mandate of countering terrorism financing. Its core body is a secretariat of experts. The FATF repeatedly states that it is essentially a 'technical body' of experts.[5] The expert secretariat, together with a satellite of external consultants, continually develop normative standards, monitor their implementation worldwide and engage in technical assistance to help states achieve compliance.[6] Having no formal legal existence as an international organization, the FATF's rules (known as 'Recommendations') are legally non-binding but practically observed nearly universally – in fact, by more states than the total membership of the United Nations.[7] The FATF states that 205 jurisdictions have so far made high-level political commitment to its Recommendations, and, by February 2020, in-depth assessment of compliance (known as 'mutual evaluation report') have been conducted in 98 states.[8]

Currently there is a discussion of possible reconstitution of the FATF into a formal (international) legal person. Member states are debating as to precisely what, if any, legal personality and/or capacity the FATF should assume. There seems to exist a consensus on the unsustainability of the current arrangement, whereby the FATF operates essentially as a 'permanent conference'[9] of its members. Taking this debate as a case-study, this chapter discusses the linkage between debates on (international) legal personhood and accountability of informal expert bodies such as the FATF. Specifically, this chapter seeks to answer the question whether formalizing the legal personality of the FATF goes some distance in enhancing its accountability.

Accountability is construed in this chapter not in the legal sense of answerability before a (quasi)-judicial forum, but in the broader socio-legal/political sense of democratic mechanisms whereby stakeholders can scrutinize the activities of an institution. I borrow this concept from two key texts, one is the International Law Association's (ILA) 2004 report on accountability of international

4 See FATF's current mandate, open-ended duration starting from 2019, adopted 12 April 2019 in Washington D.C., available at <https://www.fatf-gafi.org/media/fatf/content/images/FATF-Ministerial-Declaration-Mandate.pdf>.

5 FATF, 'Financial Action Task Force: 30 Years' (Paris, 2019), p. 15, available at <https://www.fatf-gafi.org/media/fatf/documents/brochuresannualreports/FATF30-(1989-2019).pdf> accessed 17 April 2020; Tom Keatinge, 'The Financial Action Task Force Should Embrace the Opportunity to Reform' (*Commentary*, 25 June 2019) < https://rusi.org/commentary/financial-action-task-force-should-embrace-opportunity-reform> accessed 17 April 2020.

6 See FATF mandate 2019 (n 4).

7 Remarks of David Lewis, FATF Executive Secretary, the 50th Meeting of MONEYVAL (Strasbourg, 12 April 2016).

8 FATF, 'Consolidated Table of Assessment Ratings' (13 February 2020) available at <http://www.fatf-gafi.org/media/fatf/documents/4th-Round-Ratings.pdf>.

9 To borrow a term from Richard Collins and Nigel White, 'Moving Beyond the Autonomy-Accountability Dichotomy: Reflections on Institutional Independence in the International Legal Order' (2010) 7 Int'l organizations law Review 1.

organizations,[10] the other is Ruth Grant and Robert Keohane's seminal article titled *Accountability and Abuses of Power in World Politics.*[11] The ILA report conceptualizes accountability of international organizations as a multi-level process of scrutiny involving legal, political, administrative or financial tools. One important process of accountability is described by ILA as 'the extent to which international organizations (...) are and should be subject to, or should exercise, forms of *internal and external scrutiny and monitoring*, irrespective of potential and subsequent liability and/or responsibility'.[12] The essential element in this understanding of accountability is the existence of an actor, whether inside or outside the organization, that is positioned to contest, challenge, or put procedural or substantive limitations upon the activities of the organization. In principle, this definition includes actors that do not have formal hierarchal relationship with the organization in question. In fact, ILA elaborates that sometimes the relevant actors or 'constituency' that scrutinizes or monitors the organization could include 'all component entities of the international community at large provided their interests or rights have been or may be affected by acts, actions or activities' of the international organization.[13] To undertake such scrutiny, the ILA further elaborated, binding legal standard is not necessary; instead, a set of 'principles, objectives and concepts common to all international organizations' is used as a standard. The ILA has enumerated this set of standards, which include principles such as 'good governance', 'participatory decision-making' and 'transparency'.

The widely used schematic of accountability mechanisms in global governance developed by Grant and Keohane largely corroborates that developed by the ILA. Grant and Keohane espouse that both formal international organizations and informal international bodies whose power does not derive from delegated authority could be held accountable. The difference between these two types of international organizations is, Grant and Keohane maintain, in the case of the former, accountability is mainly exercised by those (states) that have 'delegated' the authority to the organization, whereas in the latter case, a 'participation' model of accountability is exercise by those that are affected by the organization. In either case, the actors that scrutinize the international organization could be internal actors within the organization, member states of the organization, or even the general public. The important element is that such actor must have the *right* to hold the international organization to a certain standard that is 'articulated in transnational civil society', regardless of the legal character of the standard.[14] Similar to the ILA conceptualization, therefore, accountability is defined broadly in a manner that allows global public participation and the use of extra-legal standards. This means

10 International Law Association, 'Accountability of International Organizations' (2004) Final Report of the Berlin Conference, available at <https://www.ila-hq.org/index.php/committees> accessed 17 April 2020.

11 Ruth W. Grant and Robert O. Keohane, 'Accountability and Abuses of Power in World Politics' (2005) 99(1) American Political Science Review 29.

12 ILA report (n 10) 5 (emphasis added).

13 Ibid.

14 Grant and Keohane (n 11) 35.

that to ascertain the existence of accountability in light of this definition, what we need to ask is whether an actor in global society has the right to deploy legal, political, administrative, financial, or other material leverages to scrutinize the organization's adherence to generally accepted standards of behavior.

In light of this understanding of accountability, this chapter brings to light distinct promises and obstacles the formal reconstitution of the FATF holds for enhancing the organization's accountability both towards its member states ('delegated' accountability) and towards affected stakeholders in global society (participation' accountability). It does so by first moving away from an often-reflected view that conceptualizes the formal or informal existence of an (international) entity as a matter of inclusion or exclusion from the law's legitimizing purview. The assumption within this view is the visibility of an entity under the spotlight of a defined legal order directly translates into a sense of accountability. This chapter proceeds from the view that formal existence under a defined legal order is a starting point of, but not a direct proxy to, accountability. Being subject to a legal order matters, but not simply because it creates an inevitable doctrinal trigger to accountability, rather because it creates certain legal, political and institutional consequences that have relevance for accountability. The chapter fleshes out the consequences that arise from legal personality and argues that they may help enhance FATF's accountability under certain conditions, but may not help or even be counter-productive to accountability under other conditions. In this sense, the chapter presents not a doctrinal legal, but a sociolegal analysis of accountability.

The chapter begins with a brief description of the relevant organizational aspects of the FATF followed by a presentation of the possible paths for the transition of the organization into an (international) legal person. The subsequent sections analyze a number of possibilities under which the move towards (international) legal personality of the FATF could have both positive and negative contributions to the organization's accountability.

2 The FATF at present

Established by the G7 in 1989, the FATF has largely had an obscure existence, housed in the offices of the Organisation for Economic Co-operation and Development (OECD) in Paris – while being organizationally independent from the later – before being thrust into the forefront of global security governance post-9/11. The FATF has a rudimentary organizational structure, with a secretariat of less than 50 experts and administrative staff headed by an Executive Secretary. Secretariat experts are organized into five substantive working groups – Evaluation and Compliance Team, Policy Development Team, Risk, Trends and Methods Team, International Cooperation and Review Team and Global Network Coordination Team. The administrative staff includes, besides the Executive Secretary, human resources, finance and communications advisors.[15]

15 FATF, 'Annual Report 2014–2015' (Paris 2016) available at <fatf-gafi.org/media/fatf/documents/reports/Annual-report-2014-2015.pdf> accessed 17 April 2020.

Above the Secretariat is the FATF Plenary, the ultimate decision making body consisting of the finance ministers or other high officials from security or judicial apparatus of member states ('member jurisdictions' in FATF terminology).[16] The Plenary is led by a president and vice-president chosen from its own ranks, each serving a term of one year.[17] Although led by finance ministers or other high-level government officials, member states' delegations to the Plenary are also composed of experts and lower officials from those branches of government and others such as 'interior or external affairs, financial regulatory authorities, and law enforcement agencies'.[18]

The FATF falls in the category Jan Klabbers disapprovingly calls 'soft organizations'.[19] It is not established by treaty, nor does it have a formal constitutive document. Until 2019, it operated on temporary mandate delegated by ministers of its member states,[20] and since then the mandate is 'open-ended' instead of permanent – meaning it is subject to change in future.[21] The document stating the mandate makes it explicit that no legal effect is intended to be driven from it, implying that other actors cannot hold the FATF legally answerable for non-compliance with its own mandate.[22] The FATF is also not formally incorporated as a legal entity in its host state France. Listed as a 'special entity' of the OECD, the FATF shares offices with the OECD secretariat and relies upon the formal channels of the OECD for its routine corporate necessities, such as the collection of budgetary contribution from member states, the recruitment of staff and secretarial services.[23] However, it still stands independent to the OECD both institutionally (governed and run by its own set of actors delegated directly by states) and financially (funded by its own members contribution). In this sense, there is no direct institutional linkage through which the formal organization of OECD would be held accountable for the activities of the FATF.

16 E.g. the 2019–2020 president, Xiangmin Liu, is the Director-General of the Legal Department of the People's Bank of China, and the vice-president, Marcus Pleyer, is Deputy Director General of Germany's Federal Ministry of Finance.

17 The June 2017 FATF Plenary has decided to amend the term of service of these two offices to two years.

18 FATF website <www.fatf-gafi.org> accessed 17 April 2020.

19 Jan Klabbers, 'Institutional Ambivalence by Design: Soft Organizations in International Law' (2001) 70 Nordic Journal of International Law 403. But, for an alternative point of view, see Nico Krisch, 'Authority, Solid and Liquid, in Postnational Governance' in Roger Cotterrell and Maksymilian Del Mar (eds), *Authority in Transnational Legal Theory: Theorising Across Disciplines* (Edward Elgar 2016) 25–48.

20 See past mandate, covering the period 2012–2020, adopted on 20 April 2012, Washington D.C., available at <http://www.fatf-gafi.org/media/fatf/documents/FINAL%20FATF%20MANDATE%202012-2020.pdf> accessed 17 April 2020. FATF's institutional operation is guided by a confidential document titled 'Internal Governance Principles', which is not accessible to the public.

21 FATF mandate 2019 (n 4) 10.

22 FATF mandate 2012–2020 (n 20) para 48, stating: 'This Mandate is not intended to create any legal rights or obligations'.

23 FATF, '25 Years and Beyond' (Paris, 2014), 7. Generally, see FATF website <www.fatf-gafi.org>.

Overall, FATF documents often emphasize the view that the organization is essentially a conference of its member states, and hence for all its activities, is answerable only to 'its ministers'.[24] The FATF Secretariat is led by an Executive Secretary, who is answerable to a President, who in turn is appointed by and answerable to the Plenary. The FATF refers to the Plenary, and itself in general, as a policy forum and not an organization.[25] From international legal perspective, therefore, the FATF as such is not visible independently, but only as a vehicle for its member states.

Despite its institutional obscurity, the FATF has an outsized impact as the most important global body in the fight against criminal finance. It is the primary body that sets normative and technical standards on AML/CFT, identifies and analyses emerging threats of criminal finance, regularly monitors states' compliance, sanctions non-compliant states and promotes the global adoption of AML/CFT standards.[26] Compliance with FATF standards is now a crucial requirement for states' integration into the global economy. This is because the FATF membership constitutes the largest economic block in the world. FATF member jurisdictions are 39 most important economies of the world. Although the FATF technically adopts AML/CFT standards to its member jurisdictions, any other state that fails to comply with these standards will become subjected to a system of blacklisting by the FATF.[27] This blacklist restricts states' relationship with the FATF member jurisdictions, thereby effectively cutting states' access to the global financial system. Due to this economic power at its disposal, although FATF's membership consists of only 39 jurisdictions, more than 200 states in the world generally subscribe to its AML/CFT standards.

Non-member states partially participate in the deliberations of the FATF through what are known as FATF-style regional bodies (FSRBs).[28] These are regional intergovernmental organizations that operate as independent but subservient agents of the FATF by disseminating and monitoring the implementation of AML/CFT standards among their respective membership. FSRBs have associate membership status at the FATF, which allows them to attend the latter's meetings, but do not have voting rights. Moreover, while each member state of FATF is individually represented in such meetings, non-member states are represented only collectively via their respective FSRBs – given that there are nine FSRBs so far, it can be said the more

24 FATF mandate 2019 (n 4), para 50; also FATF mandate 2012–2020 (n 20), para 51.

25 FATF mandate 2019 (n 4).

26 FATF, 'International Standards on Combatting Money Laundering and the Financing of Terrorism & proliferation' (Paris, 2012–2019), available at <https://www.fatf-gafi.org/media/fatf/documents/recommendations/pdfs/FATF%20Recommendations%202012.pdf>.

27 FATF listing of 'high-risk and non-cooperative jurisdictions', <http://www.fatf-gafi.org/publications/high-riskandnon-cooperativejurisdictions/?hf=10&b=0&s=desc(fatf_releasedate)> accessed 17 April 2020.

28 See FATF (n 3).

than 160 non-member states collectively occupy only nine seats at FATF meetings. This means, the FATF exercises a lawmaking power over virtually the entire global society without having formal delegation of authority by most states or without meaningfully ensuring their participation in its decision-making.[29]

This problem of lack of representation or participation by non-member stakeholders is exacerbated by the fact that the FATF operates in a highly informal, non-transparent manner.[30] Decision-making generally follows consensus model among its 39 member jurisdictions, and much of the work is undertaken in informal consultations between national technical delegates or at times outside of the FATF framework, such as at the G20 forum.[31] The informal decision-making culture reduces FATF's accountability to its own member states, as most issues become agreed upon between experts and policy-makers working behind the scenes. The migration of some decisions to outside the FATF, on the other hand, gives *some* of its own member states, particularly the powerful economies that also are members of the G20, stronger leverage to sway FATF decision-making. This shows us that the FATF has accountability deficit towards some of its member states, in some aspects of its decision-making, and towards the majority of the global community (non-member states) in virtually all its decision-making.

3 Accountability and legal visibility

The imagery of (international) legal invisibility or 'non-existence' of an entity often evokes the feeling that the entity is legally unaccountable, or, at least, is too elusive to be held meaningfully accountable.[32] This perception animates formalistic arguments for the granting of (international) legal personhood. In other words, incorporating informal international bodies into formal legal personhood is perceived as advantageous for legal accountability.[33]

In general international law discourse, the conferral of international legal personality is seen as advantageous to accountability because of the belief in the

29 Further, see James Thuo Gathii, 'The Financial Action Task Force and Global Administrative Law' (2010) Journal of the Professional Lawyer 197.

30 Tom Keatinge, 'The Financial Action Task Force Should Embrace the Opportunity to Reform' (*Commentary*, 25 June 2019) < https://rusi.org/commentary/financial-action-task-force-should-embrace-opportunity-reform> accessed 17 April 2020.

31 E.g. the FATF adopted AML/CFT standards with respect to virtual assets in response to decision adopted at the G20, FATF, 'Report to G20 Leaders' Summit' (June 2019) <https://www.fatf-gafi.org/media/fatf/content/images/G20-June-2019.pdf> accessed 17 April 2020.

32 This corresponds to the 'nobody problem' expounded by Alessandra Arcuri and Florin Coman-Kund, 'Introduction: Breaking Taboos, Talking Accountability' (in this volume).

33 E.g. Mario Savino, 'Global Administrative Law Meets "Soft" Powers: The Uncomfortable Case of Interpol Red Notices' (2011) 43 New York Journal of Int'l Law and Policy 263–336.

constraining and legitimizing effect of actors' location within a well-defined legal order (i.e. international law).[34] This belief – generally reflected in literature on constitutionalization of international law – sees a potential solution to the accountability deficit of obscure expert governance in legal visibility, i.e. being brought to the legal spotlight.[35] The understanding is that upon gaining (international) legal personhood, the whole armor of the law (domestic and international) would be brought to bear upon the actor. In addition, some in this camp add, legal personality would just 'settle many problems',[36] such as reducing the bureaucratic obstacle from some states that may not be onboard with the organization's purpose or operation.

From the perspective of institutional analysis, however, visibility under a specific legal order constitutes only a starting point of discussion – a material fact – and not an automatic proxy to accountability. The fact that an entity is formally recognized under international law cannot be by default translated to more accountability. As Berman and Wessel note, because there is no international procedural law that automatically applies to international legal bodies, international legal personality '...is largely meaningless in relation to accountability questions'.[37] In fact, legal visibility could be a double-edged sword that disciplines not only the entity in question but also its legitimate detractors. Legal recognition consolidates the organizational status of bodies such as the FATF. If one starts from the view that the very organization represents undesirable politics or harmful policy, then the organizational consolidation of such entity could not be a welcome news for accountability because accountability in this context should have meant resistance, i.e. ensuring the entity exerts as minimum an influence as possible. The following sections, therefore, discuss the FATF's possible (international) legal personhood as a starting point and assess what advantages and disadvantages for the organization's accountability arise therein. Before delving into that directly, a brief sketch of the various models of (international) legal personality the FATF could be conferred with is in order.

34 Jochen von Bernstorff, 'Procedures of Decision-Making and the Role of Law in International Organizations' (2008) 9 German Law Journal 1939–1964.

35 E.g. Armin von Bogdandy, Philipp Dann, Matthias Goldmann, 'Developing the Publicness of Public International Law: Towards a Legal Framework for Global Governance Activities', in von Armin von Bogdandy and others (eds) *The Exercise of Public Authority by International Institutions*, vol 210, (Springer 2010); Armin von Bogdandy, Matthias Goldmann and Ingo Venzke, 'From Public International to International Public Law: Translating World Public Opinion into International Public Authority' (2017) 28(1) EJIL 115.

36 Christian Tomuscat, 'Legalization of the OSCE?' (*Volkerrechtsblog*, 1 August 2016) <https://voelkerrechtsblog.org/legalization-of-the-osce/> accessed 17 April 2020.

37 Ayelet Berman and Ramses Wessel, 'The International Legal Form and Status of Informal International Lawmaking Bodies: Consequences for Accountability', in Joost Pauwelyn, Ramses Wessel and Jan Wouters (eds), *Informal International Lawmaking* (CUP 2012) 35, 61.

4 Possible modes of FATF formalization

There is a lively debate on the issue of legal personality in connection to the Organization for Security and Co-operation in Europe (OSCE), which has an informal existence similar to the FATF.[38] The debate on the legal status of the OSCE is a perfect mirror which shows us the possible organizational models the FATF might borrow. Based on this precedent, and the discussions going on within the FATF, it seems there are three possible options to establish the FATF's legal personality: (1) granting international legal personality together with a constitutive document, (2) granting personhood only in domestic legal systems, coupled with specific privileges, immunities and capacities and (3) granting international legal personality without a constitutive document, but possibly with specific arrangements on privileges and immunities. It is my assessment that the third option is the model most likely to be adopted, and the first option being the least likely.

4.1 *Option one: International legal personality and constitutive treaty*

FATF member states could decide to grant the organization an international legal personality by adopting a treaty, which could also serve as the constitutive document of the organization. What makes this option least likely is the constitutive treaty component. The reconstitution of the FATF within strictures of a formal instrument seems to constrain the operational flexibility the body currently enjoys. A similar argument has been raised in the debate concerning the legal status of the OSCE.[39] The response to this argument was that the proposed constitutive instrument does not have to necessarily lead to operational stricture – instead, it could be a bare-bones framework addressing needed items only and loosely-defined functions.[40] Indeed, there is no international law

38 Volkerrechtsblog entries by Christian Tomuscat, Cedric Ryngaert, Isabelle Lay and Gleb Bogush, which followed an international conference organized on the theme by the Max Planck Institute for Comparative Public Law and International Law (July 2016); Mateja Platise Steinbrück, Carolyn Moser and Anne Peters (eds), *The Legal Framework of the OSCE* (CUP 2019); For a discussion at an earlier phase of the OSCE's transformation, see Miriam Sapiro, 'Changing the CSCE into the OSCE: Legal Aspects of a Political Transformation' (1995) 89(3) AJIL 631; Christian Tomuscat, 'General Course on Public International Law' (1999) 281 Recueil Des Cours/Collected Courses of the Hague Academy of International Law 146.

39 Helmut Tichy and Catherine Quidenus, 'Consolidating the International Legal Personality of the OSCE: A Headquarters Agreement with Austria' (2017) 14(2) International Organizations Law Review 403; Jasna Arsic-Dapo, 'Another Brick in the Wall: Building Up the OSCE As an International Organization One Agreement at a Time' (2017) 14(2) International Organizations Law Review 414.

40 Niels Blokker and Ramses Wessel, 'Revisiting Questions of Organisationhood, Legal Personality and Membership in the OSCE: the Interplay Between Law, Politics and Practice' in Steinbrück, Moser and Peters (eds) (n 38) 2.

obligation as to how well-defined an international organization's functions need to be. If such arrangement could plausibly be made, then this international legal personality-plus-constitutive-treaty option could be viable.

There seems to exist some interest to uplift the FATF into a full-fledged international organization-hood with a constitutive treaty.[41] However, this option still seems less likely to be adopted as it requires significant political and material commitment on the part of member states. Currently, the discussion on the legal status of the FATF is often raised in connection with the concern of efficient fulfilment of functions.[42] It is increasingly accepted wisdom that lean organizational structures are preferred for efficiency. Formal organizational status might lead to bloated or inefficient institutional structure. Furthermore, member states might be inclined to avoid the arduous process of adopting and ratifying fully-fledged constitutive treaty, and instead only address specific efficiency issues the FATF faces.

4.2 *Option two: Domestic legal personality*

Under this option, the FATF member states could agree to arrange for the domestic legal personality of the FATF in each member state (and non-member states) for the purposes of private law and to arrange specific privileges and immunities as needed. This would mainly take the form of unilateral commitments by states. For example, France, the host state of FATF headquarters, has already offered to provide the body with legal personality under French law.[43] This option would suit well the desire to keep an international body away from organizational consolidation at the expense of member states' sovereignty. This was quite visible in the case of the OSCE, where there is strong resistance to even the use of the term 'member states' – referring only as 'participating states'. In comparison, there is greater recognition of the corporate existence of the FATF by its member states, which are referred to as 'member jurisdiction' only to avoid the political inconvenience using the term 'member states' as its membership consists of regional organizations and territories with contentious or unsettled statehood.

This arrangement seems to offer a tailored solution whereby the organization would gain the specific legal capacity and other rights while not gaining an independent existence in the international legal sphere, which is said to be

41 E.g. Argentine presidency of FATF calling for strengthened 'international standing and engagement' of the FATF in connection with the discussion for legal status, see FATF, 'Objectives for FATF – XXXI (2017–2018)', paper by Argentine presidency of FATF <https://www.fatf-gafi.org/media/fatf/documents/Objectives%20for%20FATF%20XXIX%20(2017-2018).pdf> accessed 17 April 2020.

42 See, e.g. FATF, 'Objectives for FATF – XXXI (2019–2020)', paper by Chinese presidency of FATF <https://www.fatf-gafi.org/media/fatf/content/images/Objectives-FATF-XXXI(2019-2020).pdf> accessed 17 April 2020.

43 FATF's Report to G20 Leaders' Summit (July 2017), para 5, <http://www.fatf-gafi.org/media/fatf/documents/reports/FATF-Report-to-G20-July-2017.pdf> accessed 17 April 2020.

the case with the OSCE.[44] However, there is reason to believe that the need for legal personality of the FATF is connected not only to its functioning within domestic legal orders, but also within the international legal order. The specific reason for this assumption has to do with the ability to enter into international agreements and attendant privileges, which is explained in connection to option three below.

4.3 *Option three: International legal personality without constitutive treaty*

Under this model, member states could reach an agreement to confer international legal personality upon the FATF without necessarily accompanying it with a constitutive treaty. Such legal personality could come with circumscribed set of privileges, immunities and powers. It is general knowledge in international law that states can establish international organizations with varying sets of rights and duties.[45] As international organizations are not fully fledged subjects of international law like states, there is no automatic set of rights and duties they possess upon gaining international legal personality.

The reason this option may be more likely is that the discussion concerning FATF's legal status appears to be driven partly by the need to enter into international treaties. One illustration of this need is the fact that 'enhancing the effectiveness of the global network' of the FATF is mentioned as a key reason for the legal personality discussions.[46] The 'global network' of the FATF is its web of relationships with the nine FSRBs that span the globe. Currently the FATF collaborates with these FSRBs, some of which are organizations with international legal personality, by adopting bilateral memorandums of understanding that do not have legal effect. It seems some member states of the FATF desire to strengthen this web of relationships by basing them on well-defined agreements, or at least to forge some legally relevant relationship. To do so, it would need to have the ability to enter into an international agreement.

An additional illustration is the need of the FATF to enter into international agreement with states and obtain independent corporate existence. Recently, the FATF and one of its member states, South Korea, signed a memorandum of understanding for the establishment of an International Training and Research Institute (TREIN) in Busan, which is currently operational.[47] The status of such memorandum of understanding is dubious while the FATF itself is understood

44 Sapiro (n 38) 636–637. However, see Klabber's critique claiming that the enjoyment of those rights and privileges means that the OSCE indeed has international legal personality. Klabbers (n 19).

45 Jan Klabbers, *An Introduction to International Institutional Law* (CUP 2002).

46 FATF, 'Plenary Report' (June 2017) < https://www.fatf-gafi.org/publications/fatfgeneral/documents/outcomes-plenary-june-2017.html> accessed 17 April 2020.

47 FATF, 'Annual Report 2015–2016' (Paris, 2017) 6–7 <https://www.fatf-gafi.org/media/fatf/documents/reports/FATF-annual-report-2015-2016.pdf> accessed 17 April 2020.

to lack international legal personality. Due to FATF's lack of legal personality, TREIN operates as a hybrid institution, undertaking an international function (i.e. capacity building and research covering all FATF and FSRB member states), while administratively operating as a part of the Korean civil service. TREIN is administered under the Korean Financial Intelligence Unit, and internationally recruited staff are also subject to Korean income tax and Korean labor law, and are explicitly designated as not employees of FATF.[48] Given the talk about 'global network' and strengthening the effectiveness of the FATF, the ability to enter into international agreements with states also seems to be an important consideration driving the legal personality talk.

The point of departure for the following analysis is, therefore, that some kind of arrangement on international legal personality, likely resembling option 3 discussed above, would eventually be agreed upon by FATF member states. Let us now turn to the issue of what promises and obstacles such possible re-organization holds for the accountability of the FATF.

5 Promises for accountability

The formal re-organization of the FATF could give rise to three possibilities under which the accountability of the organization – both to its member states (through delegation) and to affected stakeholders in global society (through participation) – could be enhanced. These possibilities are what I call peer accountability, normative clarity and self-discipline. The commonality between these three concepts is that they entail effects that would materialize over the long term.

5.1 *Peer accountability*

Work in international relations has shown us that an important channel of legitimization for international organization is the iterative process of horizontal engagement with other international organizations, i.e. 'peer accountability'.[49] Peer accountability takes place as a form of check and balance between entities within the same network. The check and balance occurs when an entity acts in a way that is 'against the interests or principles' of other participants within the network.[50] The key ingredient here is, therefore, diversity (of interest, identity) within this institutional network.

As was mentioned at the beginning, the FATF is embedded within such global governance network. Its main peers in this network include international financial institutions (IFIs), specifically the International Monetary Fund (IMF) and World Bank, the United Nations and numerous other regional and global functional organizations with observer status at the FATF, such as the Egmont

48 Vacancy announcement for FATF ITRI, available at <http://www.fatf-gafi.org/media/fatf/documents/FATF-TREIN-Job-Vacancy-TR-Specialist.pdf> accessed 17 April 2020.

49 Grant and Keohane (n 11).

50 Ibid 39.

Group of Financial Intelligence Units, African Development Bank and Asian Development Bank.[51] There is some evidence from the practice of the FATF so far showing that the organization is not immune to peer nudge. For example, as a result of its close working relationship with the IMF and World Bank, the FATF has recently come to adopt the notions of 'sustainability', 'economic growth' and 'financial inclusion' in its work.[52] These concepts moderate the FATF's work in terms of limiting harmful spillovers from the fight against illicit finance onto the economic development efforts that the two IFIs invest in.[53]

The question here is whether re-organization into an international legal person would make any difference to this equation. This could be answered in the positive, if we proceed with the plausible assumption that legal personhood could be a catalyst in consolidating the institutional autonomy of the organization. The reference to autonomy here is not necessarily about being able to enter into an international agreement, but about the emergence of a permanent secretariat (permanent staff, headquarters, field offices, standing decision-making body) that operates independently of its member states. An independent FATF that is seen to act independently of its member states full control would more readily become a subject of criticism from its peers. In other words, it would no longer hide behind its member states.

International legal personality could also facilitate horizontal accountability by enabling the triggering of review mechanisms among peer organizations, which is difficult to achieve in the absence of a legally identifiable entity whose decisions and actions could be scrutinized. In this regard, it is important to note that the key ingredient for horizontal institutional accountability is the divergence between those institutions – i.e. institutions of non-overlapping memberships (e.g. UN v. EU), diverging power/voting structures within the same institution (e.g. UN General Assembly v. Security Council), or also within institutions of identical membership and voting structure, but diverging governmental delegation (e.g. international body consisting of national security organs v. those consisting of national economic organs).

51 FATF-style Regional Bodies (FSRBs), although officially associate members of the FATF, are too subordinate to the FATF to qualify as 'peers' in this sense. More explanation later on in section 6.3.

52 E.g. FATF, 'Financial Action Task Force: 30 Years' (Paris, 2019) 74 & 90 <https://www.fatf-gafi.org/media/fatf/documents/brochuresannualreports/FATF30-(1989-2019).pdf> accessed 17 April 2020; FATF, 'Anti-Money Laundering and Terrorist Financing Measures and Financial Inclusion' (Paris, 2013) <http://www.fatf-gafi.org/media/fatf/documents/reports/AML_CFT_Measures_and_Financial_Inclusion_2013.pdf> accessed 17 April 2020.

53 See, e.g. FATF's reception to developmental concerns of financial inclusion, FATF, 'Priorities for the Argentine Presidency of FATF 2017–18' (Paris, 2017) <http://www.fatf-gafi.org/media/fatf/documents/Objectives%20for%20FATF%20XXIX%20(2017-2018).pdf> accessed 17 April 2020. Generally, see Kenneth S. Blazejewski, 'The FATF and Its Institutional Partners: Improving the Effectiveness and Accountability of Transgovernmental Networks' (Spring 2008) 22(1) Temple International & Comparative Law Journal 1.

A very fitting illustration of horizontal accountability is the case of the scrutiny of the World Health Organization (WHO) by the Parliamentary Assembly of the Council of Europe (CoE) in connection with the WHO's management of the H1N1 flu pandemic.[54] The Parliamentary Assembly's scrutiny, specifically attacking the accountability and transparency of the WHO, took place through the appointment of a Rapporteur, and was followed by subsequent formal Resolutions seeking specific reforms on the part of the WHO.[55] It would be difficult to engage in such horizontal review against, and expect meaningful response from, a body that for all legal purposes denies its independent existence, and can deflect criticism saying the organization is nothing but only what 'its ministers' want it to be or do.[56]

An interesting line of thought in connection to this could be whether and under what condition the CoE Parliamentary Assembly could engage in the scrutiny of FATF's transparency or substantive policy problems such as concerns of financial data protection.[57] The FATF Recommendations and sectoral guidance documents encourage states to maximize information collection and exchange. At times, there has been complaint that this push for information transparency infringes on legitimate privacy concerns. For example, legal professionals have voiced this complaint vocally, pushing back against the FATF-driven obligation to reports suspicions about their clients.[58]

There is an institutional linkage for a possible CoE parliamentary oversight on matters such as data protection. A key FATF institutional partner is the Committee of Experts on the Evaluation of Anti-Money Laundering Measures and the Financing of Terrorism (MONEYVAL), which is a CoE body.[59] As MONEYVAL is essentially a monitoring body for the implementation of FATF standards, the Parliamentary Assembly could engage in direct criticism of MONEYVAL, and indirectly of FATF. This will be bound to create a Kadi-like situation where ultimately the middle actor (MONEYVAL) could evade criticism by pointing to the higher source of the norms (FATF). However, what the Kadi case has shown us is that the awkward collision of legal systems such

54 Abigail C. Deshman, 'Horizontal Review between International Organizations: Why, How, and Who Cares about Corporate Regulatory Capture', (2011) 22(4) EJIL 1089. See, further buttressing Deshman's findings, Rosa Rafaelli, 'Horizontal Review between International Organizations: A Reply to Abigail C. Deshman' (2013) 24(4) EJIL 1195.

55 Council of Europe Parliamentary Assembly, 'The Handling of the H1N1 Pandemic: More Transparency Needed', Report, Social Health and Family Affairs Committee (24 June 2010); Council of Europe Parliamentary Assembly, Recommendation No. 1929 (24 June 2010).

56 FATF (n 23).

57 See, generally, Beat Habegger, 'Democratic Accountability of International Organizations: Parliamentary Control Within the Council of Europe and the OSCE and the Prospects for the United Nations' (2010) 45(2) Cooperation and Conflict 186.

58 E.g. Duncan E. Osborne, 'The Financial Action Task Force and the Legal Profession' (2015) 59(3/4) New York Law School Law Review 421; Nathanael Tilahun, 'States' Varied Compliance with International Anti-Money Laundering Standards for Legal Professionals' (2019) 88(2) Nordic Journal of International Law 280.

59 See Council of Europe, home page <https://www.coe.int/en/web/moneyval> accessed 17 April 2020.

scenarios create likely generates political impetus for reform at the international level.[60] This means, sustained criticism from the Parliamentary Assembly could push CoE member states, several of whom are also important FATF member states, into addressing the identified problems at the FATF level.

Yet another interesting direction of thought is the possible future contact between the FATF and institutions arising from emerging economic blocks, which Ruth Gordon called the Southern Tier,[61] such as the China-backed Asia Infrastructure and Investment Bank (AIIB).[62] Such institutions might subscribe to a different set of policy priorities regarding the global financial system than those espoused by the FATF. Given its current great deference to member states' consent in its operations, the FATF might be less open to engage institutions outside of its political comfort zone. An independent FATF, on the other hand, might more readily engage AIIB and other institutions that do not necessarily fall within the political orientation of Western advanced economies, which currently constitute the core of FATF's orbit. This exposes the FATF to participation accountability: institutions such as AIIB that will enter into formal (legal) or practical working relationship with the FATF would be in a position to scrutinize and challenge the later to the extent the nature of the relationship allows. This also means that while the informal existence of the FATF facilitates stronger control of member states, and hence delegated accountability, its formalization may expose it more to participation accountability from external stakeholders.

5.2 *Normative clarity*

While there is much debate as to what international law obligations are applicable to international organizations,[63] it remains essential that for the debate to begin, the organization in question has to come out of the shadows of its

60 Antonios Tzanakopoulos, *Disobeying the Security Council: Countermeasures Against Wrongful Sanctions* (OUP 2011).

61 Ruth Gordon, 'The Dawn of a New, New International Economic Order?' (2009) Law and Contemporary Problems 72.

62 On international law aspects of AIIB, see Gerard J. Sanders, 'The Asian Infrastructure Investment Bank and the Belt and Road Initiative: Complementarities and Contrasts' (2017) 16(2) Chinese Journal of International Law 367.

63 For a recent debate see, Jan Klabbers, 'Sources of International Organizations Law: Reflections on Accountability', in Samantha Besson and Jean D'Aspremont (eds), *The Oxford Handbook on the Sources of International Law* (OUP 2017) 987; August Reinisch, 'Sources of International Organizations Law: Why Custom and General Principles are Crucial' in Besson and D'Aspremont (2017) 1007. The debate centres on Klabbers' assertion that a proper interpretation of the ICJ's jurisprudence should lead us to conclude that only secondary rules ('rules of recognition' types) of customary law are applicable towards IOs, contrary to the prevailing understanding that the 'general rules of international law' referred to by the ICJ in *WHO-Egypt* Advisory Opinion means customary rules in general or at least *jus cogens* norms. Coupled with the fact that international organizations rarely enter into international agreements except headquarters agreements with host states, Klabbers' argument concludes, there is little substantive (primary) rule in international law that binds international organizations.

member states and assume independent legal personality. The reorganization of the FATF into a formal body with independent international legal personality bridges this gap. As a formal international organization, it would be possible to speak of harm caused by the FATF as a matter of illegality.

Koskenniemi reminds us that the 'promise of justice' embedded in conceptions of law can be a useful tool of resistance for the powerless in global politics.[64] The finding of the acts of an international organization as illegal carries with it a distinctive claim of injustice, and hence illegitimacy. The articulation of criticism against FATF within defined international legal norms, thus, amplifies the critical voice. Such move shreds the conceptual hiding place/confusion of perceiving such organizations as existing outside of the law.[65] There is much debate as to what international law norms precisely are applicable to international organizations. But there is greater consensus on the view that as a minimum, an international legal person would be bound by, and scrutinized against, fundamental human rights and jus cogens norms. This means the formal re-organization of the FATF as an international organization allows for what Klabbers calls a 'more structured form of politics'[66] – i.e. legal vernacular – in claiming and contesting its legitimacy. And given that international relations scholarship has shown the role of reputation as a 'disciplinarian'[67] of international organizations, to entities for whom reputation as 'law-abiding actors' matters, a critique based on legal norms could be impactful.

5.3 *Self-discipline*

Another possibility of long-term contribution to accountability comes from the institutional consolidation that would follow FATF's reconstitution as an international legal person. The practical translation of the international legal personality would mean that the organization would have a strengthened hierarchal administration. The top leadership would be bestowed with immunities and powers to formally represent the organization. This leadership consolidation could, as Grant and Keohane show us,[68] translate into internal supervisory power, which is a form of delegated accountability mechanism towards its member states. Or as part of the consolidation of the normal operations of an organization (e.g. contractual issues with external entities, auditing, etc.) an internal legal counsel might become necessary. Given enough power and independence,

64 Martti Koskenniemi, 'What is International Law for?' in Malcolm D. Evans (eds), *International Law* (OUP 2003) 89.

65 Generally, see Fleur Johns, *Non-Legality in International Law: Unruly Law* (CUP 2013); Catherine M. Brolmann, *The Institutional Vein in Public International Law: International Organizations and the Law of Treaties* (Hart 2007).

66 Klabbers (n 19), 420.

67 Kristina Daugirdas, 'Reputation as a Disciplinarian of International Organizations' (2019) 113 American Journal of International Law 221.

68 Grant and Keohane (n 11).

such internal supervision structures help address at least conduct by officials that deviate from espoused policies of the organization.[69]

Self-discipline as a manifestation of participatory accountability could also occur through a process of learning and policy steering that is born out of a settled bureaucracy, one which is not constantly preoccupied with execution of time-bound mandates. One of the complaints the FATF secretariat raises, and is driving the legal personality question, is the high work-load and shortage of staff.[70] A further expansion of the organization, it seems, is being put off by member states who cannot yet reconcile their original plan for FATF as an informal networking forum with current demands of fully-fledged bureaucracy. If the formal reorganization and consequent organizational consolidation materializes, there is a possibility the FATF secretariat could formally establish mechanisms for entertaining complaints from external stakeholders. This means that there would be space for engaging affected stakeholders, and reviewing and addressing their complaints. The FATF currently has ad hoc forums of consultation with industry and civil society actors, and it has recently announced that it will undertake a major strategic review of its operations. However, the consultation forums take place only once a year, and the strategic review is intended to mainly assess the efficacy of its monitoring methodologies.[71] With more bureaucratic stability, there might be better organizational resource to hold participatory forums more frequently, and to undertake a review of not only efficacy, but also legitimacy of its operations.

There is an example in the work of the Security Council's Counter-Terrorism Committee (CTC) that gives us slight indication that such review could be possible. Previous research has shown that human rights-oriented reform in the work of the CTC has come about not only as a result of external resistance (e.g. the Kadi effect, whereby Court of Justice of the EU required due process in implementing Security Council sanctions on Al-Qaeda[72]), but also through the steering work of the CTC's Executive Directorate (the CTED).[73] In particular, a recent push for the inclusion of civil society actors in the work of the CTC,

69 Further, see Benedict Kingsbury and Lorenzo Casini, 'Global Administrative Law Dimensions of International Organizations Law' (2009) 6 International Organizations Law Review 319, 337.

70 Remarks of David Lewis, FATF Executive Secretary, the 50th Meeting of MONEYVAL (Strasbourg, 12 April 2016).

71 Remarks of David Lewis, FATF Executive Secretary, at the RUSI meeting on the Financial Action Task Force Strategic Review (18 November 2019).

72 Joined Cases C-402/05 P and C-415/05 P *Yassin Abdullah Kadi and Al Barakaat International Foundation v Council of the European Union and Commission of the European Communities*, European Court Reports 2008 I-06351. On resistance to the sanction regimes in general, see Antonios Tzanakopoulos, *Disobeying the Security Council: Countermeasures Against Wrongful Sanctions* (OUP 2011).

73 For a more expounded argument and empirical evidence, see Nathanael Tilahun, *Proactive Regulatory Counter-Terrorism: A Critical Appraisal of Dynamic Global Governance* (Routledge 2018).

including in reviewing states' implementation of Resolution 1373, came about through the small nudging of the CTED,[74] which in turn was influenced by the persistent work of external think tanks.[75] The evolutionary incorporation of human rights norms and actors in the Security Council's counter-terrorism system is a particularly telling manifestation of internal reform because the initial mandate of the CTC, provided under Resolution 1373(2001), did not involve human rights issues. Through incremental changes in subsequent years, both top-down from the CTC[76] and bottom up from external think tanks via CTED, human rights have become part of the regular work program of the Security Council Resolution 1373 (2001) regime.[77] This reflects that even when an international (expert) body is initially designed to steer clear of particular areas (in this case, human rights), gradual processes of scrutiny by external stakeholders (a form of participatory accountability) could lead to self-reflection and reform by an engaged secretariat.

6 Limits to accountability

There are also ways in which change in the legal status of the FATF could only remain a change in form and not in substance in terms of enhancing accountability. I discuss here three such ways.

74 Bibi van Ginkel, 'The Role of Civil Society in Implementing the Global UN Counter-Terrorism Strategy' (September 2010) Clingendael Institute and CORDAID <http://www.clingendael.nl/sites/default/files/20100909_cscp_paper_ginkel.pdf> accessed 17 April 2020; 'Engaging Civil Society in Countering Violent Extremism: Experiences with the Un Global Counter Terrorism Strategy' (2012) International Centre for Counter Terrorism (ICCT) Research Paper <http://www.icct.nl/download/file/ICCT-Van-Ginkel-Civil-Society-in-CVE-August-2012.pdf> accessed 17 April 2020; Eric Rosand, Alistair Millar and Jason Ipe, 'Civil Society and the UN Global Counter-Terrorism Strategy: Opportunities and Challenges' (September 2008) Centre on Global Counter-Terrorism Cooperation, available at <http://www.icnl.org/research/library/files/Transnational/civil.pdf> accessed 17 April 2020.

75 Examples are think tanks such as International Center for Counter-Terrorism (ICCT, <www.icct.nl>), and the Global Center on Counter-terrorism (now renamed Global Center on Cooperative Security, <www.globalcenter.org>).

76 See CTC, 'Conclusions for Policy Guidance Regarding Human Rights and the CTC', Policy Guidance PG2 of the Security Council Committee Established Pursuant to Resolution 1373 (2001) Concerning Counter-Terrorism, S/AC.40/2006/PG.2 <https://www.un.org/sc/ctc/news/document/sac-402006pg-2-conclusions-for-policy-guidance-regarding-human-rights-and-the-ctc/>.

77 Security Council Resolutions 1456 (2003), 1535 (2004), 1624 (2005) and 1805 (2008). See also, comments by Edward Flynn, the Senior Human Rights Officer of the CTED, Edward J. Flynn, 'The Security Council's Counter-Terrorism Committee and Human Rights' (2007) 7(2) Human Rights Law Review 371; 'Thematic discussion of the Counter-Terrorism Committee on the human rights aspects of counter-terrorism in the context of resolution 1373' (2001) CTED Background Paper <http://www.un.org/en/sc/ctc/docs/2010/2010_10_07_thematic-humanrights.pdf> accessed 17 April 2020; Rosemary Foot, 'The United Nations, Counter Terrorism and Human Rights: Institutional Adaptation and Embedded Ideas' (2007) 29(2) Human Rights Quarterly 489.

6.1 *Path dependency*

The first way in which the change in form could be inconsequential in terms of accountability is if the FATF's existing practice as a barely-transparent informal body remains so entrenched that it extends in its post-formalization life. Particularly, the possibilities of hierarchal or reflexive accountability through internal review body or supervision could be rendered dormant if member states insist on keeping existing 'soft' *modus operandi* and utilize legal personality only for the specific purposes of logistics (e.g. signing host state agreement). This is quite possible, and the OSCE is once again an illustration: its member states make strong effort to keep business as usual even after the organization developed internal accountability mechanisms, demonstrated by the fact that OSCE Court of Conciliation and Arbitration, established in the 'rule of law euphoria'[78] of 1990s, has not yet received a single case from member states in its two decades of existence. In addition, when member states desire to keep the organization in its pre-formalization shape, they could also take steps to that end, in addition to refraining to engage as in the case of the OSCE Court, such as preventing the organization's corporate expansion/consolidation.

6.2 *Backlash*

The accountability-enhancing consequences of legal personhood such as those discussed in the preceding section could equally trigger counter-productive reaction from member states of the FATF. Such reaction could take the form of a retreat of consequential decision-making back into less visible forums within or even outside the organization. We already know from much international relations and international law scholarship that powerful states have reason to retreat from international institutions when the gains from those institutions become not rewarding enough compared to the cost of participation. That is to say, when the organization's freedom of action becomes constrained by accountability mechanisms, its powerful member states become inclined to move away to other less constrained forums for purposes of efficiency – although we are also cautioned that in areas of 'a weakest-link good',[79] such as financial security, powerful states would less readily abandon the legitimizing and mobilizing power of working through a formal multilateral platform such as the FATF.[80]

The general understanding remains, however, that the more independent an organization becomes, the demands for its accountability increases. This is because as opposed to an informal network that admits answerability exclusively to its member states, which the FATF currently claims to be,[81] the independent

78 Remarks of Christian Tomuscat, President of the Court, in interview with OSCE (2014), available at <www.osce.org>.

79 Nico Krisch, 'The Decay of Consent: International Law in an Age of Global Public Goods' (2014) 108 AJIL 1, 20.

80 Ibid 20–25.

81 FATF (n 15).

operation of an organization raises participation accountability issues towards external affected stakeholders.[82] When participation accountability seems to slow the expediency of the organization, its powerful member states may be incentivized to re-route essential work away from the organization or scale-back the role of the organization itself.[83] The implicit insight here is that when there is a choice to be made between effectiveness and external (participation) accountability, powerful member states often prefer the former at the expense of the latter.

One possibility of re-routing in the context of the FATF is diverting key normative consensus-making work towards less inclusive and open forums such as the G7 (its original creators) or the Security Council, while the FATF secretariat would be made to concentrate on the technical work of implementation, monitoring and capacity building – a move to 'de-politicize' the FATF. [84] Another body, the G20, seems particularly potent to scale-back the role of the FATF as its 'member' states hold financial and political sway over organization. This power is interestingly revealed in the fact that although the G20 is not directly linked to the FATF (even by the informal standards of linkage between the FATF and, say, the UN Security Council or the IFIs), the FATF periodically submits report on its activities and strategic directions to the G20 (and it does not report to the Security Council or the IFIs). Financially, because the funding of the FATF is modelled after the OECD model of weighed contribution, the few powerful states of the G20 cover significant proportion of the FATF's budget. Consequently, in response to increased accountability of FATF's formalization may generate, powerful blocks such as the G20 could leverage their clout to reverse the progress of accountability or the role of the organization itself.

6.3 *Locking-in*

The last way in which the formal reorganization of the FATF could diminish its accountability is by locking-in preexisting outcomes of an unaccountable system. This is a reverse form of the manner in which states utilize international law to consolidate domestic normative achievement. In what Andrew Moravcsik calls the 'locking-in' effect, newly democratizing or post-conflict states often resort to international law, such as by acceding to human rights treaties, in order to

82 Grant and Keohane (n 11).

83 On the counterproductive effects of the institutionalization of accountability mechanisms within IOs in terms of backlash from member states, see Richard Collins and Nigel White, *International Organizations and the Idea of Autonomy: Institutional Independence in the International Legal Order* (Routledge 2010); Richard Collins and Nigel White, 'Moving Beyond the Autonomy-Accountability Dichotomy: Reflections on Institutional Independence in the International Legal Order' (2010) 7 Int'l organizations law Review 1.

84 Fleur Johns, 'Starting and Stopping Points: A Response to Gadinis' (2015) 109 AJIL Unbound, 39–43. For a similar reflection in the context of international trade law, see Robert Howse, 'From Politics to Technocracy – And Back Again: The Fate of the Multilateral Trading System' (2002) 96 AJIL 94.

ensure the non-reversal or backsliding of domestic democratic progress.[85] By pegging their systems with a system that is much harder to get out of or modify (i.e. international law), such states seek to foreclose remnant interests within their society that might seek reversal.

In a similar way, the reinstitution of the FATF as a subject of the international legal order might have the effect of locking-in and solidifying the *epistemic* and *institutional* dominance it has already gained. In terms of epistemic 'locking-in', the possession of international legal personality (and members' approval of its subsequent institutional consolidation) enables the FATF to convert itself from its current state as an under-staffed secretariat into a singular knowledge hub on AML/CTF, incubating 'insiders'[86] of the epistemic community of financial security governance. The example of the research institute (TREIN) the FATF established in South Korea comes to mind again.[87] Due to its lack of formal legal existence, the FATF has not been able to establish and run a research institute on its own. The administration of the institute under the South Korean civil service limits its effectiveness, primarily because it will not be able to attract high-caliber international staff. The reinforcement of the epistemic community through the reproduction of knowledge and practitioners is a crucial way in which the FATF would remain entrenched in its orthodoxies.

Institutionally, obtaining international legal personality could place the FATF in such a position where it would be possible to convert its regional partners (FSRBs that represent about 160 states) into permanent subsidiaries. FSRBs, several of which are formal international organizations, are officially 'associate members' of the FATF that sit in the latter's open and confidential meetings, and the FATF likes to insist that FSRBs are independent institutions that engage the FATF on 'equal terms'.[88] This is, of course, already not true. The FATF-FSRB relationship is governed by a set of principles and objectives drawn-up by the FATF.[89] A regional organization must go through an extensive process of admission before being approved as an official FSRB. The FATF 'principles and objectives' contain an astonishing level of detail regarding what the internal composition, rules of procedure, objectives and missions of the FSRB must look like before it could be recognized by the FATF. Furthermore, it is well established that the key term of partnering with the FATF as an FSRB is an unconditional endorsement and commitment to the implementation of existing and future FATF standards. Most importantly, the 'principles and objectives'

85 Andrew Moravcsik, 'The Origins of Human Rights Regimes: Democratic Delegation in Postwar Europe' (2000) 54(2) International Organization 217; Margaret Keck and Kathryn Sikkink, *Activists Beyond Borders: Advocacy Networks in International Politics* (Cornell University Press 1998).

86 In the sense Howse used it to refer to experts propping-up WTO orthodoxies, see Howse (n 84).

87 See FATF (n 26) and accompanying text.

88 FATF (n 15) 23.

89 FATF, 'High Level Principles and Objectives for FATF and FATF-Style Regional Bodies' (Paris 2012, revised 2016).

document states unequivocally that at the end of the day, the FATF alone is the sole 'guardian and arbiter' of the international AML/CTF regime.[90] By the same token, just as the FATF admits FSRBs as associate members subject to the latter's satisfactory commitment to the global AML/CFT regime, it retains the power to revoke FSRBs associate membership status should this commitment lapse.

In the legal personality discussion, the FATF has made clear that one of the key purposes of formalization is the enhancement of its relationship with the FSRBs, i.e. the 'global network'.[91] From this, and based on overall FATF discussion, it may be possible to predict that the concrete purpose here might be to convert the relationship between FATF and FSRBs into a formal agreement. In such case, it would not be farfetched to imagine that the terms of the new agreement would be entirely or largely based on the existing terms of engagement. This would mean that the existing subservient relationship would only become binding. Given that such agreement could be a take-it-or-leave-it package, and given also that opting to stay out would be a near impossible choice in the post-9/11 political environment, it could effectively silence fundamental objections to the FATF's core business of norm-development. This means that FSRBs would not be in a position to exercise serious scrutiny (participation accountability) of the FATF on fundamental issues. The end result of possessing international legal personality, therefore, could also be accountability-reducing in this sense.

The need for such fundamental reform or criticism of the work of the FATF is in fact not a far-fetched possibility. There is already research that concludes, by and large, the global AML/CTF regime as it stands is disproportionately burdensome to least-developing countries,[92] and that the regime itself is heading into misguided, wasteful or simply irrelevant direction.[93] For those in global society that are not entirely onboard with the political priorities of the FATF, or the way its rise is eclipsing or hampering other competing priorities, this locking-in effect is detrimental as it narrows the space for contestation.

7 Conclusion

A general belief in legal visibility and formalization as a pathway towards taming expert bodies may give us hope that the re-institution of the FATF as a formal international organization would enhance its accountability. This belief is rooted in the idea that unambiguously placing expert bodies under the constraining regime of an increasingly constitutionalized international legal order enhances

90 Ibid 1.

91 See FATF website <https://www.fatf-gafi.org/countries/> accessed 17 April 2020.

92 Jason C. Sharman, 'Power and Discourse in Policy Diffusion: Anti-Money Laundering in Developing States' (2008) 52(3) Int'l Studies Quarterly 635.

93 Matthew Redhead, 'Deep Impact? Refocusing the Anti-Money Laundering Model on Evidence and Outcomes' (*Royal United Services Institute*, October 2019) < https://rusi.org/publication/occasional-papers/deep-impact-refocusing-anti-money-laundering-model-evidence-and> accessed 17 April 2020; Peter Alldridge, *What Went Wrong With Money Laundering Law?* (Palgrave McMillan 2016).

their accountability. This view easily converts questions of accountability into legality, i.e. whether or not an action is answerable under a certain legal order. Consequently, the formal entry of an entity into a legal order – in the case of the FATF, acquiring international legal personality – always comes as a welcome first step that necessarily leads to better accountability.

The discussion of the FATF in this chapter illustrates that (international) legal personality may lead to more accountability of the institution under certain circumstances, but it might also produce less accountability under different circumstances. When an expert body obtains independent legal existence, relative autonomy from its member states and consolidation of its institutional body usually follows. In such case, accountability could be enhanced through participatory accountability mechanisms for external stakeholders, such as peer scrutiny, i.e. when the organization is subjected to horizontal scrutiny by other organizations. There is also the possibility for the organization itself to engage internal supervisory and hierarchal discipline as its bureaucracy matures. Furthermore, the clear reinstitution of an expert body such as FATF as a subject under the international legal order also gives a needed normative clarity both for analytic purposes and for the triggering of review mechanisms by external bodies.

On the other hand, international legal personality might simply be inconsequential or even detrimental to the accountability of the FATF. It could be inconsequential if in post-formalization life, the FATF retains its previous informal *modus operandi* (e.g. of not being reflective or transparent). In other cases, upon formalization, member states could actively suppress the organization's institutional consolidation for fear of mission creep, and refuse to establish or utilize its accountability-enhancing organs (e.g. dispute settlement body). Moreover, the consequence of the formalization of an organization could be detrimental to its external (participatory) accountability in two ways. One is when the move generates a backlash from powerful member states that prefer to have a tighter control of the organization: these states might seek to tame the organization (e.g. through funding) or substitute it with other, more exclusive/ less-accountable entities. The second is through the locking-in effect of legalization: i.e. existing contested norms produced by an unaccountable body would be transposed into and locked-in within the permanent body of international legal order, which is harder to change.

Part III

Expertise and accountability in environment, health and (food) safety law and governance

7 Expertise, trust and accountability in food safety: The evolving role of the World Trade Organization

A case study of the Japan-Korea dispute over the Fukushima nuclear disaster

Rob Howse

1 Introduction

Distrust of expertise, and rejection of the authority of experts, are often presented as symptoms of rising 'populism', a reflection of ominous irrationality in public discourse.[1] But the area of food safety has long been marked by tensions between public perception of risk and citizens' demands for risk control, on the one hand, and expert judgment and authority, on the other. At the same time, expert assessments have often proven wrong, and can be influenced by 'non-scientific' factors such as the source of research funds, disciplinary bias, political pressure and an emphasis on laboratory techniques that may not be salient to the way in which individual and collective human behaviour shapes risk. Conversely, when one takes into account that risk judgments for social and political action are inherently shaped by normative considerations and assumptions, 'popular' risk perspectives are not simply irrational.[2]

At the level of global governance, the World Trade Organization (WTO) has been front and centre in these battles. The post-war arrangement for multilateral trade, the General Agreement on Tariffs and Trade (GATT), protected regulatory diversity. The GATT required that regulations be non-discriminatory in relation to a state's trading partners; but the substantive content of the regulations

1 Michiko Kakutani, *The Death of Truth: Notes on Falsehood in the Age of Trump* (Tim Duggan Books 2018) 45, on how postmodernism prepared the ground for the notion of the contingency and situatedness of moral and political truth, and Sophia Rosenfeld, *Democracy and Truth: A Short History* (University of Pennsylvania Press 2018). See also Thomas Nichols, *The Death of Expertise: The Campaign Against Established Knowledge and Why it Matters* (OUP 2017).

2 Kristin S. Shrader-Frechette, *Risk and Rationality: Philosophical Foundations for Populist Reforms* (Berkeley, CA: University of California Press 1991).

could be completely irrational as long as the non-discrimination principle was honoured. With the creation of the WTO in 1995 a new agreement came into force binding all the WTO's Members, the Sanitary and Phytosanitary Measures (SPS) Agreement. Under the SPS Agreement it is science not public opinion that determines whether a WTO Member is permitted to restrict trade in order to protect food safety.[3] The SPS Agreement requires that food safety measures that restrict trade be based on scientific principles and a scientific risk assessment; that the measures be no trade restrictive than necessary to achieve the chosen level of protection against risk; and that 'each Member shall avoid arbitrary or unjustifiable distinctions in the levels it considers to be appropriate in different situations'.

From the earliest days of the WTO, the application of this code proved to be highly controversial. The maintenance of non-science based food safety regulations in the face of violation of WTO law may seem like a minor threat to the integrity of the multilateral trading system when compared to recent actions in the US-China trade wars in the Trump era. At the same time, introducing a level of global governance into accountability for government decision-making about food risk has the potential to correct for biases of domestic regulators and interest group capture of regulatory processes. As Dani Rodrik suggests this is a positive role for global governance. He refers to 'those, mostly procedural, obligations that enhance domestic deliberation or are consistent with democratic delegation. I have in mind procedural requirements designed to enhance the quality of domestic policy-making. Examples of such requirements would be global disciplines pertaining to transparency, broad representation of stakeholders, accountability, and the use of scientific/economic evidence in domestic proceedings'.[4]

While arguably imposing disproportionate costs on poorer countries (that might however be borne by technical assistance from development agencies), the SPS Agreement, through introducing a global level of scrutiny, creates incentives for improving the quality of expertise, and enhancing capacity for science-based decision-making at the domestic level. This is different from the apparent outcome of the Hormones and Genetically Modified Organism (GMO) cases, which highlighted the most democratically questionable feature of SPS: making science not public opinion the ultimate arbiter of risk regulation. Citizen distrust or divergence from expert conclusions about risk should not be interpreted as a nihilistic rejection of any role for scientific expertise. Instead, the outcome may be introducing greater accountability and transparency in the role of expertise in risk regulation, as well as greater attention to minority or dissenting views (along the lines already endorsed by the WTO Appellate Body in the first *EU-Hormones* ruling). Perhaps eventually this could create a genuine transnational discourse

3 See Robert Howse, 'Democracy, Science, and Free Trade: Risk Regulation Trial at the World Trade Organization' (2000) 98 Michigan L. Rev 2329.

4 Dani Rodrik, 'Putting Global Governance in Its Place' Harvard Kennedy School Working Paper (June 2019) 23.

about risk, which transcends purely domestic perspectives. As Ulrich Beck suggests: 'A global public discourse does *not* grow out of a consensus on decisions, but out of *dissent* over the *consequences* of decisions. Modern risk crises are constituted by just such controversies over consequences. Where some may see an over-reaction to risk, it is also possible to see grounds for hope. Because such risk conflicts do indeed have an enlightenment function. They destabilize the existing order, but the same events can also look like a vital step towards the building of new institutions'.[5]

At the same time, there is an important limit to the WTO SPS regime as an agent for improved public dialogue around risk. SPS imposes no obligations on the state which is posing the risk: and this comes from the overall concern of SPS with avoidance of unnecessary trade restriction, not optimizing rational and responsive regulation through global governance. Through the SPS regime, as applied in the WTO dispute process, states are only held accountable for risk regulations that have a restrictive impact on trade, and the emphasis is systematically on whether regulations are over-restrictive, from a trade liberalization perspective. The justificatory burden falls on regulations that have restrictive effects, and (unless the 'underregulation' is practiced on a discriminatory basis in favour of some states relative to others), there is no accountability for failure to regulate risk. Thus, the WTO SPS regime offers a very one-sided sort of accountability for risk decisions concerning food and agricultural health and safety.

There is perhaps one exception: Article 3.4 of the SPS Agreement creates a presumption of WTO compatibility for those SPS measures that conform to international standards, which are defined as the standards pertaining to certain international organizations like the United Nations Food and Agriculture Organization (FAO) Codex Alimentarius. Effectively in such instances accountability of domestic governance at the global level is shifted to regimes the primary focus of which is specialized standards and regulation rather than trade liberalization. At the same time the trade liberalization focus is evident even here; international standards are regarded as a common denominator such that any greater trade restrictiveness in deviating from them must be justified through the scientific risk assessment provisions of SPS.

WTO adjudicators are drawn largely (and at the Panel level) almost exclusively from the trade law and policy community. While experts provide evidence and opinions in the WTO adjudicative process, the adjudicators neither have democratic legitimacy nor specialized knowledge that would allow them plausibly to hold these experts to account.

These features of the SPS regime as applied through WTO dispute settlement suggest that the role of the regime in improving public dialogue on regulation and risk is likely to be positive where WTO adjudicators focus not on second-guessing substantive regulatory choices of states, but rather on processes and procedures.

5 Ulrich Beck, 'Living in the World Risk Society' (2006) 35 Economy and Society 329, 339.

It is in this vein that the present chapter considers the food safety dimension of the risk crisis arising from the nuclear disaster in Fukushima, Japan.

2 Fukushima: Nuclear and regulatory disaster

'On 11 March 2011, Japan experienced a massive earthquake and tsunami that triggered the Fukushima Daiichi Nuclear Power Plant (FDNPP) accident. This resulted in the release of large amounts of radionuclides into the atmosphere, including cesium-134 and -137...'.[6] Moreover, one aspect of the management of the crisis was the discharge of contaminated water into sea, raising significant concerns about the safety of human consumption of seafood from the area.[7] In response to public concerns, and despite Japan's insistence that the relevant exports of fish were safe for human consumption, based on standard scientific understandings of safe levels of radiation exposure, Korea (among other countries including China) banned imports of fish from the most highly affected areas, and imposed additional testing requirements in other cases. Japan filed a case against Korea at the WTO, alleging multiple violations of the SPS Agreement.

As will be discussed below, the context of Japan's claim at the WTO was the considerable domestic difficulties that Japan's government was facing due to massive public distrust of its contentions that food now on the shelves after the accident was indeed safe. According to Sand, 'the massive uncertainty caused by nuclear contamination' resulted in a 'breakdown' in trust in both governments and experts.[8] The fact of foreign countries banning the food only increased suspicions of Japan's own citizens that the government was in fact responding to domestic political economy imperatives to protect local agriculture and fisheries, as well as to maintain confidence in nuclear power, at the expense of the protection of human life and health. A ruling by the WTO that vindicated the government's assertions about the safety of the Fukushima-affected food supply would, in theory, support alleviate some of the public distrust. As came out in Japanese newspapers, Japan had been led to expect that it would win in the WTO. Thus, the Japanese government apparently was not concerned with the downside risk that the Panel would in fact find Korea's ban to be justifiable based upon expert evidence, and therefore that the WTO ruling would serve as

6 Nobuaki Kunji and others, 'The Knowledge and Awareness for Radiocesium Food Monitoring after the Fukushima Daiichi Nuclear Accident in Nihonmatsu City, Fukushima Prefecture' (2018) 15 International Journal of Environmental Research and Public Health 2289, 1–2.

7 Dainim Lee and others, 'Factors Associated with the Risk Perception and Purchase Decisions of Fukushima-related Food in South Korea' (2017) 12 PLOS One, 1–2.

8 Jordan Sand, 'Living with Uncertainty after March 11, 2011' (2012) 71 Journal of Asian Studies 313, 316. See also, Giulia Nicolii, 'Safe to Eat? Dealing with Food Safety after the Fukushima Disaster' (2016) 9 Reinvention.

independent evidence of the untrustworthiness of the Japanese government's pronouncement on risk and risk management strategies.

The decision of the first instance, which came down in the winter of 2018,[9] met Japan's expectations: Korea's ban on certain allegedly high-risk fish imports and additional testing on others taken in 2013–2014 were found to be an unnecessary restriction on trade. The ban was considered discriminatory in that Japanese products from the affected region were singled out, rather than all imports being held to a scientifically justified standard of safe levels of radionuclides (the Panel was more sympathetic to much earlier measures Japan had taken in the immediate wake of the disaster in 2011). Japan had established to the satisfaction of the Panel that based on repeated testing of samples, the imports in question fell well within the safe range. The panel then found that these imports should not therefore be distinguished from imported products originating from geographical areas unaffected by the Fukushima accident. Japan's government had no hesitation celebrating the victory and stating to the press that the Panel ruling was independent proof of the safety of Fukushima-affected Japanese seafood exports.

The sensitivity of the matter in terms of public opinion was such that whether to lift a ban on Japanese fish imports was put to a referendum in Taiwan. Other countries made no moves towards easing their own restrictions. Korea, for its part appealed to the WTO AB. The appeal was heard at the end of 2018. As with the first instance, Japan and Korea did not agree to the opening up of the proceedings to the public: this suggests an unwillingness to allow the WTO dispute settlement process to influence directly, unfiltered by governments, public debate about risk post-Fukushima.

The WTO Appellate Body released its Report in April 2019,[10] just weeks before the premiering of a much-anticipated TV miniseries on the previous nuclear catastrophe with widespread consequences for food safety, Chernobyl. *Chernobyl* would portray a massive governmental cover-up both in terms of the actual events at the power plant as well as their consequences for human health and safety; in *Chernobyl* the 'experts' would divide between the evil and arrogant – those complicit with government deception or even willing to risk an accident through overconfidence in their ability to work around standard risk protocols – and the saintly, represented in the miniseries by two scientist whistle-blowers who risk their careers and perhaps their lives for outing the truth.[11]

9 Panel Report, *Korea – Import Bans, and Testing and Certification Requirements for Radionuclides*, WT/DS495/R and Add.1, circulated to WTO Members 22 February 2018.

10 Report of the Appellate Body, *Korea – Import Bans, and Testing and Certification Requirements for Radionuclides*, WT/DS495/AB/R, circulated to WTO Members April 11, 2019.

11 Masha Gessen, 'What HBO's Chernobyl Got Right, and What It Got Terribly Wrong' *The New Yorker* (New York, 4 June 2019).

The Appellate Body's ruling produced shock and rage in Tokyo.[12] The AB reversed the Panel's findings on the lack of necessity of the challenged import restrictions, and on unjustified discrimination. The AB findings did not imply that Japan's science was defective or tainted: instead, through creative jurisprudence the Appellate Body had carved out a margin of appreciation that would allow Seoul to respond to public fears even without offering a contrary body of scientific evidence to support those concerns. However, the Japanese government, having initially presented victory at the WTO as a vindication of its approach to risk, now had the difficult task of explaining to the public, unaware of the nuances of WTO appellate review that the AB's ruling did not in fact constitute an evidence-based finding that the fish affected by Korea's import restrictions did in fact carry levels of radiation making them unsuited for human consumption.

Less remarked however is the Appellate Body reversal of the Panel's finding that Korea had violated requirements of transparency and regulatory dialogue. These kinds of provisions hold the promise of better transnational understandings of risk, greater accountability of national governments and their experts, and more nuanced views of the public about expertise-based risk determinations and risk management. Reversing the Panel, the Appellate Body interpreted the transparency provisions in a broad manner, finding that any assessment of violation would have to look at all factors that might be relevant, which could include not just the regulating state's responsiveness to requests for information or dialogue by the state where the risk is originating, but also the forthrightness and openness to dialogue of the risk-originating state. Here, Korea had drawn upon the resources of a civil society-based Civilian Expert Group to engage with official Japanese expertise, while taking into account perspectives of citizens and consumers. It is my argument that the Appellate Body's ruling, fundamentally correcting the Panel and taking a broader approach to risk and uncertainty, is an example of how, as Ulrich Beck suggests, a risk crisis can through global governance give rise not just to increased public insecurity and distrust (Hormones and GMOs) but to the promise of a positive global public discourse. This promise has been neglected because the ruling has been mostly viewed (both by WTO legal experts and media commentators) through the lenses of Tokyo's backfired strategic use of WTO dispute settlement as a weapon in a domestic political battle.

3 Sources of public/expert divergence on risk and the case of Fukushima

Cleavages between popular and expert approaches to risk cannot be entirely explained by the rise of populism, nihilistic embrace of irrationality, or ignorant Yahoo-like resentment and distrust of 'elites'. While expert approaches focus on

12 Japan Times, 'Japan Denounces WTO Ruling in Favor of South Korean Ban on Some Japanese Seafood' (Tokyo, 27 April 2019) <https://www.japantimes.co.jp/news/2019/04/27/business/japan-raps-wto-ruling-favor-south-korean-ban-japanese-seafood/#.XZstyEZKjIU> accessed 15 July 2020.

estimating the likelihood a risk will materialize and the range of consequences (usually in quantifiable terms) if it does materialize, a range of cognitive and contextual considerations impacts upon citizens' and consumers' approach to risk as they lead their own lives and make decisions affecting themselves and their families. Some of these factors are well-captured by Sunstein and Pildes: 'For laypeople, many contextual features are relevant: (1) the catastrophic nature of the risk; (2) whether the risk is controllable; (3) whether the risk involves irretrievable or permanent losses; (4) the social conditions under which a particular risk is generated and managed, a point that connects to issues of consent, voluntariness, and democratic control (5) how equitably distributed the danger is or how concentrated on identifiable, innocent, or traditionally disadvantaged (6) how well understood the risk process in question is, a point that bears on the psychological disturbance produced by different risks; (7) whether the risk would be faced by future generations; and (8) how familiar the risk is'.[13]

Many of these factors come into play in the case of risk from nuclear catastrophe. Dread of the consequences of radiation poisoning is deeply embedded in the public consciousness; individuals can do little or nothing obvious to avoid this risk (given how far dangerous radiation may spread after an accident, not living near a nuclear power plant is not a plausible precaution). Risk controls in nuclear power plants are not easy for laypeople to understand; many protocols are in any case secret due to legitimate security concerns. While exposure to very heavy levels of radiation can near the site of the accident may have gruesome short-term health consequences (some of which are portrayed with horrifying explicitness in *Chernobyl*), there is limited knowledge concerning and experience with very long-term consequences of lower radiation exposures that are the consequence of nuclear accidents or attacks.

The challenge of understanding these longer term effects is captured by Kamiya et al.: 'Radiation exposure increases the risk of cancer throughout life, so continued follow-up of survivors is essential. Overall, survivors have a clear radiation-related excess risk of cancer, and people exposed as children have a higher risk of radiation-induced cancer than those exposed at older ages. At high doses, and possibly at low doses, radiation might increase the risk of cardiovascular disease and some other non-cancer diseases. Hereditary effects in the children of atomic bomb survivors have not been detected. The dose–response relation for cancer at low doses is assumed, for purposes of radiological protection, to be linear without a threshold, but has not been shown definitively. This outstanding issue is not only a problem when dealing appropriately with potential

13 Cass R. Sunstein and Richard Pildes, 'Experts, Economists, and Democrats' in Cass Sunstein (ed), *Free Markets and Social Justice* (OUP 1997) 133; Sunstein and Pildes rely on the social science of for example Paul Slovic. See Paul Slovic, 'Perception of Risk' (1987) 236 Science 280; Paul Slovic, 'Beyond Numbers: A Broader Perspective on Risk Perception and Risk Communication' in Deborah G. Mayo and Rachelle D Hollander (eds), *Acceptable Evidence – Science and Value in Risk Management* (Environmental Ethics and Science Policy Series 1991) 48.

health effects of nuclear accidents, such as at Fukushima and Chernobyl, but is of growing concern in occupational and medical exposure. Therefore, the appropriate dose–response relation for effects of low doses of radiation needs to be established'.[14]

In case of food safety, long-term health risks from lower levels of radiation raise a particular concern, because many people make decisions about buying food not only for themselves as individuals but for their children, and indeed entire family. In Japan (and other parts of Asia) this is especially true, and the decision-makers are very frequently mothers.[15] A sense of responsibility for the lives and health of others, including future generations, reinforces an attitude of apprehension when making choices that may have very long-term consequences imperfectly understood.

In the context of Fukushima, as with Chernobyl, revelations of gross irresponsibility and widespread deceit by government officials and by those responsible for the nuclear power plant operation, doubtless compounded distrust of government-proffered expertise regarding the safety of the food supply, including seafood. As Kingston summarizes, 'Fukushima was preceded by a series of mishaps, cover-ups, irresponsible practices, close calls and ignored warnings...'[16] Repair and maintenance records were routinely falsified. A number of investigations and inquiries within Japan revealed that 'the government withheld information about the full danger of the nuclear disaster from the public and the international community. This belated attempt to quell public concerns about the lack of transparency actually amplified them because it has clarified how much information the government withheld from the public and how little it has divulged about the deliberations during the crisis. Apparently managing risk was more a matter of concealing chaotic and inconsistent decision-making by the government and inadequate crisis response procedures ([by the plant operator] than gleaning useful lessons about how to improve crisis response mechanisms. This lack of transparency reflects a "circling of the wagons" mindset that prevents robust risk management, ...'.[17]

One particular development that exacerbated distrust in the case of food safety is that the government itself significantly altered its own benchmark for the level of exposure to radiation in food that was acceptable for safe human consumption.[18] Distrust was far from a 'populist' rebellion against elites; Japanese consumers (as with those in Korea and elsewhere) desperately wanted reliable information about risk based on independent science; civil society groups were

14 Kenji Kamiya and others, 'Long-term Effects of Radiation Exposure on Health' (2016) 386 The Lancet 469.

15 See Nicolas Sternsdorff-Cisterna, ***Food Safety After Fukushima: Scientific Citizenship and the Politics of Risk*** (University of Hawaii Press, 2019), chapter 2.

16 Jeff Kinston, 'Mismanaging Risk and the Fukushima Nuclear Crisis' (2012) 10 The Asia-Pacific Journal 3.

17 Ibid 11–12.

18 Kunji and others (n 6) 2.

created where citizens distrustful of the government sought to gather reliable information and educate each other about the nature of the risks.[19]

3.1 *The Panel of first instance*

Despite widespread (and to some extent justified: see the analysis immediately above) distrust of Japanese Government claims about risk, Korea was unable to come before the WTO Panel of first instance with an alternative body of scientific evidence or expert opinion to establish that its import ban and additional testing procedures were necessary to achieve an appropriate level of protection of human health defined as the 'safe' level as understood on the basis of science. This level of protection was radiation exposure *below* an annual dose limit (1 mSv/year) established in international standards based on scientific analysis and experience with the consequences of the Chernobyl accident. The Panel then took this benchmark of 1 mSv/year, and considered the evidence, including that of scientific experts appearing in the WTO proceedings, concerning whether Korea's ban and additional testing requirements were necessary to achieve that benchmark. While Korea attempted to raise questions about some of Japan's data collection and analysis practices ('cherry-picking' for instance in terms of particular fish), in general, the international experts consulted by the WTO Panel, based upon the data presented, found that the established radiation levels of potentially Fukushima-affected fish imports were low enough that, with routine testing of samples, Korea could be confident of limiting the exposure of its population to the 1 mSv/year level without a ban in some cases and additional testing in others.

3.2 *The principle of precaution and SPS 5.7*

Korea had tried to justify its more stringent approach on a precautionary basis as provisional measures within the meaning of Article 5.7 of SPS, which allows measures taken temporarily in the absence of sufficient evidence to make a scientific risk assessment. But Japan's lawyers had cleverly not challenged whether Korea's measures were based on scientific principles or a scientific risk assessment. Korea therefore found it difficult to argue that it was in a situation where it did not yet have evidence to conduct risk assessments. The Panel may well have been wrong to conclude that 5.7 only applies where there scientific evidence has not reached a minimum threshold (see Paragraph 7.108); the Appellate Body in its revisiting of the Hormones dispute (its second ruling two decades after the first one, provoked by new studies presented by the EU) had found fault in a similar approach by the Panel of first instance in that case. In that report, the

19 Sterndorff-Cisterna (n 15). See also, Rika Ikeda, 'The Construction of Risk and the Resilience of Fukushima in the Aftermath of the Nuclear Power Plant Accident' in Tom Gill, Brigitte Steger and David Slater (eds), *Japan Copes with Calamity* (Peter Lang 2013) 151–176.

AB held that SPS 5.7 could be invoked to address situations where there were continuing developments concerning risk and its assessment that might affect regulatory judgments, not only ones where the evidence in the first place never passed the threshold of sufficiency to conduct a risk assessment. What might be sufficient in light of the state of affairs today and current scientific understanding might be inadequate on a deeper, more advanced scientific appreciation of the nature of the risks in question and the methodologies and data required to conduct a more adequate study of it.

Korea had argued before the Panel that the situation at the accident site was an ongoing and evolving one, which justified extraordinary precaution. And Korea was able to point to post-accident releases of contaminated water in some cases not announced or disclosed by the authorities. The Panel said it 'recognizes the importance of confidence in the regulatory authorities of the exporting country with respect to food safety and does not discount Korea's concerns about transparency as to what could be occurring…' (Paragraph 7.89) But while recognizing these concerns, the Panel disregarded them in its analysis. The Panel was simply dismissive of the notion that further unilateral (and perhaps unpredictable or unannounced) actions by Japan could alter the risk from human consumption of fish: 'Regarding the argument alleging that FDNPP remains an active and ongoing source of contamination, the experts note that a possibility of future leaks is of little relevance to the determination of food contamination, unless a significant release goes undetected, which is unlikely in view of Japan's water monitoring programme' (Paragraph 7.195). This judgment of experts might be correct, based on assumptions of best regulatory and risk management practice by Japan; but it does not take into account the evidence of Japan's past lack of transparency, and indeed outright deception, as concerns the risks from the accident and the measures required to manage the accident. The Panel's approach also did not factor in the limits to existing scientific uncertainty concerning very long-term effects of low-level exposure, as discussed above. Indeed, the Panel was dismissive (incredibly, given the small number of nuclear events from which the existing scientific understanding has been drawn) of the notion that any relevant scientific uncertainty existed: 'Although there is an uncertainty with respect to the potential for future nuclear accidents at the FDNPP or elsewhere this uncertainty does not relate to the science necessary to assess the risks associated with the consumption of contaminated food, but rather to the inherent uncertainty of life' (Paragraph 7.108).

The Panel went so far as to state that 'public concern, uncertainties, and the inability to predict the future are not, in our view' a basis for precaution-based provision measures based on SPS 5.7, which refers to acting on pertinent scientific information. Here the Panel seems to have ignored the relevance identified by the Appellate Body in *Hormones* of a broader notion of precaution than that suggested by a literal reading of the text of SPS 5.7 in isolation: 'a Panel charged with determining, for instance, whether "sufficient scientific evidence" exists … may, of course, and should bear in mind that responsible, representative governments commonly act from perspectives of prudence and precaution where risks of irreversible, e.g. life terminating, damage to harm to human health are concerned' (Paragraph 124).

3.3 'Discrimination'

The Panel also determined that Korea's measures were discriminatory in targeting Japan, and in particular exports from the areas potentially affected by Fukushima, and thus violated Article 2.3 of SPS. The Panel held that it was possible that food would contain radionuclides from non-Fukushima related sources such as nuclear testing or releases from reactors elsewhere in the world. Thus, singling out Japan was arbitrary and discriminatory (Paragraphs 7.338–7.339). The Panel here noted that the overall goal of Korea was stated as ensuring exposure did not rise to the threshold of 1 mSv/year, regardless of the source of the radionuclides.

In addition, the Panel held that certain specific testing procedures by Korea were discriminatory or unnecessarily trade restrictive (Article 7 of SPS); the Panel's analysis here largely duplicates its findings on the substantive measures adopted. Finally, however, the Panel considered Korea's compliance with transparency requirements in Article 7 of the SPS Agreement, and its Annex B. The Panel found that Korea had failed to publish its regulations in such a manner as to communicate adequately the products impacted and as well in the case of testing the tolerance levels and other standards to be applied to Japanese imports. Further, Korea had failed in its obligation to respond to reasonable questions and requests for documents by Japan (Paragraph 7.517).

The context here is interesting from the perspective of global risk dialogue. The Korean government had decided to bring into its process for responding to Fukushima a Korean/Civilian Expert Group made up of civil society actors and without a formal governmental status. '[T]he Civilian Expert Group [according to Korea] was formed as an ad hoc group of scholars, radiation specialists, nuclear experts, medical doctors, and members of NGOs' (Paragraph 7.105).

This group that sought to engage constructively with Japan's approach to risk, through reviewing Japan's documentation of risk, conducting on site-visits to Japan, and conducting an independent analysis of samples of fish and sea water. The Group seemed to be aiming at a constructive approach to risk in a context of distrust and earlier mismanagement, bringing civil society into the exercise. Korea claimed that it had delayed responses to Japanese government requests for information while the Expert Group was still conducting its examination of risk. In fact, the operations of the Group were suspended when Japan filed a claim in WTO dispute settlement. And then Korea never responded to the Japanese requests in question.

The Panel found Korea at fault here for failure to respond to Japan's requests. But the larger context was Korea's attempting to work with civil society, fearful and distrustful of Japan's management of the food safety risks in question, in an effort to close the gap between divergent perspectives on risk: public fears and perceptions of Fukushima risk vs. the official expertise proffered by Japan.

Perhaps Japanese officials were fearful of the impact of that dialogue on their own ability to manage or control risk perceptions of the domestic public (which of course so far had in case proven to be quite limited). Or it could be, more along the lines of the Panel's analysis, that the closing down of the Civilian Expert Group's operation in response to Japan going to dispute settlement was a nationalistic over-reaction; it was not appropriate for Korea to rely on this to fail to respond to Japan's requests for information. These developments, in any case occurred when political and diplomatic tensions between Japan and Korea were rising for reasons unconnected to Fukushima, above all Korea's determination to re-open a deal that the previous Administration had struck with Japan to address, and obtain closure, on Japan's mistreatment of the Korean 'comfort women' during WWII.[20] Nationalistic politics on both sides may have prevented or stymied a promising global regulatory dialogue. What is questionable is the Panel placing the blame solely on Korea. But this shows a limitation of the SPS Agreement in terms of facilitating global regulatory dialogue: the state regulating the risk has obligations to engage, but as noted in the introduction, SPS imposes no obligations on the state which is posing the risk: and this comes from the overall concern of SPS with avoidance of unnecessary trade restriction, not optimizing rational and responsive regulation through global governance.

3.4 *The appeal*

3.4.1 *Unnecessary trade-restrictiveness*

Korea appealed the main findings of the Panel that were adverse for Korea, discussed above. The AB, with (as noted, dramatic impact in Tokyo) reverse the two key findings of unnecessary trade restrictiveness and of discrimination.

On unnecessary trade restrictiveness, the Appellate Body found that the Panel had misread the level of protection chosen by Korea. The Panel had taken the level of protection to be set at the benchmark of 1 mSv/year. As the Appellate Body noted, the Panel had truncated and distorted Korea's own articulation of its level of protection as achieving exposure levels as far below this benchmark possible and in any case not above it (Paragraph 5.31). The Appellate Body affirmed that a WTO Member has the prerogative to set its level of protection according to what the AB calls the 'As Low as Reasonably Achievable' (ALARA) principle. The Panel had ignored this element of Korea's chosen level of protection, i.e. the goal of reducing radiation exposure to those 'levels that exist

20 James Griffiths, 'South Korea's New President Questions Japan "Comfort Women" deal' *CNN* (Atlanta, 5 June 2017) <https://edition.cnn.com/2017/05/11/asia/south-korea-japan-comfort-women/> accessed 15 July 2020. This controversy over transitional justice, or the lack thereof, has further intensified, leading to an unprecedented level of trade conflict between Japan and Korea; see Catherine Kim, 'The Escalating Trade War between South Korea and Japan, Explained' *Vox* (Washington D.C., 9 August 2019) <https://www.vox.com/world/2019/8/9/20758025/trade-war-south-korea-japan> accessed 15 July 2020.

in the ordinary environment'. According to the Appellate Body: 'The Panel's ultimate findings reflect an effective subordination of the elements of ALARA and radioactivity levels 'in the ordinary environment to the quantitative element of Korea's ALOP [Appropriate Level of Protection] in a manner that is at odds with the formulation of the ALOP explicitly accepted by the Panel at the outset of its analysis' (Paragraph 5.36).

It is to be noted that the Appellate Body also observed that, in principle, the Panel might have inquired into whether 'the ALARA element and the maintenance of radioactivity levels in food "at levels that exist in the ordinary environment" were insufficiently precise or otherwise incapable of serving as elements of Korea's ALOP for purposes of assessing alternative measures under Article 5.6' (Paragraph 5.35). Of course, had the Appellate Body found that given the correct legal interpretation of 5.6 and other relevant provisions of SPS, ALARA was *as such* not a permissible approach to establishing an ALOP, it could have upheld the Panel's approach regardless of the Panel's failure to address explicitly this issue. But the Appellate Body sought to leave open the possibility that in some circumstances the use of ALARA might not be compatible with SPS 5.6.

3.4.2 *Long-term consequences of low-dose radiation exposure: 'Linear without a threshold'*

In the case at hand, the Panel seems to have been swayed by Japan's argument that the trade restrictive measures challenged, even if they resulted in reduced overall radiation exposure, did not contribute to the protection of human life and health. This was because the Panel was convinced that levels of exposure that were 'safe' (i.e. well below 1 mSv/year) were achievable without Korea's challenged.

This reasoning reflects an inadequate consideration of the long-term health effects of low-level radiation exposure (albeit higher than in the ordinary environment by some discernable margin). As expressed by Kamiya et al., 'The dose–response relation for cancer at low doses is assumed, for purposes of radiological protection, to be linear without a threshold, but has not been shown definitively'.[21] Thus, even if 1 mSv/year represents an overall judgment of what is *un*safe (exposure beyond that), reducing exposures as far as possible below this quantitative ceiling is still a rational means of, at the margin, achieving positive health impact. This is the linear aspect identified by Kamiya et al. The 1 mSv/year threshold represents the best available information in the time horizons we have as concerns general populations. Persons whose lifetime levels of exposure to radiation are already high (from radiation therapy, for example) or have certain pre-existent health conditions may well have their health outcomes meaningfully

21 Rodrik (n 4).

affected by reductions that go well beyond the 1 mSv/year threshold.[22] It is entirely legitimate to take into consideration those especially sensitive or vulnerable groups through taking an ALARA approach to determining the level of protection. In practice, permitting ALARA in situations like the Fukushima one allows governments a reasonable way of taking into account factors that are important that may not be reflected in quantitative risk thresholds, even if these are determined by the best available objective and independent science.

3.4.3 *'Discrimination'*

We now turn to the Appellate Body's findings on discrimination (2.3 of SPS). The anti-discrimination provision in 2.3 refers to discrimination between products where 'similar conditions prevail' in the country of origins of the product. The Appellate Body held that the Panel erred when it failed to consider, not only the objective data concerning the radioactive content of imports from Japan and other sources, but how territorial and ecological conditions in Japan might be different in a manner relevant to determining whether the stricter treatment of Japanese imports was unjustifiably or arbitrarily discriminatory within the meaning of 2.3 (Paragraph 5.63).

According to the Appellate Body: 'the analysis under Article 2.3 thus entails consideration of all relevant conditions in different Members, including territorial conditions that may not *yet* have manifested in *products* but are relevant in light of the regulatory objective and specific SPS risks at issue' (Paragraph 5.64; emphasis added). At the same time, the Appellate Body observed, the Panel 'recognize[d] the unprecedented nature of the FDNPP accident, as the largest release of radionuclides from a nuclear accident into the marine environment'. Further, the Panel stated that 'radioactive material, mainly caesium, released [into] the atmosphere from FDNPP also contributed to global contamination levels, although the fallout has affected the East and North of Japan the most'. The Panel noted that radionuclides released from the FDNPP 'were largely dispersed by sea currents and added to existing concentration levels in the Northern Pacific, stating further that "some amounts of these radionuclides were bound to particles, sunk and settled in sediments off the Fukushima coast' (Paragraph 5.70: footnotes omitted). In other words, while well aware that risks could be affected by specific territorial or geographic conditions, the Panel completely failed to examine them as relevant under SPS 2.3. This legal error fundamentally tainted the Panel's analysis of 2.3; thus, the Appellate Body reversed the Panel's overall conclusion of the existence of impermissible 'discrimination'. At the same

22 See the discussion of 'low-dose hypersensitivity' (examining radiation from X-Rays) in Mark Little and others, 'Risks Associated with Low Doses and Low Dose Rates of Ionizing Radiation: Why Linearity May Be (Almost) the Best We Can Do' (2009) 251 Radiology 6; like other recent contributions to the literature this one emphasizes that scientific certainty about a threshold for 'safe' low-dose radiation exposure is elusive. This strongly confirms the greater soundness of the overall approach of the Appellate Body to that of the Panel.

time, the AB took pains to indicate that it offered no opinion as to what the Panel ought to have concluded concerning discrimination if it not made the legal error in question (Paragraph 5.90).

The AB's emphasis on 'consideration of *all* relevant conditions' (emphasis added) raises the question of whether relevant conditions could include Japan's early mismanagement of the risk from the accident and active deception concerning the nature and extent of ongoing and evolving risk. If so, then these conditions could easily justify greater caution and restrictiveness than in dealing with the global risk of radioactive contamination in fish stocks. There is an argument that if a WTO Member brings an SPS case attacking another Member's cautionary approach to risks it should come with 'clean hands', or at least not through its own behaviour have contributed significantly to the mistrust that fuels public perceptions of unacknowledged or concealed risk, on which democratic governments may often have little choice to but to act (even if, as in the case of Korea, attempting to open up channels for a more nuanced transnational regulatory dialogue through drawing on non-governmental civil society actors: the Korea Civilian Expert Group). The Appellate Body, as discussed, noted the requirement to take into account 'territorial conditions that may not yet have manifested in products' (Paragraph 5.64). But the AB also made it clear (footnote 218) that territorial (in the sense of geographical or ecological) differences are by no means the only, or always the most important, differences in conditions relevant to assessing discrimination under SPS 2.3.

Because, as with the AB's findings on unnecessary trade restrictiveness, its findings on discrimination impugn the legal analysis of the Panel without being dispositive of whether, on the facts, Korea may have violated the SPS provisions in question, it is still open to Japan to bring another proceeding.

The AB's reference to 'all relevant conditions' is however a warning to Japan – whether conscious or unconscious, intended or not, that reviving this dispute could result in bringing global attention to the fiascos involved in Japan's approach to nuclear safety in the first place, as well as its initial response to the accident, and thus might well backfire (as did in the end the instant dispute). As well, the announcement in September by Japanese authorities that huge additional amounts of contaminated water from the accident would have to be dumped directly into the Pacific Ocean[23] would likely provide strong support for the view that Japan, i.e. Fukushima-specific conditions are indeed relevant to assessing whether Korea's targeting of Japan in its trade restrictions is permissible discrimination.

3.4.4 *Precaution*

With respect to the Panel's finding that Korea had failed to justify its measures on a precautionary provisional basis (SPS 5.7), the AB vacated the Panel's ruling

23 Justin McCurry, 'Fukushima: Japan Will Have to Dump Radioactive Water into Pacific, Minister Says' *The Guardian* (London, 10 September 2019).

on procedural grounds. The AB found that, in fact, SPS 5.7 had not been properly raised in the pleadings as a separate matter in dispute between the parties but had only been invoked as context by Korea in explaining its arguments under the other provisions of SPS at issue. Thus, the Panel had no jurisdiction to make findings concerning the application of 5.7, and those finding were declared by the AB as without legal effect. In the past, in a situation of this nature, the AB might have been inclined to address in obiter dicta some of the Panel's interpretations of 5.7, which (as noted above) appear at odds with the AB's own approach in its second Hormones ruling. However, this Report was issued in the shadow of the US assault on the AB, which found particular fault in the appellate judges' use of obiter dicta to provide future guidance for Panels, closely connected to the Trump Administration's strong aversion to precedential authority in the WTO dispute settlement system.

This said, there are elements of the Appellate Body's analysis that communicate the relevance of precaution, especially in its statement that under 2.3 the Panel must take into account conditions that may not *yet* manifest themselves in products; and the notion of an ALARA approach to the level of protection not dogmatically relying on existing ceilings for safety, which takes into account uncertainty about very long-term health effects of low-dosage radiation exposure.

3.4.5 *Transparency*

The Appellate Body reversed the Panel's findings that Korea had violated the transparency provisions in Article 7 and Annex B (3) of SPS its failure to respond to certain of Japan's requests for information. It should be recalled that the context of this alleged failure was Korea's decision to provide an opportunity for transnational risk dialogue engaging civil society through the Civilian Expert Group and the suspension of this Group's work in the wake of Japan's decision to file a claim at the WTO. In reversing the Panel, the Appellate Body held that the Panel erred in finding a violation based on considering in isolation Korea's apparent refusal or non-responsiveness to two specific requests for information. The Appellate Body noted the relevant text in Annex B (3), observing the issue is whether 'one enquiry point exists which is responsible for the provision of answers to all reasonable questions from interested Members as well as for the provision of relevant documents' (Paragraph 6.14).

According to the Appellate Body, instead of focusing on isolated requests for information, the Panel needed to assess 'all the relevant factors' bearing upon Korea's pattern of responsiveness to Japan. This notion of 'all relevant factors' is, arguably capacious enough to include as relevant context Korea's efforts to establish a transnational dialogue inclusive of civil society through working alongside the Civilian Expert Group. As observed above, the SPS Agreement is asymmetrical or one-sided in not placing any autonomous obligations on the Member whence the risk originates to act transparently and be forthcoming in information about risk. But here, as deployed by the Appellate Body, the concept of 'all relevant factors' would be broad enough to require taking into account Japan's own behaviour in response to Korea's efforts to understanding the risks its products poses, including repeated lapses of transparency, leading to some justified level of distrust.

4 Conclusion

Despite efforts of the WTO's Appellate Body to constructively engage with public concerns and perceptions of risk through its sensitive readings of the SPS Agreement, throughout most of the history of the Agreement, the role of the WTO in food safety global governance has not been a constructive one. Instead it has pitted the public and civil society against scientific experts as the ultimate arbitrators of whether trade-restrictive food safety regulations can be justified. The Appellate Body's approach in the Fukushima dispute between Japan and Korea is a renewed effort to carve out a constructive approach, not abandoning an expertise-based scrutiny of trade restrictive measures (which is clearly required by the text of the SPS Agreement) but insisting that WTO adjudicators must conduct more holistic analyses, which bring into play, alongside scientific expertise, perspectives of governments and citizens, including concerns about trust in and accountability of experts in particular contexts. The Appellate Body, particularly in its findings regarding transparency, appeared to assess the regulating Member's compliance with such procedural requirements on the basis of some notion that both parties are under a duty to engage in good faith transnational regulatory dialogue, as far at least as exchange of information goes. The Appellate Body reversed findings of the Panel that second-guessed the substantive regulatory choices of Korea. In one, very significant dimension of its ruling, the Appellate Body took a broad view of the 'conditions' that might justify differential treatment of imports from a particular country; arguably, these conditions might include the integrity of risk regulation processes and procedures in that jurisdiction. This, along with the AB's approach to transparency just discussed, provides a window for shifting the emphasis in SPS to procedures for regulatory dialogue and decision-making The approach of not abandoning science but engaging other perspectives leaves many questions still to be answered, but it does suggest that global governance can have a positive impact in enhancing accountability for expertise-based risk decisions (as opposed to abandoning democratic accountability for rule by scientists).

Acknowledgment

I am grateful for exchanges with Antonia Eliason and Dani Rodrik concerning some of the issues discussed in this chapter.

8 Transnational radiological standards in domestic contexts[1]

Machiko Kanetake

1 Introduction

Standards that determine the safety of our daily lives are formulated by experts on the basis of both scientific and non-scientific factors. While quantitative scientific evidence informs governmental regulators which are in a position to define the safety of products and services, scientific evidence often constitutes merely *part* of the decision making processes. A wide range of safety standards are formulated through the deliberation of scientific evidence among governmental officials, industry representatives, researchers and the officials of international organizations. In the course of deliberation, researchers and officials not only gather and select what they consider would be the most credible scientific findings, but also consider their wider social, ethical and political implications. Such deliberation and standard-setting involve a range of experts in multilevel governance, as elucidated in the present edited volume's introduction by Alessandra Arcuri and Florin Coman-Kund.[2] The expert-based decision making can take place at international organizations, inter-governmental forums and the international associations of researchers, industry representatives and officials. These forums in which standard-setting takes place have been described by Oren Perez as 'transnational regulatory scientific institutions'.[3] They serve as a venue through which scientists, industry and governmental agencies deliberate and formulate what this chapter calls 'transnational science-based standards'.

Transnational science-based standards, despite the lack of any legal binding force, can be adopted at the domestic level and have profound impact on our lives. This gives rise to the question of the accountability of expert-based decision making, as outlined in the volume's framework chapter.[4] Yet

1 This chapter is based on the shortened and revised version of the author's study published earlier: 'The Dual Vulnerability of Transnational Science-Based Standards in the National Legal Order' (2017) 7(4) Transnational Legal Theory 470. All websites are accessed on 10 January 2020.
2 See Alessandra Arcuri and Florin Coman-Kund, 'Introduction: Breaking Taboos, Talking Accountability' (in this volume).
3 Oren Perez, 'The Hybrid Legal-Scientific Dynamic of Transnational Scientific Institutions' (2015) 26 European Journal of International Law 391.
4 Arcuri and Coman-Kund (n 2).

it is crucial to consider whose accountability should be subject to particular scrutiny. Attention ought to be paid not only to the decision making of transnational regulatory scientific institutions themselves; inquiry should also be made about governmental decisions as well as their interactions with transnational regulatory institutions. Governmental officials may find it convenient to rely on transnational science-based standards in order to convince their domestic audience. Governmental reliance may be combined with the active campaign of transnational regulatory scientific institutions to promote the domestic adoption of their science-based models, guidelines and recommendations.

Against this background, this chapter focuses on the domestic reception of a specific category of transnational science-based standards. The chapter's focus is directed at those transnational standards on radiation safety that are meant to protect nuclear-related workers and the general public from exposure to ionizing radiation. Scientific consensus and associated policy recommendations on radiation safety have been developed interactively through the decentralized network of research institutions, expert committees, governments, international organizations and inter-governmental forums.[5] Among such bodies, particularly influential in the field of radiation safety is the International Commission on Radiological Protection (ICRP), a formally non-governmental and non-profit expert committee.[6] The ICRP's recommendations have been widely 'incorporated' into the domestic law of many countries.

While transnational standards on radiation safety help facilitate the regulatory harmonization across different states, the domestic adoption of such standards should be subject to critical scrutiny. This is precisely because, as will be demonstrated in this chapter, that transnational science-based standards have vulnerability at both the scientific and political levels. While such vulnerability is not problematic per se, concerns may arise when the transnational standards are adopted into statute, administrative instruments and judicial decisions at the domestic level, without due regard to the characteristics of the standards. While science and politics have long been intertwined, it is necessary to unpack how the invocation of science empowers politics and what implications the political appeal to science has on accountable governance.[7]

The chapter elucidates the vulnerability of transnational science-based standards by discussing the domestic adoption of transnational radiation standards in the specific context of Japan, which encountered the Fukushima Daiichi nuclear accident in March 2011. The chapter starts with the brief overview of the web of institutions that play a role in setting the standards on radiation safety (Section 2). One of such transnationally formulated standards pertains to *dose limits* applicable to the public and professionals. In the aftermath of the

5 See Bo Lindell, 'A History of Radiation Protection' (1996) 68 Radiation Protection Dosimetry 83.

6 See Section 2.2 for further details about the ICRP.

7 Sheila Jasanoff, *Science and Public Reason* (Routledge 2012) 155.

Fukushima Daiichi nuclear accident in 2011, the transnationally recommended *dose limits* were invoked in the context of raising the legally permissible exposure limits for the general public, including children (Section 3). The government's decisions have been contested at home and internationally, which has led to a series of domestic judicial proceedings to hold the government accountable. By highlighting the domestic acceptance of, and resistance against, transnational science-based standards of radiation safety, this chapter highlights the scientific and political limits of transnational science-based standards and the domestic neglect of such limitations (Sections 4 and 5).

2 The decentralized web of transnational standard-setting bodies on radiation safety

Radiation standards, which concern the Fukushima stories I will analyse in Section 3, are developed by the decentralized web of research institutions, international expert committees, international organizations and inter-governmental forums. Among such institutions, particularly influential is the aforementioned ICRP as an international expert committee. The ICRP issues science-based recommendations that provide a further basis for the reports of international organizations. Understanding these bodies' standard-setting role is essential for the analysis presented in subsequent sections of this chapter.

2.1 *Research institutions on epidemiological studies*

In formulating radiation safety standards, it is necessary to gather reliable data that help researchers ascertain and analyse the effect of ionizing radiation on our bodies. While it is by no means a straight-forward task to gather such data, the historical context of World War II has put the Atomic Bomb Casualty Commission (ABCC)[8] and its successor, Radiation Effects Research Foundation (RERF)[9] in a position to conduct one of the most comprehensive epidemiological studies on the effect of ionizing radiation on human bodies. The ABCC was established shortly after World War II essentially with the aim of studying the effects of radiation from the Hiroshima and Nagasaki atomic bombs.

The ABCC was founded according to President Truman's directive in November 1946, and was overseen by the Atomic Energy Commission and the National Research Council of the National Academy of Sciences. The ABCC worked in close partnership with the Japan National Institute of Health established in 1947 as a governmentally-associated research institute

8 The general description of the ABCC is available at the website of the National Academy of Sciences (NAS), <www.nasonline.org/about-nas/history/archives/collections/abcc-1945-1982.html>.

9 The general description of the RERF is available at its website at <www.rerf.jp/index_e.html>.

(and was subsequently renamed the National Institute of Infectious Diseases). The ABCC was replaced in 1975 by the RERF as a joint establishment of the US and Japanese governments.[10] While the ABCC and RERF are established and have been funded by the US and Japanese governments, these entities are not formally governmental bodies, and the entities' research operations have been guided by their own decision-making boards composed of radiological scientists.[11] The ABCC commenced a major genetic study in 1949[12] and initiated the leukaemia survey in January 1950. The ABCC also launched in 1950 the subject groups for the Life Span Study which investigates the life-long health effects of radiation involving about 120,000 subjects.[13] These studies, which were the products of exceptional circumstances, have been some of the most comprehensive epidemiological findings concerning the effects of radiation to date. Needless to say, a wide range of other research institutions produce their own findings which contribute to the formulation of scientific consensus.

2.2 *Transnational expert committees*

The epidemiological findings produced through scientific research are collected by an inter-governmental body created by the UN General Assembly. The UN Scientific Committee on the Effects of Atomic Radiation (UNSCEAR) was established by the UN in 1955 in order to report and evaluate scientific findings on the effects of exposure to ionizing radiation.[14] Through the work of the UNSCEAR, various scientific findings, such as those of the RERF, would be compiled and reported and serve as a basis for further standard-setting processes at the ICRP.

The ICRP is registered as an independent charity in the UK and works as a non-profit international expert committee. A committee which is now known as the ICRP was born at the second International Congress of Radiology in 1928 under the name of the International X-ray and Radium Protection Committee

10 For the history of ABCC, see Frank W. Putnam, 'The Atomic Bomb Casualty Commission in Retrospect' (1998) 95 Proceedings of the National Academy of Sciences of the United States of America 5426.

11 The RERF was managed by a bi-national board of directors, and its scientific research activities were guided by the annual recommendations of a bi-national scientific council. Funds for RERF's operation continue to be provided by both governments. In 2012, the RERF became a Public Interest Incorporated Foundation in Japan; the bi-national Board of Councillors serves as a decision-making entity, and its scientific activities are guided by the Scientific Advisory Committee: RERF, 'Objective and History', <https://www.rerf.or.jp/en/about/establish_e/>.

12 It took a few years before the ABCC commenced the systematic study, as the ABCC had encountered budgetary problems and difficulties in securing the cooperation of survivors: Putnam (n 10) 5429.

13 RERF, Life Span Study, <https://www.rerf.or.jp/en/programs/research_activities_e/outline_e/proglss-en/>.

14 UN GA Resolution 913 (X) (Effects of Atomic Radiation) (3 December 1955).

composed of several radiological experts.[15] After the Second World War, the ICRP incrementally established its international presence and became affiliated with the World Health Organization (WHO) and the International Atomic Energy Agency (IAEA).[16] The work of the ICRP is financed by different public and private entities, including national organs and government-affiliated national bodies (such as the US Department of Energy and the US Nuclear Regulatory Commission), international organizations and inter-governmental forums (such as the IAEA, the EU and the Organisation for Economic Co-operation and Development), academic societies on radiation protection (such as the International Radiation Protection Association) and industry groups (see Table 8.1).[17]

One of the key tasks undertaken by the ICRP is to issue recommendations to regulatory and advisory agencies at the international, regional and national levels on the fundamental principles on which appropriate radiological protection can be based.[18] The ICRP's recommendations, as well as models and data employed for them, serve as the basis for the system of radiological protection at the domestic level. For instance, in the US, in one of the cases concerning the Three Mile Island nuclear accident, it was noted that the recommendations of the ICRP had become a 'primary basis for federal government regulation of the nuclear industry'.[19] The European Basic Safety Standards Directive,[20] which provides safety requirements for the nuclear and radiological sector, is likewise based on the recommendations of the ICRP.[21] The revision of the Directive

15 R.H. Clarke and J. Valentin, 'The History of ICRP and the Evolution of its Policies' (2009) 39 Annals of the ICRP 75, 78. The body changed its name as the ICRP in 1950: ibid, 78–80. For the history of the ICRP, see also Lauriston S Taylor, 'History of the International Commission on Radiological Protection (ICRP)' (2002) 82 Health Physics 789. The following presentation slides also provide a useful overview: Claire Cousins, ICRP Chair, 'ICRP Past, Present and Future', ICRP 2013 Symposium Presentations, Opening Session (2013) <www.icrp.org/page.asp?id=184>.

16 The ICPR also remedied its financial situation in the early 1960s with the grants from the Ford Foundation and the affiliated international organizations: Clarke and Valentin (n 15) 80.

17 See, for instance, ICRP, 2013 Annual Report (2014) 33–34, <www.icrp.org/docs/ICRP%20Annual%20Report%202013.pdf>; ICRP, 2012 Annual Report (2013) 42–43, <www.icrp.org/docs/ICRP%20Annual%20Report%202012.pdf>.

18 Bo Lindell, H. John Dunster and Jack Valentin, *International Commission on Radiological Protection: History, Policies, Procedures*, Swedish Radiation Protection Institute, SE-171 (1998), at 3, <www.icrp.net/docs/Histpol.pdf>. Since 2002, ICRP subjects its draft reports to public consultation which allows professional bodies to provide input to the ICRP: Clarke and Valentin (n 15) 101.

19 *In re TMI*, Nuclear Reg. Rep. P 20,571, 67 F3d 1103 (US Court of Appeals, Third Circuit) (17 October 1995) at 1112, fn 22. See, however, also (n 38) below.

20 Council Directive 2013/59/Euratom of 5 December 2013 laying down basic safety standards for protection against the dangers arising from exposure to ionising radiation, and repealing Directives 89/618/Euratom, 90/641/Euratom, 96/29/Euratom, 97/43/Euratom and 2003/122/Euratom [2014] OJ L13/1.

21 Ibid, Recitals 6–11.

Table 8.1 The web of scientific and regulatory institutions

Process	*Institutions (referred to in the present chapter)*
1 Scientific studies on the effect of ionizing radiation on human bodies	Among a wide range of research institutions: • Atomic Bomb Casualty Commission (ABCC) (1946–1975) • Radiation Effects Research Foundation (RERF) (1975–)
2 Formulation of scientific consensus	• UN Scientific Committee on the Effects of Atomic Radiation (UNSCEAR) (1955–)

3 Formulation of transnational science-based standards	• International Commission on Radiological Protection (ICRP) (1928–)
	• The ICRP is affiliated with:
	  • World Health Organization (WHO) (1948–)
	  • International Atomic Energy Agency (IAEA) (1957–)

4 Formulation of international regulatory standards and domestic laws	International organizations, such as: • IAEA • WHO • International Labour Organization (ILO) (1919–) • Food and Agriculture Organization (FAO) (1945–) National regulatory bodies

in 2013 was primarily driven by the publication of the ICRP's 2007 recommendations in which the ICRP put forward the new 'philosophy' for radiation protection.[22]

In fact, the radiation protection philosophies have undergone a series of changes, both in light of new scientific findings and the public's awareness of radiation safety. In its first series of recommendations published in 1928–1950, the ICRP's primary focus was directed at regulating occupational exposures. The recommendations set out the thresholds below which there would be no 'deterministic' effects on human health.[23] Deterministic effects mean that a person would not suffer from a particular illness unless he/she is exposed to a certain level of radiation.

Subsequently, the ICRP's recommendations have started covering non-occupational contexts, and the ICRP became more engaged in the risk-benefit assessment outside the context of nuclear-related workers. The ICRP has extended

22 Stefan Mundigl, 'Modernisation and Consolidation of the European Radiation Protection Legislation: The New Euratom Basic Safety Standards Directive' (2015) 164 Radiation Protection Dosimetry 9, 9–10.

23 See Clarke and Valentin (n 15) 87–89.

its coverage due both to scientific and political backgrounds. On the one hand, the expansion of the tasks was first driven by the new scientific findings that the effects of radiation can be 'stochastic' (non-deterministic) with regard to the induction of cancer and some other illnesses.[24] In other words, the low-level exposure, which was once considered risk-free, is understood as entailing health risks. This has placed the ICRP in the position of assessing how much risk is acceptable. On the other hand, political controversies also pushed the ICRP to get involved in non-occupational standard setting. The public became much more aware of the potential health risk of radiation particularly after the Hiroshima and Nagasaki atomic bombs in 1945, the extensive nuclear tests, and the accidental exposure of the Japanese fishing boat *Lucky Dragon* to the US nuclear test's fallout in 1954.[25] These scientific and political events situated the ICRP in a position to issue recommendations on scientifically uncertain, and publicly controversial, questions which would have consequences for the wider public.

2.3 *Recommending dose limits*

One of the ICRP's standard-setting tasks concerns the formulation of the maximum level of radiation exposure permissible for individuals. Dose limits are designed to ensure that no individual is exposed to radiation risks that are judged to be unacceptable.[26] Dose limitation materializes the principle of minimization, which is one of the pillars that sustain the system of radiation protection together with the principles of justification and optimization.[27] The principle of minimization denotes that a person's total dose should not exceed dose limit, so that no person is subject to unacceptable risk.[28]

To establish dose limits certainly requires the assessment of scientific validity of research findings on the health effects. At the same time, it is crucial to remember that it is not entirely a scientific undertaking. The setting of dose limits will require a value-judgment about the balance between what is best

24 Ibid, 93–94; see also Lindell (n 5) 88–89. More specifically, the ICRP Publication 9 issued in 1965 'substantially renewed the radiation protection philosophy by moving from deterministic to stochastic effects': Lindell (n 5) 90; ICRP, Recommendations of the International Commission on Radiological Protection (Adopted 17 September 1965), ICRP Publication 9 (1965) para 7.

25 Clarke and Valentin (n 15) 90.

26 See ibid 97.

27 See IAEA, *Handbook on Nuclear Law* (Vienna, International Atomic Energy Agency, 2003) 47. The principle of justification denotes that the radiation detriment must be justified against benefit for the exposed individuals and society. The principle of optimization is also called as the 'ALARA' principle; the exposure must be kept as low as reasonably achievable (ALARA), taking into account social and economic factors.

28 Ibid.

for society as a whole and what is best for an individual,[29] and, in formulating a recommendation, the ICRP necessarily decides on this risk-benefit balance. In such a process, the ICRP initially favoured wider societal benefits, and it has subsequently shifted its emphasis to the protection of individuals.[30]

In fact, the need for the risk-benefit consideration is explicitly explained in the ICRP's documents. For instance, the ICRP's recommendations revised in 1962 state that '[t]he Commission has balanced as far as possible the *risk* of the exposure against the *benefit* of the practice' and that '[t]he Commission...recommended a maximum permissible generic dose of 5 rems, on the basis that the resulting burden to society would be [...] *tolerable and justifiable in view of the benefits* that may be expected to accrue from the expansion of the practical application of "atomic energy"'.[31] According to the ICRP's 2007 Recommendations, '[a]ll of those concerned with radiological protection have to make *value judgments* about the relative importance of different kinds of risk and about the *balancing of risks and benefits*'.[32]

The ICRP's recommendations, based upon its own risk-benefit analysis, then provide the basis for wider international standards and domestic law. The recommendations are utilized by the IAEA in the promulgation of the

29 Clarke and Valentin (n 15) 104–105 (referring to the balance between 'utilitarian consequence ethics' and 'deontological duty ethics'). If the effect cannot be detected in a given population, the risk of the associated dose may be considered negligible.

30 The shift in emphasis occurred especially from the 1990 Recommendations found in 'Publication 60': Clarke and Valentin (n 15) 96–97, 105; Roger H. Clarke, 'Changing Philosophy in ICRP: The Evolution of Protection Ethics and Principles' (2003) 1 International Journal of Low Radiation 39.

31 ICRP, Recommendations of the International Commission on Radiological Protection: As Amended 1959 and Revised 1962, ICRP Publication 6 (Superseding Publication 1) (1964), paras 32a, 32c (emphasis added). Cf. ICRP, Recommendations of the International Commission on Radiological Protection: Adopted September 9, 1958, ICRP Publication 1 (1959), paras 17, 19, 22, 59 (more ambiguous about the Commission's own role in balancing risks and benefits).

32 ICRP, The 2007 Recommendations of the International Commission on Radiological Protection, ICRP Publication 103 (2007), para 27 (emphasis added). See also the ICRP Symposium presentation slides prepared by the ICRP Chair: C. Cousins, 'ICRP Past, Present and Future', ICRP 2013 Symposium Presentations, Opening Session (2013), <www.icrp.org/page.asp?id=184>, at 22 ('Based on science, ethical and social values, and experience'). Similarly, see the ICRP Symposium presentation slides prepared by Jacques Lochard, Chair of the ICRP's Committee 4: J. Lochard, Chair of the ICRP Committee 4, 'Application of the Commission's Recommendations: The Activities of Committee 4', ICRP 2011 Symposium, ICRP Programme of Work (24–26 October 2011), <www.icrp.org/page.asp?id=142>; J. Lochard, Chair of the ICRP Committee 4, 'Application of the Commission's Recommendations: The 2013–2017 Committee 4 Programme of Work', ICRP 2013 Symposium, Opening Session (22 October 2013), <www.icrp.org/page.asp?id=184>.

International Basic Safety Standards for radiation protection,[33] and influence standards and documents issued by the UN's specialized agencies such as the WHO, the International Labour Organization and the Food and Agriculture Organization.[34] As noted above, the ICRP's publications are widely absorbed into domestic regulation – although, as revealed by the Japanese experience explained below, the national process of adopting transnational science-based standards may overlook their scientific and political constraints.

3 Domestic deference and contestation: The use of transnational standards following the Fukushima nuclear disaster

As illustrated above, the ICRP's recommendations are some of the examples of transnational standards which are based on both scientific findings and non-scientific considerations. In many countries, a system of radiation protection builds on the ICRP's recommendations, including those on dose limits. The ICRP's presence matters, not merely in the process of designing regularly applicable safety standards, but also during the times of crisis. In the aftermath of the unprecedented nuclear accident in Fukushima in March 2011, the dose limits recommended by the ICRP were repeatedly invoked by the Japanese authorities to justify the changes in permissible dose limits. Yet the government's emphasis upon the ICRP's credibility revealed, paradoxically, some of the limits of transnational science-based standards.

3.1 *Domestic reliance on the ICRP-recommended dose limits*

The Fukushima nuclear accident, which provides a case study for the present research, was triggered by a magnitude 9.0 earthquake that hit Japan's north-eastern coast on 11 March 2011. The earthquake resulted in tsunami, which subsequently led to the loss of power in the Fukushima Daiichi nuclear

33 'The Board of Governors of the IAEA first approved health and safety measures in March 1960, when it was stated that "The Agency's basic safety standards…will be based, to the extent possible, on the recommendations of the International Commission on Radiological Protection (ICRP)"': IAEA, *Radiation Protection and Safety of Radiation Sources: International Basic Safety Standards: General Safety Requirements*, IAEA Safety Standards Series No. GSR Part 3, Jointly Sponsored by European Commission, FAO, IAEA, ILO, OECD/NEA, PAHO, UNEP and WHO (2014), at viii (preface) (original footnote omitted). Likewise, IAEA 2014 Basic Safety Standards, ibid, at xii ('the new edition of the BSS should follow, to the extent possible, the new recommendations of the ICRP') and para 1.5; IAEA, *International Basic Safety Standards for Protection Against Ionizing Radiation and for the Safety of Radiation Sources*, IAEA Safety Series No. 115, Jointly Sponsored by FAO, IAEA, ILO, OECD/NEA, PAHO and WHO (1996), preface ('The Standards are based primarily on the recommendations of the ICRP').

34 Clarke and Valentin (n 15) 102. The recommendations influence many other organizations, such as the European Commission and the Nuclear Energy Agency of the Organisation for Economic Co-operation and Development (OECD).

power plants. This was followed by the meltdown of the nuclear fuel rod, the hydrogen explosion of the buildings and the release of radiation into the air and water.[35] The radiation released by the crippled nuclear reactors has exposed people, buildings and food to radiation and still continues to do so. Ten days after the earthquake, the ICRP released an open message, in which the ICRP referred to some of its own basic recommendations applicable to the situation.[36]

Not surprisingly, the occurrence of the nuclear accident necessitated some changes to the level of dose limits set by the statute in Japan. In ordinary situations, a statutory equivalent dose limit of 1 millisievert per year is applicable and this limit regulates the maximum level of radiation exposure for the general public. A 'millisievert' is a unit of radiation dose weighted to take into account its biological effect. This statutory dose limit was set in Japan based upon the Recommendations of the ICRP in 1990,[37] which were widely adopted by some other states as well.[38] The ICRP recommended the limit, on the basis that the risk factor of cancer from radiation up to 1 millisievert per year would be 5 per 100,000 people.[39] The subsequent ICRP Recommendations in 2007 also recommended 1 millisievert per year as the protection criteria for the general public.[40]

As noted above in Section 2.3 of this chapter, the setting of dose limits requires the assessment of related risks and benefits, which involves scientific,

35 The facts and causes of the nuclear power incident have been investigated by the investigation commissions set up by the operator (TEPCO), the Japanese Cabinet, the Japanese Diet and a private-sector group, respectively. The Cabinet-led committee's reports are available in English: Investigation Committee on the Accident at Fukushima Nuclear Power Stations of Tokyo Electric Power Company, Final Report (23 July 2012), <www.cas.go.jp/jp/seisaku/icanps/eng/final-report.html>. For the Diet-led committee reports, which are also available in English: The National Diet of Japan, The Fukushima Nuclear Accident Independent Investigation Commission, Report (2012), <http://warp.da.ndl.go.jp/info:ndljp/pid/3856371/naiic.go.jp/en/report/>.

36 Christopher H. Clement and Michiya Sasaki, 'The International Commission on Radiological Protection and the Accident at the Fukushima Nuclear Power Stations' (2012) 47 Japanese Journal of Health Physics 206, 206.

37 ICRP, *1990 Recommendations of the International Commission on Radiological Protection*, ICRP Publication 60, Annals of the ICRP 21 (1–3) (1991).

38 See Jack Valentin, *Report on the Implementation of ICRP Recommendations by NEA Member States* (October 2006), 3rd NEA/ICRP Forum, Prague, online: <www.oecdnea.org/rp/prague/Implementation_of_ICRP_recommendations.pdf>, at 4–5. According to Valentin's summary, '[w]ith the exception of the United States, NEA [OECD's Nuclear Energy Agency] member states have all implemented the Recommendations in the ICRP 1990 Recommendations in *Publication 60*': ibid, 1. While the key exception may be the US, in substance, the US regulation does not conflict with the 1990 Recommendations: see ibid, 5.

39 An updated source is the 2007 Recommendations which affirmed the risk coefficient presented by the ICRP in the 1990 Recommendations: The 2007 Recommendations (n 32) para 87.

40 See The 2007 Recommendations (n 32) 116 (Table 8. Comparison of protection criteria between the 1990 and the 2007 Recommendations).

legal, ethical, economic and political considerations. This is because the limit is merely the *permissive* level, and such permissibility is about the balance of risk and benefit.[41] The benefits may include the use of nuclear power plants and the development of nuclear weapons, but the intricacy is that those who benefit from the use of nuclear power may not be the same as those who are at risk from the radiation attached to the possession of nuclear technologies.[42] The determination of dose limits thus necessarily involves social and political risk-benefit analyses, which should be in part left to the decisions of governmental bodies, workers and the wider public. In fact, the need for political and social input has been recognized by the ICPR itself. Its recommendations note that 'the factors influencing the balancing of risks and benefits will vary from country to country and that the final decision rests with each country'.[43] The ICRP's report concerning the application of its 2007 Recommendations points out that the process of selecting a dose limit 'should also be carefully balanced to appropriately include the views of all relevant stakeholders'.[44]

The national process of adopting the ICRP's recommendations, however, may not fully acknowledge the role of wider public scrutiny. This is because the reliance on the ICRP-recommended dose limits can help the government to avoid the aforementioned complex scientific and political discussions. While the scientific integrity of the ICRP induces national regulatory organs to abide by its recommendations, it could be a convenient way for governments to avoid a difficult political process to balance the benefits and risks at the domestic level.

In the aftermath of the Fukushima nuclear accident, the domestic political convenience to emphasize the authoritativeness of the ICRP standards became visible in Japan. In response to the release of radiation from the nuclear reactors, the government decided to raise the legally permissible level of radiation exposure

41 As the ICRP stated in 1959, a limitation of the exposure 'necessarily involves a compromise between deleterious effects and social benefits': ICRP, Recommendations of the International Commission on Radiological Protection: Adopted September 9, 1958 (1959) ICRP Publication 1, para 59. Radiation dose limits are about the acceptability of risk, as pointed out by the ICRP's 1965 Recommendations: 'there is a degree of risk and must limit the radiation dose to a level at which the assumed risk is deemed to be *acceptable* to the individual and to society in view of the *benefits* derived from such activities. Such a dose might be called an acceptable dose, with the same meaning as was implied by "permissible dose"' (ICRP 1965 Recommendations (n 24) para 34 (emphasis added)).

42 Nakagawa provides a critical assessment of a longstanding connection between internationally adopted radiological standards and the politics of nuclear power: Y. Nakagawa, *Hōshasen hibaku no rekishi: Amerika genbaku kaihatsu kara Fukushima genpatsu jiko made [History of Radiological Exposure: From the US's Atomic Bomb Development to the Fukushima Nuclear Power Plant Accident]* (Akashi Shoten, 2011) (in Japanese).

43 ICRP 1959 Recommendations (n 41) para 17; ICRP, 'Recommendations of the International Commission on Radiological Protection: As Amended 1959 and Revised 1962' (1964) ICRP Publication 6 (Superseding Publication 1) para 17.

44 ICRP, 'Application of the Commission's Recommendations to the Protection of People Living in Long-term Contaminated Areas After a Nuclear Accident or a Radiation Emergency', ICRP Publication 111, Annals of the ICRP 39 (3) (2009) para 49.

for the general public from 1 to 20 millisieverts per year.[45] It has done so on the basis of the ICRP's 2007 Recommendations, which allow for higher dose limits in case of emergency situations and their aftermath.[46] By way of administrative notices and instructions, the government employed the higher dose limit in restricting the use of school buildings and playgrounds in Fukushima and determining evacuation areas.

More specifically, on 19 April 2011, the government adopted 1–20 millisieverts as the interim level with which to determine the availability of school buildings and playgrounds to children;[47] it did so 'in consideration of international standards',[48] and referred to the ICRP's 2009 report[49] and its Fukushima-specific statement made shortly after the power plant incident, in which the ICRP had reiterated its recommendations on the level of dose limits.[50] The government's statement of April 2011 regarding school buildings and playgrounds immediately invited a public outcry.[51] In response, the Japanese government issued another statement on 27 May 2011 that it would use the annual dose of 1–20 millisieverts 'as a guide level' and aim to reduce the annual dose to 1 millisievert or less.[52] Yet the government still maintained the Interim Policy dated 19 April 2011,[53] which means that the May 2011 statement was issued in order to provide some assurance to the affected people about the government's long-term plan.

45 See Takeshi Oshima, 'Fukushima daiichi jiko no hinan shiji kaijo no kijun o meguru keii [Background Regarding the Standards for the Lifting of Evacuation Orders on the Fukushima Daiichi Nuclear Power Accident]' (2014) 353 Rippo To Chosa 58 (in Japanese).

46 More specifically, the 2007 Recommendations provide 20–100 millisieverts as reference levels (i.e. the level of residual dose above which it is judged to be inappropriate) for the situations of 'emergency exposure', and 1–20 millisieverts for the situations of 'existing exposure' following the emergency exposure: see The 2007 Recommendations (n 32) 15, 116–7.

47 The Ministry of Education, Culture, Sports, Science and Technology (MEXT), 'Notification of Interim Policy Regarding Decisions on Whether to Utilize School Buildings and Outdoor Areas within Fukushima Prefecture', No. 23-Monka-Su-134 (2011, Sports and Youth Bureau, MEXT No. 134) (19 April 2011), <www.mext.go.jp/a_menu/saigaijohou/syousai/1305173.htm> (in Japanese).

48 MEXT, 'Interim Policy' (19 April 2011) (n 47).

49 ICRP, 'Application of the Commission's Recommendations for the Protection of People in Emergency Exposure Situations', ICRP Publication 109, Annals of the ICRP 39 (1) (2009). The Publication 109 is to assist the application of the ICPR's 2007 Recommendations: The 2007 Recommendations (n 32).

50 ICRP, *Fukushima Nuclear Power Plant Accident*, Ref 4847-5603-4313 (21 March 2011) (available at <www.icrp.org/docs/Fukushima%20Nuclear%20Power%20Plant%20Accident.pdf>). The ICRP notes that the 'Commission continues to recommend choosing reference levels in the band of 1 to 20 mSv per year, with the long-term goal of reducing reference levels to 1 mSv per year': ibid.

51 See (n 60) below.

52 MEXT, 'Immediate Measures toward Reducing the Radiation Doses that Pupils and Others Receive at Schools, etc. in Fukushima Prefecture' (27 May 2011), <https://www.mext.go.jp/en/incident/title01/detail01/sdetail01/sdetail01/1373045.htm> (in English).

53 Ibid.

The ICRP was also invoked frequently in the context of setting out evacuation areas. On 22 April 2011, the Japanese government first employed the 'emergency exposure' level of 20–100 millisieverts in determining a 'deliberate evacuation area' (***keikaku hinan kuiki***).[54] On 26 December 2011, the government employed 20 millisieverts as a standard for revising the evacuation instruction.[55] This 'Basic Concept' is based upon the then Japanese Nuclear Safety Commission's opinions, which refer to the ICRP's recommendations.[56] The Japanese Nuclear Regulatory Authority, the successor to the Nuclear Safety Commission, continued to refer to the level of 20 millisieverts based upon the ICRP's recommendations with a stronger emphasis on the protection of individuals.[57]

3.2 *Domestic and international contestations*

3.2.1 *Contesting the 20-millisievert yardstick*

As highlighted above, the presence of the ICRP has been repeatedly referred to in the aftermath of the Fukushima nuclear accident in March 2011. For the government, it was pragmatically necessary to raise the standards to a higher level in order to limit evacuation zones and associated compensation for evacuation, and 20 millisieverts was within the ICRP's recommended range as the level of permissible exposure.[58] The government has invoked the ICRP's recommendation, presumably to provide better assurance to the affected residents and the wider public that the level of exposure stays within the internationally recognized safety criteria. In the aftermath of the disaster, the government has

54 Cabinet Office, 'The Establishment of "Deliberate Evacuation Areas" and "Evacuation-Prepared Areas in Case of Emergency"' (22 April 2011) (issued in accordance with the Act on Special Measures Concerning Nuclear Emergency Preparedness, Act No. 156 of 17 December 1999) (in Japanese), <www.kantei.go.jp/saigai/20110411keikakuhinan.html>.

55 Cabinet Office, Nuclear Emergency Response Headquarters, 'Basic Concept and Issues to be Challenged for Rearranging the Restricted Areas and Areas to which Evacuation Orders Have Been Issued Where Step 2 Has Been Completed' (26 December 2011), section 2(1)(E), <www.meti.go.jp/english/earthquake/nuclear/roadmap/pdf/20111226_01.pdf> (in English).

56 E.g. Nuclear Safety Commission of Japan, 'Standpoint of the Nuclear Safety Commission for the Termination of Urgent Protective Actions Implemented for the Accident at Fukushima Dai-ichi Nuclear Power Plant' (4 August 2011) (in English); Nuclear Safety Commission of Japan, 'Basic Policy of the Nuclear Safety Commission of Japan on Radiation Protection for Termination of Evacuation and Reconstruction' (19 July 2011) (in English).

57 E.g. Nuclear Regulatory Authority of Japan, 'Practical Measures for Evacuees to Return their Homes' (20 November 2013), section 2(A), <https://www.nsr.go.jp/english/library/>.

58 More specifically, the level of 20 millisieverts set for the evacuation area immediately after the Fukushima incident was based on the lower limit applicable to the situations of 'emergency exposure'. The level of 20 millisieverts set for the availability of school buildings and playgrounds was based on the recommended limit applicable to the situations of the situations of 'existing exposure'. See (n 46).

stressed, from time to time, that the yardstick of 20 millisieverts was recognized by the ICRP as a permissible level after the emergency.[59]

However, the government's decision, despite reliance on the ICRP's credibility, invited a public outcry. Particularly controversial was the use of the level of 20 millisieverts for school buildings and playgrounds. Not surprisingly, this has fuelled anger among the parents of the affected children.[60] Various bodies expressed their concerns about the governmental policy on schools. For instance, the Japan Federation of Bar Associations issued the statement, criticizing the way in which the government relied upon the ICRP's recommendations. The Federation indicated that the ICRP's recommendations did not accommodate

59 The government made frequent reference to the ICRP, which cannot be exhaustively listed here. To provide only a few examples, (1) the government provided the accessible Q&A to the general public in which it referred to the ICRP's reference level as an international standard: Cabinet Office, 'Q&A about Radiation Dose Standards' (2 May 2011), <www.kantei.go.jp/saigai/faq/20110502genpatsu_faq.html> at Q3 (in Japanese). (2) The ICRP has been frequently referred to in the parliamentary debate: e.g. (i) 177th Session of the Japanese Diet, House of Representatives [*shugiin*], Special Committee on Youth Affairs, Minutes No. 3 (20 April 2011), at 3 (Ikuko Arimatsu, an expert witness [*sankōnin*] for the government), Joint Committees on Economy and Industry and on Cabinet, Minutes No. 1 (27 April 2011) at 7 (Yukio Edano, Chief Cabinet Secretary), Committee on Audit and Oversight of Administration, Minutes No. 3 (27 April 2011) at 13 (Itaru Watanabe, an expert witness for the government), Committee on Education, Culture, Sports, Science and Technology, Minutes No. 8 (27 April 2011) at 11–12, 19 (Takafumi Goda, an expert witness for the government, and Yoshiaki Takagi, Minister of State); Committee on Education, Culture, Sports, Science and Technology, Minutes No. 10 (18 May 2011) at 21 (Takafumi Goda, an expert witness for the government); (ii) 177th Session of the Diet, House of Councillors [*sangiin*], Special Committee on Disasters, Minutes No. 5 (20 April 2011) at 7, 11 (Ryuzo Sasaki, Vice Minister; Yoichi Ito, an expert witness for the government), Committee on Cabinet, Minutes No. 6 (21 April 2011) at 2–3 (Yukio Edano, Chief Cabinet Secretary, referring 20 millisieverts as a lowest standard 'within international organizations'), Joint Committees on Financial Affairs, on Health, Welfare and Labour, and on Land, Infrastructure, Transport and Tourism, Minutes No. 1 (1 May 2011) at 7, 10 (Itaru Watanabe, an expert witness for the government), Committee on Budget, Minutes No. 14 (2 May 2011) at 16 (Yoshiaki Takagi, Minister of State), Committee on Education, Culture and Science, Minutes No. 8 (17 May 2011) at 11, 14 (Yoshiaki Takagi, Minister of State, noting that: 'as I have mentioned a number of times, I have determined the matter in accordance with the ICRP—within this international standard. It is one of the yardsticks, taking into account various experts' opinions'); (iii) 179th Session of the Diet, House of Councillors [*sangiin*], Committee on Economy, Trade and Industry, Minutes No. 2 (27 October 2011) at 37 (Yukio Edano, Minister of State); (iv) 180th Session of the Diet, House of Representatives [*shugiin*], Special Committee on Reconstruction after the Great East Japan Earthquake, Minutes No. 5 (7 March 2012) at 8 (Yasuhiro Nakane, Parliamentary Secretary). Just to stress, these are only a few examples.

60 See, for instance, H. Tabuchi, 'Angry Parents in Japan Confront Government Over Radiation Levels', *The New York Times* (25 May 2011), <www.nytimes.com/2011/05/26/world/asia/26japan.html?pagewanted=1&tntemail0=y&_r=2&emc=tnt>; J. Watts, 'Fukushima Parents Dish the Dirt in Protest over Radiation Levels', *The Guardian* (2 May 2011), <www.theguardian.com/world/2011/may/02/parents-revolt-radiation-levels>.

the vulnerability of children with regard to radiation-induced illness.[61] The setting of the maximum radiation dose involves the balancing of 'safety' with the 'benefit to society'. On this basis, the Federation found inappropriate and problematic the government's weighing of 'the social benefits of attending contaminated schools' against 'the dangers of radiation exposure' for school children.[62]

The adoption of the higher limit invited criticisms not only at home but also international audience.[63] Concern was also raised by the UN Human Rights Council's Special Rapporteur on the right of everyone to the enjoyment of the highest attainable standard of physical and mental health. In the 2013 report based on his mission to Japan in November 2012, the Special Rapporteur was critical of the fact that the Japanese government relied upon the ICRP's recommendations without providing nuanced explanations to the affected individuals. The Special Rapporteur levelled criticisms both from scientific and juridical perspectives. According to the Rapporteur, the government's adoption of 20 millisieverts amounts to 'disregarding' the 'causal links between long-term exposure to low doses of radiation and the increased incidence of cancer', as suggested by life span epidemiological studies of atomic bomb survivors.[64] Noteworthy, however, is that the Special Rapporteur's critique was also based on the mismatch between the philosophies of the ICRP-recommended dose limits on the one hand, and the framework of the right to health on the other. According to the Special Rapporteur, a 'risk-benefit analysis' underlying the ICRP's recommendations is 'not in consonance with the right to health framework, as it gives precedence to collective interests over individual rights'.[65]

Domestic and international criticisms have led the Japanese government to further reiterate the integrity and credibility of the ICRP recommendations. This is, for instance, illustrated by Japan's replies to the UN Special Rapporteur who had suggested that the government plan evacuation zones and exposure limits based on 'current scientific evidence' and 'human rights' rather than

61 See Japan Federation of Bar Associations, 'Statement Concerning the Government's "Provisional Guideline for the Utilization of School Buildings, Grounds, and Related Facilities in Fukushima Prefecture"' (22 April 2011), <https://www.nichibenren.or.jp/en/document/statements/20110422.html>.

62 Ibid.

63 See, for instance, T. Ruff, 'Children of Fukushima Need Our Protection', *International Physicians for the Prevention of Nuclear War* (26 April 2011), <http://peaceandhealthblog.com/2011/04/26/children-of-fukushima/>; Letter from the International Physicians for the Prevention of Nuclear War to the Japanese Minister of Education, Culture, Sports, Science and Technology (dated 29 April 2011), <http://pgs.ca/wp-content/uploads/2008/03/JapanMinistry042911.pdf>.

64 UN Human Rights Council, 'Report of the Special Rapporteur on the Right of Everyone to the Enjoyment of the Highest Attainable Standard of Physical and Mental Health, Anand Grover, Addendum, Mission to Japan (15–26 November 2012)', A/HRC/23/41/Add.3 (31 July 2013), para 10. The advanced version of the report was published initially on 2 May 2013.

65 Ibid para 47.

'a risk-benefit analysis'.[66] In response, the government of Japan noted that the evacuation areas were set 'based on the globally accepted recommendation of ICRP and discussion between domestic and foreign experts for radiation'.[67] According to the Japanese government, the Special Rapporteur's criticisms lack scientific merit, as the ICRP guidelines do not ignore the effects of low-dose exposure on health.[68]

3.2.2 *Contesting the yardstick before domestic courts*

The residents took the issue to domestic courts and challenged therein the government's decision to raise the dose limits.[69] Their actions were to directly contest the governmental failure to keep the statutory dose limit and protect the residents from radiation exposure. At the same time, the objections were indirectly raised against the ICRP's recommendations which the government treated as authoritative. In June 2011, 14 children in the city of Koriyama in the Fukushima prefecture brought proceedings against the local government. The residents claimed that the local government should not conduct its educational activities in the areas where the accumulated radiation dose would exceed the statutory annual limit of 1 millisievert. They also claimed that the local authority should evacuate the children so that the educational activities could be provided within the dose limits. While in December 2011, the Fukushima District Court rejected their claims on the basis that there was no imminent risk to the lives of the children,[70] the Court still referred to criticism levelled against the ICRP that its dose limits do not take into account internal exposure, and made reference to the European Committee on Radiation Risk which sets the lower dose limit of 0.1 millisievert per year. On appeal, the Sendai High Court in April 2013 has likewise rejected the claim that the government was obligated to evacuate children.[71]

Despite rejections, citizens continue using domestic courts in contesting the governmental use of 20 millisieverts as a yardstick with which to determine its policies on the residents' safety. In April 2015, 534 residents in the city of Minamisoma in the Fukushima prefecture brought proceedings against the

66 Ibid para 78.

67 'Comments of Japan on the Report of the Special Rapporteur on the Right of Everyone to the Enjoyment of the Highest Attainable Standard of Physical and Mental Health (15–26 November 2012), A/HRC/23/41/Add.3', A/HRC/23/41/Add.5/Rev.1 (27 May 2013) at 8.

68 Ibid 16.

69 There are a wide range of lawsuits regarding the Fukushima incident, and the citizens' action to launch collective lawsuits for the evacuation of children is one of them. The citizens' group also launched the website on the 'Fukushima Collective Evacuation Trial', <http://fukushima-evacuation-e.blogspot.jp/> (in English).

70 *Decision of 16 December 2011*, Fukushima District Court, Case No 2011(Yo)29.

71 *Judgment of 24 April 2013*, Sendai High Court, Case No 2012(Ra)12.

government.[72] After the Fukushima accident, a large part of the city was designated as part of evacuation zones (including, more specifically, a 'restricted residence area' and a 'zone in preparation for the lifting of the evacuation order'). On top of this, the government listed 142 'spots' within the Minamisoma city as specific spots recommended for evacuation since the annual dose would be higher than 20 millisieverts. In December 2014, the government decided to delist all the evacuation spots within the city of Minamisoma, on the basis that the annual dose would be lower than the yardstick of 20 millisieverts.[73] Thereafter, the residents sued the government, contesting its decision to lift the designation of these evacuation-recommended spots.

As of April 2020, the residents' claims remain pending before the Tokyo District Court. Regardless of the outcome of the litigation, the residents' claims and the government's responses are noteworthy in their own right. This is because one of the central points of contention pertains to how the government ought to interpret and apply the ICRP's recommendations. At one level, the parties' disagreement pertains to the question of which categories of 'exposure situations' (which the ICRP employs in its recommendations) should be used for the handling of evacuation-recommended spots. The government contended that 'emergency exposure' situations should be used as a basis for the decision making,[74] while the residents argued the use of post-emergency 'existing exposure' situations as the basis.[75]

At a much more fundamental level, however, the residents and government disagree with regard to the nature and status of the ICRP's science-based recommendations. According to the government, administrative policies ought to be based upon prevailing scientific knowledge, which should also serve as a basis for the judicial assessment of the governmental decisions. On this basis, the government pointed out that the effects of exposure below 100 millisieverts are not yet 'established'.[76] While the ICRP's recommendations accommodated risks for low-level exposure, the ICRP has done so, according to the government, not as a matter of established scientific knowledge, but as a matter of public health

72 Tokyo District Court, Case No 2015 (Gyo-U) 238 and 381. See Kyodo News, '530 Minamisoma Residents Sue Government over Hot Spot Delisting', *The Japan Times* (17 April 2015), <https://www.japantimes.co.jp/news/2015/04/17/national/crime-legal/530-minamisoma-residents-sue-government-hot-spot-delisting/#.Xr1MjMBS9PQ>.

73 The Local Nuclear Emergency Response Headquarters, 'On the Cancellation of the Specific Spots Recommended for Evaluation in the City of Minamisoma' (24 December 2014), <https://www.meti.go.jp/earthquake/nuclear/pdf/141224.pdf> (in Japanese).

74 Brief No. 8 by the Defendant (dated 27 September 2017) (Tokyo District Court, Case No 2015(Gyo-U) 238 and 381) at 28. The documents regarding the litigation are available from the support group's website: <http://minamisouma.blogspot.com/> (in Japanese).

75 Brief No. 18 by the Plaintiffs (dated 26 June 2018) (Tokyo District Court, Case No 2015(Gyo-U) 238 and 381) at 10.

76 Brief No. 8 by the Defendant (dated 27 September 2017) (n 74) at 19 (referring both to deterministic and stochastic effects). See (n 23–24) and accompanying text regarding the 'deterministic' and 'stochastic' (non-deterministic) effect of radiation exposure.

policies. In this sense, the government regarded the ICRP's recommendations as intertwined with 'policy considerations'. For the government, the recommendations served only as a point of reference without constituting the standards that should constraint the exercise of governmental discretion.[77]

The residents' claims fundamentally differ in terms of both the scientific nature of the ICRP's recommendations and the level of scientific uncertainty the government should embrace. The residents claimed that the ICRP's recommendations had been, and should continue to be, more than a mere point of reference for domestic law. The residents observe that citizens cannot be protected from nuclear disasters if the government relied solely upon a scientifically resolved 'common theory'.[78] The model used by the ICPR to assess health risks of low-level exposure best matches current scientific evidence.[79] According to the ICRP, as reiterated by the residents, it is recommended to use the 'lower part of the 1–20 [millisieverts per year] band' and 1 millisievert is typically used in long-term post-accident situations.[80] On this basis, the residents argued that the government's decision was contrary to the principle of justification[81] as the decision would bring serious harm to the residents without any benefit.[82] The residents further claimed that the procedure leading to the adoption of the contested decision was 'non-democratic' without public participation.[83]

Overall, the arguments by the residents and the government yet again demonstrate the dual foundations of the ICRP's recommendations. The government highlighted the policy dimension of the ICRP's guidance, which is rather ironic, I must add, in light of the government's earlier emphasis on the ICRP's scientific integrity in the aftermath of the Fukushima crisis.[84] In this case, the residents, in their attempt to contest the governmental decision making, tried to take advantage of the governmental reliance on the ICRP's recommendations. Regardless of the outcomes of the litigation, the case provides further evidence of the selective and strategic reliance by the government on the ICRP's scientific credibility.

77 Brief No. 11 of the Defendant (dated 26 March 2018) (Tokyo District Court, Case No 2015(Gyo-U) 238 and 381) at 5–9.

78 Brief No. 19 of the Plaintiffs (dated 27 June 2018) (Tokyo District Court, Case No 2015(Gyo-U) 238 and 381) at 7–8.

79 Brief No. 19 of the Plaintiffs (dated 27 June 2018) (Tokyo District Court, Case No 2015(Gyo-U) 238 and 381). The residents referred to the so-called linear-nonthreshold (LNT) model, according to which low-level exposure may still entail risks in a manner proportional to the level of exposure.

80 Complaint by the Plaintiffs (dated 17 April 2015) (Tokyo District Court, Case No 2015(Gyo-U) 238 and 381) at 32–34 (referring to the ICRP Publication 111); ICRP Publication 111 (2009) (n 44) para 50.

81 With regard to the core principles of radiation protection, see (n 27) and accompanying text.

82 Complaint by the Plaintiffs (dated 17 April 2015) (n 80) at 35–36.

83 Ibid at 38–40.

84 See Section 3.1 of this chapter.

4 Transnational science-based standards in the national legal order

The Japanese stories on the domestic reception of transnational radiation standards provide us with a much wider, and often neglected, issue which I referred to in the introduction: namely, the (1) scientific and (2) political fragility of transnational science-based standards adopted at the national level. Such standards, perhaps inevitably, suffer from scientific uncertainty and limited political input. The Japanese experiences in the aftermath of the nuclear accident illustrate these dual vulnerabilities accommodated in the transnational standards on radiation safety. What is problematic is, however, not the existence of these vulnerabilities, but the way the government adopted the standards without accountability for the implications of dual vulnerabilities at the national level.

4.1 *Scientific vulnerability*

One of the noteworthy features of the stories regarding the Fukushima accident I explained above is the Japanese government's strong deference to transnationally-recommended scientific models, findings and limits. There are perhaps good reasons for such deference. The RERF's decades of epidemiological studies involving a large number of subjects provide some valuable data on the effect of ionizing radiation.[85] The recommendations of the ICRP – in conjunction with the scientific consensus built upon by UNSCEAR and the epidemiological findings of the US-Japan institute – have been widely utilized by domestic regulatory organs,[86] the IAEA and other international organizations.[87]

Domestic contestations against the Japanese government's deference nevertheless highlight the *scientific* fragility in domestically-accepted transnational radiation standards. The scientific evidence regarding 'stochastic' (non-deterministic) effects of low-level exposure can be contradictory and the controversy cannot readily come to a closure. Amid ongoing controversies, the decentralized web of scientific and regulatory bodies, including the UNSCEAR and ICRP, extracts the best available scientific findings and endorses radiological standards which, perhaps inevitably, invite criticism from a segment of the scientific community. Despite the inevitable scientific limits, in the Japanese stories discussed above, the government regulators emphasized the scientific credibility of the international standards, which paradoxically invited more contestations from various domestic and international sectors.

85 See (n 13) and accompanying text.
86 See (n 19–22) and accompanying text.
87 See (n 33–34) and accompanying text.

4.2 *Political vulnerability*

The scientific vulnerability is accompanied by *political* fragility. Not surprisingly, transnational science-based standards can be formulated with little political input from domestic public organs, private entities and individuals, on whom the standards may have visible consequences.[88] At the transnational level, the standard-setting by non-governmental independent bodies (i.e. ICRP), by nature, allows no governmental representation. Inter-governmental bodies (e.g. UNSCEAR) may not have mixed representation from governmental regulators, workers and other potentially affected individuals. At the national level, non-binding transnational standards are not subject to parliamentary approval required for the conclusion of formal treaties. National regulators may readily defer to transnational radiation standards that serve regulatory uniformity. Judges and the general public may refrain from reviewing the governmental deference due in part to the scientific technicality of standards.

Domestic contestations against the Japanese government's deference then reveal its neglect of the political vulnerability of transnational radiation standards. The government persistently invoked the ICRP in order to alleviate public anxiety about the adoption of higher dose limits.[89] Despite the need for domestic political input, the Japanese government has yet to subject internationally-recommended standards to wider domestic political deliberation, even a few years after the Fukushima incident.

The neglect of the political and scientific limits of transnational science-based standards is problematic precisely because, as noted above,[90] radiation standards often involve not only scientific risk assessment, but also non-scientific (political, social and legal) determination as to how the risk ought to be weighed against benefits. While input for the former (i.e. science) is provided by scientific experts, the input for the latter (i.e. risk-benefit balance) can be provided by legislators, regulatory officials, judges, non-governmental organizations (NGOs) and the wider public, whose observations make a material difference to the standards.

The dual vulnerability should not be overlooked also because the deference given by the government to transnational bodies can be readily motivated, not only by their scientific expertise, but also by domestic political convenience. In the Japanese scenarios in the aftermath of Fukushima, there was a strong domestic incentive for the government to invoke transnationally accepted standards in order to convince domestic constituencies and avoided further controversy regarding the acceptability of risk. By stressing the scientific integrity of international standards, the government paradoxically augmented scepticism among those affected, their supporters, and the wider public, not only about

88 The limited domestic input is common to many other non-binding transnational standards: see Deirdre Curtin and Linda Senden, 'Public Accountability of Transnational Private Regulation: Chimera or Reality?' (2011) 38 Journal of Law and Society 163.

89 See (n 59) and accompanying text.

90 See (n 24–32) and accompanying text.

the scientific reliability of the data, but also on the government's avoidance of non-scientific deliberation in the process of bringing transnational science-based standards into the domestic legal order.

5 Conclusion

Within the complicated post-accident political climate, it is understandable that the Japanese government resorted to the ICRP's standards and stressed their credibility in order to provide assurance to those who have been affected by the nuclear incident. Noteworthy is that the ICRP itself has directly engaged with a series of 'dialogues' with the residents of Fukushima prefecture. Between September 2011 and August 2015, the ICRP has organized 12 stakeholder dialogue workshops with the residents.[91] The dialogues were in part designed to build 'trust' among stakeholders that were a 'necessary and central component of stakeholder involvement' in a post-accident recovery situation.[92]

In the post-Fukushima response, however, trust-building processes may have been significantly undermined by the narrative that emphasized the credibility of the ICRP's recommendations. As the ICRP itself openly acknowledges, the setting of permissible dose limits involves value judgment. The system of radiological protection is understood as being 'based on the foundations of social and ethical values, science, and experience'.[93] Therefore, to stress the fact that the ICRP's recommendations are internationally accepted and that they are based on scientific consensus does not provide any explanation for non-scientific grounds on which dose limits are set. The ICRP's efforts to conduct dialogues should be accompanied by the changes in the governmental narrative about non-scientific grounds on which a system of radiological protection is based.

Overall, the analysis of the domestic reliance on the ICRP's recommendations helped realize the vulnerability embedded in science-based, and transnationally adopted, standards on radiological protection. Scientific data on the effect of ionizing radiation on our bodies are produced by a number of research entities, whose results can contradict one another and create, perhaps inevitably, scientific uncertainty. The web of transnational institutions, including the UNSCEAR, the ICRP, and the IAEA, inject certain stability into this scientifically uncertain area which still requires regulation for the safety of professionals and the general public. Their much-needed standard-setting role in turn destabilizes the scientific trustworthiness of transnational radiation standards. By stressing the scientific credibility of the ICRP's recommendations, the narrative of the Japanese

91 T. Lazo, 'Involving Stakeholders in Radiological Protection Decision Making: Recovery History and Lessons from the People of Fukushima' (2016) 45 *Annals of the ICRP* 105; Jacques Lochard, *The Genesis of the ICRP Dialogue Initiative* (SAGE Publications Sage 2016).

92 Lazo (n 91) 107.

93 D.A. Cool, 'The New Mandate and Work of ICRP Committee 4' (2018) 47 Annals of the ICRP 214, 215–216.

government invited contestations, both on scientific and political grounds, from their domestic constituencies and international audience.

Although the chapter's analysis focused on the specific type of standards and their use in the aftermath of the Fukushima nuclear accident, the scientific and political vulnerability can be embedded in many other transnational standards based on scientific findings. The dual vulnerability may arise, for instance, with regard to the safety standards on chemical and industrial products. While transnational standards facilitate regulatory harmonization in a wide range of regulatory fields, it would be necessary to exercise caution when such standards are adopted at the domestic level. The domestic reception of transnational science-based standards cannot only rely on their scientific credibility. The domestic acceptance should involve the scrutiny of legal, ethical and political foundations on which transnational science-based standards are formulated and disseminated.

9 From contestation to accountability in EU pesticides regulation?

The case of glyphosate

Marta Morvillo

1 Introduction

Pesticides governance is at the centre of a thick web of interests and values. The use of pesticides is coessential to the prevailing model of agricultural production, thus playing an important role in the provision of stable food supplies globally. Pesticides are also a highly remunerative business: in 2019, the global pesticides market has reached a value of nearly 84.5 billion \$.[1] On the other hand, pesticides are chemical compounds that may pose substantial risks to both human health and the environment, including biodiversity.[2] Hence, their regulation entails striking a delicate balance between political, economic and public health and environmental considerations. Critically, all three are heavily informed by scientific evidence, with the consequence that regulatory-scientific expertise plays a key role in pesticides' legal and regulatory governance, in particular when it comes to their risk assessment.

The complexities inherent in the role of regulatory expertise, including in particular the ambiguous role expertise has often played in relation to politically contested decisions, are common to most contemporary legal and political systems.[3] When observing the European Union (EU) context, the nexus between epistemic and political authority appears particularly rich in implications. The peculiarities of the EU executive's institutional architecture and functioning, and primarily the contested nature of its democratic legitimacy, has tended to transform expertise into a source of alternative, surrogate legitimacy for the

1 The Business Research Company, 'Pesticides Market by Type (Herbicides, Fungicides and Insecticides), Opportunities And Strategies – Global Forecast To 2023', available at <https://www.thebusinessresearchcompany.com/report/pesticides-market> accessed 26 April 2020.

2 Emanuela Bozzini, *Pesticides Policy and Politics in the European Union* (Palgrave Macmillan 2017) 2 and 10.

3 For an overview of such complexities, see Alessandra Arcuri and Florin Coman-Kund, 'Introduction: Breaking Taboos, Talking Accountability' (in this volume), 3.

adoption of regulatory decisions.[4] While the salience of regulatory science's authority in the EU would in principle beg the presence of adequate accountability mechanisms, capable of exposing, if not disentangling, the intertwinement between technical and political actors' responsibilities, their development has encountered several obstacles, concerning both the most appropriate avenue to hold expert-executive determinations to account, and the need to compensate for the knowledge asymmetry between experts and non-experts. Highly technical determinations, such as those concerning pesticides regulation, tend to largely escape political-democratic accountability mechanisms (e.g. parliamentary oversight) precisely due to their complexity. Legal accountability mechanisms, on the other hand, have traditionally played a limited role with regard to complex assessments, due to the European courts' implicit reliance on the doctrine of technical discretion, which entails limited judicial review of such assessments.[5]

Against this background, the controversy surrounding the authorization of the pesticide glyphosate represents a valuable vantage point to expose the tensions characterizing EU expert governance in general, and pesticides regulation in particular.[6] It also offers the opportunity to explore the potential and limits of the EU's legal and institutional system in holding regulatory expertise to account. Glyphosate is a chemical compound used in plant protection products, and the most widely used pesticide globally. It has been at the centre of a heated political debate during the past few years, due to its allegedly carcinogenic properties, triggering scientific disagreement, societal contestation and sharp political conflict in the EU. As a result of this systemic reaction, regulatory science has been pushed back in the arena of law and politics. Different actors have mobilized in order to address the various tension between and within political and scientific considerations. The chapter analyses these developments from an accountability perspective. In particular, it investigates what accountability mechanisms have been operationalized in the context of the glyphosate dispute

4 Sheila Jasanoff, 'Constitutions of Modernity: Science, Risk and Governable Subjects', in Maria Weimer and Anniek de Ruijter (eds), *Regulating Risks in the European Union: The Co-production of Expert and Executive Power* (Hart Publishing 2017) 36. See also Maria Weimer and Anniek de Ruijter, 'Regulating Risks in the European Union: The Co-production of Expert and Executive Power' in Maria Weimer and Anniek de Ruijter (eds), *Regulating Risks in the European Union: The Co-production of Expert and Executive Power* (Hart Publishing 2017) 8.

5 For more recent developments in the sense of a closer judicial engagement with technical complexity see Patricia Dabrowska-Klodinska, 'EU Courts, Global Risks, and the Health and Environmental Safety Revisited: On Nuances of a Less Deferential Standard of Review' (2013) EUI Working Paper RSCAS 2013/63; more critically see Claudia Giulia Leonelli, 'The Fine Line Between Procedural and Substantive Review in Cases Involving Complex Technical-Scientific Evaluations: Bilbaína' (2018) 55 (4) Common Market Law Review 1217.

6 See Bozzini (n 2); Alessandra Arcuri and Yogi Hale Hendlin, 'The Chemical Anthropocene: Glyphosate as a Case Study of Pesticide Exposures' (2019) King's Law Journal; Michelle Everson and Ellen Vos, 'The Scientification of Politics and the Politicization of Science' in Michelle Everson and Ellen Vos (eds) *Uncertain Risks Regulated* (Routledge 2009).

and if and to what extent they have contributed to overcoming the challenges posed by experts' accountability: have they managed to bridge the 'language gap' affecting the dialogue between regulatory science and legal and political accountability mechanisms? Have they been successful in disentangling political and experts' roles and responsibilities? How do such mechanisms relate to each other? It will argue that while the development of a network of accountability mechanisms for regulatory expertise in the EU is possible, it is also highly dependent on the political salience of the matter at stake. It will suggest that, in the case of glyphosate, such network has been activated with regard to both the regulatory scientific and the political and institutional dimensions of the case, and that it addressed more effectively procedural rather than substantive issues.

The chapter is structured in six sections. Section 2 sketches the EU legal framework on plant protection products, with a particular focus on the principles underpinning pesticides regulation, the authorization procedure and the tensions between transparency and confidentiality in access to scientific studies. Having recounted the different phases of the glyphosate controversy (Section 3), it proceeds to map the different mechanisms that have been activated to hold both regulatory scientists (the European Food Safety Authority, EFSA) and decision makers (the European Commission) to account in the EU (Section 4). It then provides an assessment of the potentials for accountability in EU pesticides regulation in the light of the glyphosate dispute (Section 5). Section 6 concludes.

2 EU legal framework for the authorization of active substances

2.1 *Legal framework and principles*

Pesticides governance in the EU operates according to a composite legal framework. The case of glyphosate, in particular, is located at the crossroads of three bodies of legislation: Regulation 1107/2009 on the placing of plant protection products on the market,[7] Regulation 178/2002 on the General Food

7 Regulation (EC) No 1107/2009 of the European Parliament and of the Council of 21 October 2009 concerning the placing of plant protection products on the market and repealing Council Directives 79/117/EEC and 91/414/EEC [2009] OJ L309/1. The legislative framework is more articulated, including for example Directive 2009/128/EC of the European Parliament and of the Council of 21 October 2009 establishing a framework for Community action to achieve the sustainable use of pesticides [2009] OJ L309/71. The following sections will be based on the legislative framework in force at the time of the glyphosate authorization renewal (2010–2017); the innovations introduced by the General Food Law reform (Regulation (EU) 2019/1381 of the European Parliament and of the Council of 20 June 2019 on the transparency and sustainability of the EU risk assessment in the food chain and amending Regulations (EC) No 178/2002, (EC) No 1829/2003, (EC) No 1831/2003, (EC) No 2065/2003, (EC) No 1935/2004, (EC) No 1331/2008, (EC) No 1107/2009, (EU) 2015/2283 and Directive 2001/18/EC [2019] OJ L231/1) will be mentioned in footnotes where appropriate.

Law,[8] and Regulation 1049/2001 on access to documents[9] and Regulation 1367/2006 on access to environmental information.[10]

Regulation 1107/2009 constitutes the cornerstone of EU pesticides regulation. It lays down the principles and procedures for the authorization and renewal of active substances and plant protection products, including safeners, synergists, adjuvants and co-formulants, as defined in Article 3 thereof.[11] It pursues three objectives: ensuring a 'high level of protection of both human and animal health and the environment', harmonizing the rules for the placing on the market of plant protection products and improving agricultural production. Such objectives are implemented through the principles of hazard identification, substitution, sustainability, mutual recognition and precaution. The latter, in particular, should ensure coherence between these three potentially conflicting goals and is acknowledged as underpinning the entire act.[12]

By repealing Directive 414/91,[13] the 2009 Regulation represents the outcome of a ten years-long negotiation and embodies a major shift in the EU's approach to pesticides governance.[14] In particular, the legislative reform sought to address the shortcomings presented by the previous regime both in terms of regulatory efficiency and of health and environmental protection. It did so mainly by shifting from a risk- to a hazard-based approach to pesticides' safety assessment, with a view to speeding up scientific assessments, cutting administrative costs and delivering higher levels of safety.[15] While a risk-based approach focuses exclusively on the intrinsic properties of the substance, hazard-based approaches also take into consideration exposure, thus identifying 'the likelihood

8 Regulation (EC) No 178/2002 of the European Parliament and of the Council of 28 January 2002 laying down the general principles and requirements of food law, establishing the European Food Safety Authority and laying down procedures in matters of food safety [2002] OJ L31/1.

9 Regulation (EC) No 1049/2001 of the European Parliament and of the Council of 30 May 2001 regarding public access to European Parliament, Council and Commission documents [2001] OJ L145/43.

10 Regulation (EC) No 1367/2006 of the European Parliament and of the Council of 6 September 2006 on the application of the provisions of the Aarhus Convention on Access to Information, Public Participation in Decision-making and Access to Justice in Environmental Matters to Community Institutions and Bodies [2006] OJ L264/13.

11 Defined as 'chemical elements and their compounds, as they occur naturally or by manufacture, including any impurity inevitably resulting from the manufacturing process' ... 'having general or specific action against harmful organisms or on plants, parts of plants or plant products' (Articles 3(1) and 2(2) Regulation 1107/2009). While active substances – on which the following paragraphs focus – are authorized according to a centralized procedure taking place mostly at EU level (Articles 2–27), plant protection products are authorized at Member State level (Articles 28–37).

12 Article 1(1)-(3) Regulation 1107/2009.

13 Council Directive 91/414/EEC of 15 July 1991 concerning the placing of plant protection products on the market [1991] OJ L230/1.

14 Bozzini (n 2) 58, 60 speaks of a radical or paradigmatic policy change and gives an accurate account of the policy debate leading to it.

15 Bozzini (n 2) 73.

of harm in specific circumstances'.[16] As a consequence, besides being more efficient, the latter appears to ensure higher standards of protection of human health and the environment.[17] The shift from a risk- to a hazard-based approach must be read in conjunction with the adoption of four 'cut-off' criteria active substances need to meet in order to be considered for authorization (Article 4). Such criteria are detailed in Annex II to the Regulation and concern properties deemed to pose unacceptable hazards to human health (e.g. carcinogenicity and mutagenicity)[18] and the environment (e.g. persistent organic pollutants and persistent, bioaccumulative and toxic substances). Failure to cumulatively fulfil the cut-off criteria, according to a hazard-based assessment, leads to an immediate rejection of the application for authorization, without further inquiries into the compliance with the other criteria set out in Annex II.

2.2 *The authorization procedure*

In terms of regulatory design, the authorization procedure[19] for active substances set out by Regulation 1107/2009 follows the risk analysis model, generally adopted in EU risk regulation.[20] It therefore envisages a separation between the risk assessment and the risk management phase.

The scientific risk assessment begins with the applicant's submission of the dossier containing all the relevant information to the competent scientific authority of a Member State of their choice,[21] which acts as rapporteur. A first assessment is then undertaken by the Rapporteur Member State (RMS), according to the principles of independence, objectivity and transparency[22] and concluded with a draft assessment report (DAR), stating whether the substance can be expected to meet the Article 4 cut-off criteria. The procedure then moves on to the EU level, the DAR being submitted to the Commission and the EFSA for a second assessment. EFSA's role, as set out in the General Food Law, entails risk assessment tasks.[23] While its opinions are non-binding, it has been found to exert a significant

16 Bozzini (n 2) 31.

17 See Scientific Advice Mechanism (SAM), Group of Chief Scientific Advisors, 'EU Authorisation Processes of Plant Protection Products – From a Scientific Point of View' (2018) Scientific Opinion 5/2018, 41.

18 According to Annex II, points 3.6.2, 3.6.3, 3.6.4 and 3.7, Regulation 1107/2009.

19 The same provisions apply also to the authorization renewal, with few exceptions: the maximum renewal period is 15 years (Article 14(2)), the dossier must identify new data and studies (Article 15) and the Rapporteur Member State is designated by the Commission.

20 The risk analysis model was first advanced in 1983 by the US National Research Council, for the purposes of governmental management of technological risk (see National Research Council, Risk Assessment in the Federal Government: Managing the Process, 1983) and has been adopted as a framework for reference also in the EU context. See Alberto Alemanno, 'The Shaping of Risk Regulation by Community Courts', Jean Monnet Working Paper 18/2008, 7.

21 Article 7(1) Regulation 1107/2009. The dossier is immediately notified by the RMS to the Commission, EFSA and the Member States (Article 9(3) Regulation 1107/2009).

22 Ibid Article 11.

23 Articles 22 and 23 Regulation 178/2002.

influence on the Commission's risk management determinations.[24] EFSA's risk assessment includes a peer-review process and a public consultation.[25] It has been noted that, as a matter of fact, '"public participation" on highly technical toxicological dossiers is not wide' and is usually limited to 'the rather contained 'pesticide policy community' based in Brussels'.[26] This includes organizations representing the chemical industry (e.g. the European Crop Protection Association – ECPA), farmers' organizations (e.g. the Committee of Professional Agricultural Organisations – COPA) and public interest groups (e.g. Pesticide Action Network Europe – PAN). The outcome of the risk assessment carried out by EFSA is then consolidated in the Agency's (non-binding) conclusions, and transmitted to the Commission, which is entrusted with the risk management phase.

Whereas risk assessment is primarily science-based, risk management sees the emergence of other factors. According to Article 13, the Commission should in fact base its decision primarily on the DAR and EFSA's conclusions, but also on 'other factors legitimate to the matter under consideration and the precautionary principle'. In practice, this balancing exercise is, in the first place, in the hands of the Directorate General for Health and Food Safety (DG SANTE), which assists the Commission in preparing a final review report and a draft Regulation approving or rejecting the substance. The 'last word' on the authorization of the active substance is then for the representatives of Member States, sitting in the Standing Committee on Plants, Animal, Food and Feed (PAFF Committee), according to the comitology procedure.[27] In case of approval of the substance by the required majority,[28] the adopted Regulation will amend Annex I to Directive 91/414/EEC, which contains the list of the approved substances. The first approval can be for a maximum of ten years (Article 10), while renewals run to a maximum of 15 years (Article 14(2)).

2.3 *Burden of proof, transparency and confidentiality*

Regulation 1107/2009, as generally EU risk regulation in other areas, allocates the burden of proof as to the safety of the active substance on the applicant.[29] It is therefore for her to scientifically prove that the substance for which

24 Ellen Vos and Frank Wendler, 'Food Safety Regulation at the EU Level' in Ellen Vos and Frank Wendler (eds) *Food Safety Regulation in Europe. A Comparative Institutional Analysis* (Intersentia 2006) 122.

25 Article 12 Regulation 1107/2009.

26 Bozzini (n 2) 47.

27 Article 13(1) Regulation 1107/2009. See Regulation (EU) No 182/2011 of the European Parliament and of the Council of 16 February 2011, laying down the rules and general principles concerning mechanisms for control by Member States of the Commission's exercise of implementing powers [2008] OJ L55/13.

28 Article 6 Regulation 182/2011.

29 For a critical assessment of such arrangement in EU risk regulation, see Emilia Korkea-Aho and Päivi Leino, 'Who Owns the Information Held by EU Agencies? Weed Killers, Commercially Sensitive Information and Transparent and Participatory Governance' (2017) 54 Common Market Law Review, 1059.

authorization is sought complies with the statutory criteria, and in particular does not pose a threat to health and the environment. To this end, the application dossier includes scientific evidence in form of both peer-reviewed, open literature, published in the last ten years,[30] and (mostly) of studies commissioned and owned by the applicant herself.[31]

When scientific studies are privately commissioned, two further bodies of legislation are called into question, concerning respectively the generation of scientific evidence and their confidentiality and accessibility by the public. In order to ensure the independence and reliability of privately generated evidence, all studies are to be carried out according to a set of harmonized guidelines adopted at international and translational level (mainly within the OECD framework) and referred to by EU implementing regulations n. 283 and 284 of 2013.[32] If respected, such guidelines provide a guarantee of the quality and reliability of the studies and evidence supplied by the applicant, as they represent the internationally agreed state of the art in the respective fields.[33] The allocation of the burden of proof on the applicant entails another set of consequences, concerning confidentiality and access to documents. When it comes to authorization procedures, transparency is the rule.[34] The key documents on which the authorization (or renewal) procedure is based are made available to the public by EFSA: this applies in particular to the summary dossier submitted by the applicant,[35] to the DAR prepared by the RMS,[36] and to the conclusions reached by EFSA.[37]

30 Article 8(5) Regulation 1107/2009.

31 Article 8(1)(b) and (c) Regulation 1107/2009.

32 See Commission Regulation (EU) No 283/2013 of 1 March 2013 setting out the data requirements for active substances, in accordance with Regulation (EC) No 1107/2009 of the European Parliament and of the Council concerning the placing of plant protection products on the market [2013] OJ L93/1 and Commission Regulation (EU) No 284/2013 of 1 March 2013 setting out the data requirements for plant protection products, in accordance with Regulation (EC) No 1107/2009 of the European Parliament and of the Council concerning the placing of plant protection products on the market [2013] OJ L93/85.

33 See in particular the test guidelines developed by the Organisation for Economic Co-operation and Development (OECD) <http://www.oecd.org/chemicalsafety/pesticides-biocides/oecdguidancedocumentsforpesticideregistration.htm#dossier> accessed 28 April 2020 and the principles of Good Laboratory Practice (GLP), a set of guidelines also developed at OECD level. GLP principles have been transfused into EU legislation by Directive 2004/10/EC of the European Parliament and of the Council Directive on the harmonization of laws, regulations and administrative provisions relating to the application of the principles of GLP and the verification of their applications for tests on chemical substances [2004] OJ L50/44; on the GLP see also: <http://ec.europa.eu/growth/sectors/chemicals/good-laboratory-practice_en> accessed 28 April 2020. The General Food Law reform (Regulation 1381/2019) sets out additional guarantees to ensure the reliability and independence of privately funded studies, in particular by envisaging regular audits to the laboratories (Article 32a Regulation 178/2002) and by mandating the registration of all the studies commissioned to European laboratories in the context of an application for authorization (Article 32b Regulation 178/2002).

34 See also Article Regulation 1049/2001 and Article 3 Regulation 1367/2006.

35 Article 7(3) Regulation 1107/2009.

36 Ibid Article 12(1).

37 Ibid Article 12(2).

These publication requirements are, however, subject to limitations. Given the high costs entailed by active substances' research and development, the applicant often has a commercial interest in keeping the scientific studies supporting her application confidential. Confidentiality therefore receives specific protection under regulation 1107/2009.

When submitting the dossier, the applicant may request that certain information, including parts of the dossier, is kept confidential. The grounds on which confidential treatment may be invoked are set out in Article 63, and refer to the fact that 'disclosure of the information might undermine [the applicant's] commercial interests, or the protection of privacy and the integrity of the individual'.[38] A presumption is in particular established in favour of several types of information, such as methods of manufacture, information on the complete composition of a product or the specification of impurity,[39] whose disclosure may be particularly harmful to the producer. Confidentiality requests are to be assessed by the RMS and by EFSA.[40] When deciding upon requests for access to information concerning confidential documents,[41] EFSA shall therefore consider on a case by case basis whether confidentiality should prevail over the 'overriding public interest in [the documents'] disclosure',[42] taking into account the rules governing public access to environmental information.[43] In the context of access to documents, the provisions of Article 63, Regulation 1107/2009 and of Articles 38(1)(c) and 41, Regulation 178/2002 must therefore be read in the context of the EU legislation on access to documents (Regulation 1049/2001) in general, and access to environmental information (Regulation 1367/2007) in particular. The former establishes a general interest in disclosure of acts produced or retained by EU institutions, including Agencies, with a limited number of exceptions, among which the protection of commercial interests (Article 4(2)). The latter establishes the existence of an overriding public interest in disclosure when the requested documents contain environmental information, to the effect that the exceptions concerning the protection of commercial interests set out in Regulation 1049/2001 do not apply.

3 The 'glyphosate saga'

3.1 *The glyphosate's authorization renewal procedure (2010–2017)*

Glyphosate has been first authorized under Council Directive 91/414/EEC in 2002, for a period of ten years. Since then, the Monsanto-owned patent has expired and, although the corporation is still one of the main producers of glyphosate-based pesticides, several other companies have started synthesizing

38 Ibid Article 63(1).
39 Ibid Article 63(2).
40 Ibid Article 7(3).
41 Ibid Article 7(3).
42 Ibid Article 10.
43 Ibid Article 63(3).

Table 9.1 Glyphosate authorization renewal procedure

Risk assessment	
May 2010	Glyphosate Task Force submits the application for renewal of glyphosate's authorization to German authorities (BfR).
November 2010	Commission extends the approval of glyphosate until 31 December 2015 while pending the renewal procedure.
December 2013	BfR submits its Renewal Assessment Report, according to which glyphosate does not present carcinogenic properties.
January 2014	EFSA starts peer review process (further experts consultation on specific issues started in August 2016).
March 2014	EFSA starts public consultation.
March 2015	IARC finds glyphosate 'potentially carcinogenic to humans'.
April 2015	Commission invites EFSA and BfR to reconsider their findings in the light of IARC's report.
September 2015	BfR submits its Renewal Re-assessment Report in the light of IARC's findings, confirming its previous assessment.
October 2015	Commission extends the approval of glyphosate until 30 June 2016.
November 2015	EFSA presents its conclusions, according to which glyphosate is 'unlikely to pose a carcinogenic hazard to humans'.
Risk management	
February 2016	Commission proposes authorization renewal for 15 years, failing to obtain the required majority in the PAFF Committee.
April 2016	European Parliament approves a resolution calling on the Commission to renew glyphosate's authorization for seven years with restrictions.
June 2016	Commission extends the approval of glyphosate until 31 December 2017, having failed to obtain a majority in the PAFF Committee.
January 2017	European Citizens' Initiative 'Ban Glyphosate' registered.
March 2017	ECHA presents its report, where glyphosate is not classified as a carcinogen.
May–October 2017	Commission proposes authorization renewal for ten years, failing to obtain the required majority in the PAFF Committee.
October 2017	European Citizens' Initiative 'Ban Glyphosate' reaches 1,000,000 supporters and is submitted to the Commission.
October 2017	European Parliament approves a resolution calling on the Commission to phase out glyphosate by 2022.
November 2017	Commission proposes authorization renewal for five years, finally approved by the Appeal Committee.
December 2017	Renewal granted.

the compound. As of today, it is the world's most widely used pesticide (826 million kg/year as of 2014).[44] Facts surrounding the glyphosate controversy are known, but it is worth briefly recalling them (see Table 9.1).

44 EPRS, 'Authorisation of pesticides in the EU. With a focus on glyphosate' (2018) available at: <http://www.europarl.europa.eu/RegData/etudes/BRIE/2018/614691/EPRS_BRI(2018)614691_EN.pdf> accessed 28 April 2020.

In 2010, a consortium of companies (Glyphosate Task Force) filed an application for renewal of glyphosate's authorization to German authorities under the newly enacted Regulation 1107/2009. Having carried out a preliminary evaluation, the German Federal Institute for Risk Assessment (BfR),[45] in its quality of competent authority within the RMS, presented a favourable DAR to EFSA. In particular, glyphosate did not seem to present carcinogenic properties.

Pending EFSA's assessment, however, a scientific dispute over glyphosate's safety arose. Diverging views emerged, in particular with regard to glyphosate's carcinogenicity, between EFSA and the International Agency for Research on Cancer (IARC, a body of the WHO). According to the latter, glyphosate was 'probably carcinogenic'.[46] EFSA disagreed and, in its November 2015 conclusion,[47] found glyphosate 'unlikely to pose carcinogenic hazard to humans'. This finding was subsequently restated by the European Chemicals Agency (ECHA) in March 2017.[48] Relying on EFSA's assessment, the European Commission envisaged a generous 15-year renewal, without any restrictions as to the use of the active substance. The draft regulation proposed by the Commission, however, failed to meet Member States' support in the PAFF Committee in February 2016. By then, the scientific disagreement over the carcinogenic properties of the pesticide had in fact become a political dispute, resulting in the 'usual' deadlock at Committee level.[49]

The European Commission reacted by gradually reconsidering its initial proposal. Hoping to gain Member States' votes in the PAFF Committee, it first downsized the renewal to a 10-year period and, failing once again to reach the required majority, to a mere five years – the minimum according to the 2009 regulation. Only then did the Member States' Appeal Committee give the green light to the proposed regulation, which was finally adopted by the Commission in December 2017.

45 The Bundesinstitut fur Risikobewertung (BfR) is the scientific agency of the Federal Republic of Germany. It was established in November 2002 as a body under public law and reports to the Federal Ministry of Food and Agriculture. It enjoys independence in respect of its scientific assessments and research and operates under rules of good scientific practice (see <http://www.bfr.bund.de/cm/349/principles-of-good-scientific-practice-in-the-bfr.pdf> accessed 28 April 2020).

46 International Agency for Research on Cancer, 'Monograph 112' (2015) available at: <http://monographs.iarc.fr/ENG/Monographs/vol112/mono112-10.pdf> accessed 28 April 2020.

47 European Food Safety Authority, 'Conclusion on the peer review of the pesticide risk assessment of the active substance glyphosate' (2015) EFSA Journal 13(11):4302, available at: <https://efsa.onlinelibrary.wiley.com/doi/epdf/10.2903/j.efsa.2015.4302> accessed 28 April 2020.

48 European Chemicals Agency, Committee for Risk Assessment, 'Opinion proposing harmonized classification and labelling at EU level of glyphosate', 13 March 2017, available at: <https://echa.europa.eu/-/glyphosate-not-classified-as-a-carcinogen-by-echa> accessed 28 April 2020. ECHA operates under Regulation of the European Parliament and of the Council (EC) No 1272/2008 on the classification, labelling and packaging of substances and mixtures [2008] OJ L353/1.

49 Maria Weimer, 'Risk Regulation and Deliberation in EU Administrative Governance' (2015) European Law Journal 5, 622.

3.2 *Contested issues in the glyphosate dispute*

Different factors can be seen to have twisted a pesticide's authorization renewal into such a politically contentious issue. Among them, some relate more closely to risk assessment and to the embedding of science into the legal framework (e.g. those concerning the sources of scientific evidence and the assessment methodologies), while other are more political and institutional in nature (e.g. those concerning the levels and the goals of EU pesticides governance).[50]

The former are epitomized by the disagreement between EFSA and IARC. Behind the conflicting assessments of glyphosate's carcinogenicity reached by the two expert bodies lie different approaches to several elements of risk assessment.[51] A first element of discrepancy related to the very object of the assessment: while the IARC looked both at glyphosate itself, and at glyphosate-based plant protection products, EFSA considered only the former, as it is for Member States to assess the safety of the plant protection products containing it. Another element concerns the sources relied on in the two bodies' risk assessments: as seen above, EFSA bases its assessments mainly, although not exclusively, on evidence submitted by the applicants. IARC, on the other hand, adopts the opposite approach, based on the publicity of the evidence taken into account. According to the methodological section of the IARC's Monograph, 'only reports that have been published or accepted for publication in the openly available scientific literature are reviewed'.[52] Both approaches entail trade-offs: EFSA's in terms of public control over the scientific evidence's genesis and of access to scientific studies, IARC's in terms of range of evidence considered (necessarily more limited).

As to the political and institutional dimension, the glyphosate saga showed citizens' and Member States' deep distrust in EU risk regulation. Notwithstanding the extensive amount of documents published, the public consultation and the risk communication efforts put in place by EFSA and by the Commission, concerns were raised over the influence of corporate interests on the Agency's determinations.[53] The difficulties in reconciling sharply divided societal views emerged in the context of the re-authorization signalled the lack of a clear

50 As I have argued elsewhere, the tensions emerged during the glyphosate dispute can be traced back to the sources, levels and goals of EU pesticides regulation: see Marta Morvillo, 'Glyphosate Effect: Has the Glyphosate Controversy Affected the EU's Regulatory Epistemology?' (2020) 6 European Journal of Risk Regulation.

51 Scientific Advice Mechanism High Level Group, 'Explanatory note on scientific advice for the regulatory assessment of glyphosate in plant protection products', 2 February 2016, available at: <https://ec.europa.eu/research/sam/pdf/topics/explanatory_note_glyphosate.pdf#view=fit&pagemode=none> accessed 28 April 2020.

52 International Agency for Research on Cancer (n 46) 12.

53 Concerns also raised by the concomitant turmoil determined by the 'Monsanto papers' scandal, to which EFSA reacted with a 'Statement regarding the EU assessment of glyphosate and the so-called "Monsanto papers"', available at: <http://www.efsa.europa.eu/sites/default/files/topic/20170608_glyphosate_statement.pdf> accessed 28 April 2020.

prioritization among the goals pursued by Regulation 1107/2009.[54] Finally, the intertwinement of EU and Member State level throughout the procedure, instead of fostering its overall legitimacy, resulted in blame shifting between the two levels, especially in the comitology phase.[55]

What is unusual about glyphosate renewal, is that the story does not end here. Interestingly, the public and institutional concerns raised by the pesticide triggered the activation of accountability mechanisms new to the field of science-based regulation. The following section provides a typology of the mechanisms and fora that have been mobilized during and after the glyphosate's re-authorization procedure, highlighting what aspects of the dispute they have targeted, through which legal regime(s) they have been activated, and assessing whether they have resulted in enhanced reason giving or whether they have additionally led to legislative change.

4 A typology of accountability mechanisms in the case of glyphosate

4.1 *Political accountability mechanisms*

4.1.1 *The European citizens' initiative 'Ban glyphosate'*

Societal concerns over glyphosate resulted in a European Citizens' Initiative (ECI) being submitted to the Commission on 6 October 2017,[56] under regulation 211/2011.[57] In principle, the ECI can hardly be considered an accountability mechanism, being instead a participatory instrument.[58] It has been often noted that, although high hopes had been cast on the ECI in the wake of the Lisbon Treaty[59] and of the enactment of Regulation (EU) No 211/2011, its practice has not fully lived up to those expectations.[60] In particular, of the

54 Scientific Advice Mechanism, 'EU Authorisation Processes of Plant Protection Products', supra note 17, 7.

55 See Ton van den Brink, 'Danger! Glyphosate may Expose Weaknesses in Institutional Systems: EU Legislation and Comitology in the Face of a Controversial Reauthorisation' (2020) 6 European Journal of Risk Regulation.

56 The Citizens' Initiative was registered as 'Ban Glyphosate and protect people and the environment form toxic pesticides', see <http://ec.europa.eu/citizens-initiative/public/initiatives/successful/details/2017/000002> accessed 28 April 2020.

57 Regulation (EU) No 211/0211 of the European Parliament and of the Council on the Citizens' Initiative [2011] OJ L65/1.

58 But see also EPRS, 'The added value of the European Citizens' Initiative (ECI), and its revision', 2018, 47. On the relationship between participation and accountability, see Mark Bovens, Deirdre Curtin and Paul 't Hart, 'Studying the Real World of EU Accountability: Framework and Design', in Mark Bovens, Deirdre Curtin and Paul 't Hart (eds), *The Real World of EU Accountability: what deficit?* (OUP 2010) 38.

59 Article 11(4) TEU.

60 Anastasia Karatzia, 'The European Citizens' Initiative and the EU Institutional Balance: on Realism and the Possibilities of Affecting EU Lawmaking' (2017) CMLR 54, 181.

76 ECIs registered,[61] only 6 have been successful and the ECI's impact on the Commission's legislative initiative has been negligible, leading to a 'mismatch between the expectations of citizens from the ECI and the ECI's capacity to lead to legislative output'.[62] Compared to other cases, the 'Ban glyphosate' ECI seems to have been overall more successful. In serving its participatory function, it has also represented an unorthodox avenue for accountability as to the Commission's position during the authorization procedure and has led to enhanced reason giving and contributed to shaping already ongoing legislative reform processes.

With the ECI 'Ban glyphosate', proponents targeted both the regulatory-scientific and the political dimension of the glyphosate dispute and called on the Commission to take legislative action in three main areas: to 'ban glyphosate-based herbicides, exposure to which has been linked to cancer in humans, and has led to ecosystems degradation', referring in particular to the IARC report; to 'ensure that the scientific evaluation of pesticides for EU regulatory approval is based only on published studies, which are commissioned by competent public authorities instead of the pesticide industry';[63] and to 'set EU-wide mandatory reduction targets for pesticide use, with a view to achieving a pesticide-free future'. As to the first claim, addressing the scientific substance of the issue, the Commission disagreed with the ECI since 'there are neither scientific nor legal grounds to justify a ban of glyphosate', in so far as it complies with the 1107/2009 Regulation criteria.[64] While stating that it 'will not make a legislative proposal to that effect' the Commission nonetheless explained the reasons for its decision. In particular, it stressed that the renewal had been significantly shorter than initially proposed, as a consequence of having taken into consideration 'the views of the European Parliament and other legitimate factors when setting the appropriate period of renewal'.[65] Finally, it acknowledged 'that there has been considerable debate on glyphosate in the public sphere, as illustrated by this Citizens' Initiative and the two Resolutions adopted by the European Parliament on the matter'. Citizens' and EP's views are therefore (at least rhetorically) incorporated into the Commission's given reasons.

61 As of January, 2021, out of 99 ECI requests, 76 were registered. Of these, only 6 were so far successful.

62 Karatzia (n 60) 207.

63 Under this heading, proponents advanced three sub-claims: that the studies on which risk assessments are based shall be published; that they should be carried out exclusively by public bodies, given the interest of applicants, and of the laboratories on which they rely for a favourable assessment 'despite [the] stringent requirements under OECD Guidelines and the GLP standard'; and that applicants should not be able to choose the Rapporteur Member State.

64 European Commission, Communication from the Commission on the European Citizens' Initiative 'Ban Glyhosate' [2017] C(2017) 8414 final, 14.

65 Ibid 9.

The second claim concerns the private nature of the sources of scientific evidence and their confidential treatment.[66] As to the origins of the scientific data and studies, the Commission is, in principle, unwilling to question the allocation of the burden of proof on the applicant. It provides reasons for this policy option, stressing in particular that the quality and objectivity of the studies submitted by the industry is ensured through compliance with principles of good laboratory practice (GLP). Furthermore, an approach based on publicly commissioned studies alone 'may prove to be challenging given the high numbers of studies [and hence the costs] required to support all applications for active substance approval and product authorisation'. The Commission, however, committed to 'propose to amend the legislation to strengthen the governance for the conduct of such [industry] studies' providing examples of possible measures, including the involvement of public authorities in the decision as to which studies need to be conducted for an application dossier. Some of these measures, including audits and mandatory studies' registration, have indeed been included in the General Food Law reform approved in April 2019.[67]

An even more responsive approach has been followed with regards to transparency and access to documents. The Commission 'fully agrees that transparency in scientific assessments and decision making is vital to ensuring trust in the regulatory system' and accepts that 'addressing a perceived lack of transparency may require an adjustment of certain procedures' while ensuring respect for applicants' legitimate business secrets. The Commission committed to take measures to increase transparency of the risk assessment process and, more precisely, to present a legislative proposal by May 2018.[68] Also in this case, the Commission's commitment was channelled into the already ongoing reform of the General Food Law, resulting in a renewed procedure for the assessment of confidentiality claims.[69]

The third and final point of the ECI advanced a more clearly political agenda, asking the total elimination of all pesticides from the EU. The Commission stressed that 'the EU policy in the area of pesticides is not directed towards the total elimination of all pesticides', and it therefore 'does not envisage at this stage to submit a proposal to establish EU level reduction targets for pesticide use'. However, also in this case, mitigation measures are mentioned: the Commission is committed to strengthening 'efforts for the continuous and

66 An additional point raised under the second claim concerns the possibility for the applicant to choose the RMS. Having clarified that this is the case for active substances alone, whose authorization is sought for the first time, while for renewals applicants are allocated to RMS according to a work plan, seeking to maintain a balance between the Member States, the Commission considers that 'the overall system is appropriate' and did not put forward any proposal for change, European Commission, Communication from the Commission on the European Citizens' Initiative 'Ban Glyphosate and protect people and the environment from toxic pesticides', C(2017) 8414 final, 12.

67 See (n 7).

68 European Commission (n 64) 14.

69 See (n 7).

measurable reduction of risk from pesticide use', also in coordination with Member States.[70]

While originating in the specific context of glyphosate, the ECI resulted in broader challenges to the overall EU approach to pesticides regulation. It questioned the scientific substance of the decision (first claim), exposed the science-policy choices underpinning the generation and legal regime of scientific evidence (second claim), and contested the overall EU policy on pesticides (third claim). From an accountability perspective, the ECI resulted in the Commission engaging in explaining and justifying its decision and committing to legislative reform. As to the latter, the impact of the ECI should however not be overestimated. None of the measures proposed by the Commission represent a direct reaction to the ECI's requests: they are rather the outcome of an already ongoing process of policy evaluation that the Commission has been carrying out under the regulatory Fitness check of the General Food Law.[71] The Commission clearly sought to acknowledge the political relevance of the ECI, especially by stressing the importance of a European public debate on the issue, and the ECI is expressly mentioned in the preamble of Regulation 1381/2019 (para 27). The Commission seemed however to be more interested in the rhetorical impact rather than in the political implications, in so far as it only committed to the adoption of measures that were already in the pipeline, while disregarding those which conflicted with its policy agenda. In addition, when considering the legislative changes introduced by the General Food Law reform, it can be observed that they mostly relate to the procedural (and methodological) aspects of risk assessment, such as transparency and access to documents, while substantive issues (e.g. those relating to the goals of EU food governance) have not been addressed.[72] While representing an overall positive development in terms of both participation and accountability, the achievements of the 'Ban glyphosate' ECI should therefore not be overestimated in terms of agenda-setting. They can however be appreciated in terms of reason giving and justification.

4.1.2 *The European Parliament*

The proponents of the 'Ban Glyphosate' ECI were invited to present their case before the European Parliament (Article 11, ECI Regulation) during a public hearing, which took place on 20 November 2017. By then, the EP had already shown interest in the glyphosate dispute on several occasions. Besides having hosted a public hearing on the 'Monsanto papers', it had, more remarkably, voiced its views on glyphosate through two non-binding resolutions, adopted in

70 European Commission, Communication on the ECI 'Ban Glyphosate' (n 64) 14.
71 Ibid.
72 Morvillo (n 50).

April 2016[73] and October 2017.[74] The EP also established a special committee on the authorization procedure for pesticides (the PEST committee). While serving different purposes, both the resolutions and the PEST committee addressed the scientific, institutional and political dimensions of the glyphosate controversy, the former remaining anchored in the context of the individual case, the latter broadening the scope of inquiry to EU pesticides governance more generally.

The two resolutions mirrored the escalation in glyphosate's political salience. The former called for a 7-year renewal of the authorization, with limitations concerning non-professional uses and public spaces, the latter for a radical phasing out of the active substance by 2022. The resolutions addressed both the regulatory-scientific and political aspects of the dispute. In particular, the EP expressed concern as to the reliance on confidential industry studies instead of publicly available data and as to the inadequate level of protection of health and the environment.

The most remarkable action undertaken by the EP was however the setting up of the PEST committee. Established under rule 197 of the EP's rules of procedure, the special committee was composed of 30 members and operated for nine months, from February to December 2018. While its establishment drew expressly on the glyphosate dispute, its scope of inquiry extended beyond the specific case, reaching further to address broader issues of transparency and accountability of EU pesticides governance. According to its mandate, the PEST committee was expected, first, to assess whether the Commission had complied with Regulation 1107/2009 when renewing glyphosate authorization and, second, to conduct a broad-spectrum review of the whole pesticide authorization procedure, aimed at tackling its legal, institutional and (even) scientific weaknesses. In particular, the Committee was entrusted to assess the EU agencies' (*in primis* EFSA and ECHA) compliance with the relevant legislation, guidelines and codes of conduct and evaluated the procedure's transparency and independence, especially from industry. It was additionally endowed with the task of shedding light on possible conflicts of interest (at all levels, included national competent authorities) affecting the approval procedure, and of evaluating whether the relevant EU agencies were adequately equipped – both in terms of staff and financial resources – to commission and conduct independent studies. Finally, the committee had to consider the methodology and scientific quality of the procedure, including potential failures in the scientific evaluation. The PEST committee conducted eleven meetings and three missions, among which to EFSA and IARC. During the hearings, all phases of the pesticides' authorization procedure were examined and experts from over 30 organizations were heard, including both EU-level bodies and the national competent authorities operating at Member State level. The committee additionally heard stakeholders and representatives of other regulatory-scientific

73 European Parliament resolution of 13 April 2016, P8_TA(2016)0119.
74 European Parliament resolution of 24 October 2017, P8_PROV(2017)0395.

bodies of the OECD area.[75] It concluded its activities with a report, subsequently approved by the EP.[76]

The problems identified by the final report concern both substantive (e.g. insufficient protection of human health, lack of resources for national authorities, unclarity as to what entails unacceptable risks for the environment) and procedural issues (e.g. lack of transparency, conflict of interests at EU and Member State level, designation of the RMS). In terms of accountability, the PEST committee represents a valuable experience from at least two points of view. First, as it is apparent from the final report, the committee's activities allowed the EP to gain a comprehensive understanding of all the stages of the authorization procedure and the tensions they entail. In particular, the questions posed during the hearings served a double function: on the one hand, they allowed the committee members to understand the problems underpinning pesticides authorization and their embedding in the EU legal and regulatory framework; on the other hand, they made the expert (EFSA, ECHA) and political (Commission) actors involved to explain their choices in the context of the glyphosate dispute and more generally in the design and operationalization of the regulatory regime.

Secondly, the knowledge gathered by the PEST committee resulted in an empowerment of the EP, by allowing it to make a factually informed contribution to the debate, and, more specifically, to the then ongoing reform of the General Food Law. In particular, the final report suggested several courses of action with regard to both risk assessment and risk management. A few examples may help clarify. As to the former, the EP proposed the establishment of a work programme that ensures rotation among the different national authorities, so to achieve a fairer allocation of dossiers to RMSs; it additionally recommended the mandatory registration of scientific studies and their accessibility by the public, in order to strengthen transparency and independence of risk assessment. The EP also suggested the reconsideration of the approach to the evaluation of scientific evidence, in particular by calling for 'an independent reassessment of the current rules for the literature review so as to ensure that all relevant studies are considered'.[77] In particular, it suggested that the applicant should no longer be required to provide scientific, peer-reviewed open literature, instead assigning this role to the RMS, assisted by EFSA,[78] and that such literature 'should be given the equivalent weight in the assessment as GLP-based studies'.[79] As to risk management, the EP stressed, among other issues, the need to ensure a

75 See The European Parliament special committee on the Union's authorization procedure for pesticides, 'Documentation relating to the Committee's work from February to December 2018', available at <https://www.europarl.europa.eu/cmsdata/160000/COMPILATION.pdf> accessed 28 April 2002.

76 European Parliament, Union's authorization procedure for pesticides, European Parliament resolution of 16 January 2019 on the Union's authorization procedure for pesticides (2018/2153(INI)).

77 Ibid para 46.

78 Ibid para 43.

79 Ibid para 44.

consistent and uniform application of the precautionary principle and of the cut-off criteria established in Regulation 1107/2009, linked to a broader societal discussion on the goals of EU pesticides governance.[80] This resulted in recommendations to strengthen post-market vigilance, to set clearer minimum residue levels, considering in particular cumulative effects, and to ensure the protection of vulnerable groups.[81] The report additionally stressed the need to ensure political accountability for the adoption of implementing acts in the context of the comitology procedure, which appears unsatisfactory in terms of transparency.[82]

The establishment of the PEST Committee represents a powerful challenge to the assumption according to which parliamentary assemblies are ill-suited to engage with technically complex determinations. It reflects the EP's commitment to have its voice heard and to 'make use of its powers and political influence for the purposes of protecting citizens' interests',[83] in a field that would normally be considered too technical for parliamentary debates. The level of sophistication of the hearings and the report, both as to the institutional and as to the regulatory-scientific aspects of pesticides authorization, however, suggest that if a high level of political salience is reached, as in the case of glyphosate, technical complexity may represent a smaller obstacle to accountability than it is usually thought. While the EP's engagement with the glyphosate dispute resulted in a so far unprecedented opportunity for reason giving with regard to regulatory expertise, its impact in terms of consequences might have been more limited, also due to its overlap with the already ongoing reform of the General Food Law.[84]

4.2 *Legal accountability mechanisms*

Several glyphosate-related cases have been brought to European Courts in the context of the substance's authorization renewal, challenging the validity of Regulation 1107/2009,[85] the Commission's and EFSA's assessments,[86] and the confidentiality regime governing access to scientific studies.[87] While legal accountability mechanisms may not seem to be adequately equipped to review

80 Ibid paras 5–8.
81 Ibid paras 16, 55, 63 and 14.
82 Ibid para 79.
83 Karatzia (n 60) 190.
84 Neither the EP's resolutions nor the PEST Committee's activity are mentioned in the preamble of Regulation 1381/2019 (n 7).
85 Case C-616/17 *Blaise and Others* [2019] EU:C:2019:800.
86 See for example Case T-125/18 *Associazione GranoSalus v CommissionGrano Salus* [2019] EU:T:2019:92. All direct challenges to the validity of the implementing measures adopted by the Commission have so far been declared inadmissible, due to the strict standing requirements established by Article 263 TFEU.
87 Case T-716/14 *Anthony C Tweedale v European Food Safety Authority* [2019] EU:T:2019:141; Case T-329/17 *Heidi Hautala and Others v European Food Safety Authority* [2019] EU:T:2019:142.

complex technical assessments, European Courts have, for more than a decade, shown a rather proactive attitude to the review of science-based measures in the field of risk regulation, including those relating to pesticides.[88] This trend, particularly clear with regard to the General Court (GC), has seen the adoption of a less deferential standard of review and the development of new procedurally-oriented judicial tests,[89] which allow Courts to engage more closely with the factual elements of the case, including the structure and content of scientific opinions.[90] European Courts have also been called to interpret EU law provisions on access to documents, as enshrined in Regulation 1049/2001, and in particular access to environmental information, as protected by the Aarhus Regulation (Regulation 1367/2006). The latter have proved to be triggers for judicial developments whose impact is most likely to reach beyond the case of glyphosate.

Ironically enough, it is a judgment relating to glyphosate's authorization in 2002, that laid the basis for the most significant judicial developments concerning its renewal. Two environmental NGOs had sought access to scientific studies relating to the composition, manufacturing process and impurities of glyphosate. The Commission refused access, as disclosure would have harmed the producers' commercial interests. The applicants lamented the breach of the right to access environmental information, according to the Aarhus convention (and Regulation 1367/2006), in front of the GC, which upheld the claim in 2013.[91] In particular, the Court stated that the documents contained information relating to emissions into the environment and could therefore not be covered by confidentiality claims. On appeal by the Commission, the Court of Justice (CJ) set aside the judgment, as the GC had erred in considering that a 'sufficiently direct link' between the requested information and emissions into the environment was enough to allow disclosure.[92] In so doing however, the CJ established three principles,[93] clarifying the content and scope of 'emissions into

88 Alemanno (n 20); Dabrowska-Klodinska (n 5).

89 Joseph Corkin. 'Regulating Risk Regulation Judiciously. How the Court of Justice Ensures the European Community Responds to Both Popular and Scientific Voices' (2002) available at <https://www.kent.ac.uk/scarr/events/papers/Corkin.pdf> accessed 28 April 2020.

90 Case T-13/99 *Pfizer Animal Health v Council* [2002] EU:T:2002:209; Case T-74/00 *Artegodan and Others v Commission* [2002] EU:T:2002:283.

91 Case T-545/11 *Stichting Greenpeace Nederland and Pesticide Action Network Europe v. European Commission* [2013] EU:T:2013:523.

92 Case C-673/13P *European Commission v. Stichting Greenpeace Nederland and Pesticide Action Network Europe* [2016] EU:C:2016:889, para 82.

93 The same principles were stated on the same day by the Court in another case, namely a preliminary ruling on the Aarhus directive (Case C-442/14 *Bayer CropScience and Stichting DE Bijenstichting* [2016] ECLI:EU:C:2016:890). The question raised by the referring court concerned, in particular, the interpretation of 'emissions in the environment'. In addition to the principles established in the PAN case, the judgment in C-442/14 expressly established that the information must be disclosed regardless the source (be it a field or a laboratory study).

the environment' and of the relative information. Firstly, it established that the concept 'is not limited to information concerning emissions emanating from certain industrial installations'[94] but applies also to the spraying of plant protection products. Second, access to information relates not only to actual emissions, but also to foreseeable emissions, 'under normal or realistic conditions of use', which is the case of plant protection products, intended to be released into the environment.[95] This approach significantly broadened the range of disclosable documents, including in particular laboratory studies. Thirdly, and most remarkably, according to the Court, information relating to the emissions into the environment is functional to promoting 'more effective public participation in the decision-making process, thereby increasing, on the part of the competent bodies, the accountability of decision making and contributing to public awareness and support for the decision taken'.[96] For the public to be able to understand and 'to check whether the assessment of actual or foreseeable emissions on the basis of which the competent authority authorizes the product or substance in question is correct', information must be disclosed as to the 'nature, composition, quantity, date and place of the actual or foreseeable emissions' and their effects on the environment.[97]

These same principles were resumed and fully developed in two 'twin' access to documents cases, brought against EFSA in the context of glyphosate's authorization renewal.[98] In *Tweedale*, a British citizen and environmental consultant contested EFSA's denial to grant access to two 'key studies' on the toxicity of glyphosate, used to determine its acceptable daily intake (ADI). In *Hautala*, a group of MEPs acted against the agency's denial of access to the scientific studies used in the assessment of glyphosate's carcinogenicity. Among the claims raised by the applicants, in both cases the GC was asked to clarify the concept of information relating to emissions into the environment in the context of plant protection products. First, the Court clarified that environmental information is covered by an absolute presumption of overriding public interest, with the effect that an EU institution cannot refuse access to documents on the basis of the exception relating to the protection of commercial interests. Secondly, it established that, as the requested studies related to glyphosate's health effects (in particular toxicity and carcinogenicity), having access to them would allow citizens to understand the impact of glyphosate being released into the environment on human health. What is more, the Court expanded on the CJ's reasoning in

94 *Commission v. Stichting Greenpeace Nederland* (n 92) para 70.
95 Ibid paras 74–75.
96 Ibid para 80.
97 Ibid para 79.
98 For a more thorough reading of the Tweedale and Hautala cases, see Marta Morvillo, 'The General Court Orders Disclosure of Glyphosate-related Scientific Studies: Tweedale, Hautala, and the Concept of Environmental Information in the Context of Plant Protection Products' (2019) 10 European Journal of Risk Regulation 2, 419.

Greenpeace and *Bayer Cropscience*,[99] linking transparency and the democratic nature of the EU's decision-making process. It explicitly linked access to documents to the accountability of EU institutions,[100] with the effect that EFSA's refusal to grant access to the requested studies was found to breach Regulation 1049/2001 and the Aarhus Regulation. Interestingly, the Court's understanding of accountability reaches beyond the obstacle represented by technical complexity and applies also to toxicity and carcinogenicity studies in so far as they relate to human health and the environment, thus seeking to bridge the gap between regulatory-scientific and public debate.

A second judicial development triggered by the glyphosate dispute concerned the validity of Regulation 1107/2009 in light of the precautionary principle. In *Blaise*, the CJ decided on a preliminary ruling presented by a French court, concerning several provisions of the 2009 Regulation, which had been contested in the case of glyphosate (i.e. the focus on individual substances as identified by the applicant rather than on possible 'cocktail effects' of the compound, the type of studies submitted by the applicant and their independence). The CJ stressed that in order to comply with the precautionary principle the EU legislature 'ought to establish a normative framework that ensures that the competent authorities have available to them [...] sufficient information in order to adequately assess [...] the risks to health resulting from the use of active substances and plant protection products'.[101] It then assessed the compatibility of the contested provisions with the precautionary principle and found that the EU legislator did not commit a manifest error of assessment in adopting them. In so doing it carefully separated considerations on the validity of the general rules governing the approval of plant protection products, from considerations on the circumstances of glyphosate's renewal, which it excluded from its ruling.[102] While the judgment has been criticized for offering a de-contextualized application of the precautionary principle,[103] it is worth mentioning an aspect of the Advocate General's opinion which, at least partly, echoes the context in which the preliminary ruling originated. In a postscript to the Opinion, Advocate General Sharpston

99 See supra (n 92–93). The Court also recalled its reasoning in C-57/16 P *ClientEarth v Commission* [2018] EU:C:2018:660, para 75.

100 *Tweedale* (n 87) para 54.

101 *Blaise* (n 85) para 47.

102 Ibid, paras 48–49. See also Case C-616/17 *Blaise and Others* [2019] EU:C:2019:800, Opinion of AG Sharpston, para 43: 'The defendants hold up glyphosate as the exemplar of what is wrong with the PPP Regulation. Although specific EU acts have been adopted by the EU institutions affecting the use of glyphosate, the four questions referred do not mention — still less target — those acts. Instead, the focus is on the overall regulatory architecture established by the PPP Regulation affecting all plant protection products'.

103 Sophia Paulini, 'Fact or Fiction? Case C-616/17 and the Compatibility of the EU Authorisation Procedure for Pesticides with the Precautionary Principle' (2020) European Journal of Risk Regulation, 16. See also Alessandra Donati, 'The Glyphosate Saga, A Further but Not a Final Step: The CJEU Confirms the Validity of the Regulation on Plant Protection Products in Light of the Precautionary Principle' (2020) 11 (1) European Journal of Risk Regulation 152.

mentioned the report of the PEST committee and highlighted that, based on the report's findings, nothing in her opinion 'should be read as suggesting that it would be appropriate for the EU legislator to sit back complacently and pay attention when issues are raised concerning potential risks to human and animal health and the environment'.[104]

Against the backdrop of these judicial developments, it can be observed that Courts have also played a relevant role the development of (legal) accountability mechanisms in the context of the glyphosate dispute. While *Blaise* reflects a rather traditional approach, by clearly separating the validity claims raised by the referring court from the specific context of the glyphosate dispute, it nonetheless reflects the systemic activation triggered by the dispute, especially via the AG's reference to the PEST committee's report. *Tweedale* and *Hautala*, on the other hand, resulted in a widening of the documents that cannot be covered by confidentiality claims and additionally allowed the GC to put forward its own view of the accountability-enhancing function of transparency and access to documents, even when highly technical assessments are at stake. In neither of the cases the Court was asked to engage with the scientific evidence underpinning glyphosate renewal, thus remaining on an abstract (*Blaise*) or procedural (*Tweedale* and *Hautala*) level.

4.3 *Quasi-Legal accountability: The European Ombudsman*

Several complaints regarding glyphosate were filed with the European Ombudsman.[105] Although perhaps less remarkably if compared to the activation of political and legal accountability mechanisms considered above, the Ombudsman's Office has also emerged as a possible forum for questioning and exposing the EU executive's handling of glyphosate authorization. Complaints concerned mainly EFSA's and ECHA's practices with regard to public consultations,[106] access to documents,[107] and institutions' correspondence with citizens,[108] which have not so far led to findings of maladministration.

104 Opinion of AG Sharpston (n 102) paras 82–83.

105 See also Decision in case 12/2013/MDC [2018] on the practices of the European Commission regarding the authorization and placing on the market of plant protection products (pesticides) and the European Ombudsman's reply to the Public consultation on the transparency and sustainability of the EU risk assessment model in the food chain.

106 See Decision in case 952/2014/OV [2015] on the European Food Safety Authority's (EFSA) public consultation procedure for the renewal of the approval of the herbicide glyphosate.

107 See Decision in case 1259/2017/JAS [2017] on the European Chemicals Agency's handling of a request for public access to scientific studies.

108 See Decision in case 1769/2017/JAS [2018] on the European Chemicals Agency's handling of concerns regarding the herbicide ingredient glyphosate and Decision in case 1375/2016/JAS on the European Commission's handling of concerns regarding the renewal of the approval of the herbicide ingredient glyphosate.

In one case, however, a citizen's complaint led to a readjustment of EFSA's public consultation requirements and involved several considerations by the Ombudsman concerning participation, when technically complex issues are at stake. The complaint, filed by a Welsh environmental non-governmental organization (NGO), originated from the alleged complexity of the consultation procedure opened by EFSA on glyphosate's renewal, which was not sufficiently user-friendly and would have discouraged public participation, reflecting EFSA's intention to minimize, rather than maximize, public involvement. The issue was settled by EFSA by amending the requirements for public consultations, partly addressing the issues raised by the complainant. In its submissions to the Ombudsman, EFSA highlighted that the legislation on active substances does not expressly require the Agency to carry out a public consultation when assessing the safety of a substance and that, besides the right to be heard, there is 'no obligation to consult with the public when a scientific body is drawing up a scientific or technical document'.[109] EFSA had, however, decided to go beyond its legal obligation and to open the public consultation because of the importance it acknowledged to the principles of openness and transparency.

The Ombudsman generally welcomed the actions undertaken by EFSA to address the complainant's concerns. In so doing, however, it gave a different reading of EFSA's discretion on whether to open a public consultation or not. Although not provided for in Regulation 1107/2009, giving citizens 'the opportunity to make known and publicly exchange their views in all areas of Union action' is rooted in the TEU (Articles 1, 10(3) and 11)[110] and it is additionally implemented by EFSA's funding Regulation (Regulation 178/2002), whereby the authority is expected to develop effective contacts with citizens and stakeholders (Article 42). The Ombudsman linked these general provisions to EFSA's specific activities, and in particular to the provision of scientific advice and scientific and technical support on all EU legislation and policies related to food safety. It is therefore 'clear that the reference to open and public consultation [...] should be understood as also being relevant to EFSA's activities, in particular when it comes to risk analysis'.[111] By grounding the duty to consult on the broader legal framework within which EFSA operates, rather than on the sectoral pesticides legislation, the Ombudsman established that the technical and scientific nature of the Agency's activities are no obstacle to public participation, in particular through public consultations, which should anyway be ensured.

If the technical nature of the subject matter does not affect the principle of openness and participation, it may however affect the ways in which such principles are implemented in practice. The Ombudsman is in fact aware that 'the precise manner by which participatory democracy is made effective depends on the specific nature of the Union action in question', EU institutions enjoying

109 Decision in case 952/2014/OV, para 15.
110 Ibid para 31.
111 Ibid para 32.

a margin of discretion 'especially in areas which are technically complex'. Such discretion is, however, not unfettered, but its exercise should instead be duly justified,[112] involving a 'balancing exercise between, on the one hand, the complexity of the documents on which it wishes to consult the public, and, on the other hand, the real possibility for as many members of the public as possible to effectively participate in the public consultation'.[113] In the case of EFSA, the length and technical complexity of the document justified the adoption of a template for the public consultation.

5 From contestation to accountability?

The previous section has sought to map the systemic reaction triggered by glyphosate in the EU, from an accountability perspective. Such reaction ranged from courts to citizens, to the EP: the presence of different accountability fora resulted in different mechanisms being triggered and – accordingly – in different types of accountability being invoked (political, legal and quasi-legal). While operating independently from each other, synergies have developed among the various accountability fora throughout their operation. When looking at the preamble of the decision establishing the PEST Committee, it is possible to note that several references are made to European Courts' and European Ombudsman's decisions and to the ECI, showing the EP's awareness of the multiple avenues mobilized within the glyphosate dispute. The Court in *Blaise* referred to the report of the PEST Committee and the ECI 'Ban glyphosate' is mentioned in the preamble of Regulation 1381/2019, reforming the General Food Law.

Constellations of accountability fora and mechanisms emerged with regard to several of the issues contested in the context of the glyphosate dispute. In particular, the need to ensure the transparency and independence of the scientific evidence considered in risk assessment has emerged as a cross cutting issue, raised by the EP in both its resolutions and the PEST committee's final report, by the ECI, and brought under the scrutiny of the Court of Justice. Similar considerations apply to the more substantive issue of the goals and values underpinning EU pesticides' governance, which has similarly been raised across the board.

As to the object, while the transparency and independence of the scientific studies were probably the most prominent and frequent triggers of accountability, other issues were considered as well, such as the relationship between the different levels involved in the regulation of pesticides (EU and Member States), the need for a clearer prioritization of the goals of EU pesticides governance, and the scientific substance of the disagreement between EFSA and the IARC. The scope of the challenges raised against the Commission and EFSA also varied:

112 Ibid para 37.
113 Ibid para 40.

while in several cases it was originally limited to the individual case of glyphosate (such as in *Tweedale* and *Hautala*), it often resulted in further-reaching challenges to the overall regulatory scheme (such as in the case of the PEST committee and of the ECI or, less successfully, of *Blaise*).

The accountability-oriented developments analysed above have in most cases resulted in extensive reason giving by EFSA and the Commission (PEST committee, ECI), while more tangible consequences, in the sense of adjustments in legislation or institutional practices, have been more limited, and mainly resulting from judicial proceedings (*Tweedale* and *Hautala*) and, at least rhetorically, through the ECI. While this might appear disappointing, the value of reason giving should not be underestimated in the context of experts' accountability. Reason giving addresses one of the accountability challenges posed by regulatory expertise, i.e. the need to bridge the epistemic asymmetry between experts and citizens. By articulating the reasoning and the considerations that oriented risk assessors' evaluations and led risk managers to adopt the contested decisions, reason giving plays an essential role towards bridging such asymmetry. In so doing, it additionally allows to disentangle the respective roles and responsibilities of risk assessors and risk managers, by illuminating how they interact in practice. In this light, the activities of the PEST committee appear to be particularly valuable, especially since the committee operated within an institution, the EP, traditionally considered ill-suited by design to deal with technically complex issues. When the accountability mechanisms triggered by glyphosate have resulted in actual consequences, such consequences have mainly concerned the procedural aspects of the dispute, rather than its substance, focusing on participation (European Ombudsman), transparency (*Tweedale* and *Hautala*) and methodology (ECI). While substantive aspects (e.g. the implementation of the four cut-off criteria and in particular the soundness of EFSA's assessment as to the carcinogenicity of glyphosate) have been repeatedly raised (ECI and PEST Committee), they have not resulted in tangible consequences.

The difficulty for non-expert actors to effectively engage into substantive regulatory-scientific arguments therefore remains. Against this background, procedural values and guarantees can serve as important vehicles, not only to compensate for the difficulty of holding the Commission and EFSA to account for the technical substance of their determinations, but also to shape risk assessment and risk management processes in ways that are more open to public scrutiny and engagement. Reason giving, in particular, by seeking to bridge the 'language gap' between experts and non-experts, could pave the way for the development of more effective accountability mechanisms and practices also with regard to the substance of risk regulation determinations.

A further reflection concerns the developments observed with regard to the transparency and independence of scientific studies, as they seem particularly interesting in an accountability perspective. By establishing the rules and conditions according to which scientific evidence can enter the regulatory process, such legal arrangements epitomize the legally embedded nature of regulatory science.[114] The widespread contestation triggered by glyphosate has questioned the legal provisions through which regulatory science is validated by the legal system and, in so doing, it has exposed the assumptions shaping how expert authority is embedded in the legal system. In particular, it has unveiled the science-policy choices underpinning EU pesticides' governance, such as placing the burden of proof on the applicant, or adopting a hazard- rather than a risk-based approach. Having a clearer understanding of these assumptions and of the legal frameworks that embody them, is valuable from at least two points of view: on the one hand, it allows clarifying the respective roles and responsibilities of scientific and political actors; on the other hand, by exposing their interdependence, it can lead to the development of a more sophisticated approach to experts' accountability, as the activities of the PEST committee exemplify.

6 Conclusion

This chapter has sought to map the different accountability avenues explored in the context of glyphosate reauthorization at EU level. Having provided an overview of the legislative framework and the factual background, it has grouped the different fora where the Commission's and EFSA's glyphosate-related decisions have been contested, triggering different accountability mechanisms. Political accountability has been activated by the EP, through the establishment of a special committee on pesticides in charge of reviewing pesticide authorization procedures, and by way of a European Citizens' Initiative (ECI). Although the ECI is primarily a participatory instrument, it forced the Commission to articulate its choices in relation to glyphosate and, although to a lesser extent, to address some of the shortcomings that emerged during the approval procedure by taking legislative action. Legal accountability mechanisms have also played a role in the glyphosate controversy, in particular with regard to the right to access to documents containing environmental information. Finally, the European Ombudsman had the chance to consider complaints concerning glyphosate-related maladministration, in particular with regard to European agencies.

Besides the impact this systemic reaction has had on the individual case of glyphosate, the developments discussed above have additionally opened the way to a (re)integration of expert-based decision making into the field of the 'political' (i.e. related to the *polis*). A first lesson that can be learned from the glyphosate dispute is that, while expert-based measures undoubtedly present a challenge to traditional accountability mechanisms (legal and political), they are not entirely beyond their reach. Thanks to its political salience, glyphosate has in fact led to the activation of an unprecedented range of accountability avenues, included some, such as the PEST committee, which present elements of novelty. It could therefore be argued that when a high level of political salience is reached, the

114 Alessandra Arcuri, 'Glyphosate', in Jessie Homan and Daniel Joyce (eds), *International Law's Objects* (OUP 2018) 11–12.

obstacles presented by experts accountability appear less insurmountable. While the activation of such a wide range of accountability mechanisms is unlikely to become the routine in EU pesticides governance, precisely due to the usual lack of such political salience, it does however show that the accountability dynamics triggered by glyphosate are in principle generalizable to other risk regulation cases and areas.

Secondly, the glyphosate case helps us understand and characterize the ways in which the adoption of expert-based measures can be held to account, while respecting the essentially different and closely intertwined roles of political institutions and regulatory expertise. The accountability mechanisms analysed in this chapter have mainly led to extensive reason giving by EFSA and the Commission; on few occasions they have resulted in consequences addressing the procedural aspects of pesticides governance. While reason giving can play an essential role in addressing the knowledge asymmetry characterizing experts governance, the glyphosate dispute leaves open the question of how to channel such potential not only towards the procedural aspects of pesticides governance (and risk regulation more generally), but also towards more substantive issues, such as the consistent application of the precautionary principle and of the four cut-off criteria established by Regulation 1107/2009.

Whether the case of glyphosate will remain isolated or whether it will result in the consolidation of more thorough accountability of expert-based determinations in the EU is hard to predict and will likely depend on the latter's political salience. Glyphosate has, however, had the merit of opening up to scrutiny a policy field which is often regarded as inaccessible to laymen while being, at the same time, deeply controversial, and to explore avenues for reasoned discussion, which could be further developed beyond EU pesticides' governance.

Acknowledgment

My research in this field has been supported by a Marie Skłodowska-Curie grant on 'The Constitutional Place of Expertise' (CONPLEX), funded under the European Union Horizon 2020 research and innovation programme (grant agreement No. 748463). I would like to thank the volume editors, Ioanna Hadjiyianni, Matthew Canfield, and the participants to the 'Regulatory governance colloquia' seminar series, held at the European University Institute in Spring 2018, for their valuable feedback on previous versions of this chapter. All mistakes, of course, remain mine.

10 The Value Free Ideal of Science and non-epistemic values in regulatory toxicology

Osman Çağlar Dede

1 Introduction

To be able to answer complex and technical questions, we defer to the judgment of scientific experts. And, doing so is wise. We need scientists' advice to be able to take high-stake policy actions. More generally, complicated and morally consequential decisions should better be relied on empirical evidence and scientifically supported arguments rather than uninformed opinions, doxastic preferences of a handful of decision-makers, or blind ideological commitments.

As the problems of our advanced post-industrial societies and globalized affairs are becoming more complicated, common governance and regulation mechanisms are ever more dependent on scientific advisory. But, with great power comes great responsibility. Further reliance on scientific advisory to manage the current affairs leads to more pressure on scientific experts. Concerned citizens and students of science expect ever more from scientific experts. We demand scientists to be as unbiased as possible in their assessments, but we also wish them to be responsive to, and sometimes, protective of our values and ideals when they inform policies that will affect us. We expect scientific experts to be specialists. Yet, we also ask them to consider multiple dimensions of a decision problem and to take the interests of all the relevant stakeholders into account in doing so.

All these growing expectations concerning scientific advisers are in tension with our commonsensical understanding of scientists. The conventional image of a scientific expert is someone who is a specialist, policy-neutral and autonomous from societal affairs. If we need to abandon this old image of scientific experts and transcend it, we have to build a new conception of scientific expertise on solid foundations. These foundations will have to make sure that our reliance on expert judgments in the management of the current affairs is not spurious. We have to carefully and systematically ponder the grounds on which scientific experts can fulfil our pressing expectations. This edited volume provides us with helpful insights towards reaching this goal by conceptualizing the accountability of scientific experts from the perspective of socio-legal scholarship and examining the cutting-edge cases where the role of scientific advisors is salient in international law and governance. The present chapter contributes to this volume by offering a perspective from the philosophy of science.

In the following, I will review the debate about the most prominent account of science in society developed by the philosophers of science in the 20th century, which underpins the commonsensical image of scientists depicted above. This account is known as the *Value Free Ideal of Science*. The *Value Free Ideal* (VFI) suggests that non-epistemic (moral, political, environmental, economic and similar) values, commitments and aspirations have no legitimate role to play in scientific judgment-formation. This standard is quite stringent as it substantially limits what we could reasonably expect from scientific experts in the context of regulation and law. Yet, prominent contemporary philosophers of science have also proposed to abandon, or else amend, the VFI. I will introduce some of the key arguments for and against the VFI and discuss the implications of these arguments for conceptualizing the accountability of scientific experts in the context of evidence-based policy and regulation. To make the discussion more accessible to the legal scholars, I will illustrate these arguments by referring to regulatory toxicology and regulation of agricultural pesticides.

My aim is to demonstrate that the recent philosophical insights that contest the VFI do not debunk but rather revive and reconstruct the value of scientific expertise. Specifically, I argue that philosophers of science such as Heather Douglas, Philip Kitcher and Helen Longino appreciate and share the main worries of the proponents of the VFI, such as the importance of objectivity and neutrality, the need for rational argumentation in policy-making and the avoidance of technocracy. Nevertheless, they disagree with the proponents of the VFI about the premise that a genuine reliance on scientific expertise is sustainable within the boundaries the VFI defines. In the face of this problem, those philosophers who propose to transcend the VFI work towards developing an understanding of science as a reliable epistemic source for making complex and challenging (policy) decisions about the pressing and history-old problems. This emerging conception of science is not only responsive to urgent and significant non-epistemic values but also epistemically robust. Accordingly, I suggest, what contemporary philosophers of science have to say about the relationship between science and values is vital to develop any projects that attempt to critically assess the accountability of scientific experts in the contemporary contexts of law, governance and decision-making. My task in this chapter is to offer the reader a survey of some of the key recent philosophical insights for those socio-legal scholars who seek to strike the right balance between epistemic and non-epistemic dimensions of scientific expertise in developing a conception of the 'accountability of experts' in governance and law.

The rest of the chapter is structured as follows. In Section 2, I introduce an example concerning toxicological assessments of agricultural pesticides that I will use throughout the chapter. Based on this example, I review a number of contexts where scientific experts make non-epistemic value judgments in their assessments. In these contexts, the permeation of value judgments into their analysis is seen uncontroversial by the philosophers of science, regardless of their position on the debate about the VFI. In Section 3, I describe the contexts where the inclusion of non-epistemic value judgments in science is impermissible according to the proponents of the VFI and discuss the main arguments for and against the VFI. In Section 4, I illustrate some of the key concepts in the contemporary philosophy of science that challenge the VFI and transcend it by allowing non-epistemic values a more expanded role to play in scientific judgment than the VFI permits. In Section 5, I conclude by elaborating on how the debate on the VFI and the recent insights from philosophy of science contribute to the socio-legal scholars' attempts to reconceptualize the accountability of scientific experts in law and governance.

2 Revisiting the Value Free Ideal of Science when examining the role of regulatory toxicologists in protecting environmental safety

2.1 *The safety of pesticides and toxicological expertise*

Consider environmental safety regulations in agriculture. Various kinds of pesticides are used for maximizing the productive capacities of the agricultural businesses, from which we all benefit as consumers. The overuse of toxic chemicals has adverse consequences for the environment and public health. The safety of the agricultural pesticides is, therefore, systematically regulated by institutions such as the US Environmental Protection Agency (EPA) and EFSA (European Food and Safety Authority). The processes of decision making in the regulatory institutions are far from being simple as it is not always a clear-cut judgment to decide whether a type of pesticide should be regulated more or less stringently. Making consequential regulatory decisions requires an estimation of relative costs and benefits of a particular regulatory action over a number of desiderata such as ecological safety, economic efficiency and the public interest.

It is, therefore, useful to conceive regulatory decision making about a type of pesticide as a multidimensional balancing process that goes beyond the binary judgment of banning or allowing the industrial use of a toxic substance. For instance, questions of the following type need to be answered, and the pertinent trade-offs must be drawn by the regulatory decision makers. What is the threshold (expressed in terms of dosages) on which a pesticide is safe to use in agricultural production? To which produces should the pesticide in question be applied to? Does the adversity of the pesticide depend on its proper application? If so, how should the substance be applied by its users? What is the severity of the costs on health and the environment? What are the consequences of imposing more or less stringent regulatory measures on the agricultural sector and the producers of the pesticides?

Answering such questions is likely to demand some technical knowledge and skills. Accordingly, regulators must rely on toxicological risk assessment to answer them as accurately as possible. Toxicological experts who perform required testing and who run the pertinent risk models, therefore, play some key roles in the making of regulatory decisions for environmental safety. Overall, it is desirable that the environmental safety regulations are evidence-based and informed by science.

The need to examine the accountability of scientific experts in regulatory decision-making processes arises in controversial cases. Regulatory mechanisms sometimes fail to ensure the safety of people's health and the environment and even lead to disastrous consequences. For instance, the use of clothianidin[1] in agricultural production has led to the death of millions of honey bees in Germany.[2] Such cases are controversial not only because of the high environmental costs involved but also due to the severe uncertainties about what counts as the right course of regulatory action. In the case of the clothianidin, the details and the stringency of regulations have changed across time, and only after five years, its outdoor uses have been suspended in the EU. The gaps and incompleteness of the scientific advice over the malignancy of neonicotinoids for the environment (the health of bees in particular) seem to play some role in the progression of the debate over the suspension of the neonicotinoids such as clothianidin.[3]

In the face of such environmental failures caused by mis-regulation or under-regulation, it is appealing to question the role and the responsibilities of toxicological experts, and the regulatory scientists in general. More specifically, one feels compelled to ask whether regulatory toxicologists could have done better in preventing the environmental harms caused by the industrial use of the clothianidin. Perhaps, in the face of evidential gaps and uncertainties, the bits of advice for regulation could have been produced and communicated in a more precautionary manner, prioritizing the environmental safety over other concerns. For instance, regulatory toxicologists could have determined the parameters of their risk assessment models in a way that is more protective of environmental health.

But, to what extent is it justifiable to expect toxicological experts to be protective of *values such as environmental safety* in conducting their assessments? Should scientific advisors *qua* scientists endorse non-epistemic values or commitments and then let those values influence their analyses and conclusions? I suggest that philosophers of science have a lot of useful insights about these kinds of questions, and the VFI is a good place to start engaging with the philosophical perspectives on issues pertaining to the accountability of experts in governance and regulation.

The VFI is a deeply rooted analytical-philosophical view of how science relates to society. It defines clear boundaries under which non-epistemic values such as environmental health can legitimately influence scientific judgment.

1 Clothianidin is a member of the class of insecticides known as neonicotinoids. Neonicotinoids are chemically similar to nicotine but more effective as a pesticide. It is applied on plants and attacks the nervous system of the targeted insects. It is first developed by Bayer BV.

2 Alison Benjamin, 'Pesticides: Germany Bans Chemicals Linked to Honeybee Devastation' *Guardian* (23 May 2008).

3 Charlotte McDonald-Gibson, '"Victory for Bees" as European Union Bans Neonicotinoid Pesticides Blamed for Destroying Bee Population' *Independent* (London, April 2013).

Specifically, according to the VFI, value judgments such as a commitment to maximizing environmental safety, may play *some* permissible roles in conducting scientific research. However, the VFI states, non-epistemic values should *not* influence scientists' inferences from the evidence, hence the results of their analysis.[4] In the context of science-based regulation, a proponent of the VFI would suggest that expecting scientific experts to let certain value considerations to influence their results undermines the *raison d'être* of expert advice for making regulatory decisions. So, this view goes, the main reason for seeking scientific advice is to be informed about the facts of the world that are relevant for making morally consequential decisions; scientific advisors qua scientists are *not* regulators; hence scientists' judgments should not reflect any value judgments.

Accordingly, the VFI provides us with a clear benchmark that defines principles under which scientific experts can legitimately employ values such as environmental safety in their analysis. This ideal can, therefore, help us examine what we could justifiably expect from toxicologists to do in order to prevent regulatory failures, which may be partly made based on their judgments. I will now review a bit more closely what boundaries the VFI draws for the inclusion of values in science. We will then ask ourselves how those boundaries are justifiable and engage with the philosophical debates over whether and how the VFI should be transcended.

2.2 *Values in regulatory toxicology according to the Value Free Ideal*

In the face of regulatory failures in science-based regulation of agricultural production (manifested in the cases such as the regulation of clothianidin), we are interested in knowing whether non-epistemic values and commitments, such as maximizing the interest of public health or the environment, should have a more expanded role to play in the formation of scientific judgments made for regulatory action. I have suggested so far that the philosophical *Value Free Ideal of Science* provides us with a sound starting point to determine plausible ways in which values can play more or less expanded roles in science. My aim now is to offer a clear understanding of the principles of the VFI so as to proceed with a structured discussion about how regulatory toxicologists should employ value judgments in their analysis.

2.2.1 *Scientific integrity and fraud*

It is agreed by all the philosophers of science, irrespective of their position in the VFI debate, that scientists should avoid fraud. Scientific integrity is the most

4 Ernan McMullin, 'Values in Science' [1982] PSA: Proceedings of the Biennial Meeting of the Philosophy of Science Association 3.

commonly accepted (though also sometimes violated) moral principle in scientific practice. For instance, it is strictly forbidden to make up data for one's convenience. Similarly, scientists are not expected to cherry-pick a piece of evidence from a wide range of available evidential sources in a way that would favour the results they wish to obtain through their analysis. When regulatory toxicologists engage in these kinds of practices, they commit to *scientific fraud.*

Scientific experts who engage in fraudulent scientific practices causally contribute to the regulatory failures when the policy outcomes partly result from their untruthful judgments. The corruption of policy-informing experts is a genuine issue that needs to be discussed thoroughly. Indeed, many commonly known failures of expert-based regulatory advisory in environmental safety result from the violation of basic scientific integrity.[5] As extensively documented by the socio-legal scholars, the problem of fraud is most commonly observed among the so-called 'industry scientists' who are pressured to produce research results that serve the interests of large, profit-driven pharmaceutical and biomedical companies. The sources and the dynamics of indecent scientific practices need to be carefully studied by the socio-legal scholars and philosophers of science.[6]

2.2.2 *Non-epistemic values in the selection of research questions and tools*

The VFI does not suggest that non-epistemic values have no legitimate function in science. There are two contexts where value judgments are needed, and it is legitimate for scientists to employ value judgments in their reasoning, according to the VFI. Firstly, the context in which scientists choose a research question to investigate and decide how to investigate that question. It is permissible that scientists attend to certain subjective value judgments, commitments or interests when they make decisions in such initial phases of their inquiry.

For instance, a toxicologist may want to study the effects of pesticides on the population of bees because she might deem it valuable to conserve the bee population's health. Her employment of values in this way does not conflict with the VFI, as values (ecological safety of bees) do not determine the results of her inquiry. Similarly, she can attend to certain (communal or personal) value considerations in determining the methods through which she will conduct her investigation. She may, for example, want to work only with molecular-genetic tools instead of exposed animal bio-assays because she may not prefer to harm or kill animals to conduct her scientific research. Again, the VFI does allow a role for non-epistemic values in this particular sense.

5 Some prominent examples include, Hugh Lacey, *Values and Objectivity in Science: The Current Controversy about Transgenic Crops* (Lexington Books 2005); Peter Gøtzsche, *Deadly Medicines and Organised Crime: How Big Pharma Has Corrupted Healthcare* (CRC Press 2017).

6 See for a recent discussion, Liam Kofi Bright, 'On Fraud' [2017] 174 Philosophical Studies 1.

2.2.3 *No values in scientific inference*

The VFI does limit the permeation of values into science when value judgments influence results obtained by an investigation or when values change scientists' judgments. Specifically, values should not influence certain methodological decisions in science. These are decisions such as how evidence is gathered, how hypotheses are justified and accepted, and how the results are interpreted. These methodological contexts are referred to by the proponents of the VFI as the core stages of the scientific reasoning; also known as the context of justification. The context of justification is commonly contrasted with the 'context of discovery' where the research questions and methods are chosen, in which values play a permissible role. According to the VFI, the context of justification should, in principle, be free from non-epistemic value considerations.

So, for instance, regulatory toxicologists could endorse the value of protecting environmental safety and choose to examine those hypotheses that would be protective of the environment (if their judgments will then be used for justifying regulatory processes). The regulatory toxicologists' endorsement of a non-epistemic value in this particular sense complies with the standard of the VFI. However, a commitment to protect environmental safety should not influence how the same toxicologists justify the hypotheses they are assessing. In other words, values should not determine which judgments are accepted.

Moreover, scientific experts' role *qua scientist* must be distinguished from scientific experts *qua policy advisors*.[7] Qua policy advisors, scientists might make use of values in determining how they communicate their results.[8] For instance, they could permissibly emphasize certain aspects of their results to motivate a particular regulatory response. However, qua scientists, policy advisors should not allow non-epistemic value judgments to influence how they obtain their results. In short, values should be ignored in scientific interference, according to the VFI.

2.2.4 *Except epistemic values*

The so-called epistemic values are exceptional to the principle discussed above. The proponents of the VFI find it benign when various epistemic values of a hypothesis, such as its simplicity, explanatory or predictive power, accuracy, robustness and fruitfulness are used by scientists to assess that hypothesis. Thomas Kuhn, in particular, thought that scientific reasoning or hypothesis-confirmation

7 Katie Steele, 'The Scientist qua Policy Advisor Makes Value Judgments' [2012] 79 Philosophy of Science 893; Inmaculada De Melo-Martín and Kristen Intemann, 'The Risk of Using Inductive Risk to Challenge the Value-Free Ideal' [2016] 83 Philosophy of Science 500.

8 Stephen John, 'Inductive Risk and the Contexts of Communication' [2015] 192 Synthese 79.

should better be conceptualized as a process that appeals to some shared standards of epistemic values (which may differ across different communities of scientists).[9] Since Kuhn, it is commonly thought that the involvement of *epistemic* values in scientific inference does not harm the justification of scientific results or the objectivity of scientific judgment in general. The controversy has been over the status of the so-called 'non-epistemic values' in scientific justification. Kuhn's ideas about epistemic values in relation to scientific disagreement and objectivity were thought to be protective of the VFI.[10]

The VFI thereby provides us with a clear benchmark regarding how far we should expect scientific experts to be protective of certain non-epistemic values in producing their judgments for regulatory procedures. The principles of the VFI discussed so far can be summarized as follows. Non-epistemic values such as environmental safety are permissible in scientific experts' reasoning only in certain contexts that are considered to be separate from the core stages of science, such as collecting evidence and making inferences from them. Only the so-called epistemic values can influence scientists' judgments over the confirmation of a hypothesis.

These principles of the VFI are supposed to be protective of scientific objectivity, hence scientific authority for informing the processes of governance and regulation. Given this conceptual background, we now need to ask ourselves: should the socio-legal scholars adopt or abandon the VFI? In the context of specific cases such as the assessment of clothianidin, what are the limits of scientific activism of the sort that is protective of values such as environmental safety and public health? I will now review arguments for and against the VFI in order to motivate relevant philosophical insights regarding whether and how the VFI could be transcended.

3 Debating the Value Free Ideal of Science

As I have discussed in Section 2, the VFI does not leave room for any policy desiderata to play a detrimental role during the formation of expert advice for regulatory processes. This implies that if the socio-legal scholars endorse the VFI as a benchmark model of how scientific experts make judgments about policy-relevant issues, they should not expect from scientific experts to adjust their findings or judgments in order to serve for the protection of certain values. For instance, toxicologists assessing clothianidin should not be expected to produce results that are protective of the financial interests of a patent-holder company or the economic efficiency of the agricultural industry. Similarly, if the VFI is endorsed, the dangers of clothianidin-use for ecological health

9 Thomas S. Kuhn, 'Objectivity, Value Judgment, and Theory Choice', *The Essential Tension: Selected Studies in Scientific Tradition and Change* (University of Chicago Press 1977) 320–339.

10 Heather E. Douglas, *Science, Policy, and the Value-Free Ideal* (University of Pittsburgh Press 2009) Chapter 3, 44–65.

should not influence the expert's assessment of clothianidin's toxicity. However, the VFI is not free from criticisms and challenges. At least starting from the 1980s, philosophers of science have questioned the descriptive adequacy and the normative appeal of the VFI. I will now review some of the influential arguments that are used for contesting or defending the VFI.

3.1 *Contesting the Value Free Ideal*

An important type of challenge against the VFI is directed at the attainability of it as an ideal.[11] Specifically, these criticisms are about the nature of scientific reasoning and methods and the core concepts of the scientific method, such as evidence, theories and explanation. Helen Longino, for instance, argues that inferences from the evidence to hypothesis often rely on background assumptions which may encode ontological assumptions about the world, value presuppositions about what deserves to be examined, or methodological assumptions about what types of evidence are relevant to given hypotheses.[12] The problem, according to Longino, is that scientific communities' shared background assumptions may often be implicit, insufficiently examined, or not be subjected to critical scrutiny of alternative perspectives. This work has later motivated more recent studies in philosophy of science, which conceive of scientists as members of social groups and knowledge-production as a social activity characterized by a plurality of epistemic communities with varying values, interests and methods to pursue research. Given such an understanding of scientific judgment that is undetermined by evidence and laden with disagreements about background presuppositions, the VFI seems to be an unattainable ideal, if not an illusion.[13] In Section 4, I will also discuss how philosophers such as Longino make constructive suggestions about scientific objectivity while holding a descriptive view of science as a deeply pluralistic social practice.

However, the descriptive problems of the VFI are not of direct relevance to the problems examined in this edited volume. We are not interested in grand questions regarding the nature of science, scientific knowledge and objectivity. We are interested in the rules and principles that guide scientific experts when they need to attend to value judgments in their analysis for regulatory purposes. The critiques of the VFI that focus on the normative appeal of its principles are of more direct relevance to discuss the accountability of regulatory expertise. Some philosophers of science, such as Heather Douglas – whom we can see as a contemporary successor of Richard Rudner's approach to scientific reasoning – have argued against the VFI as an ideal,

11 Ibid.

12 Helen E. Longino, *Science as Social Knowledge: Values and Objectivity in Scientific Inquiry* (Princeton University Press 1990).

13 Harold Kincaid, John Dupré and Alison Wylie, *Value-Free Science?: Ideals and Illusions* (OUP 2009).

irrespective of its feasibility.[14] Heather Douglas' work has been particularly influential in recent years in pushing the argument against the VFI forward.[15]

Douglas argues against the normative appeal of the VFI on two grounds, which, when taken together, leads her to reject the VFI normatively. Firstly, Douglas emphasizes that scientific judgment often involves the risk of being wrong. That is to say, when a scientist makes an inference about a hypothesis, the available evidence does not fully confirm the hypothesis being true or false. And so, she argues, scientific confirmation actually takes place in degrees and commits to an error akin to the errors in basic statistical inferences: a false positive judgment or a false negative one (i.e. accepting p, when p is actually false; or rejecting p when p is actually true). This idea is known as the 'inductive risk' argument.[16] This is the first building block of Douglas's framework.

Douglas's second argument relies on the recognition of the pragmatic function of science in the last century. Scientific experts are increasingly playing a more authoritative role in resolving regulatory conflicts, making policies and legitimizing interventions to societies and people's lives.[17] Douglas suggests that it is better to conceive of scientific judgment-formation as a process that is not autonomous from the management of the current affairs and hence should not be governed by its own rules only.

The combination of these two ideas (the inductive risk argument and the [partial] causal dependence of policy outcomes to scientific expert judgments) compels Douglas to reject the normative appeal of the VFI as an ideal. Specifically, she claims that it is plausible for scientists to take into account the risks of being wrong in their judgments in the face of the inductive risk problem. Moreover, she argues, if the judgment made by a scientific expert influences policy outcomes (e.g. as it happens in the policy-relevant areas such as regulatory toxicology), the risks of being wrong bear on non-epistemic consequences of the policy action. For instance, as the clothianidin case suggests, a regulatory toxicologist's erroneous judgment may have consequences for the health of the bee population and the economic productivity of the pesticide-producing sector. Accordingly, Douglas suggests, it should be normatively desirable that scientists make an evaluation of such non-epistemic consequences in order to decide how much evidence is sufficient to confirm a hypothesis given that there are inductive risks in scientific judgment-formation.

14 Richard Rudner, 'The Scientist Qua Scientist Makes Value Judgments' [1953] 20 Philosophy of Science 893; Heather Douglas, 'Inductive Risk and Values in Science' [2000] 67 Philosophy of Science 559; Douglas (n 10).

15 Douglas (n 10).

16 Ibid; Matthew J. Brown, 'Values in Science Beyond Underdetermination and Inductive Risk' [2013] 80 Philosophy of Science 829; see Kevin C. Elliott and Ted Richards, *Exploring Inductive Risk: Case Studies of Values in Science* (OUP 2017) for a collection of recent philosophical debates on the inductive risk argument.

17 Douglas (n 10).

Douglas's conclusion goes against the normative appeal of the VFI. It does so because it leaves room for non-epistemic values to play a *permissible* role in the core stages of *scientific inference*. If we agree with Douglas that non-epistemic values can plausibly influence the results of scientists' judgments, we would then expect regulatory toxicologists to let values such as environmental protectionism to play a more prominent role during the formation of regulatory judgments. This idea has evaluative consequences for a case like the regulation of the clothianidin.

Suppose that a regulatory toxicologist collects data from the pathological examination of bee tissues, which are exposed to varying dosages of clothianidin in laboratory conditions. Based on the collected experimental observations, she chooses a model that describes how tissues respond to the different doses of clothianidin (typically in the form of a dose-response curve). Then, based on the predictions of the model, she makes a judgment about the hazardousness of clothianidin over a given bee tissue-type under varying dosages. This judgment is a probabilistic one such as 'clothianidin is likely/highly likely/unlikely to be malignant for the exposed tissue' (but typically with precise numbers).[18]

Now, as discussed above, Douglas's idea is that because the available evidence is not *fully* confirmatory of the hypothesis that the clothianidin is harmful, the toxicologist's judgment will be an inductively risky one, consisting of one of the following errors. *Error I* is reporting clothianidin as benign when it is actually malignant. *Error II* is reporting clothianidin as malignant when it is actually benign. But, both errors have non-epistemic consequences because they can be used for legitimizing different regulatory agendas. Committing *Error I* could motivate regulatory actions that do *not* strongly discourage the use of the clothianidin even though it should really be discouraged. This contributes to the development of adverse ecological or public health outcomes such as the collapse of the bee population. On the other hand, committing *Error II* provides justification for unnecessary over-regulation of clothianidin, leading to unwanted economic outcomes.

Douglas suggests that it should be legitimate when toxicologists consider the severity of these errors and pertinent outcomes in non-epistemic terms to decide how much evidence is sufficient to make one of the risky inferences. If failing to detect the malignancy of clothianidin has too severe environmental costs, it should be permissible for the toxicologist to confirm its malignancy *based on relatively weak evidential support*. In other words, non-epistemic values such as ecological health should be allowed in scientific reasoning to help scientists to determine *how much evidence is sufficient to confirm a given hypothesis*. If Douglas is right, then the ecological concerns should play a more extensive role in regulatory toxicologists' evaluation of clothianidin and similar toxic substances.

Douglas's normative argument against the VFI provides us with some reasons to depart from the VFI as a benchmark for evaluating experts' accountability in evidence-based law and governance. Perhaps, non-epistemic values or interests of the public or the environment should, after all, influence scientific experts'

18 Douglas (n 14).

judgments more wittingly. But, notice that Douglas's argument only criticizes the VFI but does not offer an alternative benchmark that regulates values in science. If we do not know how to replace the ideal, isn't abandoning it too costly?

3.2 *Why is the VFI normatively appealing?*

Without a new ideal that is as useful and convincing as the VFI, the permeation of values to scientific inference may be undesirable because the scientific authority could be conceived as unduly politicized when there is no normative benchmark that regulates the permeation of values into scientific reasoning. Some philosophers of science have argued that there are good reasons for not abandoning the VFI, at least until a better benchmark is proposed.[19] The defences of the VFI are based on two main concerns.

The first and the most pressing worry against the idea of abandoning the VFI is the potential loss of scientific objectivity in the context of scientific advisory. Betz, for instance, argues that the best use of scientific knowledge is to hold it detached from social and political processes, as that is the best way to keep the reliability of science intact. Disbelief in the objectivity of the scientific advisory would undermine the very reason to defer to the experts in making complex regulatory decisions.

The inclusion of non-epistemic values into scientific reasoning may lead to dogmatism; that is, unwillingness to update or replace one's predispositions, values and judgments.[20] Non-dogmatism is a characteristic commonly ascribed to scientists. Scientific experts are supposed to report what available evidence indicates regardless of whether her evidence-based inferences are in clash with her personal wishes, viewpoint or causes. A significant departure from the VFI depiction of science seems to spoil this basic feature of scientific reasoning.

Consider a regulatory toxicologist who endorses environmentalist values. She might be worried that the industrial use of clothianidin may harm biodiversity. She accordingly would wish that her assessment of clothianidin would conclude that clothianidin is extremely harmful to wild-life even when exposed in very small dosages. One could reasonably suspect that an expert endowed with such an activist mindset is likely to be more subjective in her judgments, and her conclusions are unreliable for informing regulatory processes. More generally, when a scientist makes a judgment that she prefers to be true even though there is no clear evidence supporting that judgment, she would commit to wishful

19 Gregor Betz, 'In Defence of the Value Free Ideal' [2013] 3 European Journal for Philosophy of Science 207; Liam Kofi Bright, 'Du Bois' Democratic Defence of the Value Free Ideal' [2018] 195 Synthese 2227; Gregor Betz, 'Why the Argument from Inductive Risk Doesn't Justify Incorporating Non-Epistemic Values in Scientific Reasoning' (2018) Current Controversies in Values and Science 94–110.

20 See for a review, Elizabeth Anderson, 'Uses of Value Judgments in Science: A General Argument, with Lessons from a Case Study of Feminist Research on Divorce' [2004] 19 Hypatia 1.

thinking. Wishful thinking has no legitimate role to play in genuine scientific reasoning. When scientific experts engage in wishful thinking, they will lose their reliability for informing regulatory processes.

Accordingly, the VFI could be considered as protective of the public trust in scientific authority in regulatory processes. Philosophers who propose to transcend the VFI should then have an account of how scientific inference can remain non-dogmatic and trustworthy while being influenced by non-epistemic value judgments. As I will review in Section 4, philosophers such as Heather Douglas or Elizabeth Anderson have addressed this worry, but the controversy remains up-to-date.[21]

The second argument for the normative appeal of the VFI emphasizes the inconvenience of scientists as agents of ethical and political decision-making.[22] Letting scientific results be influenced by certain non-epistemic value considerations may lead to the expansion of experts' arbitrary political power in regulatory processes. Experts can influence the policy processes by adjusting the results in accordance with their preferred policy desiderata. However, scientific experts are not considered to be legitimate political actors, at least in a democratic context. In a democratic governance structure, regulatory decisions are not supposed to be made by experts but by democratically legitimized political subjects. The acceptance of values into the production of scientific judgments is in tension with the liberal/democratic values.

This argument is underpinned by an understanding of policy-making in which the roles of democratically legitimized decisionmakers and the scientific advisors are clearly divided. According to this understanding, scientific experts are tasked with a politically neutral, advisory role which is to report the available evidence as accurately as possible. The democratically and legally legitimate decisionmakers then bear the responsibility of making any politically and morally binding value judgment. This ideal resembles the traditional model of risk management in regulatory sciences, which was critically discussed by the science studies scholars such as Sheila Jasanoff[23] as well as legal scholars who contributed to this volume.[24] The model distinguishes scientists as *risk-assessors* and decisionmakers as *risk-managers*. While the decisionmakers are responsible for managing risks and taking risky decisions, the scientific experts are tasked with assessing the risks without taking a stance on how those risks should be managed or letting that stance influence her assessment.

21 Betz, 'Why the Argument from Inductive Risk Doesn't Justify Incorporating Non-Epistemic Values in Scientific Reasoning' (n 19).
22 Betz, 'In Defence of the Value Free Ideal' (n 19).
23 See for instance Sheila Jasanoff, *The Fifth Branch: Science Advisers as Policymakers* (Harvard University Press 1990).
24 See for instance Alessandra Arcuri and Marta Simoncini, 'Scientists and Legal Accountability: Lessons from the L'Aquila Case' [2015] SSRN Electronic Journal; Alessandra Arcuri, 'Three Dimensions of Accountability for Global Technocracy' (Chapter 3 in this volume); Machiko Kanetake 'Transnational Radiological Standards in Domestic Contexts' (Chapter 8 in this volume).

For instance, toxicologists conduct research on the nature of clothianidin's toxicity and assess the scale of environmental risks resulting from the use of clothianidin. Then, they communicate their estimations of risks to the decision-making agents. They make clear when the evidence is inconclusive or in how far certain policy actions are supported by the available evidence. Only then, the decisionmakers (e.g. board of directors of private companies or regulators) make a decision about how to regulate clothianidin use (e.g. selling it, regulating it, banning it) by taking into account the risks estimated by the experts and valuation of potential adverse or desirable consequences of their decisions.[25] If this model of evidence-based regulation would be transcended, the replacing accounts of expertise in governance should also be able to respond to the democratic defence of the VFI, either by effectively arguing against it or by arguing that the new alternatives to the VFI do not harm democratic legitimacy of regulatory decision-making processes.

In this section, I have reviewed some of the key arguments for and against the VFI. A complete and widely accepted philosophical alternative to the VFI is not yet offered,[26] and how the VFI should be replaced is still discussed by philosophers of science. In the rest of this chapter, I will review a number of prominent approaches in the contemporary philosophy of science which transcend the VFI. The conceptual insights from these approaches can be insightful for the socio-legal scholars' search for the right balance between epistemic and non-epistemic dimensions of scientific expertise in developing a conception of the accountability of experts in governance and law.

4 Going beyond the Value Free Ideal while keeping scientific objectivity and experts' reliability intact

The aim of this chapter has so far been to offer a perspective from the philosophy of science on the debates about the accountability of scientific experts in the context of regulation. I have questioned how far scientific experts can and should make non-epistemic value judgments in their assessments for regulatory purposes. In response to this question, I have introduced the philosophical notion of the VFI, which permits values in science in some restricted ways. I have then discussed why we may want to move beyond or else protect the VFI. Now, in this section, I will introduce some of the key ideas in the recent philosophy of science that transcend the VFI but nevertheless respect the normative reasons for endorsing the VFI such as objectivity, the authority of the scientific judgments, and democratic governance.

4.1 *Does abandoning the VFI undermine science?*

In contrast to the VFI depiction of value-free scientific experts who are distant from societal issues and neutral towards policy outcomes, the philosophers

25 Richard C. Jeffrey, 'Valuation and Acceptance of Scientific Hypotheses' [1956] 23 Philosophy of Science 237.

26 For a very recent attempt to replace the VFI, see Matthew J. Brown, *Science and Moral Imagination: A New Ideal for Values in Science* (University of Pittsburgh Press 2020).

who are unconvinced by the VFI (such as Douglas, Longino, Anderson, Brown, Kitcher) portray a regulatory expert who is concerned with the policy outcomes and who is protective of relevant value judgments and commitments in producing her analysis. For some commentators, replacing the VFI with such a 'non-neutral' portrayal of scientific advisory might come across as a dangerous turn in the philosophy of science.

One could, for instance, forcefully argue that the VFI is too important to be dismissed and too risky to abandon because of its normative appeals. The VFI, the skeptic might argue, is an ideal that appreciates the authority of science and effectively regulates the science-society relationship in a regulatory context. Acknowledging and demanding a more expanded role to the non-epistemic considerations in scientific experts' reasoning opens the door to a lot of practical problems and may harm rational deference to experts in regulatory decision making. Similarly, one might be worried that the quest for including general public's expectations and values into expert-based regulatory decision-making may lead to a 'politicization of expertise',[27] 'tranny of ignorance or vulgar democracy',[28] or democratically unjustifiable 'epistocracy' in governance structures.[29] Moreover, leaving the VFI may trigger the erosion of the authority of science,[30] motivating unsubstantiated versions of post-truth politics and unconvincing adoptions of Paul Feyerabend's 'anything-goes' argument.[31] After all, given its broad normative appeal (reviewed in Section 3), the VFI could still be the best *normative* benchmark for evaluating experts' role and responsibilities in evidence-based decision-making (however untenable it might be as a descriptive account of science). If we allow the permeation of non-epistemic considerations into scientific reasoning and open the Pandora's box, so to say, how can we make sure that scientific experts are objective when they inform policy decisions? Does an expert who is driven to preserve values such as health-provision, environmentalism or inequality-aversion almost unavoidably lose her reliability as a neutral policy assessor? Is it not *too dangerous* to abandon the VFI as a normative benchmark for scientific reasoning? So, even if it might be an untenable ideal, why not keep the VFI as a guiding principle?

These important concerns need to be properly addressed if we are to fully replace the VFI. I do not claim that these concerns are already satisfactorily addressed by the philosophers of science. However, all I want to clarify is that the recent philosophical critics of the VFI, who seek to provide us with the foundations to go beyond it, endorse similar concerns but nevertheless believe that the best way to address these concerns, at least in the context of regulatory

27 Douglas (n 10) 113, 134.

28 Philip Kitcher, *Science in a Democratic Society* (Prometheus Books 2011) 113, 126, 140, 177.

29 Julian Reiss, 'Expertise, Agreement, and the Nature of Social Scientific Facts or: Against Epistocracy' [2019] 33 Social Epistemology 183.

30 Helen E. Longino, *The Fate of Knowledge* (Princeton University Press 2018) Chapter 1.

31 Denise Russell, 'Anything Goes' [1983] 13 Social Studies of Science 437.

sciences such as regulatory toxicology, is to transcend the VFI. In their arguments against the VFI, philosophers of science such as Philip Kitcher, Helen Longino and Heather Douglas, have explicitly addressed these concerns.

In the remainder of this section, I will introduce some of the key concepts in the literature on the values in science that move beyond the boundaries of the VFI, which nevertheless are protective of the meta-values that the VFI subscribes to such as scientific objectivity, the importance of scientific authority, democratic quality of science-based decision-making, and the avoidance of imposing values to the citizenry.

4.2 *Transcending the Value Free Ideal of Science*

I will review four recent concepts in the contemporary philosophy of science that go beyond the VFI while keeping the authority of science for democratic governance intact. These are Douglas's objectivity as impartiality or detachment,[32] Steel's notion of epistemic priority,[33] right values for science,[34] and Kitcher's account for the democratization of scientific expertise.[35]

4.2.1 *Objectivity as impartiality as opposed to value freedom*

Heather Douglas argues that the exclusion of value judgments from scientific inference is *not* the only plausible rule to protect the objectivity of scientific experts' reasoning.[36] She claims that values may, in principle, legitimately influence regulatory scientists' decisions about key methodological choices, which would then influence their results. However, she argues, permitting values in scientific inference does not necessarily imply that scientific objectivity qua impartiality is harmed. According to Douglas and Elizabeth Anderson,[37] the key to achieve objectivity in scientific reasoning while permitting non-epistemic values is that value judgments do not override scientists' evidence-based inferences, but rather *supplement them*. So, Douglas suggests, rather than banning the non-epistemic values in science as the VFI advises, we need to an account that distinguishes permissible and impermissible permeations of values into scientific reasoning. She, in turn, offers one such account. Douglas introduces a distinction between the direct and the indirect use of values in scientific inference.

32 Heather Douglas, 'The Irreducible Complexity of Objectivity' [2004] 138 Synthese 453; Douglas (n 10) 115–132.

33 Daniel Steel, 'Qualified Epistemic Priority' (2018) Current Controversies in Values and Science 49–63.

34 Daniel J. Hicks, 'A New Direction for Science and Values' [2014] 191 Synthese 3271; Janet A. Kourany, *Philosophy of Science after Feminism* (OUP 2010) 49–77.

35 Kitcher (n 28) 86–113.

36 Douglas, 'The Irreducible Complexity of Objectivity' (n 32); Douglas (n 10) 115–132.

37 Douglas, 'The Irreducible Complexity of Objectivity' (n 32) 458–461; Anderson (n 20).

When values influence scientific judgment indirectly, they supplement evidential reasoning by helping scientists decide how much evidence is sufficient to confirm a given hypothesis, under inductive risks. The scientific reasoning is in the following form: if the consequences of me failing to accept p when, in fact, p is true would be very bad (ethically, socially), then I will accept that p on the basis of weaker evidence. When the role of values is direct, values go beyond this supplementary function (helping assess the sufficiency of evidence), and instead value considerations trump over evidential ones or replace them. It would then be in this form: if the consequences of me failing to accept p would be very bad (ethically, socially), I then will accept p (irrespective of the sufficiency of the evidence).

Now, Douglas argues that there is an important difference between the two uses of value judgments: when employing values indirectly, a scientist is prepared to be non-dogmatic. That is to say, she would reject p when evidential support against p would increase (as the severity of non-epistemic consequences of errors would diminish when there is more certain evidence). The same is not the case for the direct employment of value judgments in scientific inference: in that case, the scientists' reasoning disregards evidence. Therefore, only the indirect role of non-epistemic values should be permissible in scientific reasoning, according to Douglas.

The reader might be wondering: How would this rather conceptual-theoretical distinction work in practice such that it can inform our analysis of the real cases of expert accountability? Although the individual scientist's right reasoning attitudes, social norms of transparency and peer-review are supposed to filter out the impermissible, direct uses of values in scientific reasoning, the idea of detached objectivity should be conceived as a regulative ideal that may not be fully attainable in practice, just as the VFI.

The concept of detached objectivity transcends the VFI in that it allows values to play some (indirect) role at the core of scientific reasoning. It is, however, protective of the value of objectivity as impartiality or avoidance of dogmatism, which is at the central to the VFI.

4.2.2 *Epistemic priority*

As noted in Section 2, the employment of epistemic values such as simplicity, internal consistency in making inferences in science does not conflict with the VFI but rather supports it. However, some philosophers of science, such as Rooney,[38] argue that the definitions and instances of epistemic values in science may sometimes be affected by hidden non-epistemic considerations as well. This kind of skepticism about the VFI leads to new approaches in philosophy of science that rethink the nature of the epistemic values in science and accept the idea

38 Phyllis Rooney, 'The Borderlands Between Epistemic and Non-Epistemic Values' in Daniel Steel and Kevin C. Elliott (eds), *Current Controversies in Values and Science* (Routledge 2017) 31–45.

that epistemic values may sometimes be context-dependent or not always serve for the attainment of truth.[39]

Recently, Daniel Steel suggests that some of the epistemic values that help with scientific inference (such as simplicity, consistency with what is already known, openness to criticism, following agreed-upon methodological procedures) sometimes do not serve the attainment of true beliefs.[40] Whether such epistemic values hinder or promote the attainment of truth depends on the context and the case at hand. Steel suggests that non-epistemic values may similarly help with the attainment of truth, so in some cases, their role is similar to the role of the benign employment of epistemic values.[41] The studies on the values in regulatory sciences can make use of Steel's account to judge whether experts' employment of certain non-epistemic values harms the quality of scientific advisory in a certain case. For instance, the standardization of policy-relevant scientific inquiry (e.g. through establishing agreed-upon protocols and mechanical procedures) may minimize any particular community of experts' arbitrary influence on political decision-making in some contexts but could also lead to biases in different cases, depending on the structure and the quality of the procedures.

Steel's argument is another prominent example of a recent approach in philosophy of science that goes beyond the VFI, which nevertheless is clearly protective of the core meta-values that the proponents of the VFI have subscribed to. Notice that Steel's criterion for allowing non-epistemic values in scientific reasoning prioritizes the attainment of truth as the guiding principle to decide whether the permeation of non-epistemic values in science leads to any harm in the quality of scientific judgment in a given context. Similar to the idea of detached objectivity, Steel's argument for the inclusion of non-epistemic values in science is protective of the scientific authority in an important sense.

4.2.3 *Pluralism and the right values in science*

Yet another remarkable and prominent philosophical approach to the role of values draws on feminism and the work of feminist philosophers of science who have grappled with the question: *Is a feminist science possible?*[42] In

39 See, for instance, Helen E. Longino, 'Cognitive and Non-Cognitive Values in Science: Rethinking the Dichotomy', *Feminism, Science, and the Philosophy of Science* (Springer 1996) 39–58.

40 Daniel Steel, 'Epistemic Values and the Argument from Inductive Risk' [2010] Philosophy of Science 14, 18; see Steel (n 33) for the most recent version of his overall argument.

41 Ibid 25.

42 Donna Haraway, 'Situated Knowledges: The Science Question in Feminism and the Privilege of Partial Perspective' [1988] 14 Feminist Studies 575; Anderson (n 20); Helen E. Longino, 'Can There Be A Feminist Science?' [1987] 2 Hypatia 51; Alison Wylie, 'Doing Archaeology as a Feminist: Introduction' [2007] 14 Journal of Archaeological Method and Theory 209.

advancing replies to this question, philosophers such as Alison Wylie, Elizabeth Anderson and Helen Longino, have offered compelling theories according to which scientific judgment can be value-laden but nevertheless deserve the label objective.

Famously, Helen Longino[43] argues that the plurality of views, values and background assumptions in science is not a weakness but rather constitutive of scientific objectivity and rationality. For instance, Longino has established the idea that avenues for criticism and peer review, openness to new perspectives and participants, and similar social institutions of science that facilitate rational argumentation help science progress and establish itself as an objective inquiry. Longino's account, therefore, invites us to think that non-epistemic values in scientific reasoning are not to be refrained from but to be embraced, reflected upon and to be regulated through the critical social interactions among scientists.

While Longino's account is a general one, more recent approaches in the feminist philosophy of science, such as Janet Kourany's *Philosophy of Science after Feminism*,[44] have addressed the problem in more specific terms by asking which non-epistemic values are conducive of good and responsible scientific practices. Note that venturing into an account of 'right values' is a controversial subject and may conflict with the ideals of democracy and neutrality. This kind of work is ongoing. However, Kourany's project is similar to Longino's in that she argues for a more extended role of non-epistemic values in science because she believes that cogent and responsible science cannot be realized without genuine engagement with values.

The feminist accounts of science, such as Longino's and Kourany's, invite us to assess the quality of the social dimensions of the regulatory sciences used for legitimizing policies. The relevant examples of these dimensions are pluralism, diversity of perspectives, transparency of non-epistemic values. Assessing these criteria for the quality of regulatory expertise can help socio-legal scholars detect whether and how failing to fulfil such feminist ideals in regulatory sciences hinders or obstructs the attainment of good regulatory outcomes (that are acceptable by the stakeholders and are protective of environmental safety and the public health). We can also use this kind of analysis to identify whether acceptable non-epistemic values are employed in regulatory sciences such as toxicology and pharmacology (see Hicks for an exploration).[45]

43 Longino (n 12); Helen E. Longino, *Studying Human Behavior: How Scientists Investigate Aggression and Sexuality* (University of Chicago Press 2013).

44 Kourany (n 34).

45 Hicks (n 34).

4.2.4 *Democratization and citizen participation in science*

Some philosophers of science, most notably Philip Kitcher[46] or Stephen Turner,[47] have explored these issues from a different angle by asking under what conditions citizens' and governments' deference to expertise to manage current affairs is reconcilable with liberal and democratic values. In response to this theoretical problem, the science studies scholars and philosophers of science have explored to what extent and how scientific expertise can be democratized by establishing institutionalized avenues that facilitate a deep and meaningful interaction between experts and non-expert citizens. In turn, various models of inserting citizens into science, or more generally models of democratization of expertise, have been proposed or investigated by the philosophers of science and science studies scholars.[48] This literature is also known as the democratization of science literature.

Some of the commentators in this literature, such as Kitcher and Douglas, have explicitly abandoned the VFI. But again, the point has not been to criticize the meta-normative values the proponents of the VFI subscribe to but to transcend them. Specifically, Kitcher addresses the second argument in favour of the VFI noted in Section 3. He proposes that the involvement of non-epistemic values and directions of scientific research should be decided by the informed citizens and deliberated in ideal settings. Kitcher's ideal demands that the heterogeneity of values in the public should be represented in scientific research projects. In order to avoid the arbitrary negative influence of value-laden experts over citizens, Kitcher argues in favour of reforming scientific institutions in such a way that science is properly situated in an advanced deliberative democratic settings. Trying to come closer to Kitcher's ideal of science (the *Well Ordered Science*), he argues, is not only a requirement of democracy but also a vehicle to fulfil liberal values such as people's freedom to pursue meaningful life projects and equality in doing so.

Together with Kitcher's *Well Ordered Science*, the four concepts reviewed above show us that the worries of the proponents of the VFI can, in principle, be properly addressed (see Table 10.1 for a summary). For the examination of the accountability of regulatory experts, these philosophical insights highlight that departing from the VFI does not necessarily imply an unguarded politicization of scientific expertise in regulatory governance processes. Moreover, they form a helpful pool of conceptual resources that can be used for evaluating the quality of how non-epistemic issues are addressed by scientific experts across diverse regulatory contexts in practice.

46 Kitcher (n 28).

47 Stephen Turner, 'What Is the Problem with Experts?' [2001] 31 Social Studies of Science 123.

48 See for a collection of contributions, Sabine Maasen and Peter Weingart (eds), *Democratization of Expertise? – Exploring Novel Forms of Scientific Advice in Political Decision-Making* (Springer 2006).

Table 10.1 Four key concepts from the recent philosophy of science that transcend the VFI while reclaiming the value of scientific authority in democratic governance

Concept	*Description*	*Key Text*
Objectivity as Impartiality	The permeation of pragmatic considerations into the core of scientific reasoning violates the sense of scientific objectivity as value-freedom. However, the violation of value-freedom does not imply that the sense of objectivity as 'detachment from values and evidence' is also violated.	*Science, Policy and the Value-Free Ideal* by Heather Douglas
Objectivity through Pluralism and Dissent	Proper social institutions of science (e.g. an inclusive and transparent peer-review community) may guard against the arbitrary dominance of any particular community of experts' subjective biases or hidden values over practical decision-making. Scientific objectivity is partly established inter-subjectively through learning from each other and discovering one's biases through critical peer-reviewing.	*Science as social knowledge: Values and* objectivity *in scientific inquiry* by Helen Longino
Epistemic Priority	Non-epistemic values can be included in scientific inference if we take the epistemic value of doing so as a guiding principle.	*Qualified Epistemic Priority* by Daniel Steel
Well Ordered Science	In order to keep the authority of science intact, we need to make sure that the heterogeneity of values in public is well represented in science. This would fulfil the instrumental value of science, which is to maximize societies' freedom to pursue meaningful life projects. In order to avoid the arbitrary negative influence of value-laden experts over citizens, we need to design the avenues for expert-citizen interaction in such a way that science is properly situated in an advanced democracy.	*Science in a Democratic Society* by Philip Kitcher

5 Conclusion

As reviewed, the philosophical debate over the cogency of the VFI provides the socio-legal scholars who are interested in the accountability of regulatory scientific expertise with useful conceptual insights. These insights can be used for examining individual cases such as the case of the regulation of clothianidin. Based on the relevant conceptual grounds reviewed here, we could ask, for instance, whether the VFI is followed by the regulatory toxicologists or justifiably violated.

Recognizing the fact that value-free and objective scientific judgment is, at best, an ideal should not readily pave the way for the politicization of scientific expertise in the context of expert-based governance. After all, multi-level regulation and governance need fair amount evidence as opposed to opinions; rational arguments as opposed to politics-driven wishes. This however does not imply that we must stick to an old-fashioned positivist ideal that is hardly applicable to the complex contemporary multi-level governance mechanisms in which experts' judgments play crucial roles. Scientific judgments must be produced with the awareness that their conclusions might be misinterpreted, misused by the policymaking agents. It is also important that regulatory experts genuinely serve for public's interest. What is required is an understanding of science as a reliable epistemic source that does not refrain from attending to the relevant non-epistemic issues.

In this chapter, I have considered different ways in which scientific experts can be permissibly expected to let non-epistemic value judgments to influence their assessment. In particular, I have offered that the arguments for and against the philosophical Value Free Ideal of Science provide us with a suitable conceptual ground to examine the accountability of scientific experts in addressing the relevant value considerations such as economic interest and environmental safety in their analysis. I have emphasized that the contemporary philosophical debates on the role of values in science urge us to consider ways in which values may play roles in regulatory scientists' analysis, but within certain limits that hopefully protect the epistemic and democratic legitimacy of our reliance on scientific experts in regulatory decision-making.

Acknowledgement

Many thanks to the participants at the 'Unpacking the Accountability Paradox in Expert-based Decision-making', hosted by Erasmus School of Law, Rotterdam, in November 2017, for their very insightful discussions and comments. Special thanks to the editors Alessandra Arcuri, Florin Coman-Kund and Conrad Heilmann for their comments and suggestions on the previous drafts of this chapter.

Part IV

Expertise and accountability in digitization and data protection governance

11 The concept of accountability in the context of the evolving role of ENISA in data protection, ePrivacy and cybersecurity

W. Gregory Voss

1 Introduction

Agencies are seen as ideal for managing complex and technical issues, given their high specialization and access to experts, and their being shielded from political influence. Their alleged distance from political influence allows them to take decisions based on technical considerations alone.[1] However, this same distance raises difficulties for accountability, in the sense of holding the agencies to account.[2] Furthermore, the independence of agencies' technical and/or scientific assessments has been described by the Commission as their '*raison d'être*'.[3] In the European Union (EU), agencies have been used both for operational activities and for supporting decision-making.[4] Moreover, it may be more palatable for Member States to give power to EU agencies, rather than to the Commission, as Member States have representatives on agencies' boards.[5] Nonetheless, certain contributions to the literature now nuance views of EU agencies' independence in the face of different levels of supervision and control and requirements for accountability. Agencies' dependence on the Commission and the fact that they work as part of a network with Member State counterparts are mentioned in this regard.[6]

The number of EU agencies has grown steadily, through different waves, with a first wave in the 1970s, a second in the 1990s and a third in the 2000s.[7] One EU expert agency, European Network and Information Security Agency (ENISA), is a member of the last wave, or 'third generation' of EU agencies, active in cybersecurity. ENISA was established by Regulation (EC) No

1 Madalina Busuioc, *European Agencies: Law and Practices of Accountability* (OUP 2013) 25–26.
2 Ibid 2.
3 Merijn Chamon, 'EU Agencies: Does the Meroni Doctrine Make Sense' (2010) 17(3) Maastricht Journal of European and Comparative Law 281, 283–284.
4 Florin Coman-Kund, 'Assessing the Role of EU Agencies in the Enlargement Process: The Case of the European Aviation Safety Agency' (2012) 8 CYELP 335, 335–336.
5 Chamon (n 3) 287.
6 Ellen Vos, 'EU agencies on the move: challenges ahead' (2018) 1 SIEPS 34.
7 Chamon (n 3) 283.

460/2004 (ENISA Regulation), with the original objectives of (1) enhancing the ability to prevent and to address network and information security problems, (2) providing advice to the European Commission (Commission) on network and information security issues, (3) using its expertise to stimulate cooperation between different actors and (4) assisting the Commission in technical preparatory work on legislation in the field of network and information security.[8] This translated into rather soft powers being entrusted to ENISA, which helped this agency to survive a challenge to its very existence before the Court of Justice of the European Union (CJEU). [9]

ENISA has recently received additional responsibilities,[10] which make a discussion of its accountability all the more relevant for the period after such change. This is important, because logically the level of accountability-ensuring processes applied to agencies should vary with the degree of operational responsibility that an agency holds, as is recognized by Rocca and Eliantonio's analysis of agencies based on groupings related to soft law instruments.[11]

This chapter demonstrates the increasing role of one EU agency – (ENISA), prior to discussing the challenges that this raises with respect to accountability, and the part that the evolution of ENISA's governance structures may play in meeting such challenges. The *essential research question* is whether accountability is a concern for ENISA today, given the development of its powers and governance structures, and whether recent and potential future changes to the agency's role might necessitate a re-assessment in this respect. This study is conducted using the evolving legal-analytical framework of governance of decentralized agencies, as modified by the Common Approach on EU Agencies,[12] and then handling ENISA as a legal-empirical case-study with the specificities related to its role in EU legislation and 'soft law'.

This chapter begins by providing an overview of theoretical perspectives regarding the accountability of EU agencies relevant for assessing ENISA's accountability (Section 2), followed by a brief description of ENISA as an expert body (Section 3). Next, the role of ENISA in connection with EU legislation that has developed over recent years in the areas of data protection, ePrivacy and cybersecurity, is detailed (Section 4). An early challenge to ENISA's legal basis is then discussed (Section 5), prior to detailing the evolution of ENISA's mandate, as

8 Regulation (EC) No 460/2004, [2004] OJ L77/1, Article 2.

9 *United Kingdom v Parliament and Council* [2006] Case C-217/04 EU:C:2006:279, I.

10 This is as the result of the adoption of the EU Cybersecurity Act, which is discussed later on in this chapter.

11 Penelope Rocca and Mariolina Eliantonio, 'European Union Soft Law by Agencies: an Analysis of the Legitimacy of their Procedural Frameworks' [2019] SoLaR (Jean Monnet Network on the study of EU soft law by national administrations and courts) Publication, 15–30.

12 Joint Statement of the European Parliament, the Council of the EU and the European Commission on decentralized agencies of 19 July 2012 (Common Approach on EU agencies) <http://europa.eu/about-eu/agencies/overhaul/index_en.htm> accessed 6 July 2020.

evidence of its establishment as an agency with growing importance (Section 6), and the evolution of ENISA's governance structures, as one solution to accountability challenges (Section 7). Finally, additional comments on accountability in connection with ENISA are made (Section 8), prior to concluding (Section 9).

2 Theoretical perspectives on EU agencies' accountability

The underlying concept of accountability is broad, and the quest for it has become pervasive. It may be viewed on different levels and has been seen to convey 'an image of transparency and trustworthiness'.[13] According to Curtin, accountability may be divided up into two categories: that concerned with making decision-making more democratic (political or democratic accountability), and that concerned with controlling delegated powers (administrative or bureaucratic accountability).[14] In a more granular analysis, Vos identifies five types of accountability: managerial (here the management board is important), political (involving the Parliament and the Council), administrative (where the Ombudsman is important), financial (involving the Commission's financial controller, the Court of Auditors, the Council and the Parliament) and judicial (involving the CJEU). She refers to this accountability as ex-post control and describes it as carrying out a 'retrospective process of information, discussion and evaluation of agencies' actions'.[15]

Busuioc is quick to distinguish between control and accountability, cautioning that although the two terms have been used interchangeably, the former term is broader than the latter, and may include both 'ex ante and ex-post mechanisms of directing behaviour',[16] but do not involve actors having to 'explain and justify their conduct to forums'.[17] When Busuioc refers to accountability, she refers to principals delegating power or authority to agents, instead. Furthermore, she speaks of three kinds of control: ex ante control, ongoing control and ex post control, the latter of which she sees as synonymous with accountability,[18] similarly to Vos. In the case of ENISA, one could say that ex post control has been paramount, and that any need for ongoing control, as defined by Busuioc,[19] has in a way been obviated more or less by ex-ante control, fashioned by constant repealing and replacing of the agency's foundational regulation, culminating in the Cybersecurity Act. Moreover, Busuioc highlights the importance of

13 Deirdre Curtin, *Executive Power of the European Union. Law, Practices, and the Living Constitution* (OUP 2009) 246. See on the concept of 'accountability' and its particular application in the context of multilevel governance Alessandra Arcuri and Florin Coman-Kund, 'Introduction: Breaking Taboos, Talking Accountability' (in this volume).

14 Ibid 247.

15 Vos (n 6) 42.

16 Busuioc (n 1) 48.

17 Ibid 49.

18 Ibid 52.

19 Busuioc refers to 'direct interference of the principal post-delegation' in the context of ongoing control, ibid at 51. This does not seem to apply to the ENISA case.

distinguishing between control and accountability in the case of European agencies, where independence necessitates excluding the kind of direct control that could be exercised as ongoing control.[20]

In Craig's discussion of agency accountability, control and accountability are divided into three sorts: legal, political and financial.[21] His use of the term 'legal accountability' includes judicial review,[22] which is separated out by Vos as 'judicial accountability', and of perhaps less interest to our discussion of ENISA today. This is because, although the CJEU has competence to 'review the legality of acts of bodies, offices or agencies of the Union intended to produce legal effects vis-à-vis third parties' under Article 263 of the Treaty on the Functioning of the European Union (TFEU),[23] ENISA does not make formal decisions having such effect.[24] Concerns of democratic control and the rule of law arise in the case of authorities that have direct law enforcement power;[25] but ENISA does not exercise such powers.[26] Most of our discussion on governance here (especially, Section 7) will relate to what Curtin has referred to as administrative accountability, and our earlier discussion of legislation (Section 4) will deal more with concepts of political accountability, as will our additional comments in Section 8. That having been said, we will also touch upon managerial and financial accountability, as those terms are used by Vos, and potential changes set out in our concluding remarks (Section 9) could one day make judicial accountability germane as well.

Depending on the facts relating to any particular agency, mechanisms implemented to ensure accountability (whether administrative or political) may be too extensive or inadequate, within a range going from 'high intensity', on the one hand, to 'undersight' and 'passive principals', on the other hand.[27] Busuioc states that, 'Agencies possess a variety of powers. Some have only information providing powers, whereas others can wield much more far-reaching powers. It is the latter that are more relevant from an accountability perspective. Substantively,

20 Ibid 52.

21 Paul Craig, *EU Administrative Law* (3rd edition, OUP 2012) 174–189.

22 Ibid 176–177.

23 Consolidated Version of the Treaty on the Functioning of the European Union (Oct. 26, 2012), [2012] OJ C326/47 [herein TFEU], Article 263.

24 This having been said, Craig cautions that if the Commission makes such formal decisions, in reality in most instances it follows the recommendations of the agency, and that then the agency should be subject to review, Craig (n 21) 176.

25 Miroslava Scholten, Michiel Luchtman and Elmar Schmidt, 'The Proliferation of EU Enforcement Authorities: A New Development in Law Enforcement' in Miroslava Scholten, Michiel Luchtman and Elmar Schmidt (eds), *The EU in Law Enforcement by EU Authorities: Implications for Political and Judicial Accountability* (Edward Elgar Publishing 2017) 1.

26 Ibid 25. This continues to be true following the EU Cybersecurity Act.

27 Madalina Busuioc and Martin Lodge, 'Reputation and Accountability Relationships: Managing Accountability Expectations through Reputation' (2016) 77(1) Public Administration Review 91.

accountability issues are most pertinent for the more powerful agencies'.[28] It may be argued, then, that the evaluation of the level of accountability obligations may change over time as the mandate of an agency evolves. By this it is meant that such obligations may be seen as either excessive (evidencing 'accountability overload') or inadequate, depending on the then-current mission of the agency and its powers, among other factors. Accountability becomes more important as an agency gains power, such as obtaining rulemaking authority or the ability to take actions intended to produce legal effects with respect to third parties. Furthermore, according to Vos, practices of Member States using EU agencies – for example, the European Union Aviation Safety Agency (EASA) – to represent them internationally or otherwise 'borrowing' the EU agencies, adds 'to the complexity of their accountability'.[29]

Administrative accountability could become an issue if an agency's action lacks transparency, or if it does not properly administer its budget. Furthermore, if an agency gains more actual influence, for example becomes more influential in policy-making, should it be not be subject to greater political and judicial control? For example, if an agency issues soft-law instruments such as recommendations, and these are taken up as the basis for assessment with data protection law compliance and result in sanction of a data controller, would this not become an issue of political and judicial control? These issues lead us to look to governance structures and discuss accountability in the context of ENISA further.

3 ENISA as an expert agency

ENISA's objectives led to tasks that included risk analysis, advice-giving, assistance within the scope of its objectives, enhancing and facilitating cooperation between various stakeholders and also between the Commission and Member States, organising consultations, contributing to conscience-raising, tracking the development of standards, contributing to EU efforts to cooperate internationally 'to promote a common global approach to network and information security issues', amongst others.[30] Indeed, one of the expectations for EU agencies generally is 'to ensure better involvement for stakeholders in the Union's policy fields and to develop networks, thereby stimulating the pooling of relevant information and best practices.[31] ENISA seems to fulfil this expectation. As one example, in the European Union, with respect to cybersecurity, ENISA tracked the work of Standard Development Organizations (SDOs) on standards on Network and Information Security (NIS), indicating areas where 'further work is necessary' and facilitating cooperation between SDOs

28 Busuioc (n 1) 42–43.
29 Vos (n 6) 20.
30 Article 3 Regulation 460/2004.
31 Florin Coman-Kund, *European Union Agencies as Global Actors: A Legal Study of the European Aviation Safety Agency, Frontex and Europol* (Routledge 2018) 24–25.

and relevant EU organizations and industry. It encouraged public-private cooperation in these matters.[32] Although ENISA itself is not an SDO, it participated in identifying standards. According to one scholar:

> the Commission and international bodies organized in various forms establishing initially non-binding standards, which by reference or explicit incorporation by EU agencies into Union policies can become binding.[33]

Thus, from the outset ENISA's role may have been greater than assumed at first glance. However, it still fell within the category of agencies supporting decision-making – Craig refers to it as an information and coordination agency –[34] a category perhaps less relevant from the standpoint of accountability than other categories of agencies: regulatory, decision-making and quasi-regulatory.[35] Yet, its domain of expertise has become of crucial importance today with various incidents of 'hacking' and the exposure of vulnerabilities of key computer networks and systems,[36] and we may consider that its area of expertise is of interest to each of the three former pillars, as cybersecurity involves commercial interests, security and defence, involving 'dichotomies such as 'internal/external, public/private, civilian/military'.[37]

Core operations department (COD) units through which ENISA works are the Secure Infrastructure & Services Unit, the Data Security & Standardisation Unit and the Operational Security Unit.[38] COD also includes the policy office, the public affairs team and support staff for the Advisory Group and the National Liaison Officers Network,[39] and operational staff has constituted approximately two-thirds of total staff, with the remainder being administrative staff and

32 Steve Purser, 'Standards for Cyber Security' in Melissa Hathaway (ed), *Best Practices in Computer Network Defense: Incident Detection and Response* (IOS Press 2014) 104.

33 Herwig Hofmann, 'A European Regulatory Union – The Role of Agencies and Standards' in Panos Koutrakos and Jukka Snell (eds), *Research Handbook on the EU's Internal Market* (Elgar Publishing 2016) 471.

34 Craig (n 21) 166.

35 Ibid 163–165.

36 Craig notes that ENISA was established 'because of the increased importance of communication networks and information systems to modern economic and social development. The security of such networks is important, more especially given that this can be jeopardized by accident, attack, and mistake' (ibid, 166).

37 Helena Carrapico and André Barrinha, 'The EU as a Coherent (Cyber)Security Actor?' (2017) 55(6) JCMS 1254, 1255.

38 ENISA, Annual Activity Report 2018, Annex 1 Human Resources, A.1.1 Organisational Chart, at 54, <https://www.enisa.europa.eu/publications/corporate-documents/enisa-annual-activity-report-2018>.

39 ENISA, ENISA Programming Document 2019–2021: Including multiannual planning, work programme 2019 and multiannual staff planning, Amendments, June 2019, at 51, <https://www.enisa.europa.eu/publications/corporate-documents/enisa-programming-document-2019-2021-with-amendments>.

'neutral'.[40] Stakeholder's relations and administration department units of ENISA include Corporate Services and Stakeholders Unit, Finance and Procurement Unit and Human Resources Unit.[41] ENISA provides a breakdown of its staff by activity: in 2018, approximately 15% of its actual staff (actual full time equivalents) was involved in expertise: 'anticipate and support Europe in facing emerging network and information security challenges'; close to 29% in policy: 'promote network and information security as an EU policy priority'; nearly 12% in capacity: 'support Europe in maintaining state-of-the-art network and information security capacities'; about 13% in community: 'foster the emerging European network and information security community'; and the remaining more than 31% in enabling: 'reinforce ENISA's impact'.[42] While each of these activities calls for knowledge in ENISA's domain of competence, it is perhaps the first category – expertise – which seems the most technical, involving 'collating, analysing and making available information and expertise on key NIS issues potentially impacting the EU taking into account the evolutions of the digital environment'.[43]

In order to recruit expertise, there is a 'careers' page on ENISA's website listing open vacancies for seconded national experts (SNEs), trainees, temporary agents, temporary agents-inter-agency, contract agents and undergraduate student programme.[44] A Selection Board vets applications and draws up the candidates' reserve list, for the Executive Director's decision 'in line with post and budget availability, as well as considering a geographical diversity and a gender balance'.[45] A Management Board decision lays down requirements for the recruitment of SNEs through a transparent procedure, with applications handled through Member State permanent representatives.[46] Furthermore, calls for tender/calls for expression of interest of external support and reserve NIS experts for assistance are used.[47]

40 Ibid, Annex 1 Human Resources, A.1.4 Information on Benchmarking Exercise, at 56. Information on the evolution of headcount may be found in Table 1 'ENISA Budget and Temporary Agent Posts'.
41 Ibid, Annex 1 Human Resources, A.1.1 Organisational Chart, at 54.
42 Ibid, Annex 1 Human Resources, A.1.6 Human Resources by Activity, at 58.
43 Ibid, Part I Achievements in the Implementation of the 2018 Work Programme, at 17.
44 ENISA, Careers, <https://www.enisa.europa.eu/recruitment/vacancies> (last visited on 30 January 2021).
45 ENISA, Frequently Asked Questions (FAQ) for candidates applying to selection procedures, Version No. 5, July 2019, <https://www.enisa.europa.eu/recruitment/working-for-enisa/faq-candidates> (last visited on 30 January 2021).
46 ENISA, Decision No. MB/2013/15 of the Management Board of the European Union Agency for Network and Information Security Laying Down Rules on the Secondment of National Experts (SNE) to the Agency, 17 October 2013, Article 3, at 3, https://www.enisa.europa.eu/about-enisa/structure-organization/management-board/management-board-decisions/decision-no-mb201315-signed.pdf.
47 ENISA, Public Procurement, <https://www.enisa.europa.eu/procurement> (last visited on 30 January 2021).

4 EU legislation and the role of ENISA

Cybersecurity is an important issue for creating trust in the digital environment and a strategic issue for the European Union. This has been highlighted in the Commission's digital single market strategy.[48] It results that the expertise of ENISA is important in this domain, both to be taken into account in fashioning the law, in addition to playing a role in the choice of standards and in the establishment and maintenance of a certification framework for various products and services. ENISA's power was increased through the adoption of the EU Cybersecurity Act in 2019,[49] and it now is to contribute to establishing and maintaining a certification framework through,[50] for example, preparing candidate certification schemes for adoption by the Commission through implementing acts.[51] ENISA will now contribute more generally to development and implementation of EU policy and law in the area of cybersecurity,[52] and to its implementation by Member States through expertise, advice and analyses, and 'soft law' such as opinions, guidelines and best practices.[53] However, ENISA is a non-majoritarian body and stakeholder involvement in the main governing entities is minimal, with an advisory role through the ENISA Advisory Group. Furthermore, as an expert agency in a highly scientific domain ENISA may have scientific legitimacy, but as has been noted in other agencies and sciences, this does not necessarily involve 'democratic legitimacy' or 'political responsibilities'.[54] It is there where administrative accountability, as made concrete in the foundational regulations of agencies and their governance provisions, plays a role. Weimar and Pisani speak of a control model of EU law as a model of 'administrative legitimation'. They note that, '[w]ide discretionary powers are seen as problematic, and need to be limited and controlled in order to maintain the democratic transmission between EU legislative commands and their

48 European Commission, A Digital Single Market for Europe – Analysis and Evidence, SWD (2015) 100 final. Communication from the Commission to the European Parliament, the Council, the European Economic and Social Committee and the Committee of the Regions. European Commission, Brussels.

49 Regulation (EU) 2019/881 of the European Parliament and of the Council of 17 April 2019 on ENISA (the European Union Agency for Cybersecurity) and on information and communications technology cybersecurity certification and repealing Regulation (EU) No 526/2013 (Cybersecurity Act) [2019] OJ L151/15.

50 Ibid, Recital (48) of the Preamble.

51 'The Commission, *on the basis of the candidate scheme prepared by ENISA*, should be empowered to adopt the European cybersecurity certification scheme by means of implementing acts' (emphasis added), ibid, Recital (84) of the Preamble.

52 Ibid, Article 4(2).

53 Ibid, Article 5(2).

54 Maria Weimar and Gaia Pisani, 'Expertise as Justification: The Contested Legitimation of the EU 'Risk Administration'' in Maria Weimer and Anniek de Ruijter (eds), *Regulating Risks in the European Union: The Co-production of Expert and Executive Power* (Hart Publishing 2016) 4.

administrative implementation'.[55] In this sense, coming back to the case at hand, we now investigate the level of power that ENISA exercises in connection with EU legislation.

ENISA continues playing its part in fostering cooperation between the Member States and also between Member States and EU institutions, agencies and bodies, and now in facilitating efforts for the establishment and adoption of European and international standards for risk management and for 'measurable security of electronic products, systems, networks and services'.[56] We will first investigate ENISA's role in the context of data protection legislation, including the use of 'soft law' in this regard (1), prior to expanding this to electronic privacy (or 'ePrivacy') legislation (2), NIS legislation (3), and, finally, data protection agency work on EU legislation (4), prior to concluding our discussion on EU legislation (5).

4.1 *Data protection and 'soft law'*

As the original founding legislative instrument for ENISA dates back only to 2004, Directive 95/46 (EC) (1995 Data Protection Directive)[57] precedes it by almost a decade and, therefore, makes no mention of the younger agency. Nonetheless, ENISA's role in relation to data protection has been recognized in the development of more recent legislative instruments, namely the General Data Protection Regulation.

ENISA played a role in the various consultations leading up to the Commission's proposal of the legislative instrument that was adopted, as amended, as Regulation (EU) 2016/679 ('General Data Protection Regulation', or 'GDPR'). As acknowledged in the explanatory memorandum to the Commission's 2012 draft GDPR, 'Dedicated workshops and seminars on specific issues were held throughout 2011. In January, ENISA organised a workshop on data breach notifications in Europe'.[58] Data breach notifications are new obligations for data controllers and data processors under Articles 33 and 34 of the GDPR.

Furthermore, several provisions of the GDPR make reference to 'appropriate technical and organisational measures', without defining the term. For example, this is the case in Article 25 on data protection by design and by default (although an approved data protection certification mechanism may be used

55 Ibid 7 (the authors also set forth a deliberative model of administrative legitimation, which is not developed here).

56 Recital (49) of the Preamble to Regulation 2019/881.

57 Directive 95/46/EC of the European Parliament and of the Council of 24 October 1995 on the protection of individuals with regard to the processing of personal data and on the free movement of such data [1995] OJ L281/31.

58 European Commission, 2012. Proposal for a Regulation of the European Parliament and of the Council on the protection of individuals with regard to the processing of personal data and on the free movement of such data (General Data Protection Regulation) COM(2012) 11 final, at 3.

as an element of proof of compliance). The 'security of processing' provision (Article 32) requires 'appropriate technical and organisational measures to ensure a level of security appropriate to the risk', taking into account risk-level, costs of implementation, the state of the art, impact on the rights and freedoms of natural persons and so on, although adherence to approved codes of conduct or certification mechanisms may be an element of proof of compliance. In addition, pseudonymization and encryption, elements of cyber resilience, and regular cyber security assessment processes may be considered included within the term, as appropriate.[59]

Moreover, in deciding whether to impose an administrative fine or in deciding upon the administrative fine's amount, in the case of infringement of the GDPR, supervisory authorities are to give due regard to, *inter alia*, 'the degree of responsibility of the controller or processor taking into account technical and organisational measures implemented by them pursuant to Articles 25 and 32' of the GDPR.[60]

It is in precisely these areas that ENISA has been working: creating guidelines, helping in sorting through standards, creating best practices and so on. These may be considered 'soft law', which in certain cases may have legal effects, by supplementing legal instruments such as the GDPR. One definition of 'soft law' is '[r]ules of conduct that are laid down in instruments which have not been attributed legally binding force as such, but nevertheless may have certain (indirect) legal effects, and that are aimed at and may produce practical effects'.[61] There is a trend in the European Union to an increased level of soft law instruments.[62] One source contends that they constitute 10 per cent of EU law.[63] In an EU context the term is usually reserved to instruments of the European Union – that is of the EU institutions consisting primarily of the Council and the Commission, such as recommendations and opinions,[64] although their use has grown to include instruments not mentioned in the TFEU such as notices, green and white papers, declarations, action programmes, codes of conduct and other acts.[65] Coman-Kund and Andone focus on soft law instruments adopted by the Commission 'because these seem to be most contested as to their legal

59 Regulation (EU) 2016/679 of the European Parliament and of the Council of 27 April 2016 on the protection of natural persons with regard to the processing of personal data and on the free movement of such data, and repealing Directive 95/46/EC (General Data Protection Regulation) [2016] OJ L119/1, Article 32(1)(a)–(d).

60 Ibid, Article 83(2)(d).

61 Linda Senden, *Soft Law in European Community Law* (Hart Publishing 2004) 112.

62 Verena Rošic Ferguš, 'The Growing Importance of Soft Law in the EU' (2014) 1(1) InterEU Law East 145, 146.

63 Oana Ştefan, 'Soft Law and the Enforcement of EU Law' in András Jakab and Dimitry Kochenov (eds), *The Enforcement of EU Law and Values: Ensuring Member States' Compliance* (OUP 2017) 200.

64 See, for example, Article 288 TFEU.

65 Ferguš (n 62) 146.

nature and effects'.[66] This seems to fit well to the case of ENISA's work, which to a certain extent may be compared to the use of interpretative instruments by the Commission. Such instruments may be helpful in the application of EU legislation, not aiming 'at generating legal effects other than those ensuing from the underlying law itself'.[67] However, these may be seen as going further, filling in the blanks, as it were, of 'vague or open' provisions of the law itself.[68] While not intending to be an alternative to legislation (although they are of a general and normative nature), they complement it.[69] Ferguš speaks of the theory of graduated normativity, entailing a diversity of levels between legally-binding acts and non-legally-binding statements, and where soft law instruments have normative value and give rise to legal (and not just political) effects, thus influencing individuals, institutions and Member States.[70] Furthermore, soft law has occasionally been used to interpret hard law in the courts,[71] even though its use in court has been described as 'undesirable' and coming 'at the expense of legal certainty'.[72]

Moreover, it has been recognized that is not only the principal EU institutions (the Council, the Commission and the Parliament) that issue soft law – EU agencies do as well.[73] Rocca and Eliantonio note that, 'Since soft law is not formally binding and, thus, does not create any rights or obligations, it seems to escape the limitations established by the *Meroni* judgement',[74] referring to a limitation excluding discretionary powers and general regulatory powers from what may be delegated to agencies by EU actors.[75] Dewar notes that ENISA helps its stakeholders deal with NIS problems through the publication of soft law, such as advice, assistance and guidelines.[76]

Senden identifies three main categories of soft law instruments. The first category includes preparatory and informative instruments, including Green and White Papers, action programmes and informative communications.[77] Interpretative and decisional instruments form the second category. A third

66 Florin Coman-Kund and Corina Andone, 'European Commission's Soft Law Instruments: In-between Legally Binding and Non-binding Norms' in Patricia Popelier and others (eds), *Lawmaking in Multi-level Settings. Legislative Challenges in Federal Systems and the European Union* (Nomos 2019) 174.

67 Senden (n 61) 143–144.

68 Ibid 144 (referring to interpretative acts).

69 Ibid 459.

70 Ferguš (n 62) 148.

71 Ibid 151.

72 Ştefan (n 63) 202 (references omitted).

73 Rocca and Eliantonio (n 11) 5–6.

74 Ibid 6; Case 9/56 *Meroni & Co, Industrie Metallurgiche, SpA v High Authority of the European Coal and Steel Community* EU:C:1958:7, and Case 10/56 *Meroni & Co., Industrie Metallurgiche, società in accomandita semplice v High Authority of the European Coal and Steel Community* EU:C:1958:8.

75 Ibid 5.

76 Robert S. Dewar, 'The European Union and Cybersecurity: A Historiography of an Emerging Actor's Response to a Global Security Concern' in Maria O'Neill and Ken Swinton (eds), *Challenges and Critiques of the EU Internal Security Strategy: Rights, Power and Security* (Cambridge Scholars Publishing 2017) 122.

77 Senden (n 61) 118.

category consists of steering instruments, further divided into formal and non-formal steering instruments, which 'aim at establishing or giving further effect to Community objectives and policy, or related policy areas'.[78] Roughly speaking the first category corresponds to soft law's '*pre-law function*', the second its '*post-law function*' and the third, its '*para-law function*', used as an alternative to legislation.[79]

In a first example, in the area of privacy and data protection by design, covered by Article 25 of the GDPR, ENISA has published a report on privacy and data protection by design that may be used by data protection authorities 'as a reference of currently available technologies and methods' on privacy by design.[80] ENISA has also issued a study on privacy by design involving big data, focused mainly on technology, calling for the integration of privacy enhancing technologies as part of the practical implementation of data protection legal obligations.[81] Recourse to such post-law soft law tools is necessary to complement and add flexibility[82] to hard law instruments such as the GDPR.[83] In the case of the GDPR and ENISA, this is because soft law allows for standards used in the legislation to follow the rapid evolution of scientific technique, organizational procedures and threats in the area of cybersecurity. While the use of vague or open provisions of law such as in Article 25 may cause some head-scratching,[84] without the flexibility that such provisions coupled with soft law allow, the legislation would contain requirements for security and privacy by design that would quickly become obsolete.

A second example concerns a draft Code of Conduct proposed by the Commission, where ENISA plays a guidance role. The final Draft Code of Conduct on privacy for mobile health applications has not yet been approved, as the most recent version was formally submitted to the Article 29 Data Protection Working Party (WP29) on 7 December 2017, and then rejected by WP29 on

78 Ibid 119.

79 Ibid 120. In each case, Senden primarily focusses on instruments issued by the Commission or the Council.

80 ENISA, 2014. Privacy and Data Protection by Design – from policy to engineering. December 2014. This report is cited as 'useful guidance in terms of what could constitute appropriate technical and organisational measures for the purpose of DPbD'. Lina Jasmontaite and others, 'Data Protection by Design and by Default: Framing Guiding Principles into Legal Obligations in the GDPR' (2018) 4(2) European Data Protection Law Review 168, 174.

81 ENISA, 2015. Privacy by design in big data: An overview of privacy enhancing technologies in the era of big data analytics. Final 1.0. Public. December 2015.

82 Ferguš (n 62) 146 (noting the flexibility and differentiation of soft law, with the idea that this will lead to 'greater efficiency, flexibility, legitimacy and transparency of the EU legal order', although the author opines that this is 'questionable').

83 W. Gregory Voss, 'Obstacles to Transatlantic Harmonization of Data Privacy Law in Context', [2019] 2 U. Ill. J.L., Tech. & Pol'y 405, 457 (on the potential duration of the GDPR).

84 See, for example, Woodrow Hartzog, *Privacy's Blueprint: The Battle to Control the Design of New Technologies* (Harvard University Press 2018) 181 ('What does this obligation actually mean in practice? It's not entirely clear'.).

11 April 2018.[85] The Commission seeks to have the Code of Conduct revised in order then to submit it to the European Data Protection Board (EDPB) for formal approval.[86] The final Draft Code of Conduct on privacy for mobile health applications addresses security measures necessary for such applications, pursuant to the data protection requirement 'to implement appropriate *technical and organizational measures* to protect personal data against accidental or unlawful destruction, loss, alteration, disclosure, access and other unlawful forms of processing' (emphasis added). In this respect, the draft Code of Conduct holds out ENISA documents as sources for guidance on secure smartphone app development and secure software development,[87] as well as with respect to technical mechanisms to implement privacy by design.[88] To the extent that guidance by ENISA is pointed to in a code of conduct, such guidance also helps interpreting and implementing EU soft law, as well as EU legislation. It has been recognized that private rules such as codes of conduct play such latter role in data protection.[89]

Thus, ENISA has played a role in development of specific issues in data protection legislation, and its guidance provides missing elements for provisions of legislation that have been drafted in a vague manner. In such a way, we can say that it has helped participate in the creation of 'soft law', through what Senden would see as a contribution to the pre-law function (for example, through its contribution to the work on the GDPR), and most particularly, the post-law one (for example through reports, studies and other guidance referred to in a draft code of conduct and elsewhere).

4.2 *Electronic privacy*

In our discussion of ENISA's role relating to legislation regarding privacy and electronic communications, we will first review this in connection with the ePrivacy Directive both before and after its amendment (1), prior to considering this in the context of a proposed ePrivacy Regulation (2).

4.2.1 *ePrivacy Directive*

In Directive 2002/58/EC (ePrivacy Directive), adopted prior to the creation of ENISA, while security is addressed, the legislators chose to cross-reference

85 European Commission, 2020. Privacy Code of Conduct on mobile health apps, https://ec.europa.eu/digital-single-market/en/privacy-code-conduct-mobile-health-apps (last visited on 30 January 2021).

86 Ibid.

87 European Commission, 2017. Draft Code of Conduct on privacy for mobile health applications, 7 December 2017, notes 14 and 15, http://ec.europa.eu/newsroom/dae/document.cfm?action=display&doc_id=16125 (last visited on 30 January 2021), 11.

88 Ibid 12.

89 Hofmann (n 33) 472 (at 15 in the version on SSRN), citing Article 27 of Directive 95/46 (EC).

the 1995 Data Protection Directive for security requirements in Recital 20: 'Security is appraised in the light of Article 17 of Directive 95/46/EC'. In the text of the ePrivacy Directive itself, vague references to requirements to 'take appropriate technical and organisational measures to safeguard security', are set out,[90] similarly to the case of the GDPR, discussed above, together with a reference to the 'state of the art', without giving any referential in order to evaluate these requirements. This is where guidelines, recommendations and best practices issued by ENISA may supplement the law, as we have seen above.

When the ePrivacy Directive was amended in 2009, ENISA was referred to directly in Article 2 of Directive 2009/136/EC (the 'Amending Directive') related to the ePrivacy Directive. Prior to the Commission adopting consistency 'technical implementing measures concerning the circumstances, format and procedures applicable' to new data beach notifications instituted by the Amending Directive, ENISA was given a right to be consulted (along with the WP29, an advisory group discussed below, and the European Data Protection Supervisor).[91] A draft Commission Decision implementing the personal data breach notification requirement, which was later turned into a regulation, included provisions defining which security measures are adequate to render data unintelligible (involving solutions such as encryption), were 'mainly based on the recommendations of ENISA'.[92]

In addition, ENISA and WP29 were to be consulted by the Commission before making comments or recommendations on proposed sanctions for infringement of the ePrivacy Directive to be added in member state implementing legislation, as communicated by national regulatory authorities, in particular to ensure compliance with the internal market. This follows a more general call for consultation of ENISA in the recitals of the Amending Directive:

> When adopting implementing measures on security of processing, the Commission should consult all relevant European authorities and organisations (the European Network and Information Security Agency (ENISA) ...),

90 Directive 2002/58/EC of the European Parliament and of the Council of 12 July 2002 concerning the processing of personal data and the protection of privacy in the electronic communications sector (Directive on privacy and electronic communications) [2002] OJ L201/37, Article 4.

91 Directive 2009/136/EC of the European Parliament and of the Council of 25 November 2009 amending Directive 2002/22/EC on universal service and users' rights relating to electronic communications networks and services, Directive 2002/58/EC concerning the processing of personal data and the protection of privacy in the electronic communications sector and Regulation (EC) No 2006/2004 on cooperation between national authorities responsible for the enforcement of consumer protection laws [2009] OJ L337/11, Article 2 (4) (c) and (5).

92 Article 29 Data Protection Working Party, 2012b. Opinion 06/2012 on the draft Commission Decision on the measures applicable to the notification of personal data breaches under Directive 2002/58 on privacy and electronic communications (WP 197), at 8.

> as well as all other relevant stakeholders, particularly in order to be informed of the best available technical and economic means of improving the implementation of [the ePrivacy Directive].[93]

Thus, ENISA plays an important consultative role in connection with security of processing aspects of the ePrivacy Directive, as well.

4.2.2 *Proposed ePrivacy Regulation*

Following a study on the implementation and effectiveness of the ePrivacy Directive and its compatibility with the GDPR, and public consultation, the Commission issued on 10 January 2017 a new proposed ePrivacy Regulation.[94] The European Commission acknowledges having relied on expert advice of ENISA, among other agencies, when drawing up the proposed ePrivacy Regulation.[95] For security requirements, Article 8(2)(b) of the proposed ePrivacy Regulation then made cross-reference to Article 32 of the GDPR,[96] rather than defining the requirements in the body of this instrument itself, and we have seen above the role of ENISA in helping supplement that regulation, through recommendations and guidelines. Although the ePrivacy Regulation draft proposed by the Finnish presidency of the Council was rejected on 22 November 2019,[97] work on a recast proposal continued in 2020 and 2021.

4.3 *Network and information security (NIS) directive and cybersecurity*

ENISA was consulted by the Commission prior to the proposal of the Network and Information Security Directive, and ENISA's 'continuous involvement' was seen as important element supporting the Commission and competent

93 Recital (74) of the Preamble to Directive 2009/136.

94 W. Gregory Voss, 'First the GDPR, Now the Proposed ePrivacy Regulation' (2017) 21(1) Journal of Internet Law 3.

95 European Commission, 2017a. Proposal for a Regulation of the European Parliament and of the Council concerning the respect for private life and the protection of personal data in electronic communications and repealing Directive 2002/58/EC (Regulation on Privacy and Electronic Communications) COM(2017) 10 final.

96 The 4 October 2019 draft of the ePrivacy Regulation contained this provision in its Article 8(2b). Council of the European Union, 2019. Proposal for a Regulation of the European Parliament and of the Council concerning the respect for private life and the protection of personal data in electronic communications and repealing Directive 2002/58/EC (Regulation on Privacy and Electronic Communications), 2017/0003(COD), 12633/19, 4 October 2019, Article 8(2a), at 64, <https://www.parlament.gv.at/PAKT/EU/XXVI/EU/07/70/EU_77024/imfname_10929175.pdf>.

97 Jennifer Baker, 'How the ePrivacy Regulation Talks Failed … Again' (*iapp*, 26 November 2019) <https://iapp.org/news/a/how-the-eprivacy-regulation-failed-again/> last visited on 30 January 2021.

authorities' efforts 'to facilitate a convergent implementation of the Directive across the EU'.[98] ENISA has a particularly central role to play in Directive (EC) 2016/1148 (NIS Directive). The NIS Directive has the objective of increasing network and information security,[99] and provides that Member States are to adopt a national NIS security strategy.[100] It establishes both security and notification requirements for operators of essential services (including in the sectors of energy, transport, banking, financial market infrastructures, health, drinking water supply and distribution and digital infrastructure)[101] and for digital service providers (online marketplace, online search engine and cloud computing service providers).[102]

The NIS Directive creates a Cooperation Group, of which ENISA is a member, to further cooperation between Member States, particularly through the exchange of NIS information.[103] In this context, ENISA provides assistance in implementing policies and in analysing NIS security strategies and is involved in developing guidelines for 'sector-specific criteria for determining the significance of the impact of an incident', among other responsibilities.[104] When the Commission adopts implementing acts relating to procedural arrangements necessary for the Cooperation Group's functioning, or on the security requirements for digital service providers, 'the Commission should take the utmost account of the opinion of ENISA'.[105]

The Commission or the Member States may consult ENISA regarding the application of the NIS Directive, and the agency is to provide them with expertise and advice.[106] It coordinates simulated real-time cyber incident scenario exercises as a tool for testing and drawing up recommendations for improving incident-handling.[107] ENISA is also to collaborate with Member States on the development of advice and guidelines regarding technical areas to be considered in connection with the use of technology, standards and specifications, relating to the security of networks and information systems.[108]

98 European Commission, 2013. Proposal for a Directive of the European Parliament and of the Council concerning measures to ensure a high common level of network and information security across the Union COM(2013) 48 final.
99 Directive (EU) 2016/1148 of the European Parliament and of the Council of 6 July 2016 concerning measures for a high common level of security of network and information systems across the Union [2016] OJ L194/1, Article 1(1).
100 Ibid, Article 7(1).
101 Ibid, Article 14.
102 Ibid, Article 16.
103 Ibid, Article 11(1)-(2).
104 Ibid, Recital (38) of the Preamble.
105 Ibid, Recital (69) of the Preamble.
106 Ibid, Recital (36) of the Preamble.
107 Ibid, Recital (42) of the Preamble.
108 Ibid, Article 19(2).

Furthermore, the importance of the role of ENISA in NIS and more generally cybersecurity has recently been highlighted by which the Council invited ENISA, Europol and Eurojust,

- to continue strengthening their cooperation in the fight against cybercrime, both among themselves and with other relevant stakeholders, including the CSIRTs community, Interpol, the private sector and academia ensuring synergies and complementarities, in accordance with their respective mandates and competences.
- to contribute jointly with Member States a coordinated approach for EU law enforcement response to large-scale cyber-incidents and crises to complement the procedures outlined in the relevant frameworks (citation omitted).[109]

Thus, we see that ENISA's role is central in advising the Commission and Member States in the area of NIS security and in providing guidelines, and otherwise in ensuring a coherent approach to cybersecurity throughout the European Union.

4.4 *Data protection agency work regarding EU legislation*

In addition, the work of ENISA has been considered by the Article 29 Data Protection Working Party (WP29), a European advisory group established under Article 29 of the 1995 Data Protection Directive, which has now been replaced by the EDPB, in its deliberations on various issues related to European legislation.

For example, in connection with the Commission's recommendation that Member States 'adopt and apply a template for a data protection impact assessment ('DPIA Template'), which should be developed by the Commission and submitted to the Working Party on the protection of individuals with regard to the processing of personal data (WP29) for its opinion within 12 months of publication of the Commission Recommendation', WP29 found that the proposed DPIA Template often confused risks and threats, and referred to ENISA's threat landscape.[110] About the security requirements applicable to smartphone

109 Council, 2017. Draft Council conclusions on the Joint Communication to the EP and the Council: Resilience, Deterrence and defence: Building strong cybersecurity for the EU, 20 November 2017, 14435/17.

110 Article 29 Data Protection Working Party, 2013b. Opinion 04/2013 on the Data Protection Impact Assessment Template for Smart Grid and Smart Metering Systems ('DPIA Template') prepared by Expert Group 2 of the Commission's Smart Grid Task Force (WP 205).

apps, WP29 cites ENISA guidelines as among the 'publicly available guidelines regarding the security of mobile apps'.[111]

Furthermore, WP29 cooperated with ENISA on various issues. For example, WP29 and ENISA worked together on developing a harmonized European personal data breach severity assessment methodology, following the introduction of data breach notifications under the ePrivacy Directive, as amended by the Amending Directive.[112] WP29 stated that such joint work on severity assessment should be incorporated in the breach notification form under the GDPR, as well.[113]

4.5 *EU legislation and the role of ENISA: Conclusion*

We have seen that ENISA has played a certain role in the development of EU law in the areas of data protection, electronic privacy and cybersecurity, through information providing and that it also may help 'complete' the law, by allowing a way to gauge compliance with security requirements of the law. One may see that because of the lack of expertise of the lawmaker, and as a means to allow for changes in the state of the art over time, aspects of security requirements have in essence been delegated to the standard-makers and to the agency responsible for sifting through these standards – ENISA. Thus, ENISA's role must be evaluated in the light of this power.

5 An early challenge to ENISA's legal basis

Early on in ENISA's existence, in *United Kingdom v Parliament and Council*, the United Kingdom of Great Britain and Northern Ireland applied to the European Court of Justice (ECJ) for annulment of the ENISA Regulation on the grounds that it alleged that then Article 95 EC (now Article 114 TFEU[114]) did: 'not provide an appropriate legal basis for adoption of that regulation. The power conferred on the Community legislature by Article 95 EC is the power to harmonise national laws and not one which is aimed at setting up Community bodies and conferring tasks on such bodies'.[115] The United Kingdom was the only Member State that voted against the ENISA Regulation, and this on the same grounds.[116]

The import of this argument was that, while the ENISA Regulation was adopted under one provision of the EC Treaty (Article 95 EC, which refers to

111 Article 29 Data Protection Working Party, 2013a. Opinion 02/2013 on apps on smart devices (WP 202).

112 Article 29 Data Protection Working Party, 2012b (n 92).

113 Article 29 Data Protection Working Party, 2012a. Opinion 01/2012 on the data protection reform proposals (WP 191).

114 Article 114 TFEU.

115 Case C-217/04 *United Kingdom v Parliament and Council EU:C:2006:279*, para. 11.

116 Case C-217/04 *United Kingdom v Parliament and Council*, Opinion of Advocate General Kokott, 22 September 2005, para. 50.

the procedure in Article 251 EC[117]) by qualified majority vote of the Council through the co-decision procedure with the Parliament, it should have been adopted by unanimous vote of the Council on proposal of the Commission and after consulting the Parliament instead (then Article 308 EC, now Article 352 TFEU[118]).[119] The ECJ found that the ENISA Regulation was rightly based on Article 95 EC and therefore dismissed the action, but it is interesting to note the ECJ's discussion of the role of ENISA. The Court held that, in the context of the risk of a 'heterogeneous application of the technical requirements laid down in [Directive 2002/21/EC on a common regulatory framework for electronic communications networks and services] and the specific directives', the EU legislature 'was entitled to consider that the opinion of an independent authority providing technical advice at the request of the Commission and the Member States might facilitate the transposition of the directives at issue into the laws of the Member States and the implementation of those directives at national level'.[120] The ECJ also pointed out that the mandate of ENISA was limited in time to five years and this allowed an evaluation of the effectiveness of ENISA before 'making a decision as to the fate' of that agency.

> The ECJ's emphasis on the technical nature of the work of ENISA echoes Recital 3 of the preamble to the ENISA Regulation, cited by the Advocate General in her opinion in *United Kingdom v Parliament and Council*.[121]

Yet the ECJ did not follow the opinion of the Advocate General; the latter was for an annulment of the ENISA Regulation, stating: 'Since the ENISA Regulation does not adequately define ENISA's contribution to the approximation of laws and none of the other views on the applicability of Article 95(1) prevails, the ENISA Regulation must in any event be annulled'.[122]

The submissions and claims of the parties, contained in the ECJ's opinion, regarding the role of ENISA are enlightening: the ECJ cited both the United Kingdom submission that ENISA 'must limit itself to providing non-binding advice', and the Parliament's claims on the limited role of that agency:

> According to the Parliament, the functions of [ENISA] are relatively modest in that they do not include the power to adopt 'standards'. The provision of advice by a single authoritative source of expertise at the European

117 The corresponding provision referring to the 'ordinary legislative procedure', is Article 294 TFEU.

118 Article 352 TFEU. Note that this corresponding article of the TFEU requires not just consultation with the European Parliament, but its consent.

119 See Sami Andoura and Peter Timmerman, 'Governance of the EU: The Reform Debate on European Agencies Reignited' [2008] EPIN Working Paper No. 19, 8.

120 Case C-217/04, 2006 (n 115) paras. 63–64.

121 Case C-217/04, 2005 (n 116) para. 4.

122 Ibid para. 46.

> level contributes to the adoption of common positions in situations where the Community and the national bodies cannot run the risk of receiving conflicting technical advice. The various forms of cooperation promoted by [ENISA] also facilitate the approximation of market conditions and the adoption by the Member States of measures which tackle information problems.[123]

Thus, while ENISA has had a limited role, which we have already noted may be greater than it seems, it has acted in a technically complex field, and came under fire from the start. In summary, 'ENISA has been accepted by the CJEU, because this agency was created for adopting non-binding supporting and framework measures under the condition that its tasks are closely related to the subject-matter of the relevant harmonising measures'.[124]

6 The evolution of ENISA's mandate

ENISA's original mandate of five years[125] was extended a first time until 13 March 2012 by an amending regulation.[126] In 2010, the Commission found that it was necessary to revise provisions regarding ENISA, and cited earlier studies indicating that there was a need to modernize, reinforce and further develop ENISA 'to support the Commission and Member States in bridging the gap between technology and policy, serving as the Union centre of expertise in NIS matters'.[127] This was seen as especially important because of the crucial role of ICTs in the European economy and society, highlighted by a Council Resolution called for a 'reinforced and flexible mandate' for ENISA.[128] A renewed ENISA was also called for as part of the Digital Agenda.[129] At the same time, it was felt that much debate would be required in order to revise provisions regarding ENISA so the Commission decided to ask for extension of

123 Case C-217/04, 2006 (n 115) para. 27.

124 Coman-Kund (n 31) 34.

125 ENISA's limited time character was an exception to the general rule that agencies (other than 'agencies classified as executive agencies by the Commission') were given a permanent character. Andoura and Timmerman (n 119) 9.

126 Regulation (EC) No 1007/2008 of the European Parliament and of the Council of 24 September 2008 amending Regulation (EC) No 460/2004 establishing the European Network and Information Security Agency as regards its duration [2008] OJ L293/1, Article 1.

127 European Commission, 2010b. Proposal for a Regulation of the European Parliament and of the Council amending Regulation (EC) No 460/2004 establishing the European Network and Information Security Agency as regards its duration COM(2010) 520 final, at 3.

128 Council, 2009. Council Resolution of 18 December 2009 on a collaborative European approach to Network and Information Security [2009] OJ C321/1, at 4.

129 European Commission, 2010a. Communication from the Commission to the European Parliament, the Council, the European Economic and Social Committee and the Committee of the Regions: A Digital Agenda for Europe COM(2010) 245 final, at 17.

the duration of ENISA for eighteen months to allow time for the debate. The latter was achieved through Regulation (EU) No 580/2011, extending ENISA's mandate until 13 September 2013.[130]

In May 2013, Regulation (EU) No 526/2013 (2013 ENISA Regulation) was adopted, extending the mandate of ENISA until 18 June 2020.[131] Later, Regulation (EU) 2019/881 (EU Cybersecurity Act) made ENISA's mandate indefinite as of 27 June 2019,[132] subject to evaluation and review every five years by the Commission, starting by 28 June 2024, which may include the proposal of amendment of the EU Cybersecurity Act to modify ENISA's mandate.[133] This periodic evaluation and review procedure may be considered an accountability mechanism, although the fact that ENISA's mandate is now otherwise 'permanent' gives more reason to focus on its governance structures, as another way to ensure accountability.

7 The evolution of ENISA's governing structures: One way to obtain accountability

We now turn to an analysis of ENISA's evolving governance structures. This exercise will highlight the relatively limited role for ENISA foreseen by the legislature, its classical EU regulatory agency governing structure, as well as the technically complex area in which ENISA was to intervene. Governing structures are one way used to help ensure what Curtin refers to as 'administrative' accountability, or the accountability between 'elected politicians and bureaucrats', which is the narrower category of accountability.[134] This kind of accountability includes ex ante control in the form of the original terms of the delegation of power or mandate (although this area may be placed in either the category of legal or political accountability, instead), as well as ongoing control in the lack of independence in terms of decision-making, and ex post control, through annual reports and budget discharges, etc.[135] It is concerned with controlling delegated powers,[136] and is helpful in the context of ensuring transparency, controlling the use of EU funds and guaranteeing proper governance.

Under the initial ENISA Regulation, which contained the original terms of delegation of power to the agency, ENISA was formed as a body of the European

130 Regulation (EU) No 580/2011 of the European Parliament and of the Council of 8 June 2011 amending Regulation (EC) No 460/2004 establishing the European Network and Information Security Agency as regards its duration [2011] OJ L165/3, Article 1.

131 Regulation (EU) No 526/2013 of the European Parliament and of the Council of 21 May 2013 concerning the European Union Agency for Network and Information Security (ENISA) and repealing Regulation (EC) No 460/2004 [2013] OJ L165/41, Article 36.

132 Article 68(4) Regulation 2019/881.

133 Ibid, Article 67(1).

134 Curtin (n 13) 247–248.

135 Ibid 250.

136 Ibid 247.

Community, having legal personality, and its operations were subject to the supervision of the Ombudsman. Its accounts were sent to the EU institutions, was subject to observations of the Court of Auditors, and the implementation of its budget required a discharge from the European Parliament. The bodies of ENISA consisted of a Management Board, an Executive Director and a Permanent Stakeholder Group. The 2013 ENISA Regulation retained the original governing bodies (with some changes) and added an Executive Board. All of these governance provisions applied to an agency with relatively little staff, as discussed in paragraph 6 below. In terms of governance structures, the EU Cybersecurity Act no longer refers to a Permanent Stakeholder Group, but to an ENISA Advisory Group and a National Liaison Officers Network, instead.[137] Each of these elements is detailed, prior to discussing ENISA's current status.

7.1 *The management board*

Under the initial ENISA Regulation, the Management Board was made up of representatives of Member States (one each), the Commission (three) and three non-voting representatives proposed by the Commission and appointed by the Council representing, respectively, the information and communication technologies (ICT) industry, consumer groups and academic experts in NIS.[138] Board members were appointed based on their experience and expertise in the NIS field.[139] Initially, we notice the preponderant weight of the Member States in this governance structure, and the lack of vote for stakeholders outside of the EU institutions. The Management Board elected a Chairperson and a Deputy Chairperson from its membership for a renewable two-and-a-half-year period.[140] The Commission proposed rules of procedure for adoption by the Management Board, and a two-thirds majority vote of the Management Board was necessary for their adoption, as well as for the adoption of ENISA's rules of operation, the budget, the annual work programme, and the appointment and removal of the Executive Director. Otherwise, voting was by a majority of voting members, unless provided differently.[141] Ordinary meetings were to be held twice a year, with extraordinary meetings convened at the request of the Chairperson or at least a third of the voting membership.[142]

The Management Board defined the general orientation for the operation of ENISA and ensured consistency of work with Member State and Community-level activities. The Management Board also adopted annual work programmes, ensuring that they are consistent with ENISA's scope, objectives and tasks as well as Community NIS legislative and policy priorities. Furthermore, the Management Board adopted an annual general report of ENISA's activities and,

137 Article 13 Regulation 2019/881.
138 Article 6(1) Regulation 460/2004.
139 Ibid, Article 6(2).
140 Ibid, Article 6(3).
141 Ibid, Article 6(4).
142 Ibid, Article 6(5).

after consulting with the Commission, financial rules applicable to ENISA, which were not to depart from those set out in Commission Regulation (EC, Euratom) No 2343/2002,[143] without the Commission's prior consent.[144]

With the adoption of the 2013 ENISA Regulation, the rules of procedure of ENISA were no longer proposed by the Commission; the Management Board had to consult with the Commission before adopting them, instead.[145] Thus, the EU executive gave up a certain degree of formal control over a governance structure essentially controlled by Member State representatives. In addition, the composition of the Management Board was modified to decrease the Commission representatives to two,[146] and the former non-voting members from stakeholders were no longer included among its members. The latter change was given the following justification: 'Since there is provision for ample representation of stakeholders in the Permanent Stakeholders Group, and that group is to be consulted in particular regarding the draft Work Programme, there is no longer any need to provide for representation of stakeholders in the Management Board'.[147] This move, it may be argued, hindered accountability to stakeholders outside of the EU institutions (more an element of political accountability), while at the same time also reducing control of the executive.

Furthermore, the requirement of a two-thirds majority was extended to the designation of the Chairperson of the Management Board,[148] in addition to the existing cases. This move can be seen as further ensuring Member State control in the agency. The renewable term of the Chairperson was extended to three years,[149] and the term of office of members of the Management Board was set at four years, which was renewable.[150] The Management Board was to adopt an anti-fraud strategy[151] (and a provision allowing the Court of Auditors to have the power of audit over grant beneficiaries, contractors and subcontractors who have received EU funds has been added[152]), and rules for the prevention and management of conflicts of interest,[153] among other new responsibilities. The required frequency of meetings of the Management Board was decreased to at least once a year.[154] No provision was made in the 2013 ENISA Regulation for Permanent Stakeholders Group members to attend Management Board meetings.

143 Commission Regulation (EC, Euratom) No 2343/2002 of 23 December 2002 on the framework Financial Regulation for the bodies referred to in Article 185 of Council Regulation (EC, Euratom) No 1605/2002 on the Financial Regulation applicable to the general budget of the European Communities [2002] OJ L357/72.
144 Article 6 Regulation 460/2004.
145 Article 5 (10) Regulation 526/2013.
146 Ibid, Article 6(1).
147 Ibid, Recital (48) of the Preamble.
148 Ibid, Article 9(2).
149 Ibid, Article 7(1).
150 Ibid, Article 6(4).
151 Ibid, Article 5(4).
152 Ibid, Article 20(2).
153 Ibid, Article 5(6).
154 Ibid, Article 8(2).

The Commission is represented on the Management Board by its Director, Digital Society, Trust and Cybersecurity (Directorate H), DG Communications Networks, Content and Technology, and by the Chief Information Security Officer of DG DIGIT.[155] Most Member State representatives on the Management Board come from information security/cybersecurity divisions of government ministries, with representatives of ministries of transportation and communication data, of digital governance, of the interior, of economic development, of defence, of security and justice and of public administration included. Other representatives come from specific NIS or communications regulatory bodies (including independent agencies) or computer emergency response teams (CERTs). One Member State is represented by its chief information officer. Surprisingly for an expert agency, perhaps, only one Member State (Poland) is represented by someone coming from what is described as a national research institute (Research and Academic Computer Network (NASK)).[156] Thus, industry, academia and research (for the most part), data protection authorities, consumer organizations and standardization agencies are all stakeholders absent from the Management Board, although present in the Advisory Group to varying extents.

The EU Cybersecurity Act lengthened the term of office of the Chairperson of the Management Board to four years, renewable once.[157] The frequency of ordinary meetings of the Management Board was increased to twice a year.[158] Unlike the Permanent Stakeholders Group members under the 2013 ENISA Regulation, under the EU Cybersecurity Act members of the ENISA Advisory Group may participate (without voting rights) in meetings of the Management Board by invitation of the Chairperson.[159] Although an improvement over the 2013 ENISA Regulation, the fact that Advisory Group must be invited to attend meetings and will have no vote there may still indicate a deficit of political accountability at a time when ENISA is receiving greater powers, in that stakeholders are not directly included at meetings where the agency's decisions are being made, except through invitation, and when invited, have no vote.

7.2 *The executive director*

Under the ENISA Regulation, the Executive Director represented ENISA[160] and managed ENISA and was independent in the performance of his or her duties. He or she was appointed by the Management Board for an up to five-year term, on proposal of the Commission, following an open competition, based on his or her merit and administrative and management skills and competence and experience relative to NIS. He or she chaired the Permanent Stakeholder Group[161] and

155 ENISA, List of ENISA Management Board Representatives and Alternates, Status 20 January 2021, <https://www.enisa.europa.eu/about-enisa/structure-organization/management-board/MBMemberAlternate.pdf> (last visited on 30 January 2021).

156 Ibid.

157 Article 16 Regulation 2019/881.

158 Ibid, Article 17(2).

159 Ibid, Article 17(4).

160 Article 18(3) Regulation 460/2004.

161 Ibid, Article 7.

participated in a non-voting capacity at meetings of the Management Board and provided the Secretariat.[162] Under the 2013 ENISA Regulation, the Executive Director's term was set at five years, extendable once for no more than five years, by the Management Board, acting on a proposal from the Commission, after obtaining the European Parliament's views.[163] The Executive Director now chairs the Advisory Group – the successor to the Permanent Stakeholder Group,[164] which allows a link between this group and the other instances of the agency such as the Management Board, but also may create a concern about the independence of the body, as not having proper distance and independence between the Advisory Group and the ENISA management that it advises. Lenstsch and Weingart theorize that there should be distance and mutual independence between advisers and the advised to 'avoid the mixing of particularistic interests and scientific judgements' so as not to lose credibility, authority and its legitimating function.[165]

The Executive Director position has been held by Mr. Juhan Lepassaar – who came to ENISA after six years in the European Commission, which followed his work at the Estonian Government Office – since 16 October 2019.[166]

7.3 *The executive board: a contribution of the 2013 ENISA regulation*

The reason given for the creation of a new governing body – the Executive Board – was to 'enable the Management Board to focus on issues of strategic importance' in an attempt to simplify and strengthen the organizational structure of ENISA to allow greater efficiency and effectiveness.[167] The Executive Board was intended to assist the Management Board by preparing decisions to be adopted by the latter 'on administrative and budgetary matters only', and by assisting and advising the Executive Director in implementing these decisions, and by following up findings and recommendations resulting from investigations of the European Anti-Fraud Office (OLAF), and various internal and external audit reports and evaluations. The renewable term of office for members of the Executive Board was four years, and their number five, appointed from the membership of the Management Board amongst whom the Chairperson of the latter (who may also serve as the former's chair), and one of the Commission's representatives. Meetings were to be held at least once every three months and the chair could convene additional meetings at the request of its members.[168] This structure was continued in the EU Cybersecurity Act, virtually unchanged, with the exception of a proviso that has

162 Ibid, Article 6(5).
163 Ibid, Articles 5 and 24.
164 Article 21 (3) Regulation 2019/881.
165 Justus Lentsch and Peter Weingart, 'Introduction: The Quest for Quality as a Challenge to Scientific Policy Advice: An Overdue Debate?' in Justus Lentsch and Peter Weingart (eds), *The Politics of Scientific Advice: Institutional Design for Quality Assurance* (CUP 2011) 15.
166 ENISA, The Executive Director, <https://www.enisa.europa.eu/about-enisa/structure-organization/executive-director> (last visited on 30 January 2021).
167 Recital (42) of the Preamble to Regulation 526/2013.
168 Ibid, Article 10.

been added allowing the Executive Board to take certain 'provisional decisions' in the place of the Management Board, especially on administrative matters, on an urgent basis, to be followed up by a ratification (or not) of the latter body.[169] Its current composition includes a representative from the European Commission (Director, Digital Society, Trust and Cybersecurity); as well as four from Member States: the Chair of the Management Board (who comes from France's ANSSI), the Head NCSC and Deputy director Cyber Security from the Netherlands' Ministry of Security and Justice, the Austrian Chief Information Officer and a member from Poland's Research and Academic Computer Network (NASK).[170]

7.4 *The permanent stakeholder group*

Under the ENISA Regulation, the Permanent Stakeholder Group was composed of experts representing stakeholder groups (ICT industry, consumer groups and academic experts in NIS).[171] It is important that these different groups be included, as ensuring pluralism of the technical body. The value of this pluralism is highlighted by Lentsch and Weingart: '[d]ifferent disciplines and advisers must be represented in the advisory process, adequately reflecting the topics in question. A plurality of perspectives, theories and methods safeguard the adequacy of the knowledge and the trust in it'.[172]

ENISA's internal rules of operation were to specify the number and the composition of the membership,[173] who were to serve for two-and-a-half-year terms and were not to be members of the Management Board. The Executive Director was to establish and chair the group. [174] Representatives of the Commission could attend meetings of the group and participate in its work.[175] The group could advise the Executive Director in his or her performance of duties and in drawing up ENISA's work programme and could help ensure communication with stakeholders on issues related to the work programme.[176]

Under the 2013 ENISA Regulation the Permanent Stakeholders Group could be composed of representatives from additional categories of stakeholders such as providers of electronic communications networks or services available to the public, representatives of national regulatory agencies notified under Directive 2002/21/EC, and law enforcement and privacy protection authorities.[177] In practice, in addition to representatives nominated by the Body of European Regulators for Electronic

169 Article 19 Regulation 2019/881.

170 ENISA, List of ENISA Executive Board Representatives and Alternates, Status 21 December 2020, <https://www.enisa.europa.eu/about-enisa/structure-organization/executive-board/enisa-executive-board-members> (last visited on 30 January 2021).

171 Article 8 (1) Regulation 460/2004.

172 Lentsch and Weingart (n 165) 15.

173 Article 8 (2) Regulation 460/2004.

174 Ibid, Article 8(3).

175 Ibid, Article 8 (4).

176 Ibid, Article 8(5).

177 Article 12(1) Regulation 526/2013.

Communications (BEREC), the Article 29 Data Protection Working Party and the European Union Agency for Law Enforcement Cooperation, there were certain Permanent Stakeholder Group members appointed 'ad personam'. The actual composition of such category of members on 3 November 2017 was: five members from academia; nineteen from industry (including members from Airbus, Continental Tires, Ebay, Google, Nokia, STMicroelectronics, SWIFT and others), one from a consumer group (BEUC) and five from other sectors (such as standardization and rating agencies, amongst others).[178] If we consider that BEUC represents the public, all main ENISA target stakeholders groups identified by an EP report, were represented in the Permanent Stakeholder Group or the Management Board:

> ENISA's main target group is public sector organisations, specifically EU Member States' governments and the EU institutions. The agency also serves the ICT industry (telecoms, internet service providers and IT companies); the business community, especially small businesses; network and information security specialists, such as computer emergency response teams; academia and the public.[179]

In the EU Cybersecurity Act, this structure was replaced by an ENISA Advisory Group,[180] detailed in Section 7.5.

7.5 *The ENISA Advisory Group, Stakeholder Cybersecurity Certification Group and the National Liaison Officers Networks: Modifications made by the EU Cybersecurity Act*

The EU Cybersecurity Act was meant to grant a much greater role for ENISA in cybersecurity in Europe.[181] It provides for the establishment of an ENISA Advisory Group, a Stakeholder Cybersecurity Certification Group and a National Liaison Officers Network. The first of these groups, the ENISA Advisory Group, may be seen as a successor to the Permanent Stakeholders Group,[182] while the

178 ENISA, 2017. The Permanent Stakeholder's Group, Term of office: 1st November 2017–1st May 2020, Status 3 November 2017.

179 European Parliament, Briefing, Implementation Appraisal, The European Union Agency for Network and Information Security (ENISA), Regulation (EU) No 526/2013 of the European Parliament and of the Council of 21 May 2013 concerning the European Union Agency for Network and Information Security (ENISA) and repealing Regulation (EC) No 460/2004, May 2017, at 3, <https://www.europarl.europa.eu/RegData/etudes/BRIE/2017/603231/EPRS_BRI(2017)603231_EN.pdf>.

180 Article 21 Regulation 2019/881.

181 European Commission, 2017b. Proposal for a Regulation of the European Parliament and of the Council on ENISA, the 'EU Cybersecurity Agency', and repealing Regulation (EU) 526/2013, and on Information and Communication Technology cybersecurity certification ('Cybersecurity Act') COM(2017) 477 final.

182 Indeed, ENISA refers to its Advisory Group as the 'former Permanent Stakeholder's Group'. ENISA, 2019. The Advisory Group (former Permanent Stakeholder's Group), 26 June 2019.

latter two may be seen as having been created relating to the expansion of ENISA's role into certification and an increase in its cooperation with Member States. Certain of the provisions of the EU Cybersecurity Act with respect to certification have a delayed entry into force date of 28 June 2021.[183]

Similar to the former Permanent Stakeholders Group, the ENISA Advisory Group is proposed by the Executive Director. The Management Board then acts upon this proposal. The ENISA Advisory Group's membership may come from diverse sources, much like the Permanent Stakeholders Group following the modifications made by the 2013 ENISA Regulation. In the case of the ENISA Advisory Group, these may include relevant stakeholders such as the ICT industry, providers of electronic communications networks or services available to the public, SMEs, operators of essential services, consumer groups, cybersecurity academic experts, representatives of competent authorities notified under Directive (EU) 2018/1972, European standardization organizations, law enforcement and data protection supervisory authorities. Furthermore, it is to reflect gender, geographical and stakeholder group balance.[184] However, as its name suggests, it only plays an advisory role, which does not extend to the cybersecurity certification framework.[185] Its composition on 26 June 2019 included nominated representatives of BEREC, Europol and the successor to the Article 29 Data Protection Working Party – the EDPB. In addition, there were five representatives from academia, eighteen from industry, one from a consumer group and five from other sectors. These consisted of the same persons as on the Permanent Stakeholders' Group mentioned in Section 3, with the following exceptions, all involving representatives from industry: the representative from Rohde & Schwartz Cybersecurity, who had gone to work for a German region, instead, left the Group; the representative of Philips left the Group; and a new representative from Capgemini joined the Group.[186]

While the representation of various stakeholders on the Advisory Group is laudable, the failure to automatically include certain members on the Management Board may be seen as a weakness. Thus, in the context when the role of ENISA is increasing, paradoxically stakeholders have less access to the centre of decision-making than in the original ENISA Regulation.

183 Article 69 (2) Regulation 2019/881.
184 Ibid, Article 21 (1).
185 Ibid, Article 21 (5).
186 ENISA, 2019. The Advisory Group (former Permanent Stakeholder's Group), Term of office: 1st November 2017–1st May 2020, Status 26 June 2019, <https://www.enisa.europa.eu/about-enisa/structure-organization/advisory-group/members/ag-composition-2017-2020/view>. The Management Board substantially changed the list of 'ad personam' members of the Advisory Group in June 2020, and as a result its members then included twelve representatives from industry, two representing consumers (of which one from consumer group BEUC) and four from academia. ENISA, Decision No. MB/2020/14 of the Management Board of the European Union Agency for Cybersecurity (ENISA) setting up an Advisory Group for the period 2020–2023, 25 June 2020, <https://www.enisa.europa.eu/about-enisa/structure-organization/advisory-group/members/mb-decision-2020_14_on-setting-up-the-ag-2020-2022/view>.

Table 11.1 ENISA budget and temporary agent posts

Year	*ENISA Annual Budget (in €)*	*Staff Temporary Agent Posts*
2005	6,800,000	38
2006	6,940,080	44 (38 + 6 filled during year)
2007	8,416,928	44
2008	8,355,024	44
2009	8,117,200	44
2010	8,113,988	44
2011	8,102,920	44
2012	8,550,149	47
2013	8,549,553	47
2014	9,086,354	48
2015	10,095,949	48
2016	11,060,564	48
2017	11,175,225	48
2018	11,449,000	47
2019	16,932,952	59

Source: ENISA

7.6 *ENISA's budget and staffing*

ENISA's budget has been relatively small throughout its short history, when compared to other agencies. Furthermore, its staffing has been small. ENISA's budget remained under €10 million from 2005 through 2014 (see Table 11.1).[187] The highest annual increase in its budget occurred in the most recent year – 2019 – which is the year when the EU Cybersecurity Act was adopted and political aims were to strengthen ENISA. In that year, the budget increased €5,483,952 or by nearly 50% (47.9%) over the prior year. Its budgeted temporary agent staff remained constant from 2006 through 2011 at 44, increasing by less than 10% during the following period through 2018 to 47. It was only in the last year that, in at the same time that its budget increased significantly, ENISA temporary

187 ENISA, 2019. *Annual Budgets*, <https://www.enisa.europa.eu/about-enisa/accounting-finance/files/annual-budgets> (last visited on 30 January 2021). Where there was an amended budget amount for a certain year, that amended amount was retained for this table. Decimals have been rounded to the nearest Euro, with 51 cents and more being rounded up. Certain years include a contribution from the EFTA countries, a subsidy from the Greek

Government for the rent of the offices of ENISA in Greece (set to a maximum of €640,000) (in the latter case, for the periods from 2013 through 2019, described in the earlier years as a 'subsidy from the host member State covering the hosting needs of the Agency'), and the interest on cash deposits. For a comparative view, to show just how low ENISA's budget is, Carrapico and Barrinha contrast ENISA's 2016 budget of roughly €11 million to the cybersecurity budget of the Pentagon, which requested USD 3.2 billion of cybersecurity funding, during the period when reported by those authors. Carrapico and Barrinha (n 37) 1264.

agent staff increased by over a quarter (25.53%). The EU website shows that, from a numerical perspective, ENISA has been a small agency, with 65 total staff members.[188] By contrast, EASA, which is an agency that has 'the power not only to assist the Commission in the exercise of rulemaking powers but also to directly adopt technical rules'[189] (which is not the case for ENISA today) had a budget in 2019 of €103,214,000,[190] more than six times that of ENISA's highest budget amount. EASA has a staff of 840 members,[191] nearly thirteen times that of ENISA. However, the basic governance of EASA (except for the latter's Board of Appeal)[192] is similar (but not identical) to that of ENISA, making one wonder if the administrative accountability provisions for ENISA were not, at least for the period prior to 2019 and the EU Cybersecurity Act, excessive, in the sense attributed to it by Busuioc. Indeed, a one-size fits all strategy for oversight merely results in agencies spending more time on administrative tasks related to audit requirements.[193] This pleads for a more customized set of accountability rules for agencies such as ENISA, contrary to the Common Approach on EU Agencies.

188 European Union, 2019a. European Union Agency for Network and Information Security (ENISA): Overview, <https://europa.eu/european-union/about-eu/agencies/enisa_en> (last visited on 30 January 2021).

189 Edoardo Chiti, 'European Agencies' Rulemaking: Powers, Procedures and Assessment' (2013) 19(1) European Law Journal 93, 97. EASA has been described as 'both a decision-making and a quasi-rulemaking agency'. Johannes Saurer, 'The Accountability of Supranational Administration: The Case of European Union Agencies' (2008) 24(3) American University International Law Review 429, 464.

190 EASA, 2019. Annex 1: 2019 First Amending Budget – Detailed Table, <https://www.easa.europa.eu/sites/default/files/dfu/EASA%20MB%20Decision%2006-2019%20Annex%201%20-%201st%20amending%20budget%20detailed%20table.pdf> (last visited on 30 January 2021).

191 European Union, 2019b. European Union Aviation Safety Agency (EASA): Overview, <https://europa.eu/european-union/about-eu/agencies/easa_en> (last visited on 30 January 2021).

192 Regulation (EU) 2018/1139 of the European Parliament and of the Council of 4 July 2018 on common rules in the field of civil aviation and establishing a European Union Aviation Safety Agency, and amending Regulations (EC) No 2111/2005, (EC) No 1008/2008, (EU) No 996/2010, (EU) No 376/2014 and Directives 2014/30/EU and 2014/53/EU of the European Parliament and of the Council, and repealing Regulations (EC) No 552/2004 and (EC) No 216/2008 of the European Parliament and of the Council and Council Regulation (EEC) No 3922/91 [2018] OJ L212/1, Articles 94–106. Chiti also refers to EASA having a 'rulemaking directorate', which is absent in ENISA, Chiti (n 189) 97.

193 'First, as Busuioc notes, agencies spend on average 30 per cent of their staff resources on administrative tasks—and some more then 50 per cent—due to extensive audit requirements'. Andreas Eriksen, 'Agency Accountability: Management of Expectations or Answerability to Mandate?' (2019) TARN Working Paper 02/2019, 7.

7.7 *The evolution of ENISA's governing structures: Conclusion*

Following a relevant set of taxonomies,[194] ENISA is an agency with tasks related to expertise, and information and cooperation. Although under the EU Cybersecurity Act it will now contribute to the adoption of a certification framework, it is not today involved in providing services such as registration and certification. Furthermore, it does not supervise, inspect or enforce, nor does it execute EU programmes. As we have seen, ENISA is a small agency. This fact was at the root of criticism of the Cybersecurity Act proposal by the head of France's cybersecurity agency, the *Agence nationale de la sécurité des systèmes d'information* (ANSSI), who indicated that ENISA did not have the resources (either staff or budget) to play a role of cybersecurity crisis management and response, suggesting that the priority should be working at the member state level, instead.[195] Indeed, a proposal for a European Resolution was even introduced in the French Senate, questioning the grounds for the Cybersecurity Act, and arguing that it posed difficulties with the concept of subsidiarity.[196]

Objectively, ENISA's evolving governance structure appears to have worked rather well, as evidenced by the review of the Court of Auditors. The Court of Auditors issued a clean opinion on ENISA's accounts for 2018,[197] with a reference to ENISA's internal audit report and an observation on a lack of sensitive post policy to identify sensitive functions and to define measures to mitigate the risk of vested interests,[198] and 2017,[199] with a criticism about the handing over process for an accounting officer (no hand-over report transmitted) and observations on the failure to post vacancies on the website of the European Personnel

194 Ellen Vos, 'European Agencies and the Composite EU Executive', in Ellen Vos and others (eds), *European Agencies in between Institutions and Member States* (Wolters Kluwer Law & Business 2014) 17–23. In one typology of power, ENISA is arranged in the information providing agencies category, the least powerful of the categories. Busuioc (n 1) 38–39.

195 Rolland, S., 2017. 'Cybersécurité: 'La Question n'Est Plus de Savoir Si On Va Etre Attaqué', *La Tribune Hebdomadaire*, 26 October 2017, 12.

196 Sénat (France) 2017. N° 79, Proposition de résolution européenne au nom de la commission des affaires européennes, en application de l'article 73 octies du Règlement, portant avis motivé sur la conformité au principe de subsidiarité de la proposition de règlement relative à l'ENISA, Agence de l'Union européenne pour la cybersécurité, et abrogeant le règlement (UE) n° 526/2013, et relative à la certification des technologies de l'information et des communications en matière de cybersécurité (règlement sur la cybersécurité) – COM(2017) 477 final, présentée par M. René Danesi et Mme Laurence Harribey, 9 November 2017, <https://www.senat.fr/leg/ppr17-079.html>.

197 Court of Auditors, Annual reports on EU agencies for the financial year 2018, 24 September 2019, 2019 C 417/01, 11 December 2019, 3.11. European Union Agency for Network and Information Security (ENISA) 76–77.

198 Ibid, at 77. The Court of Auditors said ENISA should adopt a sensitive post policy 'without delay'.

199 Court of Auditors, Annual reports on EU agencies for the financial year 2017, 18 September 2018, 2018/C 434/01, 30 November 2018, 3.11. European Union Agency for Network and Information Security (ENISA) 79–80.

Selection Office and to conduct an analysis of the impact of Brexit upon its organizations, operations and accounts.[200] A clean opinion was issued also for 2016, with comments that 'do not call the Court's opinion into question'. The Court concluded that core operational activities under Work Programme 2014 'have a clear connection to the legal mandate of ENISA' and that effectiveness was good. There was room to improve related to the division of ENISA between Athens and Heraklion offices, however. Its 2015 evaluation indicated that ENISA 'effectively meets its stakeholders' expectations' but that there was a need to improve communications with stakeholders.[201] A clean opinion was also issued for 2015,[202] as well as for 2014[203] and 2013,[204] with only minor points raised, such as the late payment by the Greek authorities of the rent for ENISA's Athens offices.[205] In each instance, observations allowed for corrective actions and played a necessary role in good governance.

Today, ENISA is devoid of decision-making powers to adopt binding legal instruments, although it can adopt internal documents such as recommendations, guidelines, reports, work programmes and strategic plans. In principle, it has been the kind of agency to which accountability issues are less relevant.[206] Both Member States and the Commission are represented on ENISA's Management Board, although the Member States more so, and since the 2013 ENISA regulation, ENISA has an Executive Board, as well – a governing body described generally as 'a proper solution that accommodates both needs of large size and efficiency'.[207] One could argue, then, that at least prior to the EU Cybersecurity Act, the provisions regarding ENISA's governance structures intended to ensure administrative accountability have been excessive. However, this view neglects the positive effect that governance has brought to the agency, and does not take into account the fact that such governance may have been rendered necessary, or at least desirable, as a result of the impact of the agency's creation of soft law measures.

200 Ibid, at 80.

201 Court of Auditors, Report on the annual accounts of the European Union Agency for Network and Information Security for the financial year 2016, together with the Agency's reply, 19 September 2017, 2017/C 417/25, [2017] OJ (C 417) 160, 161–162, 6 December 2017.

202 Court of Auditors, Report on the annual accounts of the European Union Agency for Network and Information Security for the financial year 2015, together with the Agency's reply, 13 September 2016, 2016/C 449/25, [2016] OJ (C 449) 138,139, 1 December 2016.

203 Court of Auditors, Report on the annual accounts of the European Union Agency for Network and Information Security for the financial year 2014, 8 September 2015, at 4.

204 Court of Auditors, Report on the annual accounts of the European Union Agency for Network and Information Security for the financial year 2013, 16 September 2014, at 5.

205 Ibid, at 6.

206 See Busuioc (n 1) 42–43.

207 Vos (n 194) 26.

8 ENISA and accountability: Additional comments

EU agencies are part of a growing executive power in Brussels that, when granted independence, may escape traditional controls and raise issues regarding accountability.[208] 'Task expansion' has resulted in agencies having regulatory (or semi-regulatory) functions, such as issuing guidelines for national application of EU law.[209] Two trends are noted regarding ENISA: first, additional provisions regarding accountability – especially administrative accountability – being added to its founding regulation. This is the case with the 2013 ENISA regulation, to which 2012 Common Approach[210] provisions have been added (some of which are mentioned above). This is also true of the EU Cybersecurity Act. Second, the tasks assigned to ENISA have increased, and with the EU Cybersecurity Act they increase greatly, although its powers still remain in the domain of soft law. As we have discussed, this latter fact would tend to indicate a greater need for accountability as ENISA evolves into a more important agency, in terms of missions, budget, size and power.

While not a rule-making agency, ENISA is involved in identifying guidelines and best practices which are part of 'soft law' that allows data controllers to show compliance with security requirements under EU data protection law. If we look to the case of a rule-making agency developing 'soft law' contained in guidelines issued by another agency, the European Medicines Agency (EMA), these guidelines are non-legally binding but may be considered to have a 'quasi-binding character that can derive from the legal basis when the guideline intends to specify how to fulfil a legal obligation'.[211] While the situation of a non-rulemaking agency issuing guidelines is different, the point being made is that because of the importance of GDPR compliance and the fact that ENISA, the EU Cybersecurity Agency, has issued guidelines on this area of compliance, it could be argued that such 'soft law' likewise takes has a 'quasi-binding character', or, as Coman-Kund and Andone would say, an 'in-between' one, astride the boundary between legally-binding and non-legally-binding acts,[212] which would seem to argue for greater political accountability. Furthermore, certain academic legal theories posit that through coercive enforcement, soft law may become hard law, through judicial intervention, for example.[213] However,

208 Busuioc (n 1) 3–4. For an interesting and nuanced approach putting forward 'hybrid multilevel accountability' as a conceptual framework to address the accountability problems of EU agencies, see Florin Coman-Kund, 'Holding Europol Accountable: The Promise and Challenges of (Hybrid) Multilevel Accountability' (Chapter 12 in this volume).

209 Morten Egeberg and Jarle Trondal, 'Researching European Union Agencies: What Have We Learnt (and Where Do We Go from Here)?' (2017) 55(4) Journal of Common Market Studies 675.

210 European Parliament, Council of the EU and European Commission, 2012. Joint Statement of the European Parliament, Council of the EU and the European Commission on decentralized agencies and Annex (Common Approach), 19 July 2012, <https://europa.eu/european-union/sites/europaeu/files/docs/body/joint_statement_and_common_approach_2012_en.pdf>.

211 Chiti (n 189) 98.

212 Coman-Kund and Andone (n 66) 178.

213 Ştefan (n 63) 211.

any such enforcement would involve an indirect path between ENISA and, say, data protection authorities, or the Commission, prior to such enforcement. That is, data protection authorities could use soft law created by ENISA in order to find that a data controller had not met security requirements or privacy by design requirements under the GDPR. While there are Member State cybersecurity agencies and standardization bodies that also issue cybersecurity guidelines, which the data protection authorities could look to, it seems that from the perspective of legal certainty related to rule of law concerns, data controllers and processors should be able to rely on ENISA soft law instruments in order to prove their compliance with provisions of the GDPR, although in another field – competition law – discretion of Member State authorities has prevailed over individual expectations, and this has led one academic to comment that 'courts do not really enforce soft law, but the legal principles and values soft law is expected to foster'.[214] Moreover, when ENISA proposes candidate certification schemes under the Cybersecurity Act, a pre-law function, these have to be adopted by the Commission under an implementing act. Thus, there is a decisionmaker between ENISA and law-making as well as enforcement, which may be looked to for political accountability and whose decisions may be judicially reviewed.

Nonetheless, Rocca and Eliantonio argue that, as there is a general lack of ex post control with respect to agency soft law, there should be some form of ex ante control, and that 'the procedure that leads to the adoption of soft law becomes an important factor to establish the legitimacy of EU agencies' soft law-making'.[215] Arriving at such legitimacy involves transparency, which also is a concern discussed in the context of ex post accountability, although here the focus is on transparency specifically in the law-making that is of concern – allowing access to the soft-law documents, knowledge of 'who is accountable for the final document and who has to be consulted in the process'.[216] Rocca and Eliantonio divide agencies into four groups, based on the kinds of soft law they issue: (1) soft law measures that contain technical and specific guidelines, which explain requirements for compliance with specific EU law (as an example, EASA is placed in this group); (2) soft law measures that come in the form of technical guidelines, mainly helping explain the process for applications for sector-specific authorizations (EMA is an example); (3) soft law aimed at disseminating comprehensible and high-quality information and (4) soft law 'in the form of technical documents mainly addressed to the Commission in order to help it develop further EU legislation', such as recommendations on possible amendments to current legislation in the information security sector by ENISA, which they put in this category.[217]

214 Ibid 210–211.
215 Rocca and Eliantonio (n 11) 6.
216 Ibid 10.
217 Ibid 12–13.

This simplification ignores the multi-faceted role of work by agencies such as ENISA, whose work product in the area of cybersecurity and privacy by design may be considered to explain requirements for compliance with the data protection legislation – the GDPR – thus falling within the first category, and whose role is also to disseminate high-quality information – consistent with the third category. Although the claim is that ENISA should be expected to have a medium level of legitimacy,[218] as the soft law is internal in that it is addressed to the Commission, it may be more appropriate to have a high level of legitimacy for its work that fits into the first category, instead. In that category there is a higher level of proceduralization, with detailed rules as to public access to documents, and indicating who is accountable for the soft law issued, and separate rules of procedure explaining which stakeholders must be consulted in the decision-making process.[219] The real difference between EASA, in the first category, and ENISA, which has been placed by Rocca and Eliantonio in the fourth, is what they describe as 'participation'. In this category, EASA is described as having '[s]eparate detailed rules of procedure on how to adopt soft law (including the stakeholders to be consulted)'[220] and ENISA as having only '[g]eneral articles in the Regulation about the transparency of the agencies' procedures',[221] instead. This argues in favour of the implementation by ENISA of greater procedural rules on the adoption of soft law measures, as ex ante controls.

Moreover, the development of ENISA has been described (before the EU Cybersecurity Act) as part of an 'institution-building strategy that was adopted in the early 2000s'.[222] In its initial years, 'some cyber security policy issues were moved away from the EU institutions, including the European Parliament, the [Commission] and the Council, to bureaucratic institutions such as ENISA',[223] a non-elected body, which raises questions of political accountability, as well. Furthermore, ENISA acts in a highly technical area, where 'Member States and EU bodies rely on its substantial expertise on cybersecurity matters'.[224] While greater expertise could be built up in the EU institutions, so that they best be able to control the work of ENISA, this would negate the value of efficiency of an agency, and perhaps its independence as well.

Members of one of ENISA's governance structures, its Advisory Group, only have a right to attend Management Board meetings when invited, contrary to the non-voting stakeholder members of the Management Board, prior

218 In fact, in testing their hypotheses, the authors determine that ENISA has a low level of legitimacy, instead (ibid 28).

219 Ibid 15.

220 Ibid 20.

221 Ibid 27.

222 Jukka Ruohonen, Sami Hyrynsalmi and Ville Leppänen, 'An Outlook on the Institution Evolution of the European Union Cyber Security Apparatus' (2016) 33 Government Information Quarterly 746, 750.

223 Ibid 754.

224 European Commission, 2017b (n 181) 15.

to ENISA's 2013 governance structure reforms. Indeed, at that time the former stakeholder representatives on the Management Board who were thus not re-appointed, became members of the Permanent Stakeholders' Group, instead.[225] Thus, experts from stakeholders are not automatically included at meetings of the Management Board where important operational decisions are made. This may be seen as a weakness, given ENISA's role and the importance of the advisers' advice and connection to stakeholders. Although these advisers include five members from academia, certain commentators have criticized ENISA saying that it 'seems to intentionally distance itself particularly from academic research'.[226]

In addition, '[t]here is no other actor at EU level that supports such broad scope of network and information security stakeholders'.[227] The European Parliament committee with responsibility for ENISA is the Industry, Research and Energy Committee (ITRE).[228] However, there are many demands on the time of the Members of the European Parliament (MEPs), and high MEP turnover, which might limit the time that specific MEPs may have to build up the technical expertise necessary for properly providing administrative oversight in this area.[229] The result is that there may be the development of an oversight problem related to the fact that the agency is more expert on cybersecurity issues than the legislature,[230] indicating a concern for political accountability. This will become truer if ENISA obtains greater powers and is an area that merits further study.

Insofar as what Vos calls financial accountability is concerned, the Parliament plays a role through the discharge procedure.[231] It 'allows for a 'written dialogue' between the Committee on Budgetary Control and the relevant agency', often based on observations of the Court of Auditors, but it may also include issues from the agency's annual activity report or other issues the Parliament considers relevant,[232] thus extending to ongoing control of the agency and limiting its autonomy. There is also a verbal exchange between the committee and

225 ENISA, Decision No. MB/2014/7 of the Management Board of the European Union Agency for Network and Information Security on the Establishment and Operation of the Permanent Stakeholders' Group, 28 October 2014, <https://www.enisa.europa.eu/about-enisa/structure-organization/management-board/management-board-decisions/mb-decision-no-mb-2014-7-on-internal-rules-of-operation-of-psg>.

226 Ruohonen, Hyrynsalmi and Leppänen (n 222) 752.

227 Ibid, at 6.

228 Francis Jacobs, 'EU Agencies and the European Parliament' in Michelle Everson, Cosimo Monda and Ellen Vos (eds), *European Agencies in-between Institutions and Member States* (Kluwer Law International 2014) 213.

229 Ibid 227.

230 Busuioc (n 1) 59.

231 Vos (n 6) 9 ('financial accountability which concerns the role of the Commission's financial controller, the Council and the European Parliament as budgetary authorities, the latter of which is also responsible for the annual budgetary discharge and the Court of Auditors').

232 Busuioc (n 1) 180.

the agency, when considered necessary.[233] If one discharge of ENISA is taken as an example, it may be noted that there is extensive discussion of the agency's budget and staffing, of the agency's future whistleblowing policy, of transparency (for example, the lack of CVs and declaration of interest of the Management Board Members, and of the need for a 'proactive lobby transparency policy'), but there is no mention of any soft law measures which might have been included in ENISA's activity report.[234]

9 Concluding remarks

Information-providing agencies such as ENISA seem less problematic insofar as accountability is concerned, and we have seen that changes in ENISA's founding regulation have brought it into line with the Common Approach on EU Agencies, providing elements of accountability and control to an agency that has stood out because of its time limited mandate. However, we have also seen that, given ENISA role as a maker of soft-law, this one-size-fits all approach may not be suitable, especially insofar as what Rocca and Eliantonio call participation. The provisions implemented in order to ensure administrative accountability of ENISA may be seen by some to have been excessive, given the limited mission and small budget and staff of the agency, although it has been shown that checks, such as observations of the Court of Auditors, have provided grounds for improvement in ENISA's case. The recently adopted EU Cybersecurity Act increases ENISA's powers, and we have seen that the role that that agency plays in EU legislation in the fields of data protection, electronic privacy and cybersecurity, particularly through the creation of soft law, give it a stronger role than might otherwise be expected, although still in the realm of a contributor to policy, and a maker of soft law. This places it squarely within what Coman-Kund has described as agencies' being 'placed 'at a crossroads' between implementation and decision-making, between expertise and policy-making, in a complex environment populated with various actors from different levels of governance.[235] Part of the solution may be to implement ex ante control in the form of a greater proceduralization of law-making, as discussed by Rocca and Eliantonio. Finally, the oversight problem that might exist with respect to

233 Ibid 181.

234 Decision (EU) 2017/1690 of the European Parliament of 27 April 2017 on discharge in respect of the implementation of the budget of the European Union Agency for Network and Information Security for the financial year 2015, 2017 OJ L 252/267, 29 September 2017, and the attached Resolution (EU) 2017/1691 of the European Parliament of 27 April 2017 with observations forming an integral part of the decision on discharge in respect of the implementation of the budget of the European Union Agency for Network and Information Security for the financial year 2015, 2017 OJ L 252/268, 29 September 2017, <https://eur-lex.europa.eu/legal-content/EN/TXT/PDF/?uri=OJ:L:2017:252:FULL&from=EN>.

235 Coman-Kund (n 31) 53.

ENISA's cybersecurity expertise warrants further study and consideration in the context of accountability.

As a final thought, the area of cybersecurity is one where there is greater and greater need for centralized action and standards. Although cybersecurity has been argued to be almost exclusively the ambit of Member States, the EU has claimed nevertheless that it is 'too complex and too transnational in nature to be left to Member States'.[236] Consistent with this thought, and with the ongoing general trend to supranationalism of EU executive power noted by Vos (amongst others)[237] this may be the natural tendency for cybersecurity, too. Historical divisions between the original pillars act as a brake to this today. If at some future point the Member States could be convinced of the desirability of handling (and not merely coordinating or facilitating) cybersecurity at the EU level, ENISA might see its mission greatly increased, at which time the question of accountability for the agency, especially related to the 'expertification of decision-making',[238] would become all the more important.

236 Carrapico and Barrinha (n 37) 1266.

237 Vos (n 6) 18–19.

238 Eriksen (n 193) 1 (referring to Vibert's term 'rise of the unelected'). See for a comparison with the accountability regime of Europol, an expert EU agency entrusted with information-related and semi-operational tasks, Florin Coman-Kund, 'Holding Europol Accountable: The Promise and Challenges of (Hybrid) Multilevel Accountability' (Chapter 12 in this volume).

12 Holding Europol accountable

The promise and challenges of (hybrid) multilevel accountability

Florin Coman-Kund

1 Introduction

This chapter examines the mechanisms and instruments for holding Europol accountable for its activities, in particular as regards its data processing activities. Since the added value of Europol in the fight against crime lies mainly with its information-related tasks, it is essential that Europol has the expertise and technical capacity to collect, process, store and exchange safely high-quality information, as well as the capacity to analyse data. At the same time, the Agency must deliver in a particularly sensitive area, where its actions may impact on Union's security strategy and have far-reaching consequences for fundamental rights. In this respect, an adequate and effective accountability system is essential to keep Europol in check and ensure that the agency lives up to the requirements and expectations set by its relevant legal-policy framework.

One recurrent concern over time was the legal review/supervision and political scrutiny of Europol's activities, in particular those pertaining to personal data processing. The 2016 Europol Regulation has redesigned the Agency with a view to align its legal regime with the Lisbon Treaty and with the 2012 Common Approach on European Union (EU) agencies.[1] Notably Article 88 TFEU commanded a new legal framework for Europol providing for 'procedures for scrutiny of Europol's activities by the European Parliament (EP), together with national parliaments'. Another important novelty in the direction of aligning Europol to other EU agencies was the takeover by the European Data Protection Supervisor (EDPS) of the supervision over Europol's personal data processing, a role previously held by the Joint Supervisory Body (JSB) composed of representatives of national supervisory authorities.

1 Joint Statement of the European Parliament, the Council of the EU and the European Commission on decentralized agencies of 19 July 2012 (referred to hereafter as the 'Common Approach on EU agencies') <https://europa.eu/european-union/sites/europaeu/files/docs/body/joint_statement_and_common_approach_2012_en.pdf> accessed 6 July 2020.

While bearing the promise of enhancing Europol's democratic legitimacy, accountability and lawfulness of data processing,[2] the operation and effectiveness of the governance framework set up by the 2016 Europol Regulation still need to be assessed. Against this background, this chapter offers a preliminary analysis of Europol's accountability system with a focus on the recent parliamentary scrutiny and data protection mechanisms enshrined in Agency's current legal framework. This analysis is contextualized with reflections on the concept of accountability in a multilevel setting and by construing Europol's accountability as a fluid and encompassing process, rather than a clearly delineated and narrow notion. While Europol is an excellent illustration of the idea of multilevel accountability within the EU, we come to the tentative conclusion that more formal accountability does not necessarily mean more genuine scrutiny over Europol's activities. More time is needed to provide a comprehensive and accurate diagnosis of the functioning and effectiveness of Europol's current accountability system.

The chapter begins with conceptual considerations regarding accountability of EU agencies and of Europol in particular (Section 2). Next the role of Europol as an expert EU agency is outlined (Section 3), followed by a general overview of Europol's accountability regime (Section 4). The chapter then focusses on parliamentary scrutiny (Section 5) as a means of holding Europol politically accountable, followed by the more specialized personal data processing supervision of Europol's activities by expert bodies such as EDPS and national data protection authorities (Section 6). Lastly, the author looks at the interlinks between the two types of Europol's accountability examined, provides a more panoramic preliminary assessment of Europol's current accountability system (Section 7) and concludes with some broader conceptual reflections regarding the accountability of EU technocratic agencies in Union's multilevel governance system (Section 8).

2 Conceptual reflections regarding the accountability of EU technocratic bodies

For more than 20 years, accountability has been the 'buzzword' in academia and public policy.[3] From a rather obscure and technical term linked to bookkeeping in financial administration, accountability has made a quantum leap under the impetus of New Public Management to become an 'icon for good governance

2 Recitals 2 and 50 of the Preamble to Regulation (EU) 2016/794 of the European Parliament and of the Council of 11 May 2016 on the European Union Agency for Law Enforcement Cooperation (Europol) and replacing and repealing Council Decisions 2009/371/JHA, 2009/934/JHA, 2009/935/JHA, 2009/936/JHA and 2009/968/JHA [2016] OJ L135/53 (Europol Regulation).

3 See Madalina Busuioc, *European Agencies. Law and Practices of Accountability* (OUP 2013) 44–45.

both in the public and in the private sector'.[4] Today accountability is a 'chameleon-like term'[5] popular among political scientists, public administration experts, lawyers, managers and politicians,[6] performing 'all manner of analytical and rhetorical tasks'.[7] As such accountability is arguably also the victim of its own success, by turning into an increasingly vague and multifaceted concept[8] up to the point that it 'resembles a garbage can filled with good intentions, loosely defined concepts, and vague images of good governance'.[9] Accountability is linked in complex ways to other concepts such as 'control', 'responsibility', 'liability', 'responsiveness', 'transparency'.[10] Often the relationship between accountability and such concepts is not fully elucidated, prompting questions on partial or total overlap between the various categories. Reasons for this fuzziness could be, at least in part: (1) the enthusiastic reception of accountability in various disciplines; (2) the readiness to see in the newcomer the potential to better express new realities or even to identify it with more traditional notions; (3) the particular features of the legal-political systems within which accountability is used.

Mulgan and Bovens count amongst the scholars who made the most significant endeavours to clarify and delineate the concept of accountability in a public context. Their preference goes for a narrower version of public accountability featuring the following essential elements: (1) a social relationship (involving exercise of authority) between an actor and a forum; (2) exchanges entailing that the actor must explain and justify conduct while the forum can ask questions and pass judgment and (3) the actor may face consequences.[11] There are some variations between these two authors regarding the more detailed understanding of the main accountability elements. For instance, Mulgan confines accountability to external scrutiny and the application of sanctions,[12] whereas Bovens insists on accountability as a form of *ex post* scrutiny and takes a broader view on the consequences the actor may face.[13] While this more narrow vision on public accountability is increasingly embraced one way or the other in the current

4 Mark Bovens, 'Analysing and Assessing Public Accountability. A Conceptual Framework' (2006) European Governance Papers (EUROGOV) No. C-06-01, 7 <http://edoc.vifapol.de/opus/volltexte/2011/2459/pdf/egp_connex_C_06_01.pdf> accessed 22 May 2020.

5 Richard Mulgan, 'Accountability: An Ever-Expanding Concept' (2000) 78(3) Public Administration 555.

6 See Luc Verhey and Monica Claes, 'Introduction: Political Accountability in a European Perspective' in Luc Verhey, Hansko Broeksteeg and Ilse Van den Driessche (eds), *Political Accountability in Europe: Which Way Forward? A Traditional Concept of Parliamentary Democracy in an EU Context* (Europa Law Publishing 2008) 9.

7 Mulgan (n 5).

8 Ibid.

9 Bovens (n 4).

10 See Mulgan (n 5), Bovens (n 4).

11 Bovens (n 4) 9; Mulgan (n 5) 555–556.

12 Mulgan (n 5) 571.

13 Bovens (n 4) 9 and 31.

accountability scholarship,[14] the concept remains relatively elusive, takes many forms and shapes and is difficult to assess.[15]

On the one hand, some academics still embrace a more extensive view on accountability by attaching a prospective or *ex ante* dimension to it, such as the setting of standards enabling accountability.[16] In this respect, also the proponents of accountability as *ex post* scrutiny admit that in practice '[t]he line between retrospective accounting and proactive policy-making can be thin' as accountability 'is not only about control' but 'also about prevention'.[17] Also Mulgan conveys that the 'policy cycle' view assigning accountability to the later 'evaluation' and 'correction' stages of the policy process is rather artificial as 'issues of external evaluation and accountability impinge at all stages of actual policy making through the "law of anticipated reactions"'.[18]

On the other hand, even in its narrowest sense, the concrete content and operationalization of public accountability depend ultimately on the theoretical perspectives behind this concept and the vision regarding the political system within which it operates.[19] First, one may identify a plethora of forms of accountability along the 'who', 'to whom', 'for what'' and 'how' questions. In one of the most extensive and systematic overviews of accountability types, Bovens

14 See for instance, Luc Verhey, Hansko Broeksteeg and Ilse Van den Driessche (eds), *Political Accountability in Europe: Which Way Forward? A Traditional Concept of Parliamentary Democracy in an EU Context* (Europa Law Publishing 2008); Busuioc, *European Agencies: Law and Practices of Accountability* (n 3); Miroslava Scholten and Michiel Luchtman (eds), *Law Enforcement by EU Authorities. Implications for Political and Judicial Accountability* (Edward Elgar 2017).

15 For some notable attempts to operationalize and measure accountability based on various indicators and indexes, see David and Keith Dixon 'The Public Accountability Index: Crafting a Parametric Disclosure Index for Annual Reports' (2004) 36(1) The British Accounting Review 79; Monica Blagescu, Lucy de Las Casas and Robert Lloyd 'Pathways to Accountability: The Global Accountability Framework' (One World Trust 2005) <http://www.oneworldtrust.org/uploads/1/0/8/9/108989709/pathways_to_accountability_the_gap_framework__lo_res_.pdf> accessed 10 June 2020; Robert Lloyd, Jeffrey Oatham and Michael Hammer, '2007 Global Accountability Report' (One World Trust 2007); Fabian Amtenbrink, 'Towards an Index of Accountability for Informal International Lawmakers?' in Joost Pauwelyn, Ramses Wessel and Jan Wouters (eds), *Informal International Lawmaking* (OUP 2012) 337–356; Mark Bovens and Anchrit Wille, Indexing Watchdog Accountability Powers a Framework for Assessing the Accountability Capacity of Independent Oversight Institutions (2020) Regulation & Governance 1–21 available at <https://onlinelibrary.wiley.com/doi/full/10.1111/rego.12316> accessed 6 July 2020.

16 See Anne Davies, *Accountability: A Public Law Analysis of Government by Contract* (OUP 2001) 81; Carol Harlow, *Accountability in the European Union* (OUP 2002) 10; Elizabeth Fisher, 'The European Union in the Age of Accountability' (2004) 24(3) Oxford Journal of Legal Studies 495, 510; Deirdre Curtin, 'Holding (Quasi-)Autonomous EU Administrative Actors to Public Account' (2007) 13(4) European Law Journal 523, 525; see also Alessandra Arcuri and Florin Coman-Kund, 'Introduction: Breaking Taboos, Talking Accountability' (in this volume).

17 Bovens (n 4) 13.

18 Mulgan (n 5) 564.

19 See Bovens (n 4) 25–27 and 30–31.

identifies political, legal, administrative, professional and social accountability (according to the nature of the forum), corporate, hierarchical, collective and individual accountability (depending on the nature of the actor), financial, procedural and product accountability (based on the nature of the conduct), and vertical, diagonal and horizontal accountability (in view of the nature of the obligation to account).[20] This reveals the image of a comprehensive accountability 'toolbox' featuring multiple channels and raising questions about the interplay between the various accountability avenues.[21] Here issues of accountability overlap, accountability overload, complementarity or mutual exclusivity of accountability mechanisms come to the fore.

Second, it is possible to take different perspectives/approaches to accountability depending on the context in which it operates and the function assigned to it. For instance, Bovens looks at accountability from a democratic, a constitutional, a cybernetic as well as a legitimacy perspective, each approach being grounded in a different theoretical setting and entailing different implications for accountability relations.[22] Multiple perspectives on accountability make it obviously difficult to evaluate accountability arrangements.[23] What is more, even within one perspective on accountability, questions arise about the concrete understanding of the yardsticks used for assessing accountability (e.g. how do we construe democratic scrutiny, checks and balances, good governance, sufficient reporting, appropriate sanctions, etc.).[24] Adding to this, accountability regimes are likely to shape differently in different institutional-political systems, be it a state, an intergovernmental organization or a multilevel polity like the EU. In this respect, the meaning, working and assessment of public accountability are inextricably linked to the understanding of the core concepts, principles and theories defining the foundations and functioning of a political system.[25]

Hence discussing accountability in the EU context entails understanding the very nature and fundamentals of the Union.[26] In our view essential features of the EU are its supranational and multilevel character. The former entails a transfer of sovereign powers from the Member States to the EU institutional framework, further shared and exercised according to principles and safeguards enshrined in the Founding Treaties. The latter highlights the composite nature of EU decision-making entailing a complex interplay between EU-level actors

20 Ibid 22.

21 See Richard Mulgan, 'The Processes of Public Accountability' (1997) 56(1) Australian Journal of Public Administration 25, 30–31.

22 Bovens (n 4) 24–27.

23 Ibid 30.

24 Ibid.

25 See ibid 30–31.

26 See Fisher (n 16) 511–512; for an excellent account of key perspectives on the nature of the EU and how these are reflected in the debates regarding the legitimacy and accountability of the Union, see Mark Bovens, Deirdre Curtin and Paul 't Hart, 'The Quest for Legitimacy and Accountability in EU Governance' in Mark Bovens, Deirdre Curtin and Paul 't Hart (eds), *The Real World of EU Accountability. What Deficit?* (OUP 2010) 9–30.

and the Member States.[27] The EU could thus be seen as a complex *sui generis* transnational governance system rather than a full-fledged political order comparable to a state.[28] This would allow dealing with most issues of democratic legitimacy at the level of Member States and focusing at EU level on the exercise of regulatory governance. This discussion, mirroring Majone's view on legitimizing EU as a regulatory state[29] would entail placing at the centre of discussion the issue of exercising and controlling EU-conferred powers.[30] This could still include an important degree of democratic control but would alleviate to some extent the inexorable EU democratic deficit accusation.

In view of the complex and varying intermingling between EU and national actors, a multilevel accountability model is perhaps best suited in the EU context.[31] Multilevel accountability would entail multiple actors, fora and channels at both EU and Member State levels corresponding to Union's shared legal order.[32] This allows using to the fullest the comprehensive accountability 'arsenal' depicted by Bovens in a variety of combinations depending on the specific situation and context. Such an encompassing accountability model raises inevitably issues of 'too many eyes' or 'too many hands'.[33] Hence the challenge is to fine-tune the accountability toolbox according to the characteristics of the actors, fora, activity scrutinized, aims pursued in such a way as to avoid accountability gaps and overkills or to get around the risks associated to having too much multi-polar accountability.[34]

The multilevel accountability model seems particularly fit for EU agencies as 'in-betweeners' positioned between EU institutions and the Member States,[35] as 'central nodes' of regulatory networks,[36] or as factors fostering 'pluralisation of the EU executive' through the exercise of powers extracted from the Member States and through the coordination of Member States' administrations within the

27 See Deirdre Curtin, *Executive Power of the European Union. Law, Practices, and the Living Constitution* (OUP 2009).
28 See Harlow (n 16) 179–181.
29 Giandomenico Majone, 'Europe's Democratic Deficit: The Question of Standards' (1998) 4(1) European Law Journal 5.
30 Fisher (n 16) 508.
31 Colin Scott, 'Accountability in the Regulatory State' (2000) 27(1) Journal of Law and Society 38, 54; on the concept and the various dimensions of accountability in present-day global governance, see Alessandra Arcuri, 'Three Dimensions of Accountability for Global Technocracy' (Chapter 3 in this volume).
32 For a discussion on accountability in a Union's shared legal order, see Miroslava Scholten, Michiel Luchtman and Elgar Schmidt, 'The Proliferation of EU Enforcement Authorities: A New Development in Law Enforcement in the EU' in Scholten and Luchtman (n 14) 12–13.
33 Bovens (n 4) 15–20.
34 See on this Harlow (n 16) 183–184.
35 See Ellen Vos, 'EU Agencies on the Move: Challenges Ahead' [2018] 1 SIEPS 6, 8, 10, 20, 45–46 available at <https://espas.secure.europarl.europa.eu/orbis/sites/default/files/generated/document/en/EU%20agencies.pdf> accessed 6 July 2020.
36 Giandomenico Majone, 'Delegation of Regulatory Powers in a Mixed Polity' (2002) 8 (3) European Law Journal 319.

framework of EU policy implementation.[37] In view of their nature, EU agencies can be said to have multiple principals (both EU-level institutions, such as the EP, the Council or the Commission, and the Member States)[38] which in turn results in multiple and complex accountability relationships. Since more often than not EU agencies are delegated powers that have been exercised previously by the Member States and they rely extensively on the cooperation of Member States for exercising their powers, it seems logical that the latter can maintain some oversight over EU agencies' activities. This is one of the main premises upon which the managerial accountability (via the management or administrative board composed mostly of representatives of the Member States) of EU agencies is premised.[39] Same goes for Europol's political accountability (via the EP and national parliaments), as shown later in this chapter. The technocratic nature of EU agencies and the limits set on their powers via the so-called *Meroni* doctrine and the principle of institutional balance[40] also result in a plethora of EU-level accountability regimes and arrangements intertwined in sophisticated ways. Thus, EU agencies are generally subject to some political accountability via the Council and the EP, to administrative accountability via the Commission, the European Court of Auditors, the European Ombudsman, OLAF and other specialized EU bodies (e.g. the EDPS), and to judicial accountability via the EU courts.[41] Hence it is argued that the hybrid (supranational and intergovernmental) nature of EU agencies entails a *hybrid multilevel accountability* system whereby both EU level institutions and Member States are involved in holding these EU technocratic bodies to account.

Finally, building on the view expressed by Harlow and Fischer, we opt for a more *fluid* understanding of the accountability of EU agencies. Such an understanding, which in our view best reflects the reality of accountability relationships, encompasses not solely an *ex post* evaluation of past conduct, but also a forward-looking perspective aimed at shaping future behaviour of these bodies. As such accountability is seen as a continuous process/cycle that entails informing and explaining, inquiring and debating, and passing judgement both over past and future conduct of the actor.[42]

37 See Herwig C.H. Hofmann and Alessandro Morini, 'Constitutional Aspects of the Pluralisation of the EU Executive through "Agencification"' (2012) 37(4) European Law Review 419, 436–438 and 441–443.

38 Curtin, 'Holding (Quasi-)Autonomous EU Administrative Actors to Public Account' (n 16) 528.

39 See Busuioc (n 3) 75–113.

40 For an extensive analysis of the principle of institutional balance and the *Meroni* doctrine, see Merijn Chamon, *EU Agencies: Legal and Political Limits to the Transformation of the EU Administration* (OUP 2016) 175–298.

41 See Busuioc (n 3) 75–113.

42 See Alessandra Arcuri and Florin Coman-Kund, 'Introduction: Breaking Taboos, Talking Accountability' (in this volume). This may happen, for instance, when the forum debates and passes judgment both over past activity reports and over actors' work programme and strategy for next year(s); for a different view, excluding agencies' work programme from the sphere of accountability due to its *ex ante* character, see Busuioc (n 3) 118.

3 Europol as an expert agency[43]

The establishment of Europol was announced by the Treaty of Maastricht, which provided in Article K.1 for a European Police Office (Europol) in the framework of an EU system of exchanging information in the field of police cooperation. Europol was established on the basis of the 1995 Europol Convention[44] and finally became operational on 1 July 1999. Thus, initially Europol was a 'fully fledged international organisation', equipped with 'full legal personality, including the capacity to enter into binding agreements under international law',[45] or at least a 'European organisation sui generis of the EU'.[46]

From the very beginning, the centre of gravity of Europol's mandate was on information processing and exchange tasks.[47] Although the tasks of Europol have been gradually expanded including the possibility to participate in joint investigation teams (JITs), this body remained essentially a non-operational support organization for the enforcement authorities of the Member States.[48] This role of Europol has been enabled in particular through the liaison officers posted by the Member States at Europol's headquarters, as well as through the Europol National Units (ENUs) established in the Member States as an interface between this body and the national competent authorities.[49]

An important milestone in the evolution of Europol was its transformation into an EU agency by Council Decision 2009/371/JHA (Europol Council Decision).[50] As a result, from 2010 Europol was financed from the EU budget, subjected to staff regulations, and all relevant EU rules.[51] However, Europol remained a somewhat special 'third pillar' agency, and its mandate, tasks and

43 The analysis in this section is partly based on Florin Coman-Kund, *European Union Agencies as Global Actors. A Legal Study of the European Aviation Safety Agency, Frontex and Europol* (Routledge 2018) 217–219.

44 Convention based on Article K 3 of the Treaty on the European Union, on the establishment of a European Police Office (Europol Convention) [1995] OJ C316/1; the Europol Convention can be best described as an intergovernmental agreement concluded by the Member States within the framework of the EU, see Conny Rijken, 'Legal and Technical Aspects of Co-operation between Europol, Third States, and Interpol' in Vincent Kronenberger (ed), *The European Union and the International Legal Order: Discord or Harmony?* (Asser Press 2001) 582–583.

45 Dick Heimans, 'The External Relations of Europol – Political, Legal and Operational Considerations' in Berndt Martenczuk and Servaas van Thiel (eds), *Justice, Liberty and Security: New Challenges for EU External Relations* (VUBPRESS 2008) 369.

46 Rijken (n 44) 583.

47 Heimans (n 45) 369–370.

48 Ibid.

49 Ibid.

50 Council Decision 2009/371/JHA of 6 Apr. 2009 establishing the European Police Office (Europol) [2009] OJ L 131/37.

51 See Steve Peers, *EU Justice and Home Affairs Law* (OUP 2011) 932.

governance did not undergo radical changes,[52] except perhaps for moving the emphasis from 'organised' to 'serious' crime as regards Agency's competence.[53]

In line with Europol's previous legal framework and practice, Article 88 (1) TFEU enshrines Europol as a supportive structure for the enforcement authorities of the Member States. Hence Agency's role is to assist the real operational actors at state level, and not to act as a 'European FBI' with full-fledged investigative and enforcement powers. Europol's current Treaty legal basis also extends Agency's mandate with the category of crimes affecting EU interests and commands interparliamentary democratic scrutiny over Europol's activities.

The 2016 Europol Regulation, based on Article 88 TFEU, maintains the core principles upon which the role and functioning of Europol are premised, but also brings some noteworthy novelties. Thus, in line with Article 88 TFEU, it supplements Europol's competence with 'forms of crime which affect a common interest covered by a Union policy'.[54] Next, it enhances Europol's analytical and operational capacity by formalizing Agency's power to set up specialized centres for combatting crime such as the European Cybercrime Centre, and by enabling the Agency to make internet referrals to online service providers.[55] Moreover, it seeks to consolidate Europol's information-related tasks by establishing an obligation for the Member States to provide information to the Agency.[56] What is more, it aims to strengthen through the involvement of the EDPS the supervision over Europol's processing of personal data,[57] and to increase parliamentary supervision over Europol's activities.[58] While important peculiarities still persist,[59] overall the Europol Regulation can be seen as an important step towards transforming Europol from a 'special' Area of Freedom, Security and Justice (AFSJ) agency into a 'regular' EU agency.

An apt understanding of Europol as an expert agency requires a closer look at Agency's mandate and tasks to pinpoint what this Agency is actually doing. Inside the crime areas included within its mandate,[60] Europol's main tasks can be roughly divided into three main categories:[61] information-related tasks; strategic/operational analysis and threat assessment tasks; and semi-operational tasks (e.g. the possibility to ask competent authorities of the Member States to

52 One of the notable upgrades brought by the Europol Council Decision pertain to the possibility for the Agency to establish new data processing systems (Article 10); see also Alexandra de Moor and Gert Vermeulen, 'The Europol Council Decision: Transforming Europol into an Agency of the European Union' (2010) 47(4) Common Market law Review 1089, 1097–1104 and 1120–1121.

53 Article 4 (1) Europol Council Decision; see also Moor and Vermeulen (n 52) 1121.

54 Article 3(1) of Regulation 2016/794.

55 Article 4 (1) (l) and (m) of Regulation 2016/794.

56 Recital (13) and Article 7 (6) of Regulation 2016/794.

57 Recitals (50)–(54) and Article 43 of Regulation 2016/794.

58 Recital (58) and Articles 51–52 of Regulation 2016/794.

59 Such as maintaining a special data processing and protection regime for Europol.

60 See Article 3(1) and Annex I of Regulation 2016/794.

61 See Article 4 of Regulation 2016/794.

initiate investigations and to participate in JITs).[62] Of all the three categories, the information-related tasks define the 'core business' of the Agency,[63] followed by its threat assessment and analysis tasks. In particular, the ability to facilitate the exchange of (personal and non-personal) information between the Member States, third countries and international organizations, as well as the capacity to process information, including intelligence, confer added value to Europol.[64] Furthermore, expertise is crucial as regards Agency's capacity to deliver high-quality threat assessments and analysis reports supporting EU policy-making in the fight against serious international and organized crime. In short, Europol's distinctive expertise lies in its capacity to act as the Union's information hub in the field of serious cross-border crime, processing and exchanging personal and non-personal data as well as providing intelligence analyses and threat assessments.[65]

With a view to fulfil its role, Europol is equipped with the Europol Information System (EIS) and a secure information exchange network application (SIENA). The EIS is a database enabling the Agency and the Member States to store and exchange criminal intelligence, and cross-check personal data regarding persons suspected or convicted for committing crimes within Europol's remit.[66] Europol and Member States via their ENUs may directly enter/retrieve data into/from the EIS; in line with the data owner principle, 'only the party which entered the data into the system may modify, correct or delete them'.[67] While most of the data in the EIS is provided by the Member States, Europol may also collect its own (personal) data from public sources (e.g. internet, online platforms) or receive data from other EU bodies, third countries and international organizations, and private parties/persons.[68] SIENA facilitates the secure exchange of information between Member States, Europol, other Union bodies, third countries and international organizations, being an essential element enabling Europol to become an EU information hub on cross-border crime.

62 See Elspeth Guild, Sergio Carrera, Leonhard den Hertog, Joanna Parkin, 'Implementation of the EU Charter of Fundamental Rights and its Impact on EU Home Affairs Agencies. Frontex, Europol and the European Asylum Support Office', Study for the European Parliament, Committee on Civil Liberties, Justice and Home Affairs (LIBE) (PE 453.196/2011) 27–29 <http://www.europarl.europa.eu/meetdocs/2009_2014/documents/libe/dv/02_study_fundamental_rights_/02_study_fundamental_rights_en.pdf>.

63 Moor and Vermeulen (n 52) 1099.

64 Guild et al (n 62) 27.

65 See European Union Agency for Fundamental Rights and Council of Europe, Handbook on European Data Protection Law (2018 edition) 300–301 <https://fra.europa.eu/sites/default/files/fra_uploads/fra-coe-edps-2018-handbook-data-protection_en.pdf>.

66 See Florin Coman-Kund, 'Europol's International Exchanges of Data and Interoperability of AFSJ Databases' (2020) 26(1) European Public Law 181, 191.

67 Handbook on European Data Protection Law (n 65) 301.

68 Articles 17 and 23–27 Europol Regulation; see also Handbook on European Data Protection Law (n 65) 301.

Europol Regulation brought a fundamental change in approach as regards data processing by the Agency.[69] It replaced the provisions on pre-defined and separate data processing systems in the 2009 Europol Council Decision (the so-called 'silo approach') with a new information structure focusing on the purposes for which data is being processed.[70] Thus, Europol Regulation enables the Agency to process personal data for the following purposes: (1) cross-checking aimed at identifying connections between information related to crimes within Europol's mandate; (2) strategic or thematic analyses; (3) operational analyses; (4) facilitating exchanges of information between Member States, Europol and other EU bodies, as well as third countries and international organizations.[71] This new data processing approach based on the 'data integrated management'[72] concept obviously offers more flexibility and increased information-related powers to Europol potentially enhancing Agency's operational effectiveness.[73] Yet this approach also raises serious concerns as regards the principles of purpose limitation and data minimization, and requires effective safeguards and controls.[74] In particular the possibility for Europol to cross-match data collected for different purposes and across different databases, as well as the extended Member States' access to Europol data[75] are problematic from a data protection perspective.[76]

The current regulation seeks to upgrade Europol as Union's information hub and centre of expertise in cross-border serious crime by granting the Agency wide possibilities to access and retrieve through computerized means information, including personal data, from EU, international and national databases.[77]

69 This paragraph is taken over and adapted from Coman-Kund, *European Union Agencies as Global Actors* (n 43) 192–193.
70 EDPS Opinion 31/13 on the Proposal for a Regulation of the European Parliament and of the Council on the European Union Agency for Law Enforcement Cooperation and Training (Europol) and repealing Decisions 2009/371/JHA and 2005/681/JHA (31 May 2013) 8–9.
71 Article 18 Europol Regulation.
72 See Daniel Drewer and Vesela Miladinova, 'The BIG DATA Challenge: Impact and Opportunity of Large Quantities of Information Under the Europol Regulation' (2017) 33 Computer Law & Security Review 298, 304–305; these authors define integrated data management as 'the possibility to use crime-related information for multiple business purposes as indicated by the data owner, allowing for its management and processing in an integrated, technology neutral manner' (305).
73 EDPS Opinion 31/13 (n 70), at 10–11.
74 Ibid, at 11–13.
75 See Article 20 Europol Regulation.
76 Coman-Kund, 'Europol's International Exchanges of Data and Interoperability of AFSJ Databases' (n 66) 193.
77 Article 17 Europol Regulation; this trend is further exacerbated by the two recent 'Interoperability Regulations' (Regulation 2019/817 and Regulation 2019/818) enabling Europol to access *inter alia* non-law enforcement databases established in the Area of Freedom, Security and Justice (AFSJ) – see Coman-Kund, 'Europol's International Exchanges of Data and Interoperability of AFSJ Databases' (n 66).

To cope with the quickly evolving digital world, Europol is also required to use new information technologies for data processing and the most efficient IT-structures for its databases 'to swiftly detect links between investigations and common *modi operandi* across different criminal groups, to check cross-matches of data and to have a clear overview of trends'.[78] In this context, the use by Europol of potentially intrusive big data in order to enhance its analytical capacity in preventing and combatting serious crime brings particular tensions as regards compliance with data protection principles and fundamental rights.[79]

The role of Europol as an expert body becomes more visible also through its specialized centres targeting crimes deemed significant and entailing a certain degree of sophistication.[80] Such centres are, most famously, the European Cybercrime Centre (EC3), but also, more recently, the European Counter Terrorism Centre (ECTC) and the European Migrant Smuggling Centre (EMSC). These specialized centres monitor and investigate trends and patterns in their area of expertise, offer forensic and technical assistance, and they provide information and analytical products supporting strategic decision-making but also law enforcement operations.[81]

As already mentioned, an important domain of Europol's expertise lies in its capacity to deliver high-quality analysis in the area of cross border crime. Europol's legal framework makes a basic distinction between strategic analysis (more generic, preventive in nature and supporting policy-making in the fight against crime) and operational analysis (more targeted in nature and aimed at supporting criminal investigations).[82] Europol's strategic analysis materializes in situation reports, thematic reports and threat assessments, such as the Internet Organised Crime Threat Assessment (IOCTA) and the Serious and Organised Crime Threat Assessment (SOCTA). IOCTA provides each year key findings on emerging threats and developments in cybercrime, and key recommendations to law enforcement, policymakers and regulators to tackle cybercrime in an effective and concerted manner.[83] SOCTA represents a comprehensive analysis of major crime threats and it recommends priority crime areas that should be the focus of EU operational response.[84] SOCTA is claimed to be 'the cornerstone of the EU Policy Cycle for Serious and Organised Crime' as the JHA Council takes

78 Recital 24 of the Preamble to Europol Regulation.
79 See for an analysis of the challenges and opportunities regarding the use of big data by Europol, Drewer and Miladinova (n 72).
80 See Article 4 (1) (l) Europol Regulation.
81 Handbook on European Data Protection Law (n 65) 301–302.
82 See Article 2 (b) and (c) Europol Regulation; see also Drewer and Miladinova (n 72) 306.
83 Europol, Internet Organized Crime Threat Assessment <https://www.europol.europa.eu/activities-services/main-reports/internet-organised-crime-threat-assessment> accessed 2 June 2020.
84 Europol, Serious and Organised Crime Threat Assessment. Crime in the Age of Technology (2017) 7 <https://www.europol.europa.eu/activities-services/main-reports/european-union-serious-and-organised-crime-threat-assessment-2017> accessed 2 June 2020.

Europol's SOCTA recommendations into account for defining the EU priorities in fighting crime for a four-year period.[85] As for Europol's operational analysis, this entails processing of personal data and intelligence to support concrete criminal investigations and enforcement operations carried out in the Member States.[86] Operational analysis currently takes place within the framework of specific operational analysis projects (OAP) subject to strict requirements regarding the purpose, the categories of data and the individuals involved, the participants, data retention period, conditions for access and any proposed transfer or use of the data concerned.

Strategic analysis is important 'to maintain an accurate picture of crime (…) and related developments, to inform decisions on priority areas for criminal investigations, the development of joint strategies to counter the main threats, and the prioritisation of resources for those purposes'.[87] Within the key focus areas identified by strategic analysis, more targeted thematic analysis can be carried out to better understand dynamics and threats with a view to finally direct the targeting of key criminal networks and processes via operational analysis.[88]

With Europol's expertise being located in the field of criminal and forensic investigation techniques in combination with information/intelligence processing and analysis in the area of cross-border serious crime, an important caveat needs to be taken into account for a proper understanding of Agency's position and operation within the EU framework. This pertains to the fact that somehow paradoxically, while Europol has been created to support Member States, it is also heavily dependent on Member States' support in order to function properly. Thus, most of the information/intelligence entered into EIS and exchanged via SIENA comes from the Member States, who remain the owners of the information provided.[89] Also the strategic/operational analysis carried out by the Agency often requires the cooperation of the Member States. In the past, Europol's effectiveness has been vigorously undercut by the lack of cooperation of national enforcement authorities, preferring to work on an informal bilateral basis rather than through Europol.[90] Europol Regulation attempts to address this by compelling Member States to provide information to the Agency and by expanding Agency's own information capacities. Yet the need for Europol to work closely with the Member States' enforcement authorities in order to fulfil its mandate will always

85 Ibid.

86 See EDPS, Annual Report 2019, 39 <https://edps.europa.eu/data-protection/our-work/publications/annual-reports/2019-annual-report-year-transition_en> accessed 2 June 2020.

87 Drewer and Miladinova (n 72) 306.

88 Ibid.

89 See Article 19 Europol Regulation.

90 Madalina Busuioc, Deirdre Curtin and Martijn Groenleer, 'Agency Growth between Autonomy and Accountability: the European Police Office as a "Living Institution"' (2011) 18(6) Journal of European Public Policy 848, 857.

be there and will remain a challenge for the Agency.[91] Thus, a multilevel approach considering the interplay between the Union and Member States is required when examining the operation of an EU technocratic agency like Europol. The same goes for the accountability of Europol, discussed in the next sections.

4 General overview of Europol's accountability regime

Europol's accountability regime over time followed Agency's evolution path from an intergovernmental body to an EU agency. From the times of the Europol Convention when Agency's scrutiny was almost exclusively the domain of the Council, Europol's Management Board and the JSB,[92] the accountability arsenal has been gradually expanded with more supranational supervisory mechanisms (EP oversight, involvement of the Commission and the Court of Auditors, judicial review) once Europol turned into an EU agency.[93] Under the current Europol Regulation, Agency's formal accountability regime has been further aligned with the Lisbon Treaty and the Common Approach on EU agencies. At present, Europol's accountability regime features, similarly to other EU agencies,[94] diverse accountability mechanisms and arrangements encompassing multiple accountability types (administrative, managerial,[95] financial, political, legal) and various accountability fora (the Council, the Commission, the EP and national parliaments, the Court of Auditors, the European Anti-Fraud Office (OLAF), the European Ombudsman, the CJEU, the EDPS, Europol's Management Board). In this context, the intensity, actual operation and interplay between the multifarious accountability processes and channels are highly relevant for assessing overloads, overlaps or gaps in Europol's accountability regime.[96]

A comprehensive assessment of Europol's overall accountability regime is beyond the scope of this chapter. Instead, the remainder of this contribution focusses on parliamentary scrutiny and data processing supervision (mainly by EDPS) over Europol's activities. The choice for these two accountability mechanisms lies in the

91 Ibid 861.

92 Established as an independent body outside the structure of the Agency, the JSB was Europol's data protection control authority – Heimans (n 45) 371. It was composed of representatives of national supervisory bodies, and its main task was to review all the relevant activities of the Agency in order to ensure that the rights of the individuals are not violated by the storage and processing of data held by the Agency (see Article 34 of the 2009 Europol Council Decision).

93 See for an informative analysis, Busuioc, Curtin and Groenleer (n 90) 854–861.

94 See for a comprehensive monographic study on the accountability of EU agencies, Busuioc (n 3).

95 According to Article 16(1) Europol Regulation, Agency's Executive Director '(...) shall be accountable to the Management Board'.

96 See Busuioc, Curtin and Groenleer (n 90) 861–863. For a comprehensive analysis of the accountability regime of another EU expert agency with somewhat lighter powers in data protection and cybersecurity, see W. Gregory Voss, 'The Concept of Accountability in the Context of the Evolving Role of ENISA in Data Protection, ePrivacy and Cybersecurity' (Chapter 11 in this volume).

fact that they are very good illustrations of the '(hybrid) multilevel accountability' concept as regards Europol, as well as in the fact that they have been recently recalibrated by the 2016 Europol Regulation in response to calls for making Europol more transparent and accountable.[97] Additionally, personal data processing supervision is really about the core of Europol's activities and therefore, it presumably scores high within Agency's accountability arsenal. Hence, looking closer at the design, working and interplay between Europol's redesigned political-democratic (parliamentary scrutiny) and the administrative-specialized data processing accountability processes may provide valuable insights regarding the success of the reforms undertaken to improve Europol's accountability as a hybrid expert EU agency.

5 The democratic accountability of Europol: Inquiring into the appropriateness of multilevel parliamentary scrutiny

One of the recurring accusations pertaining to the accountability deficit of EU agencies is the lack of sufficient democratic scrutiny, in particular by the EP, over their activities.[98] This holds especially for Europol in view of its secretive and potentially intrusive police work, coupled with its strong intergovernmental pedigree. Under the 1995 Europol Convention the accountability relationship between the Agency and the EP was almost non-existent; it amounted to no more than some form of indirect reporting[99] entailing that the Council would send the EP Europol's annual report and work programme.[100] Beside this, the EP was powerless with regard to the Agency, except perhaps for manifesting repeatedly its discontent for being brushed aside in accountability and decision-making processes concerning Europol.[101] However, the parliaments of the participating Member States had arguably a more prominent formal role in holding the intergovernmental Europol accountable. Such role could be exercised via their powers to adopt/ratify amendments to the Europol Convention and its implementing acts,[102] as well as through their eventual supervisory powers over national representatives in Agency's Management Board.[103]

Parliamentary accountability has been enhanced, at least on paper, when Europol was transformed into an EU agency. Beside extending EP's information

97 See Recitals (50)–(51) and (58) of the Preamble to Europol Regulation.
98 See Busuioc (n 3) 115.
99 Article 34 of the Europol Convention.
100 Busuioc (n 3) 118.
101 Busuioc, Curtin and Groenleer (n 90) 857–858.
102 See Valentin Kreilinger, 'A Watchdog over Europe's Policemen: The New Joint Parliamentary Scrutiny Group for Europol' (2017) Policy Paper No. 197, Jacques Delors Institut (Berlin) 9 available at <https://hertieschool-f4e6.kxcdn.com/fileadmin/user_upload/20170612_WatchdogoverEuropol-Kreilinger-1.pdf> accessed 6 July 2020.
103 Vigilenca Abazi, 'The Future of Europol's Parliamentary Oversight: A Great Leap Forward' (2014) 15 German Law Journal 1121, 1130.

rights with the external evaluation reports concerning Europol's activities,[104] the 2009 Europol Council Decision also formalized the duty of the Chairperson of the Management Board and the Director to appear before the EP at its request.[105] In practice this duty was discharged before the specialized EP Committee on Civil Liberties, Justice and Home Affairs (LIBE Committee), where the Chairperson and the Director would answer questions concerning Europol's performance and engage in a dialogue with Members of the European Parliament (MEPs).[106] What is more, the EP gained important leverage over Europol by exercising the power of the purse as a budgetary and discharge authority for the Agency.[107]

The Lisbon Treaty announced further transformations regarding Europol's democratic accountability. Article 88 TFEU further consolidated EP's position vis-à-vis Europol by assigning the role of co-legislator to the former with regard to the mandate and operation of the Agency. Most relevant for this contribution, it stipulated as an essential element for future legislative reforms the setting-up of specific procedures for parliamentary scrutiny over Europol's activities. It is for the first time that the Founding Treaties provide explicitly for parliamentary scrutiny over an EU agency.[108] More remarkably, the Founding Treaties acknowledge Europol's hybrid nature and its former 'third pillar' pedigree (things are similar for Eurojust) by subjecting the Agency to scrutiny by both the EP and national parliaments. In this respect, the involvement of national parliaments in holding Europol accountable needs to be linked to the general clause on the participation of national parliaments in Union's activities enshrined in Article 12 TEU. That provision foresees inter-parliamentary cooperation between the EP and national parliaments, and it stipulates political monitoring of Europol's activities as one of the core elements of national parliaments' involvement in the AFSJ.

The next logical step was the adoption of the 2016 Europol Regulation shaping the details of the parliamentary scrutiny clause in Article 88 TFEU. Compared to the previous legal framework, the current regulation formally enhances parliamentary scrutiny of Europol's activities. First, as a pre-condition to effective scrutiny, EP's information rights are further consolidated with the explicit possibility to gain access, under certain conditions, to sensitive non-classified information and also to classified information processed by or through Europol.[109] Second, the Joint Parliamentary

104 Article 37 (11) Europol Council Decision.

105 Article 48 Europol Council Decision.

106 See Busuioc (n 3) 122–123.

107 Articles 42–43 Europol Council Decision; in practice EP's budgetary role vis-à-vis Europol is exercised via the Committee on Budgets and the Budgetary Control Committee (CONT), see also Busuioc (n 3) 122.

108 It should be noted that beside Europol, the Lisbon Treaty inserted a similar parliamentary scrutiny provision for Eurojust (Article 85(1) TFEU), the EU agency supporting judicial cooperation between the Member States within virtually the same area of competence as Europol.

109 Article 52 Europol Regulation.

Scrutiny Group (JPSG) bringing together members of the EP and of national parliaments is created as a vehicle of multilevel interparliamentary monitoring of Europol's activities.[110] For this purpose, Europol Regulation imposes a duty on the chair of the Management Board, the Executive Director and other Europol officials to report before JPSG on Agency's activities. Moreover, an obligation is placed on Europol to transmit to JPSG various documents.[111] The outcome of the monitoring carried out by JPSG materializes in 'summary conclusions' that are submitted to the EP and the national parliaments.[112]

Before delving into the details and practice of Europol's parliamentary scrutiny, one should first inquire about the rationale and scope for holding this Agency democratically accountable. An obvious reason for subjecting Europol to parliamentary scrutiny lies in the principle of representative democracy laid down in Article 10 (1) TEU entailing that politically legitimized authorities oversee the exercise of the unelected executive power.[113] This materializes in a delegation chain of principal-actor relationships linking the people and their direct representatives to the executive bodies and public servants in charge of implementing laws and policies.[114] Another reason resides in the fundamental constitutional principles of a political system, featuring Montesquieu's separation of powers and checks and balances to prevent abuses of powers by the executive.[115]

Yet the applicability of these principles needs to take into account the hybrid nature of the EU as a mix of supranationalism and intergovernmentalism. Judging the EU by the standards applicable in democratic states will always lead to the finding that the Union suffers from a democratic deficit. Therefore, the solution is to accept a certain degree of democratic deficit (according to state models of representative democracy) as an inherent feature of the Union, emanating from the limited powers entrusted to the EU as illustrated by the principles of conferral, proportionality and subsidiarity.[116] Instead the focus should be on addressing Union's democratic deficit in a slightly different sense:

110 Article 51 Europol Regulation.

111 I.e. threat assessments, strategic analyses and general situation reports relating to Europol's objectives, the results of studies and evaluations commissioned by Europol, administrative arrangements implementing the Union's international agreements or the Commission's 'adequacy decisions', Europol's multiannual programming and annual work programme, the consolidated annual activity report on Europol's activities, Commission's periodic evaluation reports of Europol, other relevant documents – see Article 51 (3) Europol Regulation.

112 Article 51 (5) Europol Regulation.

113 See for an in-depth study on the legitimacy of executive power in general, Paul Tucker, *Unelected Power. The Quest for Legitimacy in Central Banking and the Regulatory State* (Princeton University Press 2018).

114 Mark Bovens, 'Analysing and Assessing Public Accountability. A Conceptual Framework' (2007) 13(4) European Law Journal 447, 463.

115 Ibid.

116 See Majone, 'Europe's Democratic Deficit: The Question of Standards' (n 29) 7.

tackling problems related to the delegation of powers to non-majoritarian actors, like the EU agencies.[117] From this perspective, democratic deficit 'refers to the legitimacy (…) of non-majoritarian institutions' and translates into problems related to technocratic decision-making, transparency, mechanisms of control and accountability.[118] As mentioned before, the core legal standards relevant for EU agencies' powers are the principle of institutional balance with its system of checks and balances, and the revamped *Meroni* delegation of powers doctrine demanding conditions limiting the discretion of the agency, including sufficient oversight and control.[119] Provided that EU agencies are entrusted with limited powers, it is maintained that non-majoritarian standards (e.g. expertise, transparency, accountability by performance) would be most appropriate for legitimizing their actions.[120] The fact that EU agencies have multiple principals (the Council, the EP, the Commission and the Member States) also requires holding them politically accountable via a network of complementary accountability and checking mechanisms.[121]

Against this background, parliamentary scrutiny over Europol represents an important means (though not the only one) to hold the Agency politically accountable.[122] Unlike the state level where political accountability of national law enforcement agencies may be ensured more indirectly, through the mechanism of ministerial responsibility (involving normally the ministry of internal affairs), Europol is a formally autonomous EU agency more like a national administrative independent authority or executive agency.[123] With the EP having very little influence on the designation of Europol's governing structures,[124] it becomes essential that in counterbalance there is some democratic control over the way in which the Agency is exercising its powers delegated by the EU legislator.

Democratic control is designed as a mix of complementary and partly overlapping parliamentary actors scrutinizing Europol's activities to ensure that the Agency is 'fully accountable'.[125] The idea of a joint parliamentary scrutiny mechanism is based on the assumption that Europol's activities cannot be sufficiently scrutinized neither by the EP alone nor by the national parliaments of the Member States.[126] As to the role distribution regarding scrutiny of Europol's performance and activities, the JPSG focusses on political monitoring (including

117 Ibid 14–15.
118 Ibid.
119 Coman-Kund, *European Union Agencies as Global Actors* (n 43) 36–37.
120 Majone, 'Europe's Democratic Deficit: The Question of Standards' (n 29) 28.
121 Ibid 26–27 and Curtin, 'Holding (Quasi-)Autonomous EU Administrative Actors to Public Account' (n 16) 540–541.
122 Another important political accountability channel is established between Europol and the Council, the latter also having the possibility to impose formal sanctions, such as removing Agency's Executive Director from office (see Article 54 Europol Regulation).
123 Also labelled as a 'quasi-autonomous national government organisation' (Quango) in British bureaucratic jargon.
124 See Articles 11, 13 and 54–55 Europol Regulation.
125 See Recital 58 of the Preamble to Europol Regulation.
126 Kreilinger (n 102) 3–4.

the impact of Agency's activities on fundamental rights), whereas the EP alone is equipped with important information rights[127] and supervises the budgetary-financial matters pertaining to Europol's activities. While the JPSG is not the first EU joint parliamentary body,[128] it is considered nevertheless the one with the most specific mandate and most significant scrutiny powers.[129]

The effectiveness of the new parliamentary scrutiny system laid down by the 2016 Europol Regulation depends to a large extent on the concrete design of the JPSG as well as on the synergies between JPSG and EP (in particular the LIBE Committee).[130] Moreover, there are various legal and practical factors that impact on the exercise of the scrutiny powers at different stages of the accountability process.

To begin with, the 2016 Europol Regulation entrusts JPSG with seemingly important information rights. The Agency is compelled to submit an extensive list of documents to JPSG, and the latter may also ask for additional documents from the Agency or other authorities with a view to exercise properly political monitoring over Europol's activities. As already seen, the information side of JPSG scrutiny is complemented by the EP's powers to access sensitive non-classified information and EU classified information processed by or through Europol. All this information is expected to overcome better than before the knowledge/information asymmetry between the accountability fora and the Agency, by enabling both JPSG and EP to better understand what Europol is doing and to assess its performance. Additionally, a novel element potentially enhancing parliamentary scrutiny capacity is the possibility to have a JPSG representative participating at the meetings of Europol's Management Board as a non-voting observer, though such participation is possible only on invitation by the Management Board itself.[131] The scope of interparliamentary scrutiny seems all-encompassing, in line with the fluid accountability perspective, being both retrospective (based on *ex post* activity reports, evaluations and threat assessments) and prospective (based on *ex ante* annual work programmes and multiannual programming documents).

127 Especially with a view to support political monitoring by JPSG – see Article 52 (1) Europol Regulation.

128 Other EU interparliamentary bodies preceding JPSG are the Conference of Parliamentary Committees for Union Affairs of Parliaments of the European Union (COSAC) Plenary, the Inter-parliamentary conference for the Common Foreign and Security Policy (CFSP) and the Common Security and Defence Policy (CSDP) or the Interparliamentary Conference on Stability, Economic Coordination and Governance in the European Union (SECG Conference).

129 See in this respect, Kreilinger (n 102); Ian Cooper, 'A New Form of Democratic Oversight in the EU: The Joint Parliamentary Scrutiny Group for Europol' (2018) 10(3) Perspectives on Federalism 185; Diane Fromage, The New Joint Parliamentary Scrutiny Group for Europol: Old Wine in New Bottles? (17 June 2017) TARN Blog <https://eutarn.blogactiv.eu/2017/06/17/the-new-joint-parliamentary-scrutiny-group-for-europol-old-wine-in-new-bottles/> accessed 23 June 2020.

130 See Kreilinger (n 102) 10–14.

131 Article 14 Europol Regulation.

Next, relevant in particular for the debating phase of Europol's accountability, the JPSG is entrusted with an extended right to conduct hearings,[132] largely corresponding to the rights previously entrusted to the EP under Article 48 of the 2009 Europol Council Decision.[133] The EP still remains with an own right of hearing Agency's Executive Director before taking up his/her post or on the occasion of the one-time extension of his/her mandate.[134] Here again, complementarity between the EP and the JPSG seems essential to hold Europol fully accountable, especially that, in terms of consequences, the JPSG is deprived of any hard law sanctioning powers while the EP still has a grip on the Agency in its role as a legislative and budgetary authority.

Yet in spite of the rather optimistic picture regarding access to information detained by Europol or concerning Europol, one obvious limitation of parliamentary scrutiny remains precisely the relevant information necessary to assess Agency's performance. First, the fact that most of Europol's data belongs actually to the Member States may create obvious difficulties for the EP/JPSG to access such information. The main reason is the principle of ownership of data enabling the data owner (i.e. a national enforcement authority) to classify information and restrict access rights.[135] Second, the principle of confidentiality built in Europol's legal design, provides the Agency with an important tool to further restrict parliamentary scrutiny in particular as regards its operational activities.[136] A frequent use (and sometimes misuse) of this tool is likely to contribute to keeping a high level of information asymmetry between the parliamentary fora and the Agency, making performance assessment quite difficult.[137] In any case, there is an inherent tension between parliamentary scrutiny rights and the obligations of discretion/confidentiality concerning Europol's (operational) activities,[138] and finding a fair balance between the two represents one of the biggest challenges the Agency has faced and will face in the future.

Another important element for effective democratic accountability is the actual capacity and willingness of the EP and JPSG to properly understand

132 JPSG may summon before it the Chairperson of the Management Board, the Executive Director, their Deputies, other relevant persons; quite importantly, as it will be seen later on in this chapter, also EDPS must appear before JPSG at least once a year to report on personal data protection matters concerning Europol's activities – Article 51 (2) (b) Europol Regulation.

133 Kreilinger (n 102) 10.

134 Article 54 Europol Regulation.

135 See Recitals (26)–(27) of Preamble to Europol Regulation; this could be possibly compensated at least in part by national parliamentary control over national law enforcement authorities; see for a comprehensive analysis, Abazi (n 103).

136 EP and JPSG requests for information must comply with Europol's own adopted rules on the obligations of discretion and confidentiality as well as on the protection of sensitive non-classified information and classified information, Articles 51 (4) and 52 (1)–(2) junto Article 67 Europol Regulation.

137 Abazi (n 103) 1133–1136.

138 Ibid 1133–1134. This tension is aptly illustrated by the Working arrangements under Article 52 of the Europol Regulation concluded in 2018 between the EP and Europol (on file with the author).

and evaluate Europol's performance. Thus, besides having access to sufficient information, the accountability forum must also possess and/or mobilize sufficient expertise and knowledge to alleviate the information asymmetry problem. In this respect, MEPs or national parliamentarians in specialized committees (i.e. LIBE Committee for Europol) following constantly Europol's activities, combined with reliance on sound parliamentary in-house expertise or external experts (reporting regularly or invited on an *ad hoc* basis) might significantly contribute to a meaningful scrutiny and avoid transforming accountability too much into a lobbying and 'demand for resources' exercise.[139] Also the inherent political nature of the forum entailing the tendency of parliamentarians to focus on sporadic politically loaded or sensitive issues instead of a more comprehensive and in-depth scrutiny of Agency's activities might seriously compromise the quality and intensity of the accountability process.[140]

As to the practice of Europol's democratic accountability, very much depends on how the EP and JPSG use the scrutiny powers at their disposal. In particular parliamentary hearings, questions and follow-up regarding Agency's performance are important accountability tools. Yet, just like with other EU agencies, the intensity of EP's scrutiny was rather mild in view of the fact that its specialized committees largely rely on the information sent by Europol, do not consistently use evidence from other sources, and they do not produce extensive reports after the hearings.[141] As for the JPSG, the interparliamentary scrutiny forum has effectively been established in April 2017 by the Conference of Speakers of European Union Parliaments.[142] The choice for a rather large-scale body counting up to 128 members[143] and meeting twice per year already raised doubts regarding the capacity of JPSG to exercise effective oversight over Europol.[144] Based on the guidelines enshrined by the Conference of Speakers, the JPSG became functional in March 2018 after adopting its own rules of procedure.[145]

The JPSG RoP details some important aspects that may enhance the capacity of this body to fulfil its role. First, it aims at a stable composition of this

139 See Busuioc (n 3) 124–133; for a more general argument regarding the capacity of politicians to rely on expertise to counter the expertise gap with technocratic agencies, see Majone, 'Europe's Democratic Deficit: The Question of Standards' (n 29) 16.

140 See Busuioc (n 3) 133–136.

141 Ibid 134–135.

142 Conclusions of the Presidency, Conference of Speakers of the European Union Parliaments (Bratislava 23–25 April 2017) <https://secure.ipex.eu/IPEXL-WEB/euspeakers/getspeakers.do?id=082dbcc55898c90b01589abbb37500fa> accessed 30 June 2020.

143 Each national parliament is represented by max. 4 members while the EP is represented by max. 19 MEPs – Article 2.1 JPSG Rules of Procedure (RoP).

144 Fromage (n 129).

145 Second meeting of the Joint Parliamentary Scrutiny Group (JPSG) on Europol (Sofia, 18 March 2018) <https://www.europarl.europa.eu/committees/en/product-details/20180301EOT02301> accessed 30 June 2020. JPSG Rules of Procedure have been revised in September 2019 during the Fifth meeting of the Joint Parliamentary Scrutiny Group (JPSG) on Europol (Brussels, 23.09.2019) <https://www.europarl.europa.eu/committees/en/fifth-meeting-of-the-joint-parliamentary/product-details/20190911EOT03961> accessed 30 June 2020.

body in that its membership should last for the whole parliamentary mandate of the participating MEPs and members of national parliaments;[146] this way, JPSG members would have more time to understand Europol and monitor its activities more effectively. Second, JPSG is allowed to rely on the support of relevant experts and other persons with a view to fulfil its role,[147] which may partly help overcoming the knowledge/information asymmetry problem. Third, the JPSG has the possibility to create specialized subgroups, which could boost more in-depth scrutiny over important aspects of Europol's activities.[148] Fourth, JPSG members may, individually or jointly,[149] ask Europol oral and written questions independently or linked to the topics on the meeting agenda.[150] Fifth, reflecting the multilevel hybrid accountability dimension, Europol is to send the documents intended for JPSG to the EP and national parliaments;[151] thus national parliaments become some sort of 'multi-arena players' combining 'domestic scrutiny activities with the new possibilities offered by the JPSG'.[152] Sixth, the RoP provide some details on the designation and reporting obligations of the JPSG representative in Europol's Management Board (if and when invited by the latter).[153] Finally but yet importantly, it is a welcomed development that parliaments/chambers are allowed to propose amendments and to enclose specific observations to the consensus-adopted JPSG summary conclusions,[154] thereby potentially ensuring a more nuanced and rich outcome of the democratic accountability process.

On the less bright side, one may note concerns[155] regarding the effective operation of such a large and diverse body, the smooth cooperation between its members, in particular the potential 'turf wars' between MEPs and members of national parliaments, or the rather modest output of JPSG in the form of mere (non-mandatory) 'summary conclusions' on political monitoring of Europol's activities.[156]

146 Article 2.1 JPSG RoP.
147 Article 2.3 JPSG RoP.
148 Article 3.6 JPSG RoP.
149 JPSG Written and Oral Questions. Guide for Members 1, available at <https://secure.ipex.eu/IPEXL-WEB/conference/getconference.do?id=8a8629a86e891977016ed560a58140aa> accessed 30 June 2020.
150 Article 4.2 JPSG RoP. Only written questions can be asked independently from the topics on the agenda.
151 Article 4.5 JPSG RoP.
152 Kreilinger (n 102) 15.
153 Article 5 JPSG RoP; see also Cooper (n 129) 206–207. In practice the JPSG representative may participate to two (of the four) yearly meetings of Europol's Management Board, see JPSG Summary conclusions by the Co-Chairs, Fourth meeting of the Joint Parliamentary Scrutiny Group (JPSG) on Europol (Bucharest, 24–25 February 2019) available at <https://secure.ipex.eu/IPEXL-WEB/conference/getconference.do?id=082dbcc568350fdf016837feb8770407> accessed 30 June 2020.
154 Article 4.7 JPSG RoP.
155 See more extensively Kreilinger (n 102) and Cooper (n 129).
156 See Article 51 (5) Europol Regulation.

It is still early to assess the JPSG practice on monitoring Europol, considering that, after the adoption of its rules of procedure, there were only four JPSG meetings, the last one being organized as a mere exchange of information by electronic means because of the COVID-19 situation.[157] However, at this incipient stage, JPSG monitoring over Europol's activities seemed to offer a good opportunity for Europol to familiarize MEPs and members of national parliaments with its activities and achievements, to promote its strategy and to emphasize shortcomings in budget and resources. Meetings are informed by a number of documents sent in advance by Europol according to Article 51 of Regulation 2016/794,[158] as well as by written questions for Europol and by written contributions sent in advance by the EP and national parliaments.

The meetings so far entailed conference-like presentations on Agency's activities by the Executive Director and the Chair of the Management Board, followed by questions and reactions by JPSG delegates from the EP and national parliaments. A reading of the JPSG summary conclusions suggests that reporting on Europol's performance during the JPSG meetings seems to do little more than repeating public information as well as highlighting Europol's strategic planning and achievements despite its limited resources. The questions/exchanges tend to remain quite generic, showing a rather limited understanding of Europol's mandate and activities. Sometimes questions and discussions tend to focus on few salient issues on the political agenda of the JPSG members involved, not always equally relevant for Europol's activities. The JPSG summary conclusions are mostly descriptive documents, deal quite expeditiously with core elements of parliamentary scrutiny (i.e. Q&A and debates) and provide little on follow-up actions. On the bright side, the JPSG summary conclusions reveal much more detailed and operationally oriented reporting on Europol's activities by the EDPS and the Europol Cooperation Board according to their mandate.

The JPSG needs of course more time to fully take on its supervisory role. Yet it is important for its effectiveness not to replicate common failures of parliamentary scrutiny mechanisms while building good practices of cooperation and complementarity to hold Europol fully accountable. For a meaningful scrutiny by JPSG, it seems essential to: (1) rely on sufficient information and expertise from all relevant sources and sides; (2) give enough weight to hearings, follow-up questions, debates and criticism;[159] (3) ensure some form of ongoing monitoring between the two yearly JPSG meetings and (4) prepare insightful conclusions as these may provide important input for other accountability channels.

157 The overview of JPSG meetings, including relevant documents and materials, is available on the EP website, <https://www.europarl.europa.eu/relnatparl/en/high-level-conferences/jpsg-on-europol.html> accessed 30 June 2020.

158 E.g. multi-annual programming documents, consolidated activity reports, strategy documents, threat assessments and other reports, working arrangements, replies to written questions, etc. A preliminary observation is that the information circulated by Europol seems to go little beyond what can be found on Agency's website.

159 See also Kreilinger (n 102) 12.

6 Supervising Europol's data processing: A business between experts?

In view of its mandate, Europol has always been subject to a specific regime on personal data processing and data protection.[160] The reason for such a tailored legal regime was to enable the Agency to fully and swiftly support Member States in preventing and combatting serious crime. However, extensive possibilities to process and exchange personal data in this area are likely to entail highly intrusive effects on privacy, individual freedom and other fundamental rights, and require commensurate safeguards.[161] One of the essential guarantees against abuses or misuses of personal data by Europol was through supervision of Agency's data processing activities by a specialized independent authority.

In line with the evolution of Europol, supervision of Europol's personal data processing has also followed the path from intergovernmentalism to supranationalism. Thus, since 1995 until 1 May 2017, the JSB, composed of representatives from the Member States, had been responsible for supervising data processing at Europol and ensuring that individual rights were not infringed by such activities.[162] Equipped with little formal powers beside addressing complaints to the Agency's Executive Director, referring a matter to the Management Board, issuing opinions and drawing up regular reports forwarded to the EP and the Council, the JSB was nevertheless quite an influential and effective supervisory authority in practice.[163]

The 2016 Europol Regulation replaced the JSB with the EDPS with far-reaching formal tasks and powers. In this respect, the EDPS is tasked to hear complaints, conduct inquiries, monitor and ensure the application of the relevant EU legal framework in order to protect natural persons with regard to processing of personal data by Europol.[164] Its supervisory role encompasses both legal aspects (i.e. the level of compliance of Europol with its legal framework) and technical aspects (e.g. the use of new tools and complex IT technologies for data collection/processing or information security procedures employed by the Agency).[165] The EDPS may *inter alia* warn or admonish Europol, compel the Agency to rectify, restrict, erase or destroy incorrectly processed personal data, ban Europol's processing operations, or refer a matter to the EP, the Council, the Commission or the CJEU.[166] For the purpose of carrying out its tasks, the EDPS is granted access to all necessary personal data and information detained

160 See Coman-Kund, 'Europol's International Exchanges of Data and Interoperability of AFSJ Databases' (n 66) 189–193.

161 Ibid 200–203.

162 See Article 34 Europol Council Decision.

163 See for an example, Coman-Kund, *European Union Agencies as Global Actors* (n 43) 228.

164 Article 43 (2) Europol Regulation.

165 See EDPS, Annual Report 2017, 24 and Annual Report 2019, 38 and 40 available at <https://edps.europa.eu/annual-reports_en> accessed 30 June 2020.

166 Article 43 (3) Europol Regulation.

by Europol, as well as access to all Agency's premises.[167] Two observations are opportune for further clarifying the role of EDPS vis-à-vis Europol. First, not all EDPS tasks and activities entail holding Europol accountable strictly speaking. Thus, the EDPS also fulfils an advisory function toward Europol, providing opinions and recommendations on matters concerning processing of personal data.[168] It also exercises a more *ex ante* control function, for instance with regard to *prior* authorizations of a set of transfers of personal data to third countries in derogatory situations.[169] Second, in the specific context of data protection supervision, the EDPS promotes quite a technical understanding of accountability, as 'the ability of Europol as an organisation to proactively and internally ensure and demonstrate compliance with the principles and rules for the protection of personal data'.[170]

However, in spite of the impressive tasks and powers of the EDPS, the multilevel hybrid accountability dimension is still very obvious in Europol's personal data processing supervision. Thus, the EDPS must cooperate closely with national supervisory authorities (NSAs) on all matters concerning Europol's personal data processing that involve a national element.[171] The NSAs remain competent to supervise all transfers, retrievals and communication of personal data from the Member States to Europol, and for this purpose they have access to relevant documents and information kept by the ENUs and by national liaison officers at Europol.[172] The EDPS is compelled to rely on the expertise of NSAs in carrying out its tasks, and they must assist each other in carrying out inspections and audits.[173] Quite importantly, the EDPS cannot decide on a case concerning data originating in the Member States before the relevant NSA(s) have expressed their views on the matter; what is more the EDPS must take utmost account of the views of the NSA(s) concerned.[174] Furthermore, similarly to the hybrid nature of the JPSG, a Cooperation Board, composed of one representative from EDPS and each NSA, is set up[175] as an advisory body with a broad mandate

167 Article 43 (4) Europol Regulation.
168 See Article 43 (2) Europol Regulation.
169 See Article 25 (6) Europol Regulation; 'derogatory situations' in this context entail transfers of personal data to third countries/international organizations with which there are no formal cooperation agreements concluded for such transfers, nor is there a Commission 'adequacy decision' adopted establishing that that country/organization ensures an adequate level of data protection.
170 EDPS, Annual Report 2017, 26. In this very specific and technical sense, accountability entails that 'controllers put in place internal mechanisms and control systems that ensure compliance and provide evidence – such as audit reports – to demonstrate compliance to external stakeholders, including supervisory authorities', EDPS, Data protection/ Glossary <https://edps.europa.eu/node/3095#accountability> accessed 30 June 2020.
171 Article 44 (1) Europol Regulation.
172 Article 42 Europol Regulation.
173 Article 44 (2) Europol Regulation.
174 Article 44 (4) Europol Regulation.
175 Article 45 (1) Europol Regulation.

covering all aspects related to data processing and data protection supervision of Europol.[176] The Europol Cooperation Board is intended to ensure the much-needed coordination between EDPS and NSAs in keeping Europol in check for personal data processing activities. Europol Regulation foresees nevertheless quite an influential role for the Board in practice, as the EDPS and NSAs are required to take 'utmost account' of its opinions, guidelines, recommendations and best practices.[177] What becomes evident is that effective supervision of Europol's personal data processing will very much depend on the real capacity of EDPS to fulfil its tasks, on the cooperation between EDPS and NSAs, including within the Cooperation Board, and additionally on the relationship between EDPS and Europol, in particular Europol's Data Protection Officer (DPO).

As required by Europol Regulation,[178] since 2017, EDPS has included a section on Europol supervision in its annual report. EDPS supervisory practice so far confirms a strong cooperative approach with a view to understand and assess Europol's performance regarding personal data processing. Aware of the fact that most personal data processed by Europol is provided by national law enforcement authorities, the EDPS established ties with the national data protection authorities both independently, for the purpose of joint supervisory activities, and within the framework of the Cooperation Board.[179] Moreover, regular meetings and exchanges are taking place between the EDPS and Europol's DPO and Data Protection Function (DPF) Unit in order to obtain more insights into Europol's in-house data processing and data protection matters; additional meetings have been reported between EDPS and Europol's top management, in particular Agency's Executive Director.[180] In concrete terms, EDPS supervision so far entailed: (1) a number of generic and targeted inspections and inquiries, usually followed by recommendations for improvement, (2) several opinions (on *prior* request by Europol or on own initiative) on various matters concerning personal data processing, (3) dealing with individual complaints concerning data protection breaches by the Agency,[181] and most spectacularly, (4) in one case, imposition of a ban on Europol's data processing operations.[182] EDPS supervisory activities tend to focus on selected issues concerning Europol's data processing activities, which allows in principle for more in-depth scrutiny of Agency's

176 Article 45 (3) Europol Regulation.

177 Article 45 (4) Europol Regulation.

178 Article 43 (5) Europol Regulation.

179 EDPS, Annual Report 2019, 39 available at <https://edps.europa.eu/annual-reports_en> accessed 30 June 2020.

180 EDPS, Annual Report 2019, 38–39. While such meetings are definitely useful for a better understanding and supervision of Europol's activities, they should not amount to establishing a too close relationship that might alter the impartiality of the EDPS.

181 So far, no individual complaint filed with the EDPS was successful.

182 Ultimately the ban has been suspended for one year in view of the importance of the data processing operations for combatting money laundering and terrorism financing in the EU, see EDPS, Annual Report 2019, 41.

performance.[183] In view of the strong intertwinement between Europol's data processing and the activities of the national law enforcement authorities, EDPS shares inspection reports, opinions and other supervisory output with NSAs either directly or via the Cooperation Board.[184]

Last but not least, all EDPS activity reports refer more or less extensively to the cooperation with JPSG. The participation of the EDPS at the JPSG meetings is regarded as an opportunity 'to provide the JPSG with an overview of EDPS supervisory activities, as well as to discuss more specific issues'.[185] Before the JPSG, the EDPS reports, sometimes in a quite detailed manner, on the main supervisory activities carried out and on the main findings, pointing both to positive aspects and to more problematic issues.[186] Very interestingly, but rather logical in view of the hybrid nature of Europol's data protection supervision, the Cooperation Board, normally represented by its chair, also reports before the JPSG though it does not have a legal obligation to do so.[187] The interventions of the EDPS and of the Cooperation Board are followed by exchanges with JPSG members for the purpose of obtaining more in-depth insights or clarifying certain issues. This dual reporting bears the promise of providing more complete and accurate information to JPSG with regard to Europol's personal data processing operations, by encompassing the much-needed multilevel perspective on Agency's supervision. Being so far the most insightful part of the JPSG summary conclusions, the reporting on data protection supervisory activities may significantly help JPSG to fine-tune its scrutiny on core operational aspects of Europol's activities and ensure more meaningful political accountability of the Agency.

7 Connecting the dots: The interplay between Europol's parliamentary scrutiny and data processing supervision in a multilevel setting

The analysis so far displays interesting commonalities and interlinks between Europol's democratic and specialized personal data processing accountability. Both accountability types reflect the hybrid nature of the Agency's design, tasks and activities, situated at the frontier between EU and Member States' competences. As could be seen the quasi-symbiotic relationship between Europol and

183 See EDPS, Annual Report 2018, 26–29 available at <https://edps.europa.eu/annual-reports_en> accessed 30 June 2020.
184 See EDPS, Annual Reports 2017, 2018 and 2019 available at <https://edps.europa.eu/annual-reports_en> accessed 30 June 2020.
185 EDPS, Annual Report 2018, 29–30.
186 JPSG Summary conclusions by the Co-Chairs, Fifth Meeting of the Joint Parliamentary Scrutiny Group (JPSG) on Europol (Brussels, 23–24 September 2019) available at <https://secure.ipex.eu/IPEXL-WEB/conference/getconference.do?id=8a8629a86b273e34016bae32ac2b4cb7> accessed 30 June 2020.
187 JPSG Summary conclusions by the Co-Chairs, Fifth Meeting of the Joint Parliamentary Scrutiny Group (JPSG) on Europol (Brussels, 23–24 September 2019).

national law enforcement authorities requires a commensurate hybrid multilevel accountability model bringing together EU level and national actors to ensure that Europol is held fully accountable for its actions. Also, a fluid dimension to Europol's accountability can be observed, entailing both *ex post* performance evaluation and a forward-looking assessment of Agency's planned activities. This is most obvious in the case of the JPSG, assessing and discussing during its meetings Europol's multiannual planning, yearly work programmes and various strategies.

The two types of accountability examined with regard to Europol reveal the complex interplay between EU level and national actors in holding the Agency accountable. The EP and national parliaments, on the one hand, and the EDPS and national supervisory authorities, on the other hand, are involved both in their own right and through mixed cooperation structures, namely the JPSG and the Cooperation Board, in scrutinizing Europol. There is a convoluted division of tasks between accountability fora along jurisdictional lines and stages of accountability. Thus, scrutiny by national actors is more bottom-up, indirect and circumscribed to the relationship between national law enforcement authorities and Europol. Scrutiny by the EP and the EDPS is more encompassing and targeted on the Agency, while the JPSG and the Cooperation Board represent the venue for coordination of EU level and national perspectives. The interplay between EU level and national actors is ensured at all accountability stages, but the ultimate formal decisions affecting directly the Agency at the 'consequences' stage of accountability belong to the EU level actors (e.g. EP refusing to grant discharge regarding the implementation of Europol's budget or EDPS ordering the Agency to carry out erasure of personal data processed unlawfully); in this regard, it can be observed that the mixed accountability fora (JPSG and Cooperation Board) can formally bark but not bite. All this should allow taking into consideration in the accountability process all dimensions of Europol's activities and in particular the complex interlinks with Agency's national counterparts. At the same time, taking into account the complexity of police cooperation in combatting serious cross-border crime, one important challenge is to single out, for accountability purposes, Agency's actions and powers from those of other law enforcement actors.

The relationship between the two accountability types is complementary and supportive. Thus, the more encompassing parliamentary scrutiny of Europol's activities is complemented by the more targeted and in-depth supervision of Agency's personal data processing. The latter also supports increasingly parliamentary scrutiny, in particular through EDPS and the Cooperation Board, with expertise and substantive insights into Europol's core activities. This provides a good opportunity to mitigate the 'knowledge/information asymmetry' problem between the EP/JPSG and Europol, thereby offering the prospect of a more meaningful democratic accountability of the Agency.[188]

188 See on the concept of meaningful accountability, Mark Bovens and Thomas Schillemans, 'Meaningful Accountability' in Mark Bovens, Robert E. Goodin and Thomas Schillemans (eds), *The Oxford Handbook of Public Accountability* (OUP 2014) 674–681.

For now, the new accountability system established by the Europol Regulation is too early to assess, as both the JPSG and EDPS are still at an embryonic stage as accountability fora for Europol. On paper the general impression is that both parliamentary scrutiny and personal data supervision of Europol's activities have been significantly enhanced. This offers the promise of a more accountable Europol in the EU multilevel setting. Yet challenges exist as to the actual functioning and interplay between the new accountability tools in holding the Agency effectively accountable. Much will depend on the cooperation and synergies between the EU-level and national actors involved in Europol's accountability process. Cooperation and complementarity between these actors, in line with the principle of sincere cooperation,[189] are to be preferred for a comprehensive accountability process, instead of competition/turf wars leading to fragmentary and dysfunctional oversight.[190] Also the capacity and willingness of the EDPS and the Cooperation Forum to provide substantive input for parliamentary scrutiny, combined with the preparedness of the JPSG to assess Europol's performance and development will be key to meaningful democratic accountability. More generally, legal and practical limitations faced by these supervisors in terms of resources, knowledge and access to information will also influence their capacity to properly assess Europol's performance. Finally, as could be seen, Europol's parliamentary scrutiny and personal data supervision are embedded in a much more overarching accountability system encompassing multiple channels and fora. Therefore, an accurate diagnosis of these two accountability types demands a more contextual analysis, by looking at how they fit in the bigger picture, in particular by considering their interlinks with other accountability tools and their impact on the aggregate Europol accountability.[191]

8 Conclusion

This chapter looked into the accountability of 'Europe's police agency' by examining in particular two types of accountability recently redesigned by Europol's legal framework, namely democratic accountability and specialized administrative personal data processing accountability. Acknowledging supranationalism and the multilevel character as key features shaping the EU as a complex *sui generis* transnational governance system, we argue that a multilevel accountability model, entailing multiple actors, fora and channels crosscutting EU and Member State levels, is best suited in the EU context. Multilevel accountability is particularly suitable for EU agencies, like Europol, as 'in-betweeners' between

189 Enshrined in Article 4(2) TEU.

190 See Madalina Busuioc, 'European Agencies: Pockets of Accountability', in Bovens, Curtin and 't Hart (eds), *The Real World of EU Accountability. What Deficit? (please keep the Italics)* (n 26) 87–116.

191 For a view on public accountability as a web of various accountability mechanisms, requiring to specify potential deficits in political accountability and to contextualize them by considering the likely compensatory effects of other accountability mechanisms and processes, see Richard Mulgan, 'Accountability Deficits' in Bovens, Goodin and Schillemans (eds), *The Oxford Handbook of Public Accountability* (n 188) 552–553.

EU institutions and the Member States. The obvious hybrid (supranational and intergovernmental) nature of Europol and of its expertise is captured by the term 'hybrid multilevel accountability' whereby both EU level institutions and Member States are involved in holding the Agency accountable. Observing the reality of accountability relationships, we opted for a fluid understanding of accountability, encompassing both an *ex post* evaluation of Europol's past conduct but also a forward-looking perspective aimed at shaping Agency's future behaviour. In our view the relevance of hybrid (fluid) multilevel accountability goes beyond the specific case of Europol, being valid for virtually all EU agencies and technocratic bodies whose design and operation feature a pooling of EU and national resources and powers. It is perhaps the hallmark of the current degree of administrative integration within the EU.

The two types of accountability examined with regard to Europol reveal the complex interplay between EU level and national actors in holding the Agency accountable. The EP and national parliaments, on the one hand, and the EDPS and national supervisory authorities, on the other hand, are involved both in their own right and through mixed cooperation structures, namely the JPSG and the Cooperation Board, in scrutinizing Europol. The interplay between EU level and national actors is ensured at all accountability stages, but the ultimate decisions affecting directly the Agency at the 'consequences' stage of accountability belong to the EU level actors. The relationship between Europol's parliamentary scrutiny and personal data scrutiny is complementary and supportive. This provides a good opportunity to mitigate the 'knowledge/information asymmetry' problem between the EP/JPSG and Europol, thereby offering the prospect of a more meaningful democratic accountability of the Agency.

The preliminary examination of the two types of accountability leaves a mixed impression. On paper, the general impression is that both parliamentary scrutiny and personal data supervision of Europol's activities have been significantly enhanced. However, more accountability on paper does not necessarily mean more or better accountability in practice. A number of challenges have been identified as to the actual functioning and interplay between the new accountability tools in holding the Agency effectively accountable. Much will depend on the cooperation and synergies between the EU-level and national actors involved in Europol's accountability process, as well as between democratic accountability and expert data protection supervision. In view of the complexity of police cooperation in combating serious cross-border crime, one important challenge is to single out, for accountability purposes, Agency's actions and powers from those of other law enforcement actors. Legal and practical limitations faced by parliamentary actors and data protection supervisors in terms of resources, knowledge and access to information will also influence their capacity to properly assess Europol's performance. More time is needed for an accurate diagnosis of the effectiveness of Europol's revamped accountability system.

Index

For Product Safety Concerns and Information please contact our EU representative GPSR@taylorandfrancis.com
Taylor & Francis Verlag GmbH, Kaufingerstraße 24, 80331 München, Germany

www.ingramcontent.com/pod-product-compliance
Lightning Source LLC
LaVergne TN
LVHW011111300926
849160LV00008B/350

9781032005782